W9-BCG-306

The Tax on Value Added

THE TAX ON
VALUE ADDED

Clara K. Sullivan

COLUMBIA UNIVERSITY PRESS

NEW YORK AND LONDON

Clara K. Sullivan is Research Economist, International Program in Taxation, Law School, Harvard University, and Senior Economist, International Economic Integration Program, Columbia University.

In memory of my parents, Marie and Harry Freedberg

Preface

Although the idea of value-added taxation originated over four decades ago, world-wide interest in its potentialities as a source of revenue began with the Shoup Mission's recommendation of 1949 for its use in the Japanese prefectures and with its official adoption by the French National Government in 1954. Moreover, it has been receiving increased attention since the recommendation by the Fiscal and Financial Committee of the European Economic Community in 1962 that it be employed as a means of harmonizing the sales tax systems of the member states.

In this book the character of value-added taxation is revealed primarily by exploring the manner in which such taxation is, on the one hand, related to those general levies customarily designated as sales taxes and, on the other hand, related to direct personal income and expenditure taxes. There is much need for this type of inquiry because the fact that a value-added measure may be used for any tax on income or product flows makes it necessary to distinguish among the various principles of taxation intended by any given proposal for a value-added tax.

Chapter 1 analyzes the value-added tax in terms of the various principles of taxation which it may be intended to implement. The remaining chapters of Part I describe in detail the two most significant examples of legislation applying the value-added tax, namely, the French and Japanese, analyzing them in terms of the principles which they are supposed to represent. The Michigan legislation is discussed in an appendix.

Part II probes more deeply into the nature of value-added taxation. It begins, in Chapter 4, with a consideration of the underlying philosophy.

Chapter 5 undertakes a detailed inquiry into how "value added" is defined. Chapter 6 focuses on administrative problems, especially as compared with other types of sales taxes. The analysis ends with a chapter which discusses in a very general manner some of the most significant issues involved in a consideration of the incidence and effects of the value-added tax viewed as an indirect type of personal tax. The treatment is admittedly incomplete. Especially in view of recent developments, which suggest growing interest in the value-added tax as an impersonal type of business taxation, the subject deserves more careful consideration than time has allowed and indeed warrants a separate treatise. Also, no attempt has been made to deal with the problems of interjurisdictional shifting and effects, which are also becoming vitally important.

The book began as a dissertation submitted in 1959 to the Faculty of Political Science of Columbia University, in accordance with the requirements for the degree of Doctor of Philosophy. It was prepared under the supervision of Carl S. Shoup, McVickar Professor of Political Economy at Columbia University, who also suggested the topic. As the research for the dissertation was largely completed by 1955, it has been necessary to bring much of the factual material up to date. Also, the first two chapters have been rewritten in the light of increased understanding of the issues acquired from my work at the Harvard Law School International Program in Taxation under the supervision of Oliver Oldman, Professor of Law and Director of Training of the Program.

I wish to thank Professor Shoup and Professor Oldman for their continuing cooperation and encouragement. Acknowledgments are likewise due to the members of Professor Shoup's Graduate Economics Research Workshop, who discussed part of the original manuscript, and especially to the members of Professor Oldman's International Tax Research Seminar, who have critically examined a number of my analyses over the past five years. Professors Shoup and Oldman and Dr. Richard Bird, Senior Researcher in Economics of Columbia University's International Economic Integration Program, have also been so kind as to read and comment on parts of the revised dissertation. Naturally, I assume sole responsibility for the contents of the study.

None of the work could have been accomplished without the cooperation of the librarians at Harvard University, particularly those at the Law School, the School of Public Administration, and the Widener Library. Also, I extend my appreciation to the administrative staff of the World

Tax Series, Harvard Law School International Program in Taxation, which, under the supervision of Mr. Clifford P. Greck, Administrative Director of the Harvard Law School International Program in Taxation, undertook the task of typing and proofreading the final manuscript. Finally, I am much indebted to Elizabeth M. Evanson of Columbia University Press for her splendid editorial assistance.

CLARA K. SULLIVAN

West Roxbury, Mass.
January, 1965

Contents

Part I

The Development of the Concept of the Tax on Value Added

Chapter 1

An Introduction to the Concept of the Tax on Value Added

The concept of the tax on value added has been developed through two different approaches. Through one approach the tax has been devised merely as a method of collecting a sales tax viewed as a tax on the value of a product collected from business enterprises selling it and expected to be shifted forward to purchasers by means of an increase in prices equal to the amount of the tax. Through the other approach the tax is expressly related to some version of the benefit principle of taxation, usually one formulated in terms of a benefits to business thesis. In that case, the tax may or may not be regarded as a tax on ultimate purchasers of taxable products, the concept of the tax being dependent upon the particular version of the benefit thesis involved.

Given the first approach, the value-added tax will naturally reflect one or another policy of sales taxation compatible with the view of the tax as a burden on purchasers of final products. However, no particular policy is implied through use of the value-added measure as such, except possibly that the tax applies to a wide range of products. In other words, the value-added procedure is most suitable for a general tax as contrasted with a selective sales tax or special excise.[1]

Like other sales taxes of general scope expected to be borne by final

[1] A value-added procedure is used for the limited number of products covered by the European Coal and Steel Community. However, an estimate procedure is used which appears to involve a high degree of constructive pricing and which would not be worth while in the case of the usual special excise. For a brief description of the method, see Maxime Chrétien, "Les divers problèmes fiscaux des trois Communautés Européennes," *Les problèmes juridiques et économiques du Marché Commun* (Paris, 1960), pp. 294–95.

purchasers, the value-added tax may be regarded as a kind of personal taxation and therefore compatible with some version of the ability to pay principle, albeit the indirect method of implementing the principle cannot be tailored to personal situations as precisely as the direct. Similarly, when under the benefit principle the tax is intended as a method of taxing final purchasers, it may be viewed as a personal tax distinguished by the fact that the allocation of the tax burden is designed to reflect the benefits which the final purchasers derive from governmental services rather than ability to pay considerations. The extent to which the allocation of the tax burden under the benefit principle will differ from that under the ability to pay principle will depend upon the formulas used to implement the principles. In any event, the use of the value-added procedure has no significance as such because another method of collecting the tax might have been used if the value-added procedure had not been thought to offer certain technical advantages. If the value-added tax is recommended as a substitute for profits taxation under these principles, it reflects a wish to lighten the tax burden on business profits, sometimes because shifting of the profits tax makes its retention irrational; it is not because the value-added tax is expected to rest on such profits.

On the other hand, at least one version of the benefit thesis has come to be identified with the value-added method of collecting the tax. This version conceives of the tax as a charge for the benefits of governmental services which directly benefit business enterprises—that is, services which make it possible for the concerns to lower their costs; and the tax may be recommended as a substitute for business profits taxation and all other taxes imposed on business enterprises, notably property taxes. Thus, for example, Dr. Gerhard Colm considers a value-added measure the appropriate one in the United States "only if we had *one* single tax on enterprise for federal, state, and local governments."[2] In the case of this version of the benefit principle, it is not clear what the incidence of the value-added tax is expected to be, a subject discussed in more detail in a later section of this chapter.

The importance of relating any proposal for value-added taxation to the particular principle of taxation which it is supposed to represent, or, in other words, the allocation of the tax burden among individual taxpayers

[2] Gerhard Colm, "The Corporation and the Corporate Income Tax in the American Economy," *Essays in Public Finance and Fiscal Policy* (New York, 1955), p. 99.

which it is expected to effect, is forcefully demonstrated by the case of the Japanese value-added tax designed to raise income for the Japanese prefectures. In this instance, controversy arose over whether there was any distinction between a sales tax and a business tax based on sales and, if so, the nature of the distinction. Failure to resolve the conflict became a major factor in the successive postponement of the effective date of the measure originally scheduled for January 1, 1952, and its complete abrogation in 1954, before the legislation was ever put into effect. True, even if both sides of the controversy had reached agreement on what the legislation was intended to accomplish, they might have disagreed over whether it would in fact accomplish its aims; but there was never even a meeting of minds over the principle underlying the tax.

As the issue raised in Japan persists in being the most fundamental source of confusion in thinking about value-added taxation, this introductory chapter is largely concerned with relating the value-added tax to the various principles of taxation which it is capable of implementing. We thereby seek to appraise the extent to which the distinction between a sales tax and a so-called business tax based on sales has any significance.

The chapter first presents the value-added tax merely as one method of collecting a sales tax, defined for this purpose as a tax on the value of the product expected to be borne by final purchasers, the comparison with other methods being made primarily through simple numerical examples. This first step is essential in order to make clear the general relationship of the value-added technique to other methods of collecting a sales tax which may be used to implement a given principle and also to demonstrate the implications of various methods of assessing the value-added tax itself.

The next section provides a summary explanation of the principles of indirect personal taxation which sales taxes are capable of implementing. The various methods of collecting sales taxes are compared with the aid of numerical examples in terms of the principles of indirect personal taxation which they are supposed to effect, presumably on the basis of some ability to pay or benefit thesis.

The final section examines the value-added tax as applied under different versions of the benefit principle, especially the business-benefit thesis. Emphasis is placed on the implications of the different versions for the allocation of the tax burden among individual taxpayers.

Various points raised in the course of discussion are often illustrated with reference to other general discussions of the measure and specific tax proposals or legislation. However, a detailed description of specific legislation is postponed to the following two chapters of Part I, which are concerned with the French and Japanese legislation, respectively, the laws being analyzed in terms of their effectiveness in applying the principles which they are supposed to represent. Moreover, although the discussion is concerned with tax principles and therefore problems of tax incidence, these issues are treated in summary fashion, a more detailed consideration being postponed to Chapters 4 and 7.

TAX ON VALUE ADDED AS COLLECTION DEVICE

The general turnover tax, the value-added tax, and the single-stage tax may be regarded as three methods of collecting sales taxes defined for purposes of the comparison as taxes on the value of products expected to raise prices by the amount of the tax.[3] This proposition may be illustrated with the aid of simple numerical examples.

In the first example, assume three business firms, one at the manufacturing stage, one at the wholesale stage, and one at the retail stage, with the manufacturer selling a product for $100 to the wholesaler who in turn sells it for $125 to the retailer, who finally sells it to the ultimate consumer or user for $200. With a rate of 10 percent, the different procedures of collecting the tax may be visualized as shown in Example I.

Both the value-added and single-stage procedures eliminate the multiple taxation imposed under the general turnover tax, which otherwise could be avoided only if the three independent firms had been combined into one. The correction under the value-added procedure is made through measures which, generally speaking, limit the tax liability

---

[3] "Indirect taxes" are defined as taxes on products in the Treaty establishing the European Economic Community (Arts. 95–97), as noted by Georges Vedel, "Les aspects fiscaux du Marché Commun," *Bulletin for International Fiscal Documentation*, XII (1958), 333, 337. While useful for certain analyses, this definition says nothing about the allocation of the tax burden—in fact less than the one used here, which at least assumes forward shifting. In any case, the direct-indirect terminology has been abandoned in the report of the Fiscal and Financial Committee of the EEC, which designates those taxes defined by the Treaty as taxes on products as taxes on the employment of income. See Communauté Économique Européenne, Commission, *Rapport du Comité Fiscal et Financier* (1962), p. 24, and International Bureau of Fiscal Documentation, *The EEC Reports on Tax Harmonization* (Amsterdam, 1963), p. 113.

of each firm to its contribution to the value of the final product. The correction under the single-stage procedure is effected by allowing business firms to sell intermediate products without paying tax if the purchaser supplies an exemption certificate stating the firm's intention to use the product in a manner warranting the tax-free purchase. In other words, payment of the tax is "suspended" until the product reaches the final taxable stage, that is, the retail stage, if the total value of the product is to be reached. The amount of tax on the final value of the product is the same as under the value-added procedure—$20 in Example I.

EXAMPLE I. Comparative Operation of General Turnover Tax, Single-Stage Tax, and Value-Added Tax, with 10% Rate

	Value of Product Excluding Tax	General Turnover Tax[a]	Value-Added Excluding Tax	Value-Added Tax	Single-Stage Tax
Manufacturing stage	$100	$10.00	$100	$10.00	—
Wholesale stage	125	13.50	25	2.50	—
Retail stage	200	22.35	75	7.50	$20.00
Final value of product	$200		$200		
Tax on final value		$45.85[a]	$20.00	$20.00	$20.00

[a] The general turnover tax has been imposed on the value at each stage as increased by the tax at the previous stage. Under a value-added tax, this type of multiple taxation is avoided by a legal provision that the firm's accounts register purchases net of tax.

In contrast to the single-stage method of eliminating multiple taxation of the same values, the value-added procedure may be implemented through more than one approach. Either an addition or subtraction procedure may be used to compute a firm's value added while the subtraction procedure may in turn be applied in two different ways, the "sales method" and the "tax-credit method."

The addition approach consists in adding various bookkeeping items, specifically the payments made by the firm to the factors of production employed in turning out the product, such as wages, interest, rent, royalties, and profits. Under the subtraction approach, one procedure, herein called the "sales- or cost-subtraction method" deducts a firm's outlays on intermediate products from its taxable sales. The other subtraction method, herein called the "tax-credit method" deducts the value-added tax which the firm pays on its purchases from the value-added tax due on its sales.

On the assumption that intermediate products are defined in the same way under the addition and sales procedures, the tax base is identical and therefore so is the tax liability, given the same tax rate at every stage of production. Some divergence would occur, however, if under the sales procedure no deduction were allowed on exempt products, a measure sometimes suggested, and a compensating adjustment were not made in the addition approach.

The tax-credit procedure will always give the same results as the other methods provided that the credits are allowed on products classified as intermediate under the other approaches, provided that no sales are exempt from tax, and provided that there is no other differentiation of tax rates at different stages. Given exemptions, the results under the tax-credit procedure will not coincide with those under the other methods except in the case where exemptions at earlier stages are made non-deductible under the addition and sales procedures. Given other rate differentiation, the results will never coincide.

The situation under the three procedures is best illustrated through numerical examples, as in Examples II and III, which use three stages of processing a product and values of the product at each stage of $100, $125, and $200, respectively with the total value of the product consisting of the payments made to the various factors of production. For simplification in presentation, assume in Example II that the payments to the factors of production consist of only wages and profits, with the amounts of wages and profits at the various stages as shown in the example. Then, value added at Stage I may be computed by adding the $70 of wages and $30 of profits or, alternatively, may be obtained through subtracting purchases of intermediate products (zero in this case) from sales of $100. If the intermediate product turned out at Stage II had been exempt from tax and the subtraction of purchases of exempt products had been disallowed at Stage III under the sales procedure, value added at Stage III would have been $100 rather than $75. For equivalent results under the addition procedure, purchases of exempt products would have had to be added to the tax base of the firm at Stage III.

As previously indicated, it is necessary to assume that intermediate products are similarly defined under the two procedures. If, for example, the addition procedure defined as a factor payment an item classified as an intermediate product under the subtraction approach, the results would differ. This would occur, for instance, if a firm's interest and rental payments were considered part of its factor payments under the addition approach but under the subtraction procedure were treated as purchases of intermediate products. Similarly, the results would not be the same if a firm's profits were defined under the addition approach so as to be only net of depreciation of capital investment while the subtraction procedure allowed the deduction of purchases of capital goods, thereby treating them as an intermediate product instead of a final purchase which would be capitalized and depreciated. A more detailed explanation of these accounting problems is provided in Chapter 5.

EXAMPLE II. Addition and Sales- or Cost-Subtraction Procedure of Computing Value Added

Value of Product at Each Stage	Value of Product Excluding Tax and of Components of Value	Value Added through Addition Procedure	Value Added through Sales Procedure
Stage I			
Value of product	*$100*		$100
Intermediate product	0		–0
Wages	70	$ 70	
Profits	30	30	
Value added at Stage I		100	100
Stage II			
Value of product	*125*		125
Intermediate product	100		–100
Wages	20	20	
Profits	5	5	
Value added at Stage II		25	25
Stage III			
Value of product	*200*		200
Intermediate product	125		–125
Wages	55	55	
Profits	20	20	
Value added at Stage III		75	75
Final value of product or total value added	$200	$200	$200

Given rate differentiation, including exemptions, which in effect represent a differentiated rate of zero, the most efficient method of assessing the value-added tax is through the use of the tax-credit procedure under which the effective tax rate on the final value of the product can be made equal to the rate stipulated in the legislation. This is illustrated in Example III where the tax-credit procedure is compared with the sales procedure in three cases: (1) a uniform rate of 10 percent, (2) a rate of 20 percent at Stage I and 10 percent at other stages, (3) a rate of 20 percent at the final stage and 10 percent at other stages. Example III makes it evident that, given rate differentiation, the tax burden on the final value of the product will not coincide with the tax rate intended by the legislation except under the procedure which allows tax credits for taxes imposed at higher rates on vendors than on business purchasers and which, in the case of taxes imposed at lower rates on vendors than on business purchasers, in effect limits the deductions for purchases of intermediate products commensurately with the extent to which the tax on the vendor lies below the rate imposed on the purchaser. Thus, in Example III, when the rate on the final value of the product is supposed to be 10 percent, it actually amounts to 15 percent when the sales procedure is used with a 20 percent rate at Stage I despite the 10 percent rate at later stages; and, when the legal rate on the final value of the product is 20 percent but a 10 percent rate has been imposed at earlier stages, the sales procedure yields an effective rate of only 13.75 percent. Meanwhile, the tax-credit mechanism always yields an effective rate equal to the one provided in the statute for the final value of the product.

EXAMPLE III. Comparison of Sales Procedure and Tax-Credit Procedure of Computing Value Added under Three Conditions in Rates

Value of Product at Each Stage	Value Added	Uniform 10% Rate	20% Rate at Stage I	20% Rate at Stage III
		Sales Procedure		
Stage I: $100	$100	$10.00	$20.00	$10.00
Stage II: $125	25	2.50	2.50	2.50
Stage III: $200	75	7.50	7.50	15.00
Final value: $200 Tax on final value		$20.00	$30.00	$27.50
		Tax-Credit Procedure		
Stage I: $100	$100	$10 − $0 = $10.00	$20 − $0 = $20.00	$10 − $0 = $10.00
Stage II: $125	25	12.50 − 10 = 2.50	12.50 − 20 = −7.50[a]	12.50 − 10 = 2.50
Stage III: $200	75	20 − 12.50 = 7.50	20 − 12.50 = 7.50	40 − 12.50 = 27.50
Final value: $200 Tax on final value		$20.00	$20.00	$40.00

[a] The firm at Stage II is entitled to a reimbursement for his excess tax credits of $7.50 so that he will invoice a tax of $12.50 to his customer at Stage III. Thus the final value of the product will be taxed at the rate intended by the statute, or 10%.

Any of the above procedures of collecting a sales tax may be limited to a stage prior to the retail stage. If the tax is restricted to the manufacturing level, only manufacturers are registered as taxpayers. If the tax extends through the wholesale level, manufacturers and wholesalers are registered. Then, given a general turnover tax, only registered firms are subjected to the tax. Under the single-stage tax, only registered firms are permitted to purchase in suspension of tax. In the case of the value-added tax, only registered firms are entitled to deductions or tax credits. Constructive pricing is necessary with all procedures when operations of firms at taxable stages are integrated with those at nontaxable stages. Moreover, the taxation of services creates a problem because it is impossible to limit the tax to their manufacturing or wholesale value in all instances. An even more important disadvantage of the manufacturers' and wholesalers' taxes is the impossibility of defining taxable price in such a way as to avoid including in the tax base of some firms values which are not taxed to competitors, because in the case of the latter the values are added by other firms located in a nontaxable stage.

An Improved Turnover Tax

The procedure of assessing a sales tax on the aggregate turnover of every business firm constitutes a primitive method of collection. It imposes the tax every time that a business firm sells a taxable product, that is, transfers the product to another independent business or to a non-business purchaser. In other words, the amount of tax imposed on the product at its last taxable stage varies with the number of market transfers or turnovers which have taken place at previous stages.[4] As the tax is avoided when market transfers are eliminated through the combination of independent business firms, it is obvious that it subsidizes integration. On the whole, only vertical integration is favored; but presumably some horizontal integration may be stimulated as, for example, by the tax savings which result when a firm is able to economize through purchasing large rather than small quantities.

[4] It may be noted that the current German turnover tax allows tax-free transfers among legally independent firms having the same ownership (*die Unternehmereinheit*) and also among separate enterprises deemed to be related through economic, financial, and organizational interdependence (*der Organschaft*). See Henry J. Gumpel, *Taxation in the Federal Republic of Germany* (World Tax Series, Harvard Law School International Program in Taxation [Chicago, 1963]), 16/2.3 and 16/2.4. Presumably, the rationale for these arrangements is that actual combination would otherwise occur under the pressures exerted by the turnover tax.

If the benefits from tax savings by a firm's production of its intermediate products and investment goods were not offset by internal diseconomies, one might logically expect the process of vertical integration to continue under a turnover tax imposed at every stage until the concerns which turned out a given consumer product accounted for its entire value from the raw material to the finished stage as well as for the value of all necessary plant and equipment. This certainly is not a development conducive to pure competition or, for that matter, even to workable competition, and a fortiori if the tax fosters some horizontal integration.

In practice, different industries come to be characterized by different degrees of integration and within each industry individual firms experience discriminatory tax treatment. The differential tax treatment of various products in effect converts a general measure into a conglomeration of special excises or selective sales taxes. In conjunction with the unequal treatment of firms within an industry, the tax may be assumed to interfere with the optimum allocation of resources.[5] The competitive inequities and inefficiencies caused by the cumulative nature of the general turnover tax were responsible for the first proposal for value-added taxation, that of Dr. Wilhelm von Siemens, a German businessman and governmental consultant, who called his proposal the "improved turnover tax" or "the refined turnover tax."[6] The improvement consisted in the subtraction of previous outlays from taxable sales[7] with the result that the tax base of each firm would be reduced to the value which it added to the product.[8] Thus the von Siemens proposal apparently uses the sales procedure with subtractions not limited to previously taxed items.

[5] For a concise exposition of the welfare criteria as affected by special excises, see Richard A. Musgrave, *The Theory of Public Finance* (New York, 1959), pp. 142–54. On pp. 149–52, Professor Musgrave presents the theoretical case for special taxes designed to improve the allocation of resources, given market imperfections or an elastic supply of effort. However, there is no reason to suppose that a general turnover tax implements that philosophy.

[6] See Gerhard Colm, "Methods of Financing Unemployment Compensation," *Social Research,* II (May, 1935), 161.

[7] A description of the proposal may be found in "Nr. 200, Vorläufiger Reichswirtschaftsrat," *Verhandlungen des Reichstags, Anlagen zu den Stenographischen Berichten* (1920/21).

[8] Various terms are used in German for value added, including *Nettoumsatz, Wertzuwachs, Mehrwert, Werterhöhung, Wertschöpfung.* See Günter Schmölders, "Die Veredelung der Umsatzsteuer," *Public Finance,* IX, No. 2 (1954), 110, 111, 119; Hanya Ito, "Theorie und Technik der Nettoumsatzsteuer in Japan," *Finanzarchiv,* XV, No. 3 (1955), 447. It should be noted that on occasion some of the terms have a special connotation, such as *Wertschöpfung* which may mean "value originating within a given area."

The value-added tax recommended by the Shoup Mission for use by the Japanese prefectures and considered in some detail in Chapter 3 of this book was combined with the recommendation that the national transactions tax, a general turnover tax, be abolished. Strictly speaking, however, the yield of the value-added tax was intended to replace the receipts from a profits tax rather than a sales tax.

Use of the value-added technique to avoid the multiple taxation which would occur when every market transfer is taxed may be found in the sales tax legislation of a few countries. For example, the system is used under the manufacturers' sales taxes in the Argentine, the Philippines, and Greece. In the case of the Argentine, the 8 percent manufacturers' sales tax, in force since 1935, when it replaced a general turnover tax, allows a subtraction for sales of previously taxed "physical ingredients," that is, materials and parts.[9] The Philippine manufacturers' sales tax, which replaced a general turnover tax in 1939 and which contains a high degree of rate differentiation according to the type of product, allows the manufacturer to reduce his taxable sales by the cost of previously taxed materials.[10] The Greek manufacturers' sales tax introduced in 1933 in the general turnover form is currently imposed at the general rate of 6 percent and since 1948 has provided that the taxable gross receipts of industrial enterprises, artisans, and suppliers of electricity and gas be reduced by outlays on materials previously subjected to tax when purchased from other firms or imported. Taxpayers are required to keep a sales tax account in their books which debits the amount of tax paid to suppliers or the Treasury and credits the amounts collected on sales of the articles.[11]

An instance of a somewhat different view of the value-added procedure as an improvement over the general turnover method is provided by a proposal once made by the Société pour la Défense du Commerce et de l'Industrie, Marseille, to substitute the value-added system for the French 2 percent general turnover tax of the twenties.[12] Instead of being sug-

---

[9] For a description of the Argentinian tax, see Dino Jarach, "L'impôt sur les ventes dans la République Argentine," *Impôts sur transactions, transmissions et chiffre d'affaires,* ed. by M. Masoin and E. Morselli (Paris, 1959), pp. 51–56.

[10] *Tax Systems of the World,* 13th ed. (Chicago, 1952), p. 471.

[11] M. A. Nezis, "Rapport de M. A. Nezis, Directeur au Ministère grec des Finances," *Cahiers de droit fiscal international,* XXIV (Paris, 1953), 63–64. For a more detailed description of the legislation, see Panayotis B. Dertilis, "L'impôt sur le chiffre d'affaires en Grèce," *Impôts sur transactions, transmissions et chiffre d'affaires,* pp. 201–24.

[12] See Carl S. Shoup, *The Sales Tax in France* (New York, 1930), p. 318.

gested as a remedy for the subsidy to integration, it had been advanced as a means of correcting the discrimination in favor of highly finished goods as compared with coarser goods retailing at the same price exclusive of tax and undergoing the same number of market transfers. For example, assume two products selling for $100 without tax which are turned out in two stages of economic activity, the first stage involving the production of materials and the last stage combining finishing and distribution of the final product. Let value added at the first stage in the case of Product I be $75 and, in the case of Product II, $25. Then the general turnover tax will discriminate against Product I while the value-added tax will not. This is illustrated in Example IV, where a 4 percent turnover tax, which imposes a burden of 7.12 percent on the final value of Product I, is compared with a 7.12 percent value-added tax.

Under the value-added tax, the tax burden will be the same regardless of varying proportions of value added at different stages. Under the general turnover tax, the larger the proportion of value added at earlier stages the greater will be the burden, because of the multiple counting of the previous values. Thus, in Example IV, the general turnover tax of 4

EXAMPLE IV. Comparative Tax Burden on Products Having Varying Proportions of Value Added at Different Stages under General Turnover Tax and Value-Added Tax

	General Turnover Tax (4%)				Value-Added Tax (7.12%)			
	Product I		Product II		Product I		Product II	
	Value of Product	Amount of Tax	Value of Product	Amount of Tax	Value Added	Amount of Tax	Value Added	Amount of Tax
First stage	$ 75	$3.00	$ 25	$1.00	$ 75	$5.34	$ 25	$1.78
Second stage	100	4.12	100	4.04	25	1.78	75	5.34
		$7.12		$5.04	$100	$7.12	$100	$7.12

percent imposes a burden on the final product of 7.12 percent when 75 percent of the value has been added at the first stage, and only 5.04 percent when 25 percent of value has been added at the first stage. Meanwhile, the burden under the value-added tax of 7.12 percent is the same regardless of the distribution of value at different stages. It is interesting to note that this type of discriminatory impact under the general turnover tax is currently receiving consideration, not with respect to coarser and more finished products or with respect to products involving varying proportions of value added at the distributive stages as compared with the manufacturing stage or at the retail as compared with the wholesale stage of distribution, but with respect to capital intensive and labor intensive output.[13]

A Substitute for a Single-Stage Tax

As a method of correcting the multiple taxation of successive turnovers, the value-added tax becomes an alternative to the single-stage method of collecting a sales tax. To the extent that sales taxes are viewed as taxes on products or as indirect personal taxation, choice between the single-stage and value-added procedures involves only administrative issues, which are discussed in detail in Chapter 7. Generally speaking, the value-added method possesses an administrative advantage over the single-stage approach only with respect to the exemption of small firms. However, the value-added procedure appears to be the appropriate method for taxing internationally traded products when the jurisdictional principle of origin is to be applied. Thirdly, certain principles of business taxation imply use of the value-added procedure. Both jurisdictional principles and the view of the value-added tax as a business tax are discussed later in this chapter.

An example of the replacement of a single-stage procedure by the value-added method is provided by France which, through a decree of September 25, 1948 (Decree No. 48-1493), based on Article 12 of the law of September 24, 1948 (Law No. 48-1479), replaced the single-stage method of collecting its manufacturers' sales tax imposed at a general rate of 11 percent and reduced rate of 4 percent with the value-added procedure. The new system was called "fractional payments"

[13] See Bela Balassa, *The Theory of Economic Integration* (Homewood, Ill., 1961), p. 240. It is held that the general turnover tax will discriminate against capital intensive industries as compared with labor intensive industries. In other words, capital goods are regarded as values added at early stages of production and, assuming the same number of market transfers as in the case of labor intensive products, the turnover tax overburdens the capital intensive products. In reality, the number of market transfers is likely to be much less than in the case of labor intensive products. However, there is no doubt that the general turnover tax imposes burdens in an exceedingly erratic manner as compared with the value-added procedure. The treatment accorded capital goods under various principles of sales taxation are discussed later in this chapter, and the issues involved are discussed in more detail throughout Part II.

(*paiements fractionnées*), the tax being imposed on sales of all manufacturers of taxable products with a credit for the taxes paid on their purchases of various items currently expensed. In line with usual practice in sales tax legislation, the avoidance of multiple taxation was not provided for all items currently expensed; in the French legislation, it was limited to physical ingredients, sales for resale, and items consumed on first use, while items rapidly consumed were deductible from taxable sales up to 50 percent of their value.

Although advanced as a method of accelerating tax collections, the new procedure in itself merely substituted the value-added technique for the suspensive system under which tax was paid only by the manufacturer who sold his product to the distributive sphere or used it for investment in his own business; and the taxes collected at earlier stages reduced the taxes due at later stages. For the most part, accelerated collections resulted from a special provision in the legislation which provided that the tax on sales could only be reduced by credits arising from purchases in the previous month. As no credits against the tax on sales were available in the first month of the new tax, the tax applied to gross sales and hence brought increased receipts of about 20 to 25 billion francs as compared with an annual yield from the production tax of around 300 billion francs.[14] Also, a slight additional yield may have been obtained to the extent that excess tax credits derived from inventory purchases were not reimbursed immediately but were carried forward to subsequent months, a carryforward being required under the "buffer rule," as explained in Chapter 2.

Another example of the choice of the value-added technique of collection in preference to a single-stage tax is provided by the recommendation of the value-added tax in Japan. Here, the recommendation for the value-added procedure was made only after consideration had been given to the possibility of using a single-stage retail sales tax, the latter being rejected because of the difficulty of ensuring payment by the tremendous number of small retailers who by making purchases in suspension of tax would endanger the collection of tax on the entire value of the product rather than only value added at the retail stage.

---

[14] See Roger Giraudeau, "Considérations sur les récentes fluctuations saisonnières du rendement des taxes sur le chiffre d'affaires," *Revue de science et de législation financières*, XLI (Paris, 1949), 472 ff.

Survey of Methods of Computing Value-Added Tax

Although, in the absence of a uniform rate,[15] the tax-credit procedure seems to be the more efficient method of computing the value-added tax if the tax is expected to be shifted forward through an increase in product prices by the amount of the tax, it has not been universally applied either in practice or in theory. The credit method was first suggested by Thomas S. Adams, a professor at Yale University and governmental consultant who, in recommending a value-added measure, defined it as a "sales tax with a credit or refund for taxes paid by the producer or dealer (as purchaser) on goods bought for resale or for necessary use in the poduction of goods for sale."[16]

The French legislation uses this approach although, as explained in the following chapter, special provisions have interfered with the complete implementation of the credit. The Greek system also seems to apply the credit approach through its administrative arrangements, but details of the operation of the system have not been available in general treatises. On the other hand, the Argentine and Philippine laws use the sales procedure while restricting deductions to previously taxed items. Rate differentiation is not extensive in the Argentine although it is in the Philippines. In the case of the Japanese value-added tax, the sales procedure was adopted, and without limiting deductions to previously taxed items. However, in the law as finally adopted, the rate of tax was low and the differentiation moderate, consisting of a limited number of exemptions and a 3 percent rate for extractive industries, professions, and personal services as compared with a 4 percent general rate. Also, the value-added proposal for intermember trade in the European Economic Community assumes use of the sales procedure combined with a minimum of domestic and intermember rate differentiation.[17]

Most of the proposals for value-added taxation advanced in the United States, chiefly for use by state governments as "business taxes" but oc-

[15] The rate of differentiation in the law will be stated in terms of different commodities or different types of activities; but, of course, this involves rate differentiation at different economic stages because a product bought for final use by some purchasers will be treated as an intermediate item by others.

[16] "Fundamental Problems of Federal Income Taxation," *Quarterly Journal of Economics,* XXV (Aug., 1921), 553.

[17] International Bureau of Fiscal Documentation, *The EEC Reports on Tax Harmonization,* p. 175.

casionally considered for federal use, seem also to have taken it for granted that the sales procedure would be used. This was the case of a proposal for a "production tax" to be imposed on incorporated and unincorporated firms in New York State.[18] Similarly, during the early thirties, the Brookings Institution recommended a value-added tax designated as a tax on "net value product" in the states of Alabama and Iowa in conjunction with a net income tax on business profits and a minimum lump-sum tax for both incorporated and unincorporated firms. The business concern would be liable for the tax yielding the greatest amount or for the value-added tax in the event that its bookkeeping were inadequate to assess the income tax but its tax liability exceeded the minimum tax.[19] As in the case of the proposal for New York, the Brookings' recommendation limited subtractions to previously taxed outlays.

In an essay which recommends the value-added tax as a general business tax, Professor Studenski assumes the sales procedure without indicating that he would restrict the subtractions to previously taxed items.[20] Professor Colm makes a similar assumption, also noting that the tax base may be derived through the procedure of adding payments to factors of production—wages, interest, and profits.[21] Both assume proportional rates, but the extent to which they would allow exemptions is not clear.

As recently as 1953, a committee of the National Tax Association recommended that state policymakers consider the value-added tax as a possible substitute for the heterogeneous taxes on tangible personal property used in business.[22] Calling the tax the "income production" tax, the committee apparently assumed it would employ the sales procedure adopted by the Japanese legislation.[23]

[18] Presented by J. F. Zoller, tax attorney for General Electric, Charles J. Tobin, of the New York State Bar, and John J. Merrill, a member of the New York State Tax Commission. *Proceedings of the Twenty-Second Annual Conference of the National Tax Association, 1929* (Columbia, S. C., 1930), pp. 104–26.

[19] See Brookings Institution, *Report on a Survey of the Organization and Administration of the State and County Governments of Alabama* (Montgomery, Ala., 1932), IV, Pt. III, 341–398; and Brookings Institution, *Report on a Survey of Administration in Iowa: The Revenue System* (Washington, D.C., 1933), pp. 120–54.

[20] Paul Studenski, "Toward a Theory of Business Taxation," *The Journal of Political Economy*, XLVIII (Oct., 1940), 648.

[21] Gerhard Colm, "Methods of Financing Unemployment Compensation," *Social Research*, II (Apr., 1935), 161.

[22] "Report of the Committee on Personal Property Taxation on Possible Substitutes for Ad Valorem Taxation of Tangible Personal Property Used in Business," *Proceedings of the Forty-Sixth Annual Conference of the National Tax Association, 1953* (Sacramento, Calif., 1954), p. 364.

[23] *Ibid.*, pp. 390–91.

The Michigan Business Activities Tax adopted in 1953 uses the sales procedure for its version of value-added taxation and allows the subtraction of purchases from exempt concerns, presumably in conformity with the view of the Committee of the National Tax Association. This tax is imposed at an exceedingly low rate of 7¾ mills with a reduced rate of 2 mills for public utilities.

To some extent the correlation between use of the sales procedure and the concept of the value-added tax as a business tax may merely reflect use of the origin principle for products traded among independent political jurisdictions—a principle discussed in detail later in this chapter and which may be roughly defined as the rule which taxes exported products and exempts imported products. For example, the Fiscal and Financial Committee of the EEC assumes the sales procedure for the value-added tax proposal because the tax is to be imposed on the origin principle. The committee maintains that, if rates differ between two jurisdictions, value added in the importing country imposing the lower rate would be undertaxed because of the excess tax credits arising under the tax of the exporting country and vice versa for value added by importers in the higher taxing country.[24] The solution to this technical problem appears simple, however. It is merely necessary that the importer be allowed to use the taxable value underlying the amount of tax and apply the tax rate of his own country in computing the tax credit. Of course, this procedure assumes agreement on the rules of origin employed in allocating the value of the import and the manner in which they have been applied.

Whether use of the sales procedure reflects varying views on incidence of the tax is a more profound matter. Its use is frequently assumed for the application of various business-benefit concepts; but as indicated in the section dealing with these concepts, it seems essential in only one case, provided that the economic system is not dominated by administered prices.

TAX ON VALUE ADDED AS A METHOD OF IMPLEMENTING INDIRECT PERSONAL TAXATION

The comparative methods of collecting sales taxes can best be understood in terms of the general principles of taxation which they are

[24] International Bureau of Fiscal Documentation, *The EEC Reports on Tax Harmonization*, p. 130.

supposed to implement. Probably sales taxes of any significance have been intended as indirect methods of personal taxation. In other words, they are used as a substitute for taxes assessed on individual income recipients in conformity with some concept of individual ability to pay or, alternatively, with some assumption regarding the distribution among individuals of the benefits derived from governmental outlays.

In most cases the taxes have probably been intended as a substitute for the direct expenditure tax—that is, they have been regarded as a method of taxing individuals in accordance with their consumption outlays. Given the income inequality which characterizes most economic systems and the general rule that the proportion of consumption expenditures to income varies inversely with income levels, taxes which rest on consumption outlays only are regressive. Nevertheless, such taxes are deemed compatible with the ability to pay principle by those who define income as consumption and even by those who, accepting conventional income concepts, regard consumption as an index of ability to pay. When imposed under the benefit principle, the benefits from governmental services are presumably viewed as having been distributed regressively.

Sales taxes may be designed to approximate income taxation rather than expenditure taxation. In that event, they will be constituted so as to avoid regressiveness by reaching individual savings as well as consumption. They will then also be capable of implementing either some ability to pay principle or a benefit principle in which the distribution of the tax burden is assumed to coincide with the expected distribution of the governmental benefits among individuals.

Usually, the ability to pay principle has implied a progressive distribution of the tax burden among individual income recipients. On the other hand, it has probably been conventional to assume that most public expenditures are made only if their benefits are expected to be distributed generally among individual income recipients in such a way as to justify a proportional distribution of the tax burden.[25] However, as explained in Chapter 4, no theoretical proof of the correctness of these assumptions is available, so that the distributional policy becomes a matter for governmental decision, however derived.

[25] Even if the assumption is made that the benefits are distributed proportionately, a progressive tax rate may conceivably be justified on the ground that the government is in a monopolistic position and therefore able to charge differentiated prices—a point made by Antonio de Viti de Marco, *First Principles of Public Finance,* trans. by Edith Pavlo Marget (New York, 1936), pp. 171–72.

In any case, the problem here is not to discuss the justification of any particular distribution of the tax burden. Rather it is to demonstrate the manner in which sales taxes can be used as a substitute for taxes assessed directly on income recipients, given the decision as to how the tax burden is to be allocated.

The relationship of personal concepts of sales taxation to expenditure and income taxes imposed on individual income recipients will first be examined in terms of a closed economy, that is, one in which products and factors of production do not move across the borders of independent political jurisdictions. Secondly, it is assumed that because of imperfect competition and rigidities of prices and costs, equivalence between the indirect and direct technique of assessing individual incomes requires that product prices be allowed to rise by the amount of the tax. In other words, the position taken coincides with that of Professor Schmölders when he says that forward shifting must be assumed if a sales tax is to possess the character of a *Verbrauchsteuer*,[26] which is usually translated as "consumption tax" but is herein translated as "purchase tax" in order to encompass purchases of products destined for final investment use as well as ultimate consumption.

After examining the personal tax concepts in a closed economy, consideration will be given to the appropriate treatment of imports and exports. On the other hand, little attention will be paid to the issues raised when allowance is made for interjurisdictional factor movements. Such issues may range in significance from marginal considerations to those of vital importance, but there is neither time nor space to do justice to the subject in this study.[27]

[26] "Der Überwalzung der Umsatzsteuer mit deren Gelingen ihr Charakter als Verbrauchsteuer steht und fällt. . . ." (The forward shifting of the sales tax with whose success its character as a purchase tax stands or falls [*my translation*].) Günter Schmölders, *Organische Steuerreform, Grundlagen, Vorarbeiten, Gesetzentwürfe* (Berlin and Frankfurt, 1953), p. 128.

[27] Interesting and valuable work is being done in this area, especially by some European scholars, notably Professor James E. Meade of the University of Cambridge as well as Dr. Maria-Dolores Schulte and Professor Hans Möller of the University of Munich. See, for example, James E. Meade, *The Theory of International Economic Policy, Trade and Welfare* (London, 1960), Vol. II; Maria-Dolores Schulte, Die Wirtschaftspolitischen Grundlagen des Bestimmungsland- und des Ursprungslandprinzips, paper given at Institut International de Finances Publiques, Luxembourg Congress, 1963, and Den Einfluss unterschiedlicher Steuersysteme auf den Wettbewerb innerhalb eines Gemeinsamen Marktes, doctoral dissertation, Univ. of Munich, 1961; and Hans Möller, "Das Ursprungs- und

Closed Economy: Consumption Principle

If the government wishes to impose a tax on individuals in their capacity as consumers, it may do so by requiring that each individual report the amount of his expenditures during a given period and apply a given tax rate to this amount.[28] Thus, suppose that an individual with an income of $2,200 reports spendings of $2000 during a given period. He may be required to pay a tax of, say, 10 percent on his $2,000 of consumer spendings, or $200. On the other hand, rather than assess him in this manner, the government may for some reason prefer to impose a 10 percent sales tax so as to reduce the real value of his $2,200 income through an increase in the price of the products which he purchases.[29]

To do this for every consumer in the community and thus reach the aggregate consumption of the area, it is necessary to impose the sales tax on all products purchased by ultimate consumers whether in the form of goods or services. Therefore, under a general sales tax, all independent producers of such goods and services should be defined as business enterprises and the 10 percent sales tax should be collected from these business concerns, which are expected to raise prices by the amount of the tax.

The prices of final consumption products may be expected to rise by 10 percent on the average; and the monetary policy necessary to permit this rise must be adopted.[30] Not all prices will rise by 10 percent over their pretax level given the fact that the income elasticity of consumer demand will differ from industry to industry and not all industries are char-

---

Bestimmungslandprinzip" (1962), in which Möller applies to this problem the tools of analysis developed by Meade, Schulte, and Professor Richard A. Musgrave, *The Theory of Public Finance* (New York, 1959).

[28] For a detailed analysis of the concept of direct expenditure taxation, see William Vickrey, *Agenda for Progressive Taxation* (New York, 1947), *passim*. Professor Vickrey gives a concise explanation of how expenditures are measured on pp. 4–6. In brief, a true expenditure tax requires that the taxpayer report all receipts available for expenditure and subtract amounts saved or invested. It differs from a true net income tax in that increases in net worth during the period are nontaxable. For another astute analysis, see Nicholas Kaldor, *An Expenditure Tax* (London, 1955).

[29] The 10% sales tax amounts to 9.1% of price including tax just as the 10% direct spendings tax amounts to 9.1% of income including tax. Assuming that the individual maintains the same amount of real expenditures after the sales tax is imposed, he will spend $2,200 rather than $2,000.

[30] See Musgrave, *Theory of Public Finance*, pp. 365–71.

acterized by constant costs.[31] Moreover, the amount sold by all or some industries will have to decline in order to release resources for governmental use. However, the situation should be about the same as if a direct spendings tax had been imposed and the taxpayer proceeded to make adjustments in his outlays on consumption goods. In other words, the effect should be the same as if under a system of administered prices a 10 percent additional charge had been added to the prices of consumption goods, and the ultimate consumer had then been allowed to make adjustments in his outlays in the same way as if he had been subjected to a direct expenditure tax of 10 percent.

It must be borne in mind that the indirect method of expenditure taxation does not allow the refinements in the tax measure possible under the direct approach through personal allowances and planned rate progression. Of course various arrangements are possible whereby personal allowances and progression can be effected under sales taxes through credits under income taxes imposed simultaneously with sales taxes. Also, progression might be attempted through the device of issuing coupons to individual consumers. However, these schemes are very cumbersome. Besides, under an indirect approach it is difficult and often impossible to reach individual incomes which are "hoarded," that is, held in the form of cash or assets regarded as close substitutes for cash and deemed to be a sterilization of funds, rather than a productive use, albeit the indirect approach does penalize such nonproductive uses of funds by business firms. The most rational basis for use of the indirect procedure is that of superior administrative efficiency under certain circumstances.[32]

If a sales tax is to be designed to reach only purchases by ultimate consumers, it must in effect exempt from tax not only the products bought by taxable business firms which are customarily expensed but also their purchases of items destined for investment within the business, thereby indirectly exempting the savings of the individual income recipients who are the actual taxpayers. This may be accomplished either through use of the value-added procedure or through the single-stage method of collecting a sales tax.[33]

---

[31] A more detailed discussion of how the price rise may be expected to take place is postponed to Chapter 7.

[32] The various hypotheses used to justify the indirect approach are considered in Chapter 4.

[33] In one sense, a general turnover tax may be considered a consumption type of sales tax insofar as purchases of investment goods are either taxed relatively

The sales, tax-credit, or addition methods of computing the value-added tax may be used. As previously explained, the tax-credit procedure is the only adequate one, given rate differentiation. Both the sales and addition procedures cause the rate on the finished product to vary from the rate stipulated in the legislation if different rates are applied at different stages of production or distribution. Moreover, the ability of business firms to shift the tax forward may be impaired because an individual business firm cannot assume that the amount of tax on its contribution to the product's value is the appropriate amount by which to raise its prices when rates at earlier stages are higher or lower. Of course, the tax could be quoted under the sales or addition procedures, but then why not use the tax-credit method?

Assuming a uniform rate, the value-added method of collecting a consumption tax merely requires that the taxable business firms be permitted to subtract from their taxable receipts their outlays on products purchased from other business firms whether these items are customarily expensed or capitalized. With the tax-credit method they are allowed to subtract the tax on such purchases from the tax due on their sales. In either case, the idea is that the concerns will raise their prices by the amount of the tax imposed on their sales rather than the amount of tax imposed on their value added because the former sum represents the tax on the value of the product through that stage. In addition to the firm's tax on its value added, it has paid a tax on its purchases equal to the taxes paid by all firms contributing to the value of the product along the way. The addition procedure would merely add the various factor payments.[34] with the important proviso that profits be defined in a special manner, mainly through adding to conventional net profits the amount of depreciation and subtracting the outlays on purchases of investment goods.

Under the single-stage procedure the same result is obtained by

---

lightly because they experience only one or two turnovers or, more important, because many firms, especially the very large ones, may be able to avoid the tax by producing the items within their own enterprise. However, the tax burden is imposed so irrationally that the general turnover tax will not be considered an adequate method of implementing a personal concept of sales taxation in this study. Moreover, it is impossible to apply the general turnover tax to interjurisdictional trade in a satisfactory manner.

[34] Or Musgrave's "income sources." See *Theory of Public Finance*, pp. 355–64. Musgrave's analysis with respect to the equivalence of general taxes on personal income, cost payments, business gross receipts on sales, and consumer spendings is not applied here because it relates to a model of perfect competition and zero savings.

exempting from tax all sales of products to other business firms provided that such business customers have given their suppliers exemption certificates certifying that they intend to use the products within the business. Of course, under all procedures, the tax must be applied when business firms produce items for their owners' personal consumption.

The collection of a consumption-type sales tax or an indirect spendings tax is illustrated in Example V. The example compares the application of the sales and tax-credit subtraction procedures of computing the value-added tax and the single-stage method with a 10 percent tax rate.[35]

Assume two independent business firms, A and B, which between them turn out a finished consumer product, say, cloth. In addition to manufacturing the raw material, Firm A also happens to own a patent on machinery for dyeing cloth and manufactures such machinery. It sells both the raw material and the machinery to Firm B for $10,000 and $3,000 respectively; and B in turn sells the cloth, which it dyes and finishes, to ultimate consumers for $14,000. Then the application of the various methods of collecting the consumption tax may be illustrated as shown in Example V.

EXAMPLE V. Comparison of Value-Added Methods (Sales and Tax-Credit) and Single-Stage Method of Computing Consumption-Type Sales Tax, with 10% Rate

				Value-Added Tax		Single-Stage Tax
		Value of Product at Each Stage	Value Added	Sales Method	Tax-Credit Method	
Firm A	Machine	$ 3,000				
	Cloth	10,000				
	Total	$13,000	$13,000	$1,300	$1,300−0 =$1,300	E. C.*
Firm B	Finished cloth	$14,000	1,000	100	1,400−1,300= 100	$1,400
Final value		$14,000	$14,000			
Tax on final value				$1,400	$1,400	$1,400

  * E.C.=exemption certificate.

[35] The addition procedure is not presented here because an adequate exposition of the relationship between the addition and subtraction methods requires the use of detailed accounting formulas. Therefore, the discussion of this procedure is postponed for both the consumption and income types of value-added measures until Chapter 5.

The example makes evident the equivalence between the results under the two value-added methods and the single-stage procedure; the tax amounts to $1,400. Furthermore, it is apparent that under both the sales and tax-credit procedures of computing the value-added tax the manufacturer of the machine merely advances part of the tax due on the final consumer product. The machinery is treated as an intermediate product along with the raw material.

Closed Economy: Income Principle

If instead of seeking to tax the consumption outlays of individuals in the community, the government decides to tax individual income receipts, it may do so by having the individuals report their incomes and apply the appropriate tax rate to the amount reported. Thus, if an individual has an income of $2,200 during the taxable period for which the appropriate tax rate is 9.1 percent, he will pay a tax of $200, thus reducing his income to $2,000.[36]

However, rather than assess his income directly, the government may decide to use an indirect approach. In that event, it will impose a sales tax of 10 percent, which is expected to result in a commensurate increase in the prices of the products which he purchases and thereby reduce his real income to $2,000.

As contrasted with the consumption taxes, the income principle requires that the tax reach the savings and investments of individuals as well as their consumption. With direct assessment of individual incomes, the tax is imposed on the individual's total income receipts whether the income is destined for savings and investment or for consumption. Therefore, under the indirect approach it is necessary that the sales tax apply to sales of investment goods destined for final business use as well as to sales of products destined for ultimate consumption. In other words, the tax applies to business purchases of goods customarily capitalized and depreciated rather than expensed. Thus the savings of individuals are reached indirectly through their use by business firms in purchasing investment goods. The tax on a given asset becomes incorporated in the asset's value and is thus included in the amounts which

---

[36] The 9.1% rate is used in order to arrive at a tax rate of 10% on income excluding tax, thus providing equivalence with a 10% sales tax discussed in the following paragraph.

a firm charges to depreciation as the value of the asset is used up in producing goods. If the sales tax grants an allowance for depreciation, the tax paid at time of purchase of the asset is no longer part of the depreciation charges because the tax otherwise due on the final product is reduced by the amount of tax represented in the depreciation granted on the investment good.

If depreciation is disallowed, the income type of sales tax may be termed a gross product or gross income type of tax. If depreciation is allowed, it may be designated as a net product or net income type of tax. Under the direct income tax, the allowance for depreciation reduces the taxable receipts of individual income recipients or the income of corporations under the corporate income tax.[37] Under the sales taxes, the taxable sales of business firms are reduced by the same depreciation allowances which would have been used under a direct income tax; as indicated above, the business purchaser of investment goods and indirectly the individual saver is reimbursed for the tax paid on the original purchase of the investment good.[38]

If in a closed economy the measure underlying the consumption taxes encompasses the aggregate consumption of the community, the income taxes may be regarded as reaching the community's aggregate production or aggregate income.[39] If depreciation is disallowed, the tax base is

[37] To the extent that it is not integrated with the personal income tax, the corporate income tax has become an anomalous measure which in certain circumstances is thought to operate more like an imperfect sales tax than an income tax.

[38] Although in principle the allowance should be the same under the income and sales taxes, differences might be introduced in actual legislation. For instance, some German authorities hold that the depreciation guidelines would differ under the two taxes. See Der Bundeskanzler, Bundesrepublik Deutschland, *Überprüfung des Umsatzsteuerrechts* (Bonn, Dec. 20, 1958), pp. 12 f.

[39] Although in a closed economy the aggregate tax base for the individual income tax is reasonably approximated by community net product or income produced within the community, the measure of social income often assumed to underly the personal income tax is community personal income. The differences between personal income and income produced which are most significant for the base of the personal income tax are the exclusion of undistributed corporate profits gross of income tax and the inclusion of transfer payments from government. Unlike the case of a direct spendings tax, undistributed corporate profits should be included in the base of a direct individual income tax, albeit in practice the corporate profits tax is not integrated with the personal income tax in most legislation. Transfer payments should be taken into account in both taxes. Meanwhile, a sales tax based on income produced within the community would reach individual incomes inclusive of undistributed profits and transfer payments, provided that individuals spent all their incomes in purchasing consumption and investment goods from the business firms in the community.

equivalent to gross community product. If depreciation is allowed, the tax base is equivalent to net community product or net community income.

Like the consumption principle, the income principle may be applied in conformity with some version of the ability to pay or benefits thesis. If the benefits thesis is used it will be concerned with the distribution of governmental benefits to individuals who are expected to bear the tax either directly or through their purchases of taxable products. The benefits might be considered in terms of benefits to savers and consumers; but they will more likely be related to income levels, an attempt being made to decide whether they are distributed proportionately or progressively.

Like the indirect consumption taxes, the indirect income taxes cannot be patterned to the requirement of individual situations with the precision possible under the direct personal tax. Thus neither personal allowances nor planned rate progression are feasible. The net product concept in effect implements proportional taxation and, although the gross product concept may be assumed to be progressive, the rate pattern is indeterminate. These issues are discussed further in Chapter 7.

Like the consumption type of sales tax, the income type of sales tax may be implemented through either a value-added or single-stage procedure. However, the application of the tax to final purchases of investment goods means that under the sales procedure only currently expensed purchases should be subtracted while under the tax-credit method the credits should be restricted to taxes paid on currently expensed goods and services. The addition procedure merely requires the addition of factor payments for wages, interest, rent, and profits. Given rate differentiation, the tax-credit procedure is the most efficient. Under the single-stage procedure, the same result is obtained through the limitation of the use of exemption certificates to purchases of currently expensed items, the business vendor being required to pay the tax on his sales destined for final investment use by his business customers.

Any depreciation allowance must be taken by the taxable business firm which purchases the investment goods whether the value-added or single-stage method is used; and the allowances reduce the taxable receipts of vendors subject to the tax. In either procedure the depreciation allowance is attributed to the firm's capital account, thus reducing the cost of capital assets including tax by the amount of the depreciation allowance.

As in the case of the indirect spendings tax, forward shifting of the tax must be assumed, although the quantity purchased will be reduced so as to release resources to the government. In other words, the situation should be the same as if the prices of all final products had been increased by the amount of the tax, say 10 percent, and income recipients were then allowed to adjust their outlays in the same manner as if their incomes had been reduced directly through a personal income tax of, say, 9.1 percent.

To illustrate the implementation of the income type of sales tax, assume the same situation as in Example V. Then the situation under the income-type sales taxes which do not allow depreciation is the one depicted in Example VI.

The tax collected on the final value of the product amounts to $1,700 under both procedures of computing the value-added tax and under the single-stage method. The machine accounts for $300 of the tax; and in both instances is advanced by the vendor. Firm B's value added has increased by $3,000 over that in Example V because only purchases of unfinished cloth may be subtracted. The value of finished goods in the community has increased by $3,000 over that in Example V because the machine has been treated as a final rather than an intermediate product.

If depreciation had been allowed, the following situation might be

EXAMPLE VI. Comparison of Value-Added Methods (Sales and Tax-Credit) and Single-Stage Method of Computing Income-Type Sales Tax, with 10% Rate

| | Value of Product at Each Stage | Value Added | Value-Added Tax | | Single-Stage Tax |
			Sales Method	Tax-Credit Method	
Firm A	Machine $ 3,000				
	Cloth 10,000	$13,000	$1,300	$1,300− 0=$1,300	E.C.+$ 300[a]
	Total $13,000				
Firm B	Finished cloth $14,000	4,000	400	1,400−1,000= 400	1,400
Final value	$17,000[b]	$17,000[b]			
Tax on final value			$1,700[a]	$1,700[a]	$1,700[a]

[a] $300 represents the tax on the machine. In the case of the single-stage procedure, Firm B provides Firm A with an exemption certificate (E.C.) for the $10,000 purchases of unfinished cloth.

[b] $3,000 of this represents the machine.

visualized. In the taxable period following the one illustrated, Firm B is entitled to a depreciation allowance of $600 for the machine in which it had invested, having purchased it for $3,000 from Firm A. Then, with the same turnover as in the first period, Firm B's taxable sales would amount to $14,000 less $600, or $13,400; and its tax would be $1,340 rather than $1,400.

In contrast to the consumption concept, the income concept of sales taxation makes it necessary to apply the tax to any production of investment goods made within the firm for its own use. Also, inventory accumulation is in principle taxable under the income concepts. A detailed discussion of the numerous problems involved in defining a consumption and income type of tax base is deferred to Chapter 5.

Interjurisdictional Trade

When sales taxes are imposed according to some general principle of taxation, their application to products traded across the boundaries of independent taxing jurisdictions, whether independent nations or political subdivisions, should conform with either of two jurisdictional principles —that of the destination of taxable products or that of their origin. According to the destination principle, all products having the same destination, that is, area of use, should be taxed equally regardless of their place of production. According to the origin principle, all products having the same origin, that is, place of production, should be taxed equally, regardless of where they are used. This means that under the destination principle, imported products should be taxed in the same way as domestically produced goods and services while exports should be completely exempt from tax. Meanwhile, under the origin principle, the tax is applied to exports rather than imports.[40]

[40] There are cases where both exports and imports are taxed, as in the Argentine Republic, although the government has in certain instances granted temporary exemptions to encourage exports. See Dino Jarach, "L'impôt sur les ventes dans la République Argentine," *Impôts sur transactions, transmissions et chiffre d'affaires,* p. 59. There have also been instances where both exports and imports have been exempt, as in the German general turnover tax of the twenties. See Alfred G. Buehler, *General Sales Taxation* (New York, 1932), pp. 97–98, 105. Such arrangements, which either overtax or undertax international trade, may reflect special considerations. According to Professor Buehler, the German legislation reflected a policy of encouraging the export trade and a view of imports as prime necessities. The reason for the taxation of both exports and imports in the Argentine is not given in the reference cited. Sales taxes, whether general or selective, are

DESTINATION PRINCIPLE. The destination principle has been the jurisdictional rule most often applied in sales taxation and in fact constitutes the logical method of implementing indirect personal taxation whether imposed according to some ability to pay or benefits to individuals thesis. Thus, for example, if the consumer spendings or the incomes of individuals residing in a community are to be reached through a tax which raises the prices of the products which they purchase, there is no reason why they should be allowed to buy items from business firms located abroad without paying tax; the fact that values produced abroad are taxed is an irrelevant consideration in the case of the principle of indirect personal taxation, attention being focused on the actual taxpayer, that is, the ultimate purchaser. On the other hand, as the sales tax is not intended to reach the consumer spendings or income of individuals who do not belong to the community, there is no reason why exported products should be taxed.

Therefore, under a general indirect spendings tax, the tax should be imposed on all imports of final consumer goods. On the assumption that residents use all their consumer purchases in their own jurisdiction, the tax reaches the same purchases which would be reached under a direct spendings tax. With a general indirect income tax, the tax should be imposed on all imports for final use, whether the products are purchased by ultimate consumers or by business firms which intend to use the purchases for investment within the business enterprise. On the assumption that residents use all their purchases in their own jurisdiction, the tax reaches the same incomes as those assessed under the direct personal income tax. The corporate income tax distorts the conceptual equivalence between an income type of sales tax imposed on the destination principle and a direct personal income tax imposed on the residence principle to the extent that the corporate income tax represents an independent profits tax rather than a withholding of income tax on undistributed corporate profits. In this case, the corporate tax is likely to be viewed as a type of product tax imposed on the origin principle— a concept which may be extended to business profits taxes generally.

From the viewpoint of the community as a whole, the destination

often applied to exports in Latin America, perhaps sometimes without having given more thought to the matter than that the export constitutes a convenient taxable object. However, the application of export taxes in Latin America often implements a policy of fiscal controls or the view that the taxes constitute a substitute for direct profits or income taxation of businesses engaged in foreign trade. See Jonathan V. Levin, *The Export Economies: Their Pattern of Development in Historical Perspective* (Cambridge, Mass., 1960), pp. 263–66.

principle applied to a consumption type of sales tax reaches total community consumption provided that all the members of the community use the consumer goods which they purchase in their own jurisdiction. The tax does not reach consumer purchases which are made abroad and used abroad. Thus the scope of the tax is more limited than that of a direct expenditure tax, which could be made to apply regardless of where the purchases are used. Moreover, under the direct procedure, expenditures could presumably be defined so as to reach more readily than under the indirect approach funds which individuals held in cash or assets regarded as close substitutes for cash and which were judged to be economically nonproductive.

Similarly, the income type of sales taxes reach the aggregate incomes of members of the community provided that the members utilize their purchases of investment or consumer goods within their own jurisdiction. It is far more limited in scope than the direct personal income tax imposed on the residence principle, which reaches the incomes of individuals whether they use their purchases at home or abroad. Moreover, as in the case of consumption taxation, the sterilization of funds by individuals is more effectively reached under the direct approach.

Either a value-added or single-stage procedure may be used to implement the destination principle of sales taxation. Assuming domestic rate differentiation, the tax-credit procedure of computing value added is preferable.[41]

Under a value-added tax imposed through the retail stage, imports need be taxed only when purchased directly from firms located abroad and for final consumption or use because, to the extent that they enter into the value of taxable products, no tax credit would be available while under the sales procedure no subtraction would be allowed. Exports are completely freed from tax by exempting the export transaction and reimbursing the amount of tax credits to which the exporter is entitled because of his purchase of taxable products. With the consumption-type measure, the exporter is entitled to credits on his purchases of all products from other taxable business firms whether the products are expensed or

[41] The enforcement difficulties arising when rates differ between jurisdictions or when rates are very high and customs barriers do not exist or are ineffectual constitute administrative problems which are not discussed here. For some consideration of these issues, see Carl S. Shoup, "Taxation Aspects of International Economic Integration," *Travaux de l'Institut International de Finances Publiques, 1953* (Frankfurt, 1953), pp. 96–98.

capitalized in his accounts. Given the income-type measures, tax credits are limited to purchases of products currently expensed.

With the single-stage procedure the tax must also be applied when imports are purchased directly by ultimate consumers or final users of investment goods. Meanwhile, exports are automatically exempt by means of the suspensive system. If the tax is of the income rather than the consumption type, exporters, like other business purchasers, are entitled to buy in suspension only those products destined to be expensed rather than capitalized and depreciated in the firm's accounts.

Difficulty arises if the tax, however collected, is limited to a stage prior to the retail stage. Imports should in principle be taxed only up to the value covered by the law, that is, wholesale or manufacturing value; but this is never done, the tax on imports being applied to the total value of the import at the time of importation even if this is retail value. Exports should be completely exempt even if made from the nontaxable stage. Therefore, exporters should be registered as taxpayers even if they would normally operate in the nontaxable stage or, alternatively, an effort must be made to refund the amount of tax estimated to be incorporated in the price of the exports. As in the case of domestically produced goods and services, it is difficult to define taxable price of imports so as to avoid favoring certain enterprises and impossible to limit the tax on services to the manufacturing or wholesaling stage in all instances.

ORIGIN PRINCIPLE.   As explained above, the destination principle is the more logical rule for the implementation of indirect personal taxation. With the origin principle, given the realistic assumption that taxable firms immediately add the tax to their prices,[42] purchasers would be faced with products turned out by domestic firms increased by the tax while they could purchase nontaxed products from firms located abroad. Thus the tax would no longer be a general levy on the consumer spendings or incomes of individuals in the community. Moreover, foreign business firms are given a competitive advantage over domestic producers in both the domestic and foreign markets.

It is sometimes maintained that, abstracting from the effects of the sales tax on factor movements, the origin principle amounts to the same

[42] See John F. Due, *Sales Taxation* (Urbana, Ill., 1957), pp. 12–14. In a situation of pure competition, prices remain unchanged when the tax is first imposed but producers reduce their supplies because their receipts are not enough to cover cost including tax, and prices eventually rise until receipts are adequate to provide the amount demanded.

thing as the destination principle in the long run. This is the position taken in a report on the sales tax systems of the European Coal and Steel Community prepared by the Committee of Experts under the chairmanship of Professor J. Tinbergen.[43] The committee concluded that the origin principle would be equivalent to the destination principle if, with a sales tax imposed under the origin principle, a rise in the prices of the taxing country's products was achieved through a depreciation of its exchange rate. For example, if a 10 percent sales tax were imposed on the origin basis and the tax discouraged exports and encouraged imports, the resulting trade deficit might be allowed to effect a depreciation of the exchange rates. When such depreciation amounted to 11.1 percent, the prices of exports in terms of domestic currency would have risen enough so that after tax the exporter's receipts would be the same as before the tax had been imposed. Meanwhile, those who imported products from abroad would find that in terms of their own currency the tax-free foreign products were no longer cheaper than taxable domestic products. An alternative avenue of adjustment visualized by the Tinbergen report was through fixed exchange rates and deflation of money incomes within the taxing community until costs of the factors of production, including tax, were the same as the incomes before tax.[44]

Abstracting from the problems raised by the export and import of labor and capital and by transfer payments, and assuming perfect competition, which means perfect price flexibility, mobility of factors within the economy, and therefore full employment, it is valid to regard the destination and origin principles as equivalent measures. However, such equivalence does not hold with the structural rigidities characterizing real economies. Then, as a trade deficit develops under a sales tax applied on the origin principle, it is difficult to predict with any degree of certainty that the final equilibrium will approximate the results which would have been achieved under the destination principle, and a fortiori if consideration is given to exports and imports of factors of production.[45]

---

[43] High Authority, European Coal and Steel Community, *Report on the Problems Raised by the Different Turnover Systems Applied within the Common Market,* Report prepared by Committee of Experts set up under Order No. 1–53 of the High Authority, dated Mar. 5, 1953, p. 24.

[44] A more intensive analysis, which arrives at the same conclusion, has been worked out by Schulte, "Die Wirtschaftspolitischen Grundlagen des Bestimmungsland- und des Ursprungslandprinzips," pp. 12–18, and Möller, "Das Ursprungs- und Bestimmungslandprinzip," pp. 45–49.

[45] Möller stresses the fact that in the absence of factor movements, flexible exchange rates would eliminate much of the adjustment required if exchanges are fixed. Möller, p. 49.

If, however, various competing jurisdictions apply equal rate sales taxes under the origin principle, then the only difference from the destination principle is that the tax receipts accrue to the jurisdiction where the products have been produced rather than the jurisdiction where they have been utilized. In other words, ultimate purchasers would pay the same amount of tax whether they bought the items from firms located at home or abroad but, when they purchased from the latter, the taxes would accrue to the treasury of the foreign jurisdiction. Meanwhile, domestic business firms would not be placed at a tax disadvantage as compared with their foreign competitors as the foreign competitor would be paying an equal tax to his own government.

It is this version of the origin principle which would underly the proposal for its use in the European Economic Community if each member state were content with the arrangement. Each member state is to apply the same rate while the destination principle is to be used in the case of imports and exports to third countries. It is also the version which was probably intended in the case of the Japanese value-added tax.

As contrasted with the destination principle, which seeks to reach the aggregate consumption of individuals within the community or, under the income concept, aggregate consumption and investment, the origin principle is designed to reach aggregate production. Thus the aggregate tax base under an income type of sales tax imposed on the origin basis is conceptually equivalent to the concept of community income generally designated as domestic product or income.[46] The consumption type of sales tax would, of course, differ from the income type insofar as investment outlays within the community would be expensed rather than capitalized and depreciated.

Like the destination principle of sales taxation, the origin principle will not reach the aggregate incomes of individuals. Under the income type of sales tax it is applied to the same values as the source principle of income taxation, although equivalence with the direct approach is achieved in a roundabout manner and, in the real world, probably only through an increase in the prices of products purchased out of incomes. Thus it may be contrasted with the residence principle of direct income taxation which reaches an individual resident's total income regardless of the jurisdiction in which it is earned or utilized. Similarly, the con-

---

[46] See United Nations, *Statistics of National Income and Expenditure* (New York, Statistical Office, Sept., 1955), ST/STAT/Sec./18, General Note to Table 3, p. 35.

sumption type of sales tax imposed on the origin or destination basis may be contrasted with the direct expenditure tax imposed on the residence basis, which reaches consumer outlays regardless of where they are made.

The value-added procedure is the appropriate one for applying the origin principle of sales taxation and, as always, the tax-credit procedure is preferable in the event of domestic rate differentiation. Abstracting from the problem raised by source rules, which is discussed in the paragraph below, the importing business firm must calculate the amount of tax credit to which it is entitled by applying the tax rate of its own jurisdiction to the value of the imported purchases.

Although the origin principle is easily visualized in general terms, its actual application may become quite complicated because of the requirement that exports be taxed only up to their export value and imports be exempted only up to their import value. Unfortunately, there is no neat cut-off at the frontier which divides the value of a product according to whether it has been produced within one jurisdiction or another. In view of the complexity of modern business structures where, for example, manufacturing enterprises straddle frontiers with branch, assembly, and distributive establishments while the subsidiary form permits varying degrees of interrelationship between concerns located in one jurisdiction with those in another, who is to determine where the export value ends and the import value begins? Obviously, the problem is substantially the same as the one confronted under the income tax applied according to the source principle.[47] The origin of the value added by the exporting and importing concern will have to be determined according to rules which attribute the value to the respective jurisdictions in terms of the payments to the factors of production which make up the value of the product, namely, wages, rent, interest, profits, etc. Of course, the solution to the allocation problem which is most easily administered is through the use of allocation formulas based on such criteria as value of assets, payrolls, and sales. However, the formulas would have to be uniform in order to avoid multiple taxation and loopholes, and this means that the independent jurisdictions concerned would have to reach an agreement on the issue, which is not usually an easy matter.

It is conceivable that the origin principle might be applied through a

[47] For a more thorough analysis of this issue, see Clara K. Sullivan, *The Search for Tax Principles in the European Economic Community* (Chicago, 1963), pp. 45–48.

single-stage tax. The statute would provide that exports could not be made in suspension of tax; and source rules could be applied to allocate value between the exporting and importing country. However, imports would seem to create some difficulty under the single-stage procedure when the imports were purchased by business firms and were resold in the same form or after additional processing to business customers who in turn bought in suspension of tax. There would have to be some certificate attached to the suspensive sales indicating the amount of value to be excluded because it arose in the exporting country in order that the final taxable sale would be reduced by the amount of that value.

Unlike the destination principle, the origin principle becomes less difficult to apply when a sales tax is restricted to the stage prior to the retail stage. Exports made from the nontaxable stage are automatically taxed on the values covered by the legislation, either wholesale or manufacturing, while imports at the nontaxable stage are automatically exempt. Nevertheless, the problems of defining taxable price are the same as in the case of domestic firms and the same as under the destination principle, a fact which argues for the extension of a tax through the retail stage even under the origin principle.

TAX ON VALUE ADDED AS A BUSINESS TAX

When the value-added tax is proposed as a business-benefit tax some benefit principle of taxation is obviously implied. However, there is more than one version of the benefit theory; and value-added tax proposals can only be understood in terms of the particular version which they are supposed to represent.

The different versions of the benefit theory may be grouped into three main categories based upon the expected distribution of benefits from the governmental services financed by the tax and the expected incidence, that is, the distribution of the tax burden. One category consists of taxes which actually represent the same benefits to individuals principle applicable to the personal indirect taxes previously discussed. The tax is supposed to raise the prices of products purchased by ultimate consumers or income recipients by the amount of the tax and thus approximate a direct spendings or income tax. The second group consists of those taxes which are regarded as a charge for the benefits derived from governmental services which can be considered of direct benefit to business firms as such, that is, services which lower business costs. Generally speaking, the proponents of this type of measure are less concerned with forward shifting than those in the first group. The third category consists of taxes definitely not expected to be shifted forward, thereby encompassing the least conventional concepts of sales taxation. Usually it is hoped that the tax will rest on profits and thus on the owners of the business, presumably on the assumption that they have received the benefits from the governmental expenditures. Of course, the tax is due even if the firm earns no profits, in which event it is not clear how the tax burden is supposed to be distributed, but possibly it is expected to be a sort of capitalized charge on net profits.[48] Finally, within the category of nonshifted taxes may be placed the proposals which are expected to effect direct personal income taxation through backward shifting, the tax being regarded as a personal income tax withheld at the source of income receipts, that is, the factor payments made by business firms, with the proposals reflecting the benefits to individuals thesis relevant to personal taxation.

In all cases the tax may be presented as an alternative to the taxation of business profits or even other taxes collected from business. However, except for the profits-tax concept, the intention is to relieve the burden on business profits or on those thought to bear the burden of shifted profits and other business taxes.

Business-Benefit Tax Equated with Indirect Personal Taxation

Instead of imposing a sales tax in accordance with some principle of personal ability to pay or benefits to individuals, the value-added tax may be presented as a business-benefit levy although neither the measure of the tax, its rate, nor any other feature distinguishes it from other sales taxes regarded as taxes on ultimate consumers or users. Similarly, a number of retail sales taxes in the states of the United States are levied on the "*privilege* of doing business at retail" although they are in fact

---

[48] The concept of a business tax as a "vague, usually unexpressed intent on the part of the state to levy a permanent, capitalized rent-charge on the net profits of business firms in lieu of taxation proper," was once noted by Shoup. See Carl S. Shoup, "Business Taxes," *Encyclopaedia of the Social Sciences* III (New York, 1930), 124.

indistinguishable from those in which emphasis is placed on shifting the tax forward to the consumer.[49] Likewise, the proposal for the value-added tax in Japan, which was to replace the prefectural profits taxes, was in part based on the hypothesis that "Some kind of prefectural tax on enterprises is justifiable in order that the businesses and their patrons shall help defray the cost of government services that are made necessary by the existence of the business and its employees in that local area."[50] Thus the tax was expected to operate as a sales tax in the sense that ultimate consumers or users of the goods and services produced by the taxable business firms were intended as the actual taxpayers.

Although the business-benefit thesis is implied in the above legislation, there is no attempt at a specific allocation of the benefits from governmental services. Rather the benefit thesis represents a vague justification for collecting part of the community taxes through business firms. In fact, if all the members of the community can be assumed to spend their money on goods and services produced by firms within the jurisdiction and the sales tax is expected to be shifted forward to the individual purchasers, the choice between collecting the tax directly from them in the form of a direct spendings or income tax rather than a sales tax would seem to involve only questions of comparative administrative efficiency.

Even if it could be assumed that the same governmental expenditures were directly occasioned by business firms or of direct benefit to them, there would be no point in attempting a specific allocation between expenditures which benefit consumers or users and expenditures which benefit business firms. There would be some point in allocating benefits between ultimate consumers and final purchasers of investment goods. Instead, however, the tax is likely to reflect a rough judgment of the distribution of benefits by income levels or, in other words, of whether the benefits are distributed regressively, proportionately, or progressively.

In a closed economy, the concept may be implemented through either the consumption- or income-type measures previously discussed. Moreover, either the value-added or single-stage procedure of collection may be used. In the case of the value-added procedure the tax-credit method is preferable, given rate differentiation.

Under the sales taxes in the states of the United States, most of

[49] See Due, *Sales Taxation*, p. 302.
[50] Shoup Mission, *Report on Japanese Taxation* (4 vols., Tokyo, 1949), II, 201.

the measures may be classified as a version of the gross product type of income measure, although the use of the consumption-type concept has been increasing in recent years. The Japanese value-added tax allowed a choice between the consumption and income type of measures.

As in the case of the indirect personal taxes, the destination principle should be applied to interjurisdictional trade for the implementation of the business-benefit principle which assumes that the tax will actually be paid by ultimate consumers or users. As previously indicated, the destination principle of sales taxation is likely to have a much more limited scope than the residence principle of direct income or expenditure taxation in view of the possibility that individuals may purchase and use products abroad. Furthermore, the analogy between the destination principle of sales taxation and the residence principle of income taxation abstracts from the problems presented by the taxation of business profits under the direct income tax.

Again, as in the case of the principles of indirect personal taxation, the origin rule may be regarded as equivalent to the destination principle if the independent jurisdictions concerned agree to accept the same tax rates. In this event, the only difference between the origin and destination approach is that the allocation of the tax receipts would differ from those under the destination principle to the extent that imports and exports were not equal. This was presumably expected to be the situation in the case of the Japanese value-added tax.

Business-Benefit Tax as a Charge for Governmental Services Rendered to Business Firms as Such

A version of business-benefit taxation which should be sharply distinguished from the business-benefit concept discussed above is that which presents the tax as a price paid for the benefits of governmental services rendered to business firms. As explained in more detail in Chapter 4, this concept implies a definite attempt to allocate the benefits from public outlays between benefits to individuals in their capacity as ultimate consumers and benefits to individuals as organized through productive enterprises or business. Moreover, the cost or presumed value of the benefits to business is to be apportioned among firms through a tax viewed as a price paid for such services. The tax is regarded as a cost

similar to other business costs, being analogous either to the prices paid
for goods and services purchased from outside business firms or to payments for internal factors of production employed in turning out the
product.

Hence, this principle of taxation contrasts with the more conventional
view which holds that, whatever the direct benefits of the expenditures
to individuals or organizations, public outlays should be made only if
the indirect benefits may be assumed to be distributed among the individuals in the community in such manner that the expenditures may be
considered of general benefit. Moreover, the payment for such benefits
is to be made through a tax regarded as a contribution from individual
income recipients rather than as a charge which resembles a price or a
fee.

Although thus far no legislation has implemented the concept of a
business tax viewed as a price, it obviously underlies some proposals for
value-added taxation. This is notably the case of the proposals made by
Professors Colm and Studenski, who emphasize the analogy between the
value-added tax and the cost of business purchases of factors of production, with Professor Colm specifying in addition that the governmental
services may resemble supplies of goods or services by outside business
firms.[51] Also, Thomas S. Adams' proposal for value-added taxation, the
first recommendation for value-added taxation in the United States, is
compatible with this view.

The advocates of this concept realize that the value-added tax is a
type of sales tax and can therefore be expected to be shifted forward in
product prices. Nevertheless, they apparently place much less emphasis
on forward shifting than those who regard the tax as indirect personal
taxation. In part, the absence of concern with the allocation of the tax
burden among individual taxpayers reflects the *quid pro quo* envisaged
by the tax, the assumption being made that the tax is merely merged with
other business costs, presumably variable costs to the extent that it applies to current expenses and fixed costs when it applies to investment
goods. However, there also seems to be the implication that, if for some
reason the benefits from the public outlays do not result in lowering
costs to individual purchasers of final products but instead benefit various

[51] Gerhard Colm, "Public Revenue and Public Expenditure in National Income,"
Studies in Income and Wealth, Conference on Research in National Income and
Wealth (National Bureau of Economic Research, New York, 1937), I, 205.

owners of productive factors who turn out the product, the forces which led to a particular distribution of benefits will also lead to the same allocation of the tax burden, so that part of the tax will not be shifted forward.

Adams recommended his measure, which he termed a tax on "approximate net income" or "modified gross income" as a substitute for the proportional rates of the direct personal income tax,[52] which he suggested was shifted.[53] Although Adams considered net income as the more equitable measure, he objected to the administrative complexities involved in its computation. Colm once suggested his measure as a substitute for the social security taxes and has also advocated it to replace all business taxes. Studenski presents his measure as the most rational form of business taxation.

Although the value-added procedure of collecting a sales tax has come to be identified with the view of the tax as a price paid for governmental services to business, other methods of collection are appropriate when problems of applying the measure to interjurisdictional trade are ignored. In fact, Adams considered using the general turnover tax, rejecting it only because of its effect in encouraging business integration.[54]

The income type of sales tax measure seems to be the appropriate one for application of the concept, a matter considered in more detail in Chapter 4. In any event, it has thus far been the one universally suggested. A gross product type of measure was the basis of Adams' value-added tax proposal. Also, Colm and Studenski have apparently considered use of the gross product type of base but Colm raises the question of whether depreciation should be allowed;[55] and Studenski has also accepted the possibility of deducting depreciation.[56] Adams' proposal uses a tax-credit method of collecting the tax while, as indicated above, Colm and Studenski assume the sales procedure, perhaps because they assume uniform rates. There seems to be no reason why the tax-credit procedure should not be used, especially if much intrajurisdictional rate differentiation were allowed.

[52] Adams, "Fundamental Problems of Federal Income Taxation," *Quarterly Journal of Economics,* XXV (1921), 553.

[53] *Ibid.,* p. 549.

[54] *Ibid.,* pp. 552–53.

[55] Colm, "Methods of Financing Unemployment Compensation," *Social Research,* II (Apr., 1935), 161.

[56] Paul Studenski, The Place of a "Value-Added" Tax in a War Time Fiscal Program (Preliminary Memorandum, mimeo., Apr. 6, 1942), p. 4, n. 3.

To the extent that they give any indication of how interjurisdictional transactions should be treated, proposals based on this concept seem to assume the origin principle, presumably on the ground that enterprises located abroad do not receive the governmental benefits concerned. In other words, the aggregate tax base of the community would be considered as commensurate with the area's domestic product; and it is perhaps this aspect of the measure which resulted in the assumption that the value-added procedure would be used for its implementation.

Nevertheless, Adams is the only advocate of this principle of value-added taxation to stress the interjurisdictional aspects of the measure. He regards it as a substitute for the source principle of income taxation and justifies such taxes as a payment for the cost of governmental services occasioned by business establishments, whether domestic or foreign, carrying on their productive activities within the market or for the value of the benefits derived from the use of the market—a valuable social asset maintained by the community.[57]

Business-Benefit Tax not Expected to be Shifted Forward

PROFITS TAXATION. Some sales taxes are apparently expected to rest on business profits and therefore on the owners of the business, so that, generally speaking, the incidence of the tax is expected to coincide with its impact. The usual version of this concept is the one which Due ascribes to "a business occupation or license tax measured by gross receipts" and which he explains as follows:

From the standpoint of the structure of the tax and probable economic effects, this type of levy is essentially identical with a sales tax. The basic difference between the two is primarily one of legislative intent—not always reflected in the law, and not always easy to ascertain. In the case of a sales tax, it is presumed that the tax will be shifted forward to the consumer, the business firm merely being regarded as a tax collecting agent. With the business-occupation gross-receipts tax, on the other hand, the tax is regarded as charge for the privilege of carrying on business activity, and is presumably intended to be a burden on the business, as such, and thus on its owners, although actually, of course, such a tax is likely to shift forward in the same manner as a sales tax. In practice the major difference between the two types of

[57] Adams, "The Taxation of Business," *Proceedings of the Eleventh Annual Conference of the National Tax Association,* 1917 (New Haven, 1918), p. 187; and "Fundamental Problems of Federal Income Taxation," pp. 541–42.

levies is in the level of the rate, the business occupation taxes in virtually all cases having rates which are a fraction of one per cent.[58]

As previously noted, this is the type of tax which may be expected to constitute a capitalized overhead cost.

The Michigan value-added tax might constitute an example of the use of this concept of profits taxation. The law imposes a general rate of only 7¾ mills and a special rate on public utilities of 2 mills. The concept also underlies some minor state sales taxes. It is also appropriate for some license taxes in the southern states of the United States, the French *patente,* and the German *Gewerbsteuer;* but these taxes, which are sometimes more than nominal levies, are based on the value of all or part of a firm's capital as well as all or some of the components of value added, the various elements in the tax base being subjected to differing rules of taxation, and therefore they do not really take the form of a sales tax.

Aside from the Michigan value-added tax, the general turnover tax is used to implement this concept in the rare instances of its application by a state in the United States presumably because under a single-stage tax some firms would make a large proportion of their sales in suspension of tax and thus their profits would not be reached. However, the value-added approach would be preferable in order to avoid favoring integration, and an income type of measure would seem to be the appropriate one because otherwise firms making large purchases of capital goods would have much smaller taxable profits than under conventional definitions of profits. Also, a sales procedure is implied because otherwise a firm's value added would be increased by lower rates imposed at earlier stages or decreased by higher ones. In any event, the Michigan tax may be characterized as an income type of measure which allows depreciation, although its application is confused, given the allowance of a minimum deduction equal to 50 percent of gross receipts in computing value added, a tax credit up to a maximum of 25 percent of tax computed by dividing 1 percent of gross receipts by net business income, and the nontaxation of interest, which is subjected to a special tax. As noted above, the origin rather than the destination principle seems the appropriate one for this concept insofar as the tax is intended to reach the profits of business firms located within the jurisdiction; and the Michigan tax uses an accounting formula which reflects the origin princi-

[58] Due, *Sales Taxation,* p. 4.

ple. The formula requires the taxpayer to average the three following percentages: (1) his gross receipts from sales of tangible personal property and services made within the state as a percent of his total sales, (2) his payrolls within the state as a percent of his total payrolls, and (3) the net average value of his real and tangible personal property during the taxable period as a percent of the net average value of all his real and tangible personal property. The average percentage is then applied to the taxpayer's aggregate value added as defined in the Michigan statute.

DIRECT PERSONAL INCOME TAXATION. One view of the value-added tax regards it as a method of withholding a personal income tax. The tax is said to be withheld at the source but not in the sense of a tax imposed on the income receipts of individuals through withholding by the business payer, with the amount of tax ultimately established by individual returns from the income recipients. Instead, the tax, being measured by payments to owners of factors of production employed within the firm, is expected to be allocated among the owners of the factors in proportion to their contribution to the value of the product. As this view of the tax has rarely been expressed in the case of practical proposals for value-added taxation, it is surprising to read the statement that "The standard view in public finance, in contrast to that used for convenience in the text, is that the value-added tax differs more fundamentally from the turnover tax in that it is passed backward as an income tax, while the turnover tax is passed forward."[59]

This view of the tax makes sense in a perfectly competitive economic system, as explained in Chapter 7; but it is impossible to understand in the imperfectly competitive real world. It is one thing to maintain that a sales tax may be substituted for a direct personal tax through an increase in the prices of products equal to the tax, although, of course, the indirect approach is the cruder one. It is another thing to say that a tax assessed on the value added of every business firm could be allocated among the owners of the factors of production employed by the firms in proportion to their incomes, barring a highly developed system of administered prices, whether effected through private monopolies or through governmental regulation.

In 1937 Professor Roscoe Arant of Iowa State Teachers College

[59] Charles P. Kindleberger, *International Economics,* 3d ed. (Homewood, Ill., 1963), p. 428, n. 1.

recommended the use of a value-added tax, which he called a "net value-product tax," as the chief source of revenue for the state governments in the United States, the tax being applicable to all concerns whether incorporated or not and whether they produced goods or services.[60] It should be noted that the benefit thesis of taxation in this instance is not one which precisely allocates the benefits to business but merely a general benefit thesis similar to the benefits to individuals principle previously discussed.

Arant evidently assumes that the concept can be implemented by a gross product measure, referring to Adams' definition of value added as the tax base. Strictly speaking, however, proportional taxation would require a net product concept which allowed depreciation if conventional accounting concepts were accepted.[61] Given perfect competition and abstracting from the technical problem of applying the tax to interjurisdictional trade, a single-stage tax could be used as readily as a value-added procedure—a fact recognized in the analysis of Professor Harry Gunnison Brown.[62]

A consumption-type measure could conceivably be used. Maintaining the assumption of perfect competition, the tax would not only be proportionately allocated among factor earnings but would effect a relative rise in the prices of consumption goods, as demonstrated by Musgrave.[63]

Given rate differentiation, the tax-credit procedure of computing value added remains the appropriate one under this principle. The sales procedure would only make sense if the payments to factors of production reflected a system of administered prices and the tax was allocated to these payments by the taxable business firms rather than distributed through market forces.

The origin principle of sales taxation is the appropriate jurisdictional rule for this principle because the value of imports should be exempt as covering incomes paid to individuals located outside the taxing jurisdiction while export values should be taxed as covering incomes paid to in-

[60] Roscoe Arant, "The Place of Business Taxation in the Revenue Systems of the States," *Taxes—The Tax Magazine*, XV (Apr., 1937).

[61] That Arant may not have accepted conventional definitions is suggested by his reference to Ricardo's definition of social net income, which, as explained further in Chapter 5 of this book, implies the need to expense certain consumer expenditures as well as business outlays in arriving at a true definition of net income. *Ibid.*, p. 198.

[62] See H. G. Brown, "The Incidence of a General Output or a General Sales Tax," *Journal of Political Economy*, XLVII (Apr., 1939), 256.

[63] *Theory of Public Finance*, pp. 379–82.

dividuals located within the taxing jurisdiction. In other words, this view of the tax assumes an identity between the origin principle of sales taxation and the source principle of individual income taxation; and the aggregate tax base may be viewed as equivalent to the community's domestic product.

SUMMARY AND CONCLUSION

The foregoing discussion makes evident that the concept of the value-added tax encompasses a variety of tax principles. These principles may be conveniently grouped into three major categories distinguished primarily by the incidence assumptions underlying the tax.

One category represents indirect personal taxes as applied in accordance with some version of the ability to pay principle or benefits to individuals thesis, the taxable business firm being viewed merely as a collecting agent. With the income type of value-added measure, the tax is expected to be shifted forward to ultimate purchasers of the taxable consumption products or investment goods and thus approximate a direct personal income tax which applies to savings as well as consumption outlays. Given the benefit principle, the benefits from the expenditure of the tax proceeds are expected to be distributed in accordance with the anticipated incidence of the tax. A certain distribution of benefits in terms of income levels may be visualized, although no planned rate progression is possible with the indirect approach. On the other hand, the benefits might conceivably be analyzed in terms of their distribution among individuals in their capacity as consumers or savers.

If a consumption type of measure is used to implement indirect personal taxation, it may reflect an assumption that the benefits have been distributed regressively. It would also be used if conventional income definitions, which regard savings as part of income, were replaced by the definition of income as consumer spending, as suggested by John Stuart Mill and Irving Fisher.

The destination principle is the appropriate rule for applying the indirect personal taxes to interjurisdictional trade. Thus the tax is limited to individuals who use their purchases in the taxing community.

The second major group of principles comprises those taxes which require a classification of governmental outlays according to whether they benefit business enterprises—that is, individuals as organized in producing units—or whether they benefit individuals in their capacity as consumers. Thus, in contrast to the application of the benefit principle in the first group, a specific allocation of governmental outlays is required rather than some rough judgment.

In the case of this principle, the tax may not be expected to be shifted in its entirety to ultimate purchasers. Instead, it may be expected to rest in part on the incomes of owners of various factors of production in accordance with their absorption of the benefits from the governmental services concerned.

An income-type measure has invariably been assumed for the application of this concept—a matter considered further in Chapter 4. Moreover, as the governmental services are supposed to increase the efficiency of businesses located within the taxing jurisdiction, it is logical to apply the origin rule rather than the destination principle used for the indirect personal taxes.

The principle reflects an impersonal rather than a personal view of taxation, for the tax is concerned with individuals only as they are organized in producing units, not with individuals as such, although, of course, individuals must in the final analysis bear the burden of the tax. It is even less personal than the source principle of income taxation insofar as the latter is definitely imposed on individual income receipts.

The third group of taxes are those intended to rest on business profits or to effect personal taxation through backward shifting. These concepts are the most difficult to understand. Unless imposed at nominal rates, a sales tax intended as a profits tax would probably not rest on profits unless some system of administered prices prevented its forward or backward shifting. Likewise, the sales tax intended as a backward-shifted personal income tax implies a system dominated by administered pricing.

Of course, any tax may be substituted for a profits tax. However, only the business-privilege taxes definitely expected to rest on profits are a conceptual substitute in the strict sense of the word. The other taxes are suggested as a replacement for profits taxation only if profits taxes are considered excessive or if they no longer conform to their rationale because of forward shifting. If they are being shifted forward, they may be logically replaced either by the type of business-benefit taxation suggested in Japan or by the type of tax which is viewed as a charge for the benefits from governmental services specifically allocated to businesses.

The principle of benefits to producing units has come to be identified with use of the value-added procedure probably because of the use of the origin jurisdictional rule. Also, assuming that it is at all practicable, the profits-tax principle seems to require the value-added procedure. In the case of the remaining principles, the single-stage method is equally appropriate.

When a value-added tax is used to implement the business-benefit principles other than profits taxation, either the tax-credit or sales procedure may be used, with the tax-credit procedure being the superior one, given rate differentiation. In the case of the profits-tax principle, the sales procedure seems to be required. Also, the sales procedure would be the appropriate one if the sales tax were viewed as a nonshifted levy implementing a personal income tax with factor payments the result of administered prices rather than market prices.

Generally, it should be emphasized that only the principles of indirect personal taxation or the principle of benefits to producing units are compatible with economic systems in which prices are determined primarily by imperfect market forces. The principles which assume nonshifted sales taxes other than a low-rate privilege tax either involve the unrealistic assumption of perfect competition or imply that the system is dominated by administered prices.

Chapter 2

The Tax on Value Added in France[1]

The French value-added tax is the mainstay of the general system of indirect taxation imposed by the French national government as a means of taxing the consumer expenditures of individuals residing in France; in fact the system is officially described as "taxes on consumption" (*impôts sur la consommation*).[2] In other words, the value-added tax constitutes the major component of a system intended to implement the principle of an indirect spendings tax.

The value-added tax (*taxe sur la valeur ajoutée*), which applies only to sales of commodities and certain building construction, is supplemented by a separate tax on services (*taxe sur les prestations de services*), partly integrated with the value-added tax, as explained below. In addition, there are several special excises, designated as *taxes uniques,* which have been adopted as levies in lieu of the value-added or service tax otherwise due on the products or related services concerned, specifically, taxes on certain light alcoholic beverages, meats, coffee, and tea, and vehicles used for freight transportation.

[1] The preparation of this chapter has been greatly facilitated by the extensive analysis of the French sales taxes undertaken by Mr. Martin Norr for the World Tax Series International Program in Taxation, Harvard Law School, material which will comprise Chapter 14 of the forthcoming publication of the World Tax Series, "Taxation in France."

[2] See "Recettes budgétaires de l'Etat," as reported in the monthly publication of the Ministry of Finance, *Statistiques et études fiancières* as, for example, in issue No. 179 (July, 1963), p. 749.

NATIONAL SALES TAXES

These three groups of taxes comprise the general system of national sales taxes, such taxes being termed *taxes sur le chiffre d'affaires*. They are collected from all persons, whether individuals or legal persons who "habitually or occasionally buy to resell or undertake transactions relating to a commercial or industrial activity" (Code général des Impôts, art. 256-1). The taxes thereby reach almost all those engaged in what are usually considered business activities except for agricultural and professional occupations.

In addition to the sales taxes, the national system contains some special excises called indirect taxes (*taxes indirectes*), notably those on alcoholic beverages, on sugar and beets, and on the tobacco and matches sold through the public monopolies. The indirect tax system also includes the customs which, of course, differ from the other categories of consumption taxes because of their differential impact on foreign products. Finally, it is necessary to take account of the local tax (*taxe locale*), primarily a retail sales tax, collected by the national government for the benefit of the political subdivisions—the departments and communes. This tax also belongs to the category of *taxes sur le chiffre d'affaires* and is related to the value-added tax because of the option given wholesale distributors to choose between payment of the value-added and local tax.

Of the total national tax and nontax budgetary receipts in 1962, equaling 74,569 million NF (New Francs), the value-added tax contributed some 21,753 million; the service tax around 2,559 million; the *taxes uniques* 2,347 million; the indirect taxes, proper, 3,845 million; and the customs 8,929 million.[3]

The relative budgetary importance of various categories of national tax receipts is shown for 1938 and the postwar years beginning in 1949 in Table 1. The contribution of the "consumption taxes," that is, the indirect tax system discussed above, amounted to 53.1 percent in 1962. It may be compared with the 30.4 percent yielded by taxes on income

---

[3] The customs include the petroleum taxes collected when sold on the domestic market rather than on importation. These taxes are classified in the same way as indirect excises on domestic sales rather than as customs by the Fiscal and Financial Committee of the European Economic Community. See International Bureau of Fiscal Documentation, *The EEC Reports on Tax Harmonization* (Amsterdam, 1963), p. 114.

and wealth, taxes usually considered direct in the sense that they are supposed to be borne by those on whom they are assessed.[4] The relative importance of the consumption taxes as compared with the taxes on income and wealth has grown substantially since the prewar year 1938, largely because of the adoption of the special tax on wages and salaries, a payroll tax which replaced the income tax on wage earners. In postwar years the percentage of aggregate receipts yielded by both the consumption and income and wealth taxes has shown considerable variation from year to year. However, this variation has primarily reflected only the changes in the category of exceptional receipts, notably interest and amortization of loans extended by the government.[5]

Receipts from the local tax, not shown in Table 1, amounted to 2,998 million NF in 1962.[6] They supply a significant portion of local resources, over 30 percent in 1962.

Value-Added Tax

CONSUMPTION-TYPE WHOLESALERS' SALES TAX. The value-added tax, imposed at a general rate of 25 percent,[7] represents a consumption

[4] The taxes on income and wealth include taxes on capital transfers which may sometimes represent indirect taxes, that is, taxes collected from vendors with the the expectation that purchasers will be the actual taxpayers. The special tax on wages and salaries is considered a type of indirect tax by some authorities. Others consider it a nonshifted tax of the consumption type. See, for example, Maurice Lauré, *La taxe sur la valeur ajoutée* (Paris, 1952), p. 41, and André Garrigou-Lagrange, "Evolution du système fiscal français au vingtième siècle, *Revue de science et de législation financières,* LIII (1961), 208. It should be noted that a nonshifted wage tax is applied to savings of wage and salary earners exempt under the usual consumption-type taxes. However, as the tax is not applied to the income from savings and investment, it may properly be regarded as a form of consumption tax. There is also a resemblance between a nonshifted tax on wages and salaries and a consumption tax to the extent that the bulk of consumption expenditures are made by wage earners, but the consumption tax would be more regressive because of the exemption of savings. Meanwhile a shifted wage tax would presumably involve the same type of double taxation as a sales tax on both investment and consumers' goods.

[5] Since 1960 amortization is no longer reported in the general revenues, being now included in the accounts of loans and finances.

[6] Ministère des Finances, *Statistiques et études financières,* No. 175 (July, 1963), p. 754.

[7] In France as in many European countries, the effective rate of sales taxes is higher than the nominal rate specified in the statutes because the tax itself must be included in the tax base. The effective rate is calculated through the formula $t/(100-t)$, where t is the nominal rate of tax. Thus a 20% nominal rate equals a 25% effective rate. See Appendix B of this book for a list of equivalent nominal and effective rates. Unless specified otherwise, effective rates are used throughout this book.

TABLE 1. Percentage Contribution of Taxes to French National Budgetary Receipts in 1938 and 1949–62[a]

	1938	1949	1950	1951	1952	1953	1954	1955	1956	1957	1958	1959	1960	1961	1962
A. Consumption taxes (total)	48.3	59.5	54.6	53.0	53.2	49.1	48.3	48.5	47.9	43.5	46.8	48.9	51.7	52.3	53.1
1. Production tax, value-added and service taxes, including replacement taxes (taxes uniques)	16.1	32.6	30.1	32.2	33.4	31.2	30.5	32.0	33.9	29.6	31.6	32.3	35.0	35.3	35.8
2. Transactions tax, including wool replacement tax	—	9.5	8.1	7.9	7.6	6.9	6.7	4.4	—	—	—	—	—	—	—
3. Indirect taxes[b]	10.2	3.6	2.5	2.1	1.9	1.9	1.6	1.6	1.5	1.6	1.5	1.6	1.7	5.1[b]	5.1[b]
4. Customs[c]	14.4	6.9	7.7	8.0	7.9	8.0	8.1	9.5	10.2	10.4	12.3	11.2	11.7	11.7	12.0
5. Monopolies and industrial exploitations	7.6	6.9	6.2	2.8	2.4	1.1	1.4	1.0	2.3	1.9	1.4	3.8	3.3	0.2[b]	0.2[b]
B. Special tax on wages and salaries[d]	—	7.2	6.8	6.6	7.2	6.8	6.8	7.3	7.3	6.4	7.2	6.8	7.3	7.3	7.4
C. Taxes on income and wealth[e]	39.7	24.7	28.6	29.4	25.9	28.9	26.1	25.6	27.6	25.9	31.9	31.2	32.1	31.5	30.4
D. Other revenues (including miscellaneous receipts such as those from domains, lotteries, taxes on gambling, foreign aid, and other exceptional receipts, notably interest and amorization of loans made by governments)	12.0	8.6	10.0	11.0	13.7	15.2	18.8	18.6	17.2	24.2	14.1	13.1	8.9	8.9	0.1
Total Revenue	100.0	100.0	100.0	100.0	100.0	100.0	100.0	100.0	100.0	100.0	100.0	100.0	100.0	100.0	100.0

[a] Taken from publication of Ministère des Finances, *Statistiques et études financières*, Supplément statistiques No. 11–12 (Paris, 1951), Annexe I, 5, B, pp. 260–61; figures from 1951 calculated from absolute amounts reported in *Statistiques et études financières*, No. 82 (Oct., 1955), pp. 1053–57; No. 104 (Aug., 1957), pp. 940–42; No. 121 (June, 1959), p. 85; No. 133 (June, 1960), p. 56; No. 145 (Jan., 1961), p. 40; No. 160 (Jan., 1962), p. 642; No. 179 (July, 1963), p. 749. The classification is the one used by the French Ministry of Finance, designated as the economic classification.
Statistics exclude receipts belonging to Special Treasury Accounts and to independent public establishments with legal personality.
[b] From 1961 includes special taxes on products of tobacco and match monopoly which had previously been recorded under monopolies and industrial exploitations.
[c] Includes petroleum taxes, which are collected when the products are sold on the domestic market rather than on importation and which account for most of the customs receipts, over three fourths in 1962.
[d] The Ministry of Finance explains that it has segregated this tax from the income taxes because some regard it as an indirect tax on consumption. See Ministère des finances "Recettes budgétaires de l'état," *Statistiques et études financières*, No. 175 (July, 1963), p. 749, n. 7.
[e] Includes taxes on capital transfers.

type of sales tax applied through the tax-credit subtraction procedure. The value-added tax paid on purchases of products for business use is credited against the value-added tax due on sales; and credits are granted not only for purchases of items customarily expensed but also for those usually capitalized so that, generally speaking, the tax is imposed only on sales for ultimate consumption.

The scope of the tax is limited, however. In the first place, it applies only to sales of commodities and building construction, which is in effect taxed at the reduced rate of 13.64 percent through the discount of 40 percent allowed in the computation of the tax base of building contractors. In the second place, it does not reach that portion of the value of commodities added at the retail stage. Moreover, if a wholesaler elects to pay the local tax of 2.83 percent on his total receipts rather than the value-added tax, it even excludes values added at the wholesale stage. In other words, the tax may be characterized as a wholesalers' sales tax in principle although in practice it may sometimes be restricted to manufacturing values. The option to pay the local tax has no rationale other than that of a concession to wholesalers with wide profit margins and few outlays on creditable investments.[8]

A MODIFIED CONSUMPTION-TYPE TAX. Furthermore, the French value-added tax has apparently been conceived as a modified type of pure consumption tax because it rests on certain business outlays, whether current expenses or investment purchases. The fact that firms engaged in activities excluded or exempt from the tax are entitled to no tax credits means that the tax applies to both the current expenses and investment outlays of such enterprises as those engaged in agriculture, the professions, or nonprofit activities, concerns engaged in turning out products subjected to special excises, including the *taxes uniques,* retail distributors not selling to other payers of the value-added tax or for export, exempt governmental monopolies, such as the explosives monopoly, and public utility concessions for water and compressed air.[9]

[8] See Maurice Lauré, *Au secours de la T.V.A.* (Paris, 1957), p. 25. Lauré claims that the concession was not the result of the political power of the wholesalers involved but of the opinion of the legislature that there would otherwise be an excessive burden on such concerns when the tax was extended through the wholesale level. In view of the extreme shifts in the allocation of the tax burden among business firms which must have occurred under other changes in the law effected by the adoption of the value-added tax, it is difficult to understand why this limited number of wholesalers should have been permitted to disrupt the rationality of the legislation.

[9] For an example illustrating the possible hidden burden on exempt enterprises caused by the inability to credit the value-added tax on investment outlays and

Furthermore, some business investment made by firms subject to the value-added tax is burdened because tax credits are denied in the case of the purchases of various categories of investment goods including commercial buildings, most transportation equipment, and office furnishings.

REASONS FOR DENIAL OF TAX CREDITS. In part the denial of credits to certain business outlays reflects the administrative consideration that these purchases could easily be transferred to personal use or, as in the case of denial of tax credits to nontaxable firms, the fear of excessive impairment of revenues. The noncreditability of transportation vehicles is intended primarily to avoid a discriminatory burden against transportation enterprises ineligible for tax credits because exempt or subject to the special tax on transportation vehicles.[10]

The disallowance of credits for commercial buildings is reported to have reflected concern over the fact that independent distributors not subject to the value-added tax would be at a disadvantage as compared with payers of the value-added tax performing distributive functions in conjunction with their taxable activities.[11] More precisely, the discrimination would have been between firms eligible for the regime of the value-added tax which made taxable distributive sales and those not entitled to tax credits because their distributive sales were not subject to the value-added tax. For example, a manufacturer would have been entitled to tax credits for purchases of commercial buildings related to his wholesale sales subject to the value-added tax; but he would have been entitled to no credits to the extent that the commercial building was used for sales on which he had elected to pay the local tax. He would have been required to prorate his credits in accordance with the relative importance of the two types of sales. Wholesalers would have been in the same position with respect to sales subject to local tax, as would all those entitled to enter the regime of the value-added tax voluntarily, including retail distributors. Those retail distributors required to pay the value-added tax because they combined retail and wholesale sales or had multiple stores would presumably have had to prorate the

---

the double imposition of taxes when the products of exempt enterprises are sold to other taxpayers, see Lauré, *Au secours de la T.V.A.*, pp. 37–40. The example relates to Électricité de France, a public agency now subject to the value-added tax, but it still illustrates the basic issue.

[10] See John F. Due, *Sales Taxation* (Urbana, Ill., 1957), p. 129, and Lauré, *Au secours de la T.V.A.*, p. 82.

[11] Lauré, *Au secours de la T.V.A.*, p. 83.

credits both with respect to wholesale sales for which they had elected payment of the local tax and with respect to retail sales, which in a sense were not effectively subject to the value-added tax because taxed only on their wholesale value.

CONCEPT OF PRODUCTIVITY.   There is some evidence that the restrictions on the credit in part reflected the view that certain business outlays are more "productive" than others, that is, would lead to a greater output in a given period of time with the same amount of effort. For instance, the administrative instructions concerning one of the first laws to grant tax credits to investment goods describes the legislation as a concession to "certain productive investments" (*certains investissements productifs*),[12] and states that "the very purpose of the measure is to exempt 'productive investments.' "[13] Furthermore, the concessions to investments were granted in conjunction with the Monnet Plan, the system of economic planning through the establishment of production goals arrived at through the cooperative efforts of governmental officials, representatives of various sectors of economic activity, and organized labor.[14] In fact, the law provides that limitations on the tax credits under the value-added tax must be established by decrees to be taken after consultation with the General Planning Commission (C.G.I., art 267-1B).

The planners emphasized that higher standards of living in France required higher productivity per worker, which depended upon increased savings and investment in capital goods, technological advance, and improved organization of effort.[15] The exemption of investment goods from the value-added tax was regarded as an essential part of the program of stimulating savings and investment. However, it should be emphasized that the predominant view as expressed by M. Maurice Lauré, then Inspecteur des Finances, a high post in the General Tax Administration, was not that such exemption favored savings and investment but rather that it corrected the lack of structural neutrality under

[12] Administrative instructions concerning decrees no. 53–942 of Sept. 30, 1953, and no. 53–1003 of Oct. 7, 1953, as reported in "Taxe à la production: déduction des investissements; taxe à la production: régime des entrepreneurs de travaux immobilières," *La revue fiduciaire: monographies,* No. 48 (Oct. 12, 1953), p. 4.

[13] *Ibid.,* p. 5.

[14] A detailed description of how this system was established and the nature of its organization is provided by Professor Shepard B. Clough, "Economic Planning in a Capitalist Society: France from Monnet to Hirsh," *Political Science Quarterly* LXXXI (Dec., 1956), 539–52.

[15] *Ibid.,* p. 544.

the income concepts in the sense of unequal treatment of different products and therefore different business firms. This distortion was held to be caused by the fact that concerns are required to pay tax both on their purchases of capital goods and again when the depreciation of the investments enters into the prices of the final consumer good, while employment of direct labor is taxed only once.[16] In other words, the taxes were supposed to effect neutrality rather than fiscal intervention.

In general this view reflects the Mill-Fisher thesis that a tax on savings and investments as well as income derived from them constitutes overtaxation by reducing the returns from such savings and investment as compared with what they would be in the absence of a tax.[17] A closer examination of this position is postponed to Chapters 5 and 7 of this book.

BUSINESS PURCHASES VIEWED AS ULTIMATE CONSUMPTION.   Another way of looking at the taxation of certain business purchases is to regard them as a form of ultimate consumption[18]—a position taken by some French authorities with regard to the taxation of sales of products destined for final business use.[19] The tax on sales to exempt enterprises destined for resale is, of course, regarded as a tax on sales to ultimate consumers in the usual sense of the word, the tax being merely imposed on value prior to the exempt stage. This is also the view taken with regard to all sales to those engaged in nonprofit activities, whether such sales are of products destined for resale or for investment by the non-

[16] See, for example, Lauré, *La taxe sur la valeur ajoutée,* pp. 9, 44–47; and Dr. Charles Campet, *The Influence of Sales Taxes on Productivity,* Project No. 317 of the Organisation for European Economic Co-operation (Paris, 1958), pp. 60–62.

[17] For the most adequate exposition of this position, see Carl S. Shoup, "Theory and Background of the Value-Added Tax," *Proceedings of the Forty-Eighth Annual Conference on Taxation Held under the Auspices of the National Tax Association, 1955* (Sacramento, Calif., 1956), pp. 13–14.

[18] This concept is used in the Swedish retail sales tax "levied on any one in the business of selling goods or rendering services to consumers," but which applies to sales to business not destined for "(1) resale or (2) use as material in the production of goods for sale or in the rendition of taxable services." Martin Norr, "The Retail Sales Tax in Sweden," *National Tax Journal,* XIV (June, 1961), 176.

[19] See, for example, "Guide des taxes sur le chiffre d'affaires," *La revue fiduciaire,* Vol. IV, No. 399 (Oct., 1961), pp. 155 f. Here a distinction is made between retail sales and consumption sales. The commentary points out that retail sales as defined by French law always constitute consumption sales because they never include sales destined for resale but that consumption may refer to a wholesale sale because a consumption sale, unlike a retail sale, may involve wholesale prices or wholesale quantities or relate to objects not generally used by individual consumers.

profit enterprises; nonprofit institutions are in effect regarded as collective consumers and therefore receive purchases burdened with the sales taxes while their own nonprofit activities are exempt.[20] Moreover, the law provides that "agencies having a social or philanthropic character" (*organismes à caractère social ou philanthropique*) whose rates have been approved by the public authorities are exempt from tax even if they have been permitted to earn profits provided that such profits are utilized in the improvement of buildings, equipment, or other real estate (C.G.I., art. 271-44). The precise requirements for the exemption are to be established by decrees.[21]

"BUFFER RULE." In this exposition of the character of the French value-added tax, attention should be called to a legal provision which has been applied so as to impair somewhat the principle of the tax as an indirect form of personal taxation. The provision merely states that "Except in the case of exportation, the deduction envisaged [the tax credit] may not result in a reimbursement, even a partial one, of the tax having burdened a given commodity" (C.G.I., art. 273-1, 1).[22]

In itself, the provision seems fairly innocuous, for interpreted liberally it would seem merely to prohibit a cash refund of excess tax credits arising from domestic sales but to allow a carryforward of any excess credits. Of course, even a carryforward may give rise to some problems, a matter discussed in the section below dealing with the details of application of the sales taxes; but a carryforward is at least compatible with the basic character of the tax. Meanwhile, apparently focusing on the problem of the type of evasion which takes the form of underestimating sales and therefore permitting excessive reimbursement of taxes paid on purchases, the tax administration interpreted the provision to deny any type of reimbursement in certain situations with a view to creating a block or buffer against evasion,[23] hence the designation of the provision as the *règle du butoir,* or "buffer rule."

Had the application of the rule been limited to specific cases where there was evidence that sales were being understated, there would again

[20] It may be noted that certain health and medical establishments are classified as nonprofit institutions even when they earn profits if they engage in transactions "not revealing any gainful purpose" (*ne présentant aucum caractère lucratif*), provided that their fees have been approved by public authority (C.G.I., art. 271–31).

[21] No decrees seem to have been issued as yet, although apparently the exemption is being enforced. "Guide des taxes sur le chiffre d'affaires," *La revue fiduciaire,* IV, No. 399, 30. Also, see Norr, "Taxation in France," n. 55.

[22] My translation.

[23] Letter from M. Maurice Lauré, Budget Ministry (July 27, 1953).

have been no impairment of the principle of the tax. However, the administration went further than this, denying tax credits in excess of those due on sales even when in principle the taxpayer was entitled to such credits and in effect had received such credits under the previous legislation, that is, the buffer rule modified the tax base applied under the single-stage procedure. Although the administrative position was later invalidated by the high court, the Conseil d'État,[24] it was subsequently upheld through a legislative decree of April 22, 1960 (no. 60-381).

The enumeration of the types of situations in which the rule has taken effect is postponed to the section below on the application of the sales taxes. Generally speaking, except for cases of outright evasion, the buffer rule upsets the functioning of the tax credit with respect to the purchase of certain items currently expensed when the amount of tax on a particular transaction is less than the amount of tax on the purchase relating to the transaction.[25] Since any form of reimbursement is denied for excess credits arising from such purchases, the tax credit no longer eliminates all multiple taxation; and as the rule applies when rates on sales are below those on purchases, the rate of tax on the value of the final product will not coincide with the reduced rates indicated in the statute.[26]

Those who support the buffer rule are apparently concerned to some extent with the comparative situation of taxable and nontaxable enterprises. This is indicated in the quotation below of a governmental reply to a question raised by the legislature:[27]

[24] See Requête no. 41.410: Sté Martinet et Cie et Requête no. 20.458: Sté Closet et Pagés du 20 novembre 1959, as reported in *Droit fiscal,* No. 49 (Dec. 4, 1959), pp. 2–4 of the cover.

[25] A carryforward is allowed on items other than the "physical deductions," that is, physical ingredients and items disappearing on first use in the production process. It is also allowed even in the case of ingredients when the excess credits are merely derived from inventory accumulation.

[26] The rule also prevents the reimbursement of tax on excess credits resulting from sales excluded or exempt from the regime of the value-added tax; but at least this does not modify the previous system and has been accepted as necessary for reasons of revenue. In any event, the law prohibits reimbursement of all tax credits with respect to purchases by nontaxable enterprises, because it specifically limits the application of the credits to those subjected to the value-added tax (C.G.I., art. 273–1, 1). Lauré points out the discrimination which results against nontaxable firms as compared with those subjected to tax because of the inability of the nontaxable firm to obtain credits on investment purchases and because of lack of credits on all purchases when it sells to other taxpayers. See *Au secours de la T.V.A.,* Chap. 3.

[27] Ministerial Reply no. 6321, *Journal officiel, Débats, Assemblée nationale* (Sept. 17, 1960), p. 2399, as translated by Norr, "Taxation in France," 14/2.5e.5.

The purpose of the buffer rule is to assure the neutrality of the tax burden, primarily in the application of the value-added tax to the manufacture of products and to the accomplishment of construction contracts. In effect, in the hypothesis in which the amount of the taxes having struck the constitutive elements of a product or a piece of work is higher than the value-added tax applicable to the price of the finished product, non-respect for this rule would result in an actual subsidy to enterprises subject to the value-added tax, who would, paradoxically, be better treated than enterprises not so subject. It might happen, for example, that certain activities enjoying a reduced rate, or a reduction in the tax base, would suffer a tax burden less than that of exempt activities.

The statement that in the absence of the buffer rule enterprises producing items subject to a reduced rate will be favored over some firms turning out nontaxable products is, of course, correct. Focusing on items currently expensed, because the buffer rule does nothing to offset the advantage derived from tax credits on investment purchases granted to taxable firms, it may be said that the exemption from the value-added tax applies only to the value added by the exempt enterprise. If this value added is sufficiently low while the firm's purchases are taxed at the full rate, its products will be burdened more heavily than if sales had been taxed at a reduced rate and any excess tax credits arising from taxable purchases had been fully reimbursed. On the other hand, in the case of sales to nontaxpayers, the nontaxable firm is still favored as compared with enterprises whose sales are subject to the general rate. Moreover, the burden apparently conforms to legislative intent, for the nontaxable products could have been subjected to the reduced rate. On the other hand, there is definite discrimination to the extent that the nontaxable enterprises sell to other value-added taxpayers because the exemption has interfered with the mechanism of the tax credit, thereby causing double taxation; but the buffer rule merely adds more firms to the group discriminated against while firms not subject to the rule continue to receive full credit for taxes paid on their purchases. Moreover, the buffer rule does nothing about the discrimination against nontaxable firms relative to firms taxable but at a reduced rate arising from the former's ineligibility for tax credits on purchases other than ingredients—notably, investment goods.

The governmental statement concerning the buffer rule would also be consistent with the concept of the tax as a business tax in the sense of one not expected to be shifted forward to ultimate purchasers. However, this is certainly not the concept underlying the French sales taxes.

Service Tax

The service tax, which supplements the French value-added tax, is imposed at the rate of 9.29 percent on the gross receipts of service enterprises or, in other words, on their gross sales of services. The reduced rate may in part reflect an attempt to apply the tax to wholesale values, that is, a reduced rate is used instead of a discount from the retail level.

As no tax credits are allowed concerns subject to the service tax, the tax is a cumulative one to the extent that they purchase items from other service enterprises; and, besides, the service tax is superimposed on any value-added tax incorporated in the price of the firm's purchases. On the other hand, the service tax may be credited against the value-added tax liability of value-added taxpayers so that the superposition of different taxes is avoided in this instance.

The failure to effect a complete integration of the service tax and value-added tax is probably largely the result of a reluctance to undertake the administrative task of applying the value-added regime to the mass of small service enterprises. Service enterprises are free to enter the value-added tax regime voluntarily if they find it worthwhile, whether to avoid multiple taxation or to enjoy tax credits on investment purchases.

PROGRESSION UNDER VALUE-ADDED AND SERVICE TAXES. There is extensive rate differentiation under the value-added tax, ranging from exemptions or reduced rates of 6.38 percent and 11.11 percent on products regarded as necessities and on certain producers' goods, notably fuel, other forms of energy, and various agricultural producers' goods, to increased rates of 29.87 percent and 33.33 percent on items considered consumer luxuries. In certain instances the service tax of 9.29 percent may be regarded as a reduced rate on consumer services; and there are also various exemptions for services rendered in connection with products exempt or subjected to reduced rates under the value-added tax. Also, there is an increased rate of 13.64 percent on services considered luxuries. In addition, the various special excises effect rate differentiation. Such differentiation with respect to consumer goods reflects the view that a progressive spendings tax can be achieved through the indirect approach by varying the rates of the taxes collected on consumer items in accordance with their relative importance in the budgets of different income classes.[28] As indicated in Chapter 1, a planned rate progression is impossible with this method and, moreover, an effective progression is unlikely, given the exemption of sales of investment goods; but rate differentiation will mitigate the degree of regression and will even effect some progression as among certain income brackets.

Special Excises

The special excises, whether in the form of *taxes uniques* or other selective sales taxes, usually entail an exemption from the value-added or service taxes otherwise due. Exceptions to this rule are the excises on alcohol or on petroleum products prior to the distributive stage, which are imposed in addition to the value-added tax which is collected through the suspensive system in the case of petroleum products.

Generally speaking, the special excises are not creditable against the value-added or service taxes, nor are the value-added or service taxes creditable against the special excises. Thus, the special excises are superimposed on the general taxes. This means that the rates of the general taxes are in effect increased by the amount of the special excises paid on a firm's purchases or sales. Insofar as the superposition of taxes is limited to items currently expensed, this arrangement is consistent with the concept of a consumption-type tax, although important administrative issues are involved. However, inconsistency arises when the special excises involve exemption from the value-added tax; for, as in the case of all products exempt or excluded from the value-added tax, investment goods purchased by the firms subject to such excises are taxed.

Local Tax

The local tax imposed at a general rate of 2.83 percent is primarily a single-stage retail sales tax of the consumption type. Of course, when

[28] See Jean Dellas, "Taxes sur le chiffre d' affaires dans l'économie contemporaine," *Revue de science et de législation financières,* XL (1948), 87 f.; and André Garrigou-Lagrange, "Évolution du système fiscal français au vingtième siècle," *Revue de science et de législation financières,* LIII (1961), 210.

wholesalers elect payment of the local tax instead of the value-added tax, the local tax becomes a cumulative levy in the distributive sector.

The tax applies to all retail sales of commodities because the law provides that the local tax is due on all sales of commodities not subject to the value-added tax, thus reaching independent retail distributors. It also provides that the tax is due on sales benefiting from the discount which reduces taxable price from retail to wholesale value, thus reaching sales by integrated and multiple-store retailers as well as retail sales of manufacturers and wholesalers.

In addition, the local tax applies to sales of products exempt or excluded from the value-added tax or the service tax. In the case of sales of commodities exempt or excluded from the value-added tax the suspensive system is applied, that is, those who buy to resell are allowed to present vendors with exemption certificates. The tax applies to products not destined for resale even if bought by business firms. However, to the extent that the products are of a type likely to represent producers' goods rather than consumer items, there are specific exemptions from the local tax.

Like the other sales taxes, the local tax applies rate differentiation. Certain products regarded as consumer necessities and various producers' goods are exempt while an increased rate equal to that of the general rate of the service tax, 9.29 percent, is applied to certain entertainment activities, to eating and drinking establishments, and to rentals of furnished lodgings.

International Transactions

French sales taxes, whether general or selective, are imposed in accordance with the destination principle, the rule appropriate for personal concepts of indirect taxation. With respect to imports the taxes are collected on importation, except for the local tax which is collected only when the imports are sold on the domestic market.

The manner in which exports are exempt from the general taxes is explained in more detail in the section of this chapter dealing with the application of the taxes. For the most part the exemption is complete. In other words, not only is the export transaction exempt but all taxes paid prior to the export stage are either exempt or reimbursed. The exceptions consist of products excluded or exempt from the value-added and service taxes whether subjected to special excises or not, for there are no tax credits available to exporters of nontaxable items. However, the administration has allowed agricultural enterprises to purchase products used in conditioning exports free of value-added tax;[29] and it permits certain other taxpayers exempt or excluded from the value-added tax, especially those subject to special excises, to purchase ingredients or packages free of the value-added tax when they export.[30] Meanwhile, the petroleum tax, the combination of customs duty and excise, which reaches ingredients purchased by petro-chemical manufacturers subject to the value-added tax, has apparently been refunded by the customs administration whether the chemicals are destined for export or sale on the domestic market.[31] For the most part, however, the special taxes and general taxes are not integrated with each other so that exports cannot be completely freed from tax.

HISTORICAL DEVELOPMENT OF THE SALES TAX SYSTEM

The current French system of indirect taxation has emerged as an outgrowth of experimentation with a great variety of collection procedures, none of which prior to the value-added tax of 1954 effectively implemented the consumption-type concept usually intended by the government. This experimentation has reflected a struggle to establish a measure of wide scope capable of yielding the large amounts of revenue required, amenable to efficient administration, and acceptable to the taxpayers. The struggle is not yet over; and an appraisal of the extent to which progress has been made requires at least a brief review of the evolution of the sales tax system since its introduction following the First World War and current proposals for further reform.

General Turnover Tax of the Twenties

Although sales taxes in France have probably always been regarded as taxes on ultimate consumers—that is, they have been supposed to

[29] Instruction No. 168 of Sept. 4, 1958, "Guide des taxes sur le chiffre d'affaires," *La revue fiduciaire,* No. 399, p. 193.
[30] Instruction No. 213 of Nov. 24, 1958, *ibid.*
[31] See, for example, the case of the petroleum tax in Lauré, *Au secours de la T.V.A.,* p. 43.

implement the principle of an indirect spendings tax—the general turn-over tax enacted on June 5, 1920, was solely the result of a desperate attempt to raise sorely needed revenues with the least administrative and political opposition.[32] However, the legislature assumed that the tax would be shifted forward to consumers,[33] and by 1925 the legislation was being openly supported on the ground that a tax on consumer expenditures implementing the principle of personal ability to pay was preferable to a direct income tax which would be limited to certain economic classes and would strike savings.[34]

Initially imposed at a general rate of 1.1 percent, of which .1 percent was collected for the benefit of the local governments, it was increased to a rate of 2 percent in 1926. From the beginning luxury taxes, usually collected at the retail stage, had been imposed on certain articles and on the services of luxury hotels and eating and drinking establishments, with the rates reaching a maximum of 13.6 percent on luxury articles and 14.9 percent on luxury services by 1926.

As has been the case throughout French sales tax history, the tax applied only to business firms defined as *commerçants,* a term which excludes agriculture and the professions.[35] Also, artisans, that is, those engaged in small family enterprises using little or no machinery, were exempt.

From 1925, various taxes called "replacement taxes" or, alternatively, because collected from manufacturers, "production taxes" were substituted for the turnover tax.[36] The introduction of such taxes had been considered from the first year of the general turnover tax. Later called single taxes (*taxes uniques*), they represented an application of the "estimated lump-sum" procedure, or the *Pauschalierung* used extensively under the Austrian tax. Thus, they were taxes collected at a single stage, that of manufacture or importation, supposed to effect the

---

[32] Shoup, *The Sales Tax in France,* p. 106.
[33] *Ibid.,* p. 102.
[34] *Ibid.,* pp. 37, 40.
[35] A *noncommerçant* may be taxable if his transactions are considered commercial under the French Code of Commerce. On the other hand, his transactions may be exempt as accessory to a noncommercial activity. Fine distinctions become necessary in this area. Like the professional sector, agriculture has caused difficulty. Farmers are exempt on any normal prolongation of their activity, such as minor processing, but not if they go beyond this.
[36] Shoup, *The Sales Tax in France,* p. 279.

same tax burden on the finished product as if the article had undergone the average number of market transfers and had been subjected to the turnover tax.

The substitution of the production or single taxes for the general turnover tax on numerous commodities reflected the political power of small taxpayers who had apparently not been satisfied with the *forfait* procedure of assessment under which the tax was assessed through external signs while the taxpayers were permitted to dispense with all record keeping.[37] In addition to the unequal burden on small firms resulting from the subsidy to vertical integration, the transformation of wholesalers and retailers into commission merchants, taxable only on their commissions rather than gross receipts, worked against the interest of small manufacturers unable to bear the risk or provide the capital needed for investment in inventories previously supported by independent merchants.[38] Moreover, small merchants were probably less able to convert to a commission business than larger establishments because they did not have a close relationship with large manufacturers who would have accepted the risk and provided the necessary credit. It is understandable, therefore, that small firms welcomed the replacement taxes, which avoided a general subsidy to integration and made it possible to collect the tax mainly from larger enterprises.

The collapse of the general turnover tax system has been attributed primarily to its dualism, the combination of the general tax and single or production taxes, rather than to the single taxes as such. It is true that the single taxes in themselves involved difficult administrative and compliance problems because each was subject to particular rates and methods of assessment, but this defect could be remedied by the adoption of a unifying principle. Consequently, when in the early thirties the number of replacement taxes increased to the point where the administrative and compliance problems became intolerable, a solution was sought through the concept of a "general single tax" (*taxe unique globale*), imposed at the production or manufacturing stage.[39] Moreover, the limitation of the tax to the manufacturing stage made it possible to concentrate administrative resources on a relatively small group of taxpayers.

[37] *Ibid.,* p. 126.
[38] *Ibid.,* p. 316.
[39] Émile Larguier, *Traité des taxes à la production* (Paris, 1939), pp. 21–22.

The Production Tax of 1936

The fundamental refoim of the sales tax system was effected through the law of December 31, 1936, which introduced a "production tax" (*taxe à la production*) consisting of a manufacturers' single-stage sales tax imposed under the destination principle at a rate of 6.38 percent on sales of commodities, supplemented by an independent tax on services of 2.04 percent due whenever the services were rendered in France. Except for frequent rate changes, this system endured as the mainstay of the national sales tax system until the end of 1948.

As in the previous system, agriculture and the professions were excluded and artisans were exempt. Also, small producers were allowed to use a *forfait* procedure of computing the tax although this meant that they could not purchase in suspension of tax; and, unlike the previous regime, the procedure required some record keeping.[40]

Stimulus to integration from multiple taxation was avoided under the manufacturers' sales tax through the system of allowing firms defined as manufacturers and designated as tax-producers or taxable producers to purchase commodities in suspension of tax. The purchasing manufacturers either provided vendors with exemption certificates or quoted their number in the Directory of Producers compiled by the tax administration and kept up to date quarterly.[41] Also, to avoid the superposition of tax which would result if products entered the distributive or service stages and then reentered the manufacturing stage, business firms were permitted voluntarily to enter the regime of the single-stage tax when they sold to taxable producers. They were also allowed to do so if they exported products in order that the tax on their purchases might be permanently suspended.

The tax applied to the wholesale value at the manufacturing stage. Direct sales for retail were adjusted to the wholesale level by a discount from retail price, originally 30 percent and later reduced to 20 percent with an option to use a discount of two thirds of gross profit margins in the preceding year.

On the other hand, there was no suspensive regime allowed under

[40] See J. Patouillet, "La notion de producteur dans la taxe à la production," *Recueil Dalloz: Chronique, 1946* (Paris, 1946), p. 69.

[41] Larguier, *Traité des taxes,* p. 563.

the independent service tax, which was therefore a cumulative type of tax to the extent that service enterprises made purchases from other service enterprises. Moreover, there was no integration of the regime of the manufacturer's sales tax and the service tax so that manufacturers could not buy services in suspension of service tax while service enterprises could not buy commodities in suspension of manufacturer's sales tax, a fact which encouraged the integration of manufacturing and service enterprises. In the case of brokerage services, however, multiple taxation was avoided under the manufacturers' sales tax by an exemption for such services relating to taxable commodities, whether the services were rendered before or after the taxable stage. Also, the services of jobbers (*façonniers*), were exempt when rendered for taxable producers.

Certain distortions resulted from the unequal rates of the manufacturers' sales tax and service tax. A conspicuous case was that of prefabricated construction subjected to the relatively high rates of the manufacturers' sales tax as compared with construction on the premises treated as the rendering of a taxable service.

Although the new national sales tax system, like the general turnover tax, was supposed to be a consumption tax,[42] it actually implemented a gross product type of concept. In addition to the fact that the purchases by service enterprises inclusive of investment goods were subject to tax, the suspensive system under the manufacturer's sales tax was limited to the purchase of certain categories of items currently expensed. The categories included items physically incorporated in the finished product or consumed on first use. Moreover, unlike the general turnover tax, the production tax applied to products manufactured by the firm for its own use within the business, under the concept of the producer's delivery to himself (*livraison à soi-même*). By a decree of August 24, 1939 (art. 6), the suspensive system was in effect extended by allowing a deduction from taxable gross sales of one half the purchase price of "products rapidly consumed" (*produits de consommation rapide*), that is, articles which survived only a few uses in the manufacturing process, such as polishing products, grease, oils, etc., the items being listed in decrees.

A further lightening of the tax burden on products utilized in business

[42] According to the economic classification of the Ministry of Finance as indicated in Table 1. Also see Patouillet, "La notion de producteur dans la taxe à la production," *Receuil Dalloz: Chronique, 1946*, p. 71.

was effected through the tolerance of the tax administration. "Special tools" (*outillages speciaux*), such as designs, sketches, models, forms, and molds were treated as services rather than manufactured products when a producer manufactured such items for his own business, so that only the purchases of raw materials were taxed.[43] Moreover, the administration refrained from applying the tax to "partial or internal fabrications" (*fabrications partielles ou internes*), that is, items produced in the course of turning out the firm's final product. If, for example, a manufacturer whose final product was machinery utilized parts of the machine within his own plant, the administration did not bother to apply the concept of a delivery to himself.[44] Similarly, the tax was not imposed if it was customary business practice to manufacture the product on the premises for use in the enterprise as in the case of cement blocks used by construction contractors or cakes manufactured by a restaurateur for the meals which he served on the premises.[45] As contractors and restaurateurs were subjected to the 2.04 percent service tax on their services, they purchased such products from outside firms burdened with the manufacturers' sales tax.

Until the war years, there was little rate differentiation under the production tax aside from the 2.04 percent reduced rate on services, a rate also applied to a few commodities which the legislature wished to favor, and aside from the exemption of certain necessities. During the war, luxury taxation was attempted but with limited success because of black market dealings;[46] and the increased rates were abandoned by a decree of March 30, 1948.

A number of special excises had been carried over from the old sales tax regime; but a movement to eliminate them gradually began in 1938. Finally, a law of January 8, 1948, abolished all of them but the tax on petroleum. However, a special production tax at rates of 4.17 percent and 33.33 percent had been instituted in 1945 and applied to a number of products previously subject to both the excises and the manufacturers' sales tax.[47] The special production tax was collected through the same

[43] J. Patouillet, "La suppression du régime de la suspension de taxe en matière de taxe à la production," *Recueil Dalloz: Chronique, 1949* (Paris, 1949), p. 14.

[44] *Ibid.*, p. 13.

[45] Larguier, *Traité des taxes*, p. 96.

[46] Henry Laufenberger, "Finances et fiscalité de guerre," *Revue de science et de législation financières*, XXXVIII (1940–46), 197.

[47] *Les lois nouvelles, 1946* (Paris, 1946), Pt. III, p. 117.

suspensive procedure as the manufacturers' sale tax but applied in addition to it. The products concerned encompassed such items as beer, mineral water, vinegar, vanilla, and playing cards.

General Turnover Tax of 1939

The requirements of war finance presented the occasion for the revival of the turnover tax as a supplementary sales tax measure. This was effected by a decree law of April 21, 1939, based upon a general law of March, 19, 1939. Originally called the "armament tax" (*taxe d'armement*), its name was later changed to the "transactions tax" (*taxe sur les transactions*).[48]

Imposed at the rate of 1.01 percent and due regardless of liability under any other sales tax, the levy was almost identical in subject, scope, base, and rules of collection as the old turnover tax. However, it possessed no surtax for the benefit of local governments, no luxury rates except for a brief period during the war, and only one replacement tax, that on wool. Also, unlike the original, the *forfait* for small enterprises required some record keeping, being the same as under the production tax. Moreover, the tax reached artisans, treated some cooperatives more severely, and provided an additional tax on integrated retail distributors, those distributors whose wholesale sales amounted to a certain proportion of total turnover or having more than two retail establishments. The tax on these concerns was first imposed at 1.01 percent on deliveries to retail branches or outlets and later at 1.83 percent on retail sales, thereby implying a retail profit margin of about 20 percent. The new law also introduced a tax on purchases by retailers from those beyond the scope of the law, later extended to such purchases by all business firms in order to reach farmers' sales of argricultural products which short-circuited the distribution process.[49]

The absence of a local tax ended with a law of November 6, 1941, which granted municipalities the option of enacting an independent local tax on retail sales destined for ultimate consumption and on services. The tax was collected by the national administration in charge of the transactions tax at the rates of 0.1 and 0.25 percent depending on the

---

[48] "Décret d'application du 13 mai 1939," *Les lois nouvelles, 1939* (Paris, 1939), Pt. III, pp. 802–4.

[49] *Les lois nouvelles, 1948* (Paris, 1948), Pt. III, p. 90.

size of the locality. No tax was imposed on imports at the time of importation, on purchases, or on jobbing operations for the account of tax-producers. With the intention of simplifying administrative problems, the law of December 22, 1947, (law no. 47-2359 art. 6) converted the local tax into a surtax on the transactions tax and substituted the concept of a final sale for that of a sale to ultimate consumers, thereby applying the tax to sales for business use.

A decree of December 9, 1948 (decree no. 48-1986, art. 50) reorganized the local surtax into a form maintained until the latest general revision in 1955. It established a compulsory local tax at a regular rate of 1.52 percent (increased by 0.25 percent if voted by the municipal councils) on all tranactions subject to the national transactions tax except imports, purchases, jobbing operations for the account of taxable producers and sales by taxable producers. The latter were taxed only when they made direct retail sales, which under the manufacturers' sales tax benefited from a discount reducing them to the wholesale price level and were defined to exclude most sales for business use.

The local tax thus became a cumulative levy on the distribution of commodities and services. Products exempt from the production tax but not the transactions tax, such as unprocessed farm products and certain prepared foods, were especially burdened by the new law. Moreover, agricultural products were said to be more heavily taxed than industrial products because the number of intermediaries was greater.[50] In response to these criticisms, the tax burden on agricultural products was lightened by the law of July 31, 1949, (law no. 49-1034, art. 1) through a 50 percent reduction in taxable sales of products destined for resale made by those subject to the purchase tax under the national transaction tax.

To meet the objection that the local tax provided a general subsidy to integration, the reform of December 9, 1948, increased the rate of the local tax to 2.04 percent on the sales of integrated retail distributors subject to the 1.83 percent rate of the national transactions tax. The increased rate of the local tax was raised to 2.88 percent by the law of July 31, 1949 (no. 49-1034, art. 1).

The three groups of taxes just described comprised the sales tax system immediately prior to the abandonment of the single-stage method

[50] J. Grossetête, "Chronique de législation fiscale," *Revue de science et de législation financières,* XLI (1949), 223.

of collecting the manufacturers' sales tax in favor of the adoption of the value-added procedure through the law of fractional payments; and the general characteristics of this system may be briefly summarized. Two of the groups constituted the production tax, namely, the manufacturers' sales tax and the cumulative tax on services. The manufacturers' sales tax was currently imposed at a general rate of 11.11 percent and a reduced rate of 4.17 percent on selected commodities including various fuels, meat products, and slightly processed agricultural products. The service tax was imposed at a rate of 3.63 percent. Furthermore, an additional manufacturers' sales tax at rates of 4.17 percent and 33.33 percent was imposed on certain commodities, such as carbonated beverages, spices, playing cards, etc. The third group comprised the national transactions tax and local surtax whose rates had remained at the level of 1.01 percent for the transactions tax and were soon to be established at 1.52 percent for the local surtax.

Although an improvement over its disorganized predecessor, the system was excessively complicated, difficult to administer, and burdensome to the taxpayers. The cumulative taxes, that is, the service tax and transactions tax, subsidized integration as did the fact that the service tax was not applied when a payer of the value-added tax produced services for use within his enterprise, such as transportation services, although he had to pay the service tax when he bought the services from outside concerns. The different groups of taxes were superimposed on one another, that is, the taxes paid on purchases were not creditable against those due on sales. Moreover, the national transactions tax was imposed simultaneously with other taxes, that is, it was assessed on the same transactions in addition to the other national sales taxes; and in the case of service enterprises, the local tax applied as well. A variety of special provisions and some excessive exemptions made it inevitable that certain firms would suffer a discriminatory impact.[51]

Meanwhile, the production tax contained only one provision designed to equalize the situation of commodities transferred through various channels of distribution, that of a discount on direct sales by manufacturers to ultimate consumers. There was no discount on direct sales to retailers and no attempt at an uplift for manufacturing functions trans-

---

[51] For a discussion of the excessive exemptions, notably those concerning artisans, agricultural cooperatives, and various public agencies, see Lauré, *La taxe sur la valeur ajoutée,* pp. 69–74, 95–96.

ferred to the distributive or reduced rate service stages. However, it should be noted that a number of functions performed by independent firms made them taxable producers, such as other than normal packaging and the use of trade marks.

Emergence of the Value-Added Tax

FRACTIONAL PAYMENTS.   As previously noted, the value-added procedure of collection instituted by the law of fractional payments through the decree of September 25, 1948, effected no radical change in the former system. It merely substituted the value-added method of collection for the single-stage procedure of collecting the manufacturers' sales tax. In other words, the tax remained a gross product type of indirect income tax but, instead of being collected from the final manufacturer, that is, the one who sold the product to distributors or ultimate users, it was collected at every stage of the manufacturing process through taxing each firm's sales but allowing a credit for taxes paid on certain purchases. The only significant modification from the previous legislation was caused by the buffer rule, noted above.

TRANSITION TO THE CONSUMPTION-TYPE TAX.   From September 1953, the French manufacturers' sales tax underwent a series of modifications which gradually transformed the gross product type of tax to a consumption-type measure. Legislation of September 30 and October 7, 1953, introduced the first tax credits on investment goods and reduced the tax burden on building construction.[52] The new legislation was adopted for the stated purposes of increasing production and employment through a temporary decrease in the amount of the production tax burdening certain "productive" investments acquired by taxable producers, and of lowering construction costs through reducing the taxes on building construction, a measure which would also favor productive investments. The new provisions were scheduled to expire on March 31, 1954, in anticipation of a general reform of the sales tax system. The only indication of the nature of the general reform was that it would

[52] Decrees No. 53–942 of Sept. 30, 1953 and No. 53–1003 of Oct. 7, 1953, according to the instructions of the General Tax Administration, Indirect Taxes, No. 255, B 2/1 and No. 226 B 2/1, as reported in *La revue fiduciaire: monographies,* No. 48 (Oct. 12, 1953), pp. 1–14.

not include identical provisions in favor of fixed investment (decree no. 53-942, art. 2). This suggested the possibility of less generous treatment, probably because of doubt as to the consequences of the measures and perhaps in the hope of inducing taxpayers to take immediate advantage of the new legislation. As it turned out, the new measures were less liberal than the eventual general reform.

The transitional measures consisted in the allowance of tax credits equal to one half the tax paid on purchases and on a concern's production for its own use of certain investment goods delivered between October 1, 1953, and March 31, 1954. Investment goods were defined as products customarily entered in a fixed-asset account and capable of depreciation. The administration called attention to the concept employed under the income taxes and noted that depreciation was only applicable when the durability of the goods exceeded one year.[53] The creditable investments consisted of all producers' goods other than commercial buildings, most transportation equipment, and office furnishings.

Creditable investment purchases were to be entered in the taxpayer's fixed asset account at cost less tax credits, thereby ensuring that the tax credits would appear as a reduction in capital costs rather than current expenditures. The incorporation within the tax statute of this accounting requirement when tax credits were extended to investment goods had been emphasized in a plan for a general tax reform submitted to the French legislature in 1952 so as to ensure that concerns undertaking large capital outlays would not seem to have abnormally low current costs as compared with their competitors.[54]

The lightening of the tax burden on building construction under the new legislation consisted in allowing all contractors undertaking fixed construction, whether new buildings or the maintenance or repair of old ones, to adopt the status of taxable producer for all or part of their activities if they wished to do so and, moreover, to reduce their gross sales by a discount of 30 percent in computing their tax base. Thus the effective rate of the tax was reduced from the prevailing rate of 18.13 percent to 12.03 percent. Furthermore, the discount was not to result in incurrence of liability for the local surtax as was the case with the discount on retail sales, although the transactions tax was still due.

[53] *La revue fiduciaire: monographies,* No. 48 (Oct. 12, 1953), pp. 6 f.
[54] Assemblée nationale, deuxième législature, 1952, *Projet de loi portant réforme fiscale,* No. 4579 (Paris, 1952), p. 14.

Under the regime applicable to all construction contractors prior to the new system, entrepreneurs were permitted to elect the regime of taxable producers rather than pay the service tax and local tax when their customers were tax producers, the national transactions tax being applicable in any event. However, they were taxed on their total sales without any discount unless the administration classified their work as retail sales entitled to the discount of 20 percent or two thirds of the average percentage of gross profits, a practice to be discontinued under the new regime.[55] The contractor who did not sell to taxable producers was ineligible for the regime of the tax of fractional payments and hence had not been entitled to a discount for retail transactions, being subject to the lower rate service tax.

Although not mentioned in the administrative instructions, several other reasons were advanced in explanation of the new measures.[56] The discount was described as a means of inducing building contractors to elect the status of taxable producer in order to ensure tax credits for their producer customers, thereby implying that they had not always been alert to this problem. Also, the new system was supposed to end the penalty against prefabrication in the case of fixed construction because the option to elect the status of taxable producer was independent of the methods employed—an aim undermined to some extent by the buffer rule, as explained later in this chapter. As the equivalent of a reduced rate whose benefit is lost when it reduces the credits of payers of the value-added tax subject to a higher rate, the discount favors purchases which the tax treats as final rather than intermediate outlays, notably commercial and residential construction.

ADOPTION OF THE CONSUMPTION-TYPE TAX. Apparently encouraged because the limited experience with the tax credit on investment goods had been accompanied by an upturn in the production index and little reduction in revenues, the legislature enacted a general reform as envisaged in the decree of September 30, 1953, which introduced a consumption-type concept of value-added taxation (law no. 54-405 of April 10, 1954). The tax credits of 50 percent allowed on purchases of investment goods were raised to 100 percent from April 1, 1954, to July 1, 1954 (art. 23). On July 1, 1954, the tax of fractional payments was

---

[55] *La revue fiduciaire: monographies,* No. 48 (Oct. 12, 1953), p. 12.

[56] "Commentaire des dispositions législatives et réglementaires concernant la taxe sur la valeur ajoutée," Preface by M. Lauré, *Recueil Sirey, 1954* (Paris, 1954), pp. 4, 8 f., 12.

officially designated as a value-added tax (*taxe sur la valeur ajoutée*) (art. 1), which extended tax credits to general expenditures (art. 8-2) and was applied to all contractors undertaking fixed construction except artisans (art. 41). Service enterprises, regardless of the tax status of their customers, were permitted to pay the value-added tax voluntarily on all or part of their sales of services (art. 4-2). Also, rate reductions were allowed on sales of some agricultural producers' goods and the government was required to lower the prices of farm equipment through subsidies of 15 percent (art. 22)—a concession later extended to equipment purchased by exempt publications.[57] Finally, the definition of situs for the service tax was made consistent with the destination principle, that is, services were taxable when utilized or exploited in France (art. 2).

The rates of the taxes were increased to 20.26 percent for the general rate of the value-added tax and 8.11 percent for its reduced rate while the service tax remained at 6.05 percent. The discount for building construction was increased to 35 percent which largely compensated for the increase in the rate of the value-added tax; and an exemption from the national transactions tax was added to the exemption from the local tax (art. 10).

The transition to the consumption type of tax was completed by a decree of April 30, 1955 (no. 55-465), which effected some important changes in the sales tax system as established by the reform of 1954 and left it in substantially the same form as it exists today. The only really significant changes since that time have been the introduction of luxury rates in 1957 and various changes in rates and exempt categories.

The reform of 1955 took the important step of elminating the concurrent application of more than one type of sales tax. The transactions tax was abolished, including the local surtax; and the system was left with only two groups of national sales taxes and a separate local tax.

The national taxes comprised the value-added tax and the service tax. The value-added tax was extended in principle through the wholesale stage but wholesalers were granted the option of paying the local tax instead of the value-added tax.[58] Also, tax credits were now made available on purchases subject to the service tax.

The value-added tax was imposed at a general rate of 24.22 percent.

[57] See Lauré, *Au secours de la T.V.A.*, p. 29.

[58] The government has attributed its failure to extend the value-added tax through the retail stage to the accounting problems of retailers. "Réforme fiscale," *Journal officiel* (May 3, 1955), p. 4371.

Concerns undertaking fixed construction were allowed a discount of 39 percent, thus taxing them in effect at the rate of 13.49 percent. The discount was increased to 40 percent by an ordinance of December 30, 1958, a rate of 13.64 percent, which remains applicable to the present day.

The 1955 legislation provided two reduced rates on commodities instead of one. A rate of 11.1 percent was imposed on products previously taxed at the reduced rate of 8.11 percent, notably energy, soil nutriments, and other agricultural producers' goods, certain farm products which would have been exempt if they had not been slightly processed, and food preserves of which at least 20 percent were composed of meat products subject to a newly established *taxe unique* to be collected instead of the value-added tax on meats. The other reduced rate equaled 13.64 percent and applied to various food products widely consumed, which since the 1954 legislation had been taxed only on their value net of the value of the exempt products of which they were composed by allowing the food producers to compute a fictitious tax credit on their purchases of exempt products.

The service tax was imposed at a rate of 9.29 percent, in effect a reduced rate. However, no provision was made for tax credits on purchases by firms subject to the service tax, so that the previous regime was maintained.

Luxury taxation under both the value-added and service taxes was introduced by a decree of July 29, 1957 (No. 57-845, in application of C.G.I., art. 258). The rates were 29.87 percent or 33.33 percent for commodities and 13.64 percent for services, the same as the current rates.[59] Eventually, the additional value-added tax on certain products, such as mineral waters, spices, and playing cards, was abandoned by an ordinance of December 30, 1958 (no. 58-1374, art. 41), the items concerned being integrated with the regular value-added tax or luxury taxes.

The 1954-55 legislation also introduced a number of single taxes to

[59] For a brief period during which the country was subject to inflationary pressures, luxury rates were manipulated to implement a policy of fiscal controls. They were even applied to business and residential construction other than low-cost housing for a few months in 1958. The luxury rates on construction were introduced by a decree of Aug. 4, 1958 (no. 58–685, art. 4) but abandoned by a decree of Dec. 31, 1958 (no. 58–1425). Also, the maximum rate of the value-added tax reached a level of 37.93% for a brief period, having been instituted by an ordinance of Dec. 30, 1958 (no. 58–1374, art. 32) which also increased the rates applicable to luxury services to 17.64%.

replace the value-added tax imposed on certain commodities. They consisted of the taxes on wines and ciders, meats, and tea and coffee.[60] The service tax on freight transportation by rail, road, and inland waterway was eliminated by a decree of September 19, 1956 (no. 56-933) and was replaced by a special tax on freight transportation by road and inland waterways, with railroad transportation favored by an exemption. The replacement tax took the form of a vehicle tonnage tax.

One rather interesting provision of the 1954 legislation (law no. 54-404, art. 8-3) was introduced as a safeguard against the possibility that the tax credits under the value-added tax might unduly stimulate investments nonessential to productivity or might result in technological unemployment, thus indicating that some legislators—the Socialist party, according to one source—had certain reservations on the basic philosophy underlying the new measures. The provision allowed the government to refuse tax credits not only by types of products but also by categories of activities, on advice of the Planning Commission. Furthermore, it empowered the government to subordinate all or part of the tax credits to the full employment of personnel or the reclassification of the individuals threatened with unemployment because of investment. However, the provision was never utilized and was dropped in a rewording of the ordinance of December 30, 1958 (no. 58-1374, art. 39), which merely stated that decrees would establish the exclusions and restrictions with respect to the tax credits, the decision apparently having been made to tolerate any unemployment necessary for development.

The local tax established by the 1954–55 legislation was essentially the same as the current one briefly characterized in the previous section —a retail sales tax on sales to ultimate consumers but a cumulative tax in the distributive stages to the extent that wholesalers elected its payment. The only difference from the present legislation was that the general rate of the 1954–55 reform was 2.72 percent; the increased rate was 9.29 percent, the same as in the current legislation.

Prospect for Further Evolution

The foregoing review of the history of French sales taxes reveals considerable progress in the direction of legislation based on a general

[60] Lauré, *Au secours de la T.V.A.,* p. 29.

principle of taxation implemented in a rational manner. Of course, there are glaring departures from an adequate application of the underlying concepts, notably the treatment of wholesalers and the buffer rule. Moreover, in addition to the inequities among business firms engaged in similar activites caused by these discrepancies, a number of cases of discriminatory treatment can be traced to the special regime for services and the failure to extend the tax through the retail stage.

Nevertheless, aside from the brief uprising by small taxpayers in 1955,[61] the last decade has witnessed a number of encouraging developments. One is the fact that no special excises in lieu of the general sales taxes have been adopted since 1956. Another is the increasing extent to which exemptions have been receiving critical examination, thus leading to the elimination of the exemptions for agricultural cooperatives using industrial or commercial methods and for certain governmental enterprises and agencies. Still another is the absence in recent years of proposals for the extensive determination of tax due through external signs and indexes of potential productivity rather than actual records as in the governmental reform project of 1953.[62]

Even more important is the evidence that the present government is alert to the need for further improvement in the methods of assessment and collection. This is indicated by the reform project placed before the National Assembly in 1960.[63] The major aspect of the proposal is that the value-added tax should be extended to service enterprises while the

[61] The revolt was led by M. Pierre Poujade, owner of a small stationery business. See "Revamping France's Taxes," *Business Week,* No. 1333 (Mar. 19, 1955), p. 154, and "Poujadists Leap from Street Brawls to Parliament," *ibid.,* No. 1376 (Jan. 14, 1956), p. 30. This uprising was responsible for the introduction by the 1955 reform of an extensive estimate procedure or *forfait* for assessing small taxpayers defined as those with sales of commodities not in excess of 15 million old francs and sales of services not in excess of 4 million old francs. In addition to the simplified method of assessment, which, however, requires some bookkeeping, the chief concession to the small taxpayers has been that, even in the case of outright evasion, only the penalty for late payment is due, although the *forfait* is then canceled.

[62] "External signs" were to be used to compute an index of "normal productivity." This form of *patente* was presented as a direct tax and was to be substituted not only for the proportional rates of the personal income tax in the case of small and medium-size concerns but also for all the sales taxes imposed on distributors. See *La revue fiduciaire, feuillets hebdomadaires d'information,* No. 321 (Nov. 23, 1953), pp. 6–7.

[63] For a summary of the proposals, see "La réforme des taxes sur le chiffre d'affaires," *La revue fiduciaire, feuillets hebdomadaires d'information,* No. 635 (June 5, 1960), pp. 1–8.

local tax should be abolished, so that all wholesalers will be obliged to pay the wholesalers' sales tax.[64]

Immediately after the reform of 1955, Shoup expressed the opinion that "The way is being cleared for extension of the value-added principle over the entire economy, but it would be premature to predict such a move. The large number of small retail shops poses an administrative problem for the value-added tax although a lump-sum exemption might remove most of this difficulty without undue effects on competition."[65] Although the 1960 reform project stops short of this goal, it is obviously a step in that direction; and it is noteworthy that for the first time in the history of the French sales taxes, an exemption rather than an esti-mate procedure has been seriously considered for very small taxpayers, those with sales under 25,000 NF, with a graduated assessment of those with sales between 25,000 NF and 50,000 NF.

APPLICATION OF THE SALES TAXES

As explained above, the sales taxes designated as *taxes sur le chiffre d'affaires* encompass all economic enterprises classified as business or commerce—*commerçants* under the French legal system. Thus they reach all economic activities other than those of agriculture, the professions, and nonprofit institutions.

However, as is customary in sales taxation, the nature of the trans-action rather than the status of the taxpayer primarily determines tax-ability; and the crucial test is whether the transaction constitutes a commercial act as defined in the French commercial code or any other act relating to commercial or industrial activity. A transaction may incur tax merely because it is accessory to the activites of a business, such as the purchase of insurance for use in a business although the insurance

[64] A number of features of the proposal are best appreciated in relation to particular aspects of the application of the sales taxes which they are designed to correct and will therefore be discussed in the following section rather than here. Although the government had scheduled the reform for Jan. 1, 1962, at the latest, it has not yet been enacted, probably largely because of the reluctance of local governments to abandon their independent local tax in favor of surtaxes on the national value-added tax.

[65] Carl S. Shoup, "Taxation in France," *National Tax Journal,* VIII (Dec. 1955), 340.

contract in itself is considered noncommercial in character.[66] On the other hand, it may escape tax as accessory to a nonbusiness enterprise, such as the provision of food and lodging to pupils provided by the head of an educational institution participating in the teaching of the pupils.[67] Isolated transactions are taxable if their repetition would constitute business activity as, in principle, is the case of an individual who constructs his own home although in this instance specific exemptions have been provided.[68]

The taxes apply to all deliveries of commodities and fixed construction in France or services utilized in France (C.G.I., art. 259 and art. 1574). France includes all of metropolitan France and Corsica.[69]

[66] Art. 632, Code de Commerce, Livre I, Titre I, *Petits Codes Dalloz*, 58th ed. (Paris, 1962), p. 605.

[67] *Ibid.* Also, see Sieur Tordeau, Nov. 18, 1949, *Recueils des arrêts du Conseil d'État, Tables 1949*, p. 642. However, obviously commercial transactions are taxable regardless of the status of the entrepreneur; and a mutual aid society was declared taxable when it operated a restaurant and bar for its members even when it earned no profits or used profits for charitable purposes. "Société de prévoyance de la préfecture de police," Jan. 10, 1949, *Recueils des arrêts du Conseil d'État, Tables 1949*, p. 684.

[68] Art. 260–4° of the Tax Code exempts certain low-cost housing constructed by individuals for their own use or by groups for the personal needs of members while an administrative decision exempts homes constructed by any individual who can prove the use of the building for his personal and permanent occupancy or that of his family even if the homes do not conform with the requirements of the "Plan Courant" (Decisions no. 6,179 and no. 1,779 of Oct. 12 1954 and Mar. 31, 1955). A recent law, which applies the value-added tax to a number of transactions involved in residential construction previously subjected mainly to the registration taxes (law of Mar. 14, 1963, no. 63–214, art. 27) limits the exemption to houses constructed by individuals for their own use or that of their families provided that the individual acts as his own entrepreneur instead of being assisted through intermediaries. If the home is taxable, an 80% discount is applied to taxable price in computing the tax base, or an effective rate of 4.166%, rather than the usual 40% discount, or effective rate of 13.64%, provided that the individual intends to use it as his chief dwelling and the area occupied does not exceed 2500 square meters or the legal limit in the locality. The law has been put into effect through the administrative decree of July 9, 1963 (no. 63–675). The legislation is intended to simplify the application of sales taxes to residential construction, to equalize the tax burden regardless of different legal forms of organization of promoters and builders and the relative importance of different elements of cost as well as to eliminate the discrimination against wholesale dealers which results under the cumulative taxes. The value-added tax is now applied not only to the value of the building but also to the value of the site. In other words, production of a new residence is held to include the value of land as well as that of the building. See "La réforme de la fiscalité immobilière," *Impôts et sociétés* (Aug.-Sept., 1963), esp. pp. 15, 19, and 30.

[69] Monaco is also covered because it adopted legislation which applies the French sales taxes and, by agreement, the taxes are assessed as if France and Monaco were one country. The French overseas departments are treated as foreign

To ensure the implementation of the destination principle, the rule of situs given above is supplemented by provisions which ensure the application of the taxes to imports and the exemption of exports. Thus importation, that is, crossing the customs barrier, incurs taxability even if delivery has taken place abroad (C.G.I., art. 277).[70] On the other hand, exportation is exempt even if delivery has occurred in French territory (C.G.I., art. 272, and art. 1575-2, 13°).

APPLICATION OF THE VALUE-ADDED TAX

Taxable Subjects

As the value-added tax is only one component of the sales tax system, the law must identify those who are subject to its particular regime. Such taxpayers are divided into two groups. The first group consists of those who are automatically included within the concept of a wholesalers' sales tax, that is, manufacturers and wholesalers. The second group encompasses those permitted to enter the system if they find it worthwhile to do so. The taxable subjects, designated in articles 263 and 264 of the Tax Code, may therefore conveniently be classified as compulsory and voluntary taxpayers although the position of wholesalers is such that they may be assumed to belong to either group.[71]

The list of compulsory taxpayers includes the following:

1. Producers (*producteurs*), defined so as to include wholesale liquor dealers (*marchands en gros de boissons*).
2. Wholesalers (*commerçants grossistes*).
3. Building contractors or entrepreneurs of fixed construction (*entrepreneurs de travaux immobiliers*).

---

countries, that is, sales to them are regarded as exports while purchases from them are considered imports. This is also the case with Andorra. A sales tax system identical with that in France is applied in the overseas departments (Gaudeloupe, Martinique, and Réunion) although the value-added tax is imposed at lower rates while only the local tax is used in Guiana.

[70] The local tax is to some extent an exception because it is not collected at the frontier. However, the tax does reach sales of imported products on the domestic market. Meanwhile, the export transaction is exempt; and to the extent that the tax is a retail sales tax, purchases made by exporters are received in suspension of tax and thus exempt.

[71] In addition, article 1654 of the Tax Code provides that, unless specifically exempt, all governmental enterprises, agencies, and public concessions are liable for the taxes which would be applicable to private enterprises undertaking the same transactions.

4. Taxable retailers.

5. All purchasers of certain items.

6. Importers.

MANUFACTURERS OR PRODUCERS. The definition of a producer in the Tax Code is as follows (C.G.I., Annexe III, art. 69):

Producers or manufacturers (*fabricants*), in the sense of article 263-1 of the Code are those who, within the conditions established by article 264 of said Code, manufacture products, prepare or transform them as finishers (*confectionneurs*), or entrepreneurs of manufacture (*entrepreneurs de manufacture*), with the intention of giving the product its final form or the commercial appearance (*présentation commerciale*), with which it will be delivered to the consumer to be utilized or consumed by him.[72]

The Tax Code (art. 264) lists three categories of producers or manufacturers in addition to wholesaler liquor merchants and excludes artisans, those engaged in family enterprises using little mechanized equipment. The three categories are defined as follows:

a) Persons or companies who, as principals or accessories, manufacture products or have them prepared (*subir des façons*) with or without the use of other material either in the manufacture of the products or their commercial presentation.

b) Persons or companies who are substituted in fact for the manufacturer either in his factories, or even outside his factories, in order to undertake all operations relating to the manufacture or final commercial presentation of products (placing them in packages or receptacles, transportation, storage) whether or not the latter are sold under the mark or name of those who undertake the operation.

c) Persons or companies who have third parties undertake the operations visualized in paragraphs a) and b) above.[73]

This exceedingly comprehensive definition of manufacturing reaches not only all forms of business organization and methods of manufacture, including the use of preparers or jobbers (*façonniers*), who work on materials belonging to others but also most types of activity which might conceivably be undertaken by a manufacturer. Thus it is impossible to escape tax by transferring such activites to a nontaxable stage or to a service enterprise subjected to a lower rate. Transportation services are a special case, however; they are part of a manufacturer's activities only

[72] My translation.
[73] My translation.

if the manufacturer is in charge of the transportation, an issue discussed below in the section on taxable price.

Although one who merely puts a name, mark or label on a product does not become a legal producer, he will if he holds the exclusive rights to the sale of the product or if the brand assures the final presentation of the product or presents the distributor as the manufacturer.[74] Similarly, mere division into small quantities, packaging, and conditioning, not usually undertaken by manufacturers of the products concerned, and conditioning not requiring important equipment or numerous and specialized help does not make a manufacturer; but anything beyond these limits does.[75]

WHOLESALERS.   Wholesalers are defined as those "who resell commodities without further processing under circumstances other than retail" (C.G.I., art. 263-1, 5°). While wholesale liquor dealers are classified with manufacturers and must therefore pay the value-added tax, other wholesalers are allowed to elect payment of the local tax if they find it advantageous.

BUILDING CONTRACTORS.   Those engaged in fixed construction, including public works and demolition, who must pay the value-added tax, are not defined in the Tax Code but rather by the tax administration. While certain activities obviously represent building construction, it has proved impossible to derive a definition which neatly segregates fixed construction from moveable construction, that is, the installation of moveable items, which is taxed as a combination of sales and services.[76]

Consequently, in those situations where the administration has had difficulty in deciding where to draw the line, it has allowed the taxpayer to elect the system which he prefers. In other words, he may choose the category of fixed construction, thereby being liable for the value-added tax with the reduced rate resulting from the discount applied to taxable sales. On the other hand, he may choose the regime of installation, thereby paying the service tax on his installations. The situations eligible for the option include the installation of items which lose their moveable character because either permanently attached to the building or practically inseparable from it as, for example, electrical heating, air conditioning, ventilators, refrigerators, telephones, clocks, television,

---

[74] "Guides des taxes sur le chiffre d'affaires," *La revue fiduciaire,* No. 399, p. 36.
[75] *Ibid.*
[76] The installation incurs the service tax while the item installed is subjected to the value-added tax.

antennas for general use, factory installations composing an entire industrial system, and apparatus for handling and transporting merchandise within an enterprise.

TAXABLE RETAILERS. Retailers are defined as those who make "resales without further processing (*reventes en l'état*), under retail circumstances" (C.G.I., art. 263-1, 6°). They are required to pay the value-added tax on the basis of the wholesale value of their sales if they possess more than four retail stores or if they combine retail and wholesale sales and their wholesale sales exceed half of their aggregate turnover in the preceding year. The purpose of this provision is to effect some equalization of the tax burden when distributive functions are transferred to the nontaxable retail stage, a matter considered below in the discussion of taxable price.

ALL PURCHASERS OF CERTAIN ITEMS. In a few cases where the vendor lies beyond the scope of the value-added tax, the tax is applied to purchases, even those made by individuals, in order to prevent a loophole in the law (C.G.I., art. 261). The purchases concerned are precious jewelry unless sold at public auction, where a registration tax is applied, alcohol, and food preserves. The provision with respect to alcohol and food preserves is intended to reach the manufacturer of such items by farmers.

IMPORTERS. Except for those importing collectors items, antiques, and industrial designs or plans, which are subjected to the service tax, all importers of commodities are liable for the value-added tax by art. 277 of the Tax Code, the tax being applied at the same rates as on domestic sales of similar articles (C.G.I., art. 279). In addition, all importers must pay the value-added tax if related to nonresident enterprises, regardless of what their taxable status would be otherwise (C.G.I., art. 263-1, 4°) —a provision intended to prevent the type of evasion which occurs when a nontaxable firm purchases at fictitiously low prices from a related taxable enterprise. The provision also applies in the case of interdependent domestic firms, as discussed below.

Voluntary Taxpayers

Voluntary payment of the value-added tax has been granted primarily in order to prevent any interruption in the line of tax credits when products subjected to value-added tax are transferred to the nontaxable retail stage or the service stage and are then resold to a payer of the value-added tax or are exported. Therefore, all business firms are allowed to enter the regime of the value-added tax with respect to all or part of their sales when they sell to other payers of the value-added tax and export, unless the firm sells products exempt from the value-added tax because of a specific exemption or an excise or because the enterprise is engaged in an excluded activity.[77]

Generally speaking, any enterprise not subjected to the value-added tax finds it to its advantage to elect payment if its customers are payers of the value-added tax entitled to tax credits while its own purchases have been burdened wih the value-added or service tax. Only through such voluntary payment is it possible to avoid multiple taxation under the value-added tax of items currently expensed or superposition of the value-added and service taxes on such items, and to effect the complete exemption of creditable investment purchases. Similarly, only by voluntary payment can such a concern enjoy the credits for the value-added and service tax paid on its purchases needed to turn out products shipped abroad.

Even local governments undertaking building construction are allowed to elect payment of the value-added tax, the option being used in cases where the local government constructs factory buildings for sale to payers of the value-added tax. Also, wholesalers and all service enterprises are in the position of being allowed to elect payment of the value-added tax even if their customers are not payers of the value-added tax or if they do not sell for export. Whether or not they elect payment on sales to nontaxpayers or on sales of items which their customers may not credit will depend on their situation under the regime of the value-added tax as compared with the regime to which they would otherwise be subjected.

Thus, wholesalers must compare their situation under the value-added

[77] In the case of sales of nonferrous metals, the law requires that the suspensive system of tax collection rather than the value-added method be used (C.G.I., art. 266, and Annexe IV, art. 24D). Those who purchase such metals are required to provide their suppliers with exemption certificates stating that the purchases are destined for resales subject to the value-added tax. As a result of this arrangement, the purchasers are entitled to no tax credits. Presumably this arrangement was introduced in order to stop some types of evasion as, for example, the kind of swindling which Lauré claims went on in the case of dealers in iron scrap. See Lauré, *Au secours de la T.V.A.,* p. 197. Offhand, a direct attack on the evasion would seem more sensible.

tax with the alternative local tax imposed on their aggregate sales. Other things being equal and given the effective rate of the value-added tax of 25 percent and of the local tax of 2.83 percent, the amount of tax would be identical under the two systems if a wholesaler's profit margin equaled 11.32 percent; the tax is less under the local tax if the profit margin is higher and vice versa.[78]

However, the wholesaler must also take into consideration any value-added or service tax imposed on his own purchases and which he might credit under the value-added tax but not the local tax.[79] Also, he must consider his situation with regard to purchases of investment goods creditable under the value-added tax. The situation of service enterprises is similar except that they must compare the service tax on the aggregate sales of services of 9.29 percent with the situation under the value-added tax. Thus, other things being equal, the amount of tax is the same under either system if the profit margin is 37.16 percent; the service tax is less than the value-added tax with higher profit margins and vice versa.

Tax Rates

As previously noted, rates range from complete exemption, herein designated as a differentiated rate of zero, to the maximum rate on certain luxuries of 33.33 percent.[80] Most products are subjected to the general rate of 25 percent.[81]

[78] The formula is $x = L/v$, where x equals the profit margin, L the local tax rate, and v the rate of value-added tax.

[79] The complexities introduced in certain situations by the buffer rule are discussed below in the section explaining the computation of the value-added tax liability.

[80] Except for the exemptions granted because of replacement taxes listed in art. 265-II of the Tax Code, most exemptions are enumerated in art. 271. Products taxed at a reduced rate are noted in art. 262, while the increased rates to be established by decree according to art. 258 are found in Annexe III, art. 69. The application of the replacement taxes will not be described in this study. They consist of the taxes on three categories of commodities: (1) wines, ciders, perries, and meads; (2) meats; (3) tea and coffee. Freight transportation by land and inland waterways, which would otherwise be subjected to the service tax, is also exempt, a vehicle tonnage tax replacing the service tax in the case of transportation by road and inland waterways (C.G.I., Annexe II, art. 016A). Each group of replacement taxes has its own special regime of assessment and collection. The one characteristic they have in common is that they are specific rather than ad valorem.

[81] The 1960 reform project suggests an increase in the general rate to 29.03% and in the maximum luxury rate to 36.99%, with the possibility of somewhat lower

EXEMPTIONS AND REDUCED RATES.   Two reasons account for most of the rate concessions granted certain products or activities under the value-added tax. On the one hand, the concessions are intended to lighten the burden on products considered consumer necessities or on certain types of consumption which the government wishes to encourage. On the other hand, they are intended to lighten the burden on producers' goods purchased by enterprises exempt or excluded from the tax and therefore ineligible for tax credits or on certain types of producers' goods not creditable even by those paying the value-added tax. These concessions have reflected not only the application of the fundamental principle of the tax, that of a tax on the consumption expenditures of a society's residents applied with some degree of personal progression, but also a concern with maintaining price stability, an effort being made to reduce taxes on products represented in the cost of living indexes to which wage contracts have been tied.[82]

One concession of some significance which cannot be fitted into either of these categories is the exemption granted to charitable and social organizations with respect to activities beyond their noncommercial functions, a provision obviously intended to favor the nonprofit organizations concerned even if their activities compete directly with those of private enterprise. The activities are exempt provided that there are no profits and the prices charged have been approved by public authority. Furthermore, they are exempt even if there are profits, provided that the profits are used for improving their equipment and buildings. The exemption of artisans is a further example of a concession to a particular group.

The exemption of second-hand articles and industrial waste also has a special explanation. These items are exempt because it proved impossible to prevent excessive evasion.[83] Only the transfer in an unprocessed

---

rates if the yield exceeds expectations. The rate increases are intended merely to recoup the revenue loss expected from the abolition of the service and local taxes.

[82] See *La revue fiduciaire, feuillets hebdomadaires d'information,* No. 346 (June 1, 1954), pp. 7–8, and No. 350 (July 12, 1954), pp. 1–3; *"La réforme du régime des taxes sur le chiffre d'affaires, La revue fiduciaire,* No. 311–12 (July-Aug., 1954), p. 46; Lauré, *Au secours de la T.V.A.,* pp. 27–28, 53.

[83] "Commentaire des dispositions législatives et règlementaires concernant la taxe sur la valeur ajoutée," *Recueil Sirey, 1954,* p. 20. It should be noted, however, that the exemption can be justified on the principle that mere exchanges of assets should not be taxed.

condition is exempt from tax; any items manufactured from the second-hand material or waste are taxable.

The exemption of certain naval and aircraft construction is designed to enable the high-cost French firms to compete against foreign producers.[84] The exemption concerns only construction of vessels other than warships and planes used by French companies engaged in international transports. It encompasses the construction of pleasure craft provided that the French Federation of Yachting certifies that the boats are used in the open sea.

The exemption of the governmental gunpowder and stamp monopolies as well as the public concessions providing water and air in part reflects the fact that their prices are regulated by the public authorities. However, there is no reason why these activities cannot be taxed, with the authorities allowing a rise in price by the amount of the tax. On the one hand, unless there is a wish to favor such products over other consumers' goods, they should be taxed. On the other, if they represent producers' goods, they ought to be taxed so as not to break the line of tax credits, unless of course they are items used mainly by exempt or excluded activities. Although traditionally exempt from the French sales taxes, the tobacco and match monopolies as well as the public concessions in electricity and gas are now taxed.[85]

CONCESSIONS TO CONSUMER GOODS. The consumer goods exempt from the value-added tax consist largely of food products. In addition to the exclusion of sales by farmers of their own products even when they engage in some processing, the law specifically exempts sales of eggs and poultry, which would be excluded otherwise only if the farmer supplied his own fodder, sales of fresh and frozen fish and all distributive sales of the farm and fish products concerned. Ordinary bread, milk, cream, butter, and cheese are also exempt.

The reduced rate of 6.38 percent applies to various food products widely consumed and, moreover, they are taxed only at the manufacturing stage. Baby foods, water ice, household soap, and brooms are taxed at 11.11 percent. The rate is also applied to all agricultural products which have undergone only a slight transformation. The purpose is to avoid too sudden a jump from the zero rate applied to sales by farmers

---

[84] Lauré, *Au secours de la T.V.A.*, p. 51.
[85] Lauré vigorously supported the taxation of public enterprises and public service concessions. See *La taxe sur la valeur ajoutée*, pp. 71–74.

and the general rate of 25 percent applicable to processed foods. Similarly, the 11.11 percent rate is applied to preserves of which at least 20 percent of the net weight is composed of meat products which have been subjected to the replacement tax on meat. Such foods would be heavily burdened if the 25 percent rate had been imposed on sales in addition to the special excise applied to the meat ingredients. Books are also subject to this reduced rate.

As explained above,[86] residential construction conforming to certain requirements for low-cost housing is exempt from the value-added tax, provided that it is undertaken by an individual for his personal needs or by any group for the personal needs of its members. Likewise, an administrative decision has extended the exemption to all residential construction undertaken by individuals for their personal use; but some modifications in this arrangement have been introduced by the 1963 legislation. Moreover, the tax is not applied to certain public and semi-public associations working for local governments in providing equipment needed to urbanize certain areas as well as to various other associations in charge of construction programs for themselves, their members, or local governments provided that they do not engage in actual construction.[87]

Newspapers and periodicals are exempt on their sales of subscriptions, issues, and waste products as well as on composition and printing provided that they conform with certain requirements, notably that of having a character of general interest in the diffusion of information, instruction, education, and recreation. A similar exemption applies to films and photographic records as well as to publications of philanthropic organizations or those whose purpose is devoid of special interest, and to periodicals published by organizations for family gardens. All activities of agencies of local governments dedicated to social, cultural, educational, or travel programs are exempt provided that such activities do not compete with private enterprise in the locality. The list of exemptions of consumer items is completed by the exemption of supplies sold by certain health and medical establishments to those admitted into their care and the exemption of monuments to the war dead.

INCREASED RATES ON CONSUMER GOODS.   The increased rate of 33.33

[86] See note 68, above.
[87] Administrative instruction no. 95 of May 11, 1959.

percent applies to a long list of products classified as luxuries. They encompass such categories as ornaments and jewelry, perfumes and beauty products, furs, photographic equipment other than that used by professional photographers, smokers' supplies, watches, mirrors and glass, various alcoholic and nonalcoholic beverages including mineral waters, certain luxury foods (truffles, pâté de foie gras, caviar, and all food preserves not subjected to a reduced rate), certain publications on special paper and of limited circulation, as well as all components and articles used in conditioning the luxury items.

The rate may be reduced to 29.87 percent and even 25 percent when the industries concerned have entered into an agreement with the Ministry of Finance to increase their exports (C.G.I., Annexe III, art. 69 N-2). This encouragement to exports, in effect since January, 1959, has been used in a number of cases. The 29.87 percent rate is applied in the case of ventilators, waxers, and washing machines, various games and sporting or athletic equipment, trunks and ornaments, motion picture apparatus and supplies, floral and decorator pieces, and yard goods whose price exceeds 70 NF a yard. The regular rate of 25 percent now applies to refrigerators and household equipment other than ventilators, waxers, and washing machines, and to tapestries, motorcycles, crystal ware, clocks, and a few other items.

CONCESSIONS TO PRODUCERS' GOODS. The fact that enterprises engaged in turning out products exempt or excluded from the tax are denied tax credits on their purchases of producers' goods has been responsible for a long list of exemptions and reduced rates. This is the explanation of exemptions relating to grains and flour used in making exempt bread, of materials and supplies used in exempt publications, of sales of straw and fodder, calcium soil nutriments for agricultural use, and engines and fishnets sold to the fishing industry. It accounts for the reduced rate of 11.11 percent on various forms of fuel and energy, on turpentine, resin and insecticides for agricultural use, soil nutriments, sulphur and copper sulphate products destined for agricultural use as well as copper granules used to manufacture these items.

The reduced rate of 11.11 percent applicable to sales of gas and electricity, whether or not produced by public concessions, benefits all activities ineligible for tax credits because the activities are excluded or exempt from the value-added tax or because the purchases of gas and electricity are used with respect to categories of purchases denied tax credits, such as commercial buildings. It also benefits all those regarded as ultimate consumers, whether individuals or groups. The same can probably be said for the 11.11 percent rate on sales of water, compressed air, and steam used in central urban heating produced by enterprises not operating under a public concession.[88]

Likewise, the discount allowed building contractors, which results in a reduced rate of 13.64 percent, is for the benefit of all who purchase buildings but who are ineligible for credits because engaged in excluded or exempt activities or because the buildings belong to an excluded category of purchases, such as commercial buildings. Thus, it benefits various business and nonbusiness purchasers who invest in buildings as well as ultimate consumers.

Computation of Tax Liability

The taxpayer computes his tax liability by subtracting from the amount of tax due on his sales (or taxable deliveries of items produced for personal or business use) the taxes imposed on his purchases and quoted on invoices rendered by his suppliers. Generally speaking, sales are measured by actual sales prices except in the case of direct retail sales which must be reduced to the wholesale level, while constructive pricing must be used for items manufactured for own use.

The payer of the value-added tax is eligible for credits on almost all his purchases of goods and services subjected to the value-added or service taxes, whether the items are currently expensed or capitalized. Naturally, he is entitled to no credits for purchases obtained for his personal consumption. Also, he is entitled to no credits for the categories of business purchases to which credits have been specifically denied.

Only the value-added tax or the service tax are creditable. Thus no credits are available on purchases from enterprises excluded or exempt from the value-added and service taxes, whether or not the purchases have been subjected to the local tax or a special excise.

---

[88] Sales of water and compressed air by public concessions are favored by a complete exemption. However, if the prices charged by such concessions are the same as those charged by private concerns, the exemption must benefit the concessions.

TAXABLE PRICE. The value-added tax is assessed on the "amount of sales" or, in the case of barter, "the value of objects remitted in payment" (C.G.I., art. 273-1). This provision has been interpreted to mean that the taxable price encompasses almost all charges inclusive of any outlays—for example, packaging, transportation, finance,[89] warranty, installation, and advertising charges. Also, the value-added tax itself is included in taxable price at the nominal rate, that is, 20 percent in the case of the general rate, although in practice the tax is usually applied at the effective rate to price excluding tax.[90]

When a sales tax does not encompass the service and distributive spheres of economic activity, the problem always arises that some elements of price charged by taxable firms will include items which would escape tax or be taxed at a lower rate if produced by separate enterprises. As previously noted, the definition of manufacturer under the value-added tax is sufficiently broad to encompass many of those items when produced by independent firms, such as packaging beyond the simplest form and the imposition of trade marks or brands. On the other hand, some of the accessory charges noted are subjected to the reduced rate of the service tax if rendered by separate firms while in the case of most freight transportation, only the special tax on transportation vehicles or the exemption for railroad transportation is applicable.

Apparently, in those cases in which discrimination among various methods of doing business is most evident, taxable firms have been allowed to exclude certain charges from their tax base, largely as a result of administrative discretion.[91] Thus, transportation charges are excluded if the responsibility for the transportation has been assumed by the purchaser rather than the vendor, which should interest all those not making purchases eligible for tax credits. Similarly, a manufacturer may subtract from taxable price his payments to distributors holding the concession for his brand and servicing his customers, especially with respect to warranties. Likewise, certain finance charges are deductible. This is the case of interest and discounts on automobile credit after a decree of September 30, 1953 (no. 53-968), provided that the taxpayer can prove that the purchaser has paid him in cash and that the taxpayer has not

---

[89] Interest on late payments is deductible on the assumption that rewards for damage should not be taxed.

[90] "Guide des taxes sur le chiffre d'affaires," *La revue fiduciaire*, No. 399, p. 50.

[91] *Ibid.*, pp. 50–52.

intervened in the credit transaction. Also deductible are amounts paid to banks to whom the taxpayer has delegated responsibility for collection of his accounts as well as the bank discount on the vendor's receivables.

Packages may be invoiced separately provided that they are sold without expectation of return. This arrangement is useful when packages are taxable at the general rate while the contents are taxable at increased rates.

Discounts and rebates granted in accordance with the sales contracts are deducted in computing taxable price, as are canceled sales, unpaid sales, and packages sold on consignment unless they are not returned. In the case of unpaid sales, however, the credits taken on purchases relating to the sales are disallowed in accordance with the buffer rule, as explained below, so that only the fraction of tax paid by the vendor is reimbursed.

The taxable price is the wholesale price. When the taxpayer has made a direct retail sale he is allowed to reduce the retail price by a 20 percent discount or by a fraction equal to two thirds of the average percentage of gross profits of the preceding year (C.G.I., art. 273-1).[92]

The definition of a retail sale is that of a sale made at a retail price involving quantities not execeeding "the normal private needs of a consumer" (C.G.I., art. 273-1).[93] A sale is never considered a retail sale if it is a sale for resale, if it concerns products which by their character or use are not generally used by ordinary consumers, or if the price is the same whether the items are sold at wholesale or retail.

In addition to direct retail sales made by manufacturers or wholesalers, the retail discount applies in the case of those retailers who are required to pay the value-added tax, that is, retailers with multiple stores and those combining retail and wholesale sales. The requirement that these retailers pay the value-added tax is, of course, intended to eliminate the discrimination which occurs under manufacturers' and wholesalers' sales taxes when larger retailers assume certain functions ordinarily rendered at the taxable manufacturing or wholesaling stage.

---

[92] In some special cases, presumably because of their importance to the export industry, the discount is increased to three fourths of the average percentage of gross profits. The enterprises benefiting from this provision are those making quality products, such as *haute couture* and various ornaments and jewelry.

[93] The administration has established various criteria for determining retail prices and quantities.

In other words, it is intended as a substitute for the "uplift" used in the British purchase tax. However, the use of profit margins to determine the amount of the discount seriously impairs the effectiveness of the provision, since retailers assuming distributive functions have greater profit margins. It is for this reason, presumably, that the 1960 reform project recommends that the use of profit margins be abandoned and limits the discount to 20 percent for all taxable retailers. The reform project proposes the imposition of the value-added tax on all retailers with sales exceeding 400,000 NF so that only larger establishments will be taxed, as contrasted with the present situation under which the criterion of number of stores and wholesale sales exceeding a certain percentage of retail sales often reaches rather small enterprises.

There is no retail discount available for building contractors. Instead they are entitled to the 40 percent discount from their taxable receipts in computing the tax base. Similarly, there is no discount allowed service enterprises electing payment of the value-added tax.

The value-added tax must be applied to a firm's manufacture of products for its own use, of items produced for the personal consumption of the owners, and of items not eligible for credits or creditable only in part because used in an exempt or excluded activity. Although the production for own use of items fully creditable against the value-added tax does not in principle require the application of the tax, the administration has apparently decided that it is convenient to apply it even in these instances,[94] although this merely means that the firm's tax credits are commensurately increased.

In the case of self-deliveries, the taxable price is defined as the "normal wholesale sales price of similar products" (C.G.I., art. 273-4). When the concern does not sell similar products on the market, the administration uses the cost price of the articles including the share of overhead costs, plus a markup for "normal selling profit," although if the items are not normally sold on the market, the administration settles for cost price excluding profits.[95]

When a vendor is affiliated either with another domestic firm or with a foreign enterprise the tax must be paid by the vendor on the basis of

---

[94] Instruction No. 176 of Sept. 11, 1959, and Rép. min. Mariotte No. 6293, *Journal officiel, Débats, Assemblée Nationale,* Aug. 13, 1960, p. 2282.

[95] "Guide des taxes sur le chiffre d'affaires," *La revue fiduciaire,* No. 399, pp. 60–61.

the selling price of the related purchasing firm unless the vendor customarily sells to third parties at the same price as he sells to the related enterprise (C.G.I., art. 273-2). If the related purchaser is a payer of the value-added tax, the administration allows the vendor to pay the tax on the basis of his sales price, since in that instance any fictitious price practiced by the vendor would not occasion a loss to the treasury.[96]

Affiliation, which is defined by the administration, means actual interdependence regardless of the legal form or organization. Such interdependence occurs whenever one firm directly or indirectly exercises the power of decision over another or possesses the largest share of the capital or a majority of the votes in the meetings of the members or shareholders (C.G.I., Annexe I, art. 26).

TAX CREDITS.   The tax applied to sales in conformity with the above procedure is then reduced by the tax credits available on purchases. There is a monthly lag in the application of the credits, that is, the credits may only be applied to the tax on sales due in the month following that of purchase (C.G.I., art. 273-1-1°). As previously noted, this provision was introduced to obtain extra revenues at the time when the law of fractional payments was adopted. It is reported to inconvenience various categories of taxpayers;[97] and its abolition is contemplated by the 1960 reform project.

Credits are allowed for the value-added or service taxes paid on purchases, including imports, and on self-deliveries of items needed by the taxable business firms (C.G.I., art. 267). No distinction is made as to whether the items are currently expensed or depreciated. Although the Code continues to refer to physical ingredients and items disappearing on first use, distinguishing them from other objects, products, goods, and services, the only reason for the distinction seems to be that any restrictions on the eligibility of purchases for tax credits may not apply to physical ingredients or items disappearing on first use.[98]

In addition to products purchased for the personal needs of ultimate

[96] Instruction No. 161 of Aug. 18, 1958.

[97] In fact, the administration will consider granting exceptions in cases where the lag causes serious difficulty (Decision no. 4907 of Sept. 21, 1955). Presumably the hardship cases are those with fluctuating sales.

[98] The Council of Ministers, after consulting the Planning Commission, determines the categories of products not entitled to the credits (C.G.I., art. 267B).

consumers,[99] various categories of durable goods as well as any goods or services used in their upkeep or operation have been declared ineligible for credits. While credits are allowed on industrial buildings and their equipment and the places and equipment required for compulsory social services (infirmaries, cloak rooms, showers, etc.), they are denied to all other buildings, such as selling establishments, administrative and commercial offices, accounting offices, and noncompulsory social services. No credits are allowed for transportation equipment other than that used in the internal handling of merchandise. Although general business equipment is creditable, such as typewriters, calculating machines, duplicating machines and files, credits are denied on most furnishings which might serve equally for personal use, including tables, chairs, bookcases, desks, draperies, rugs, wardrobes, showcases, mirrors, etc. Naturally no credits for the service tax are available for purchases of sevices used in conjunction with excluded products.

When creditable purchases are used in turning out exempt as well as taxable products, it is necessary under the French law to prorate the credits because they are not allowed with respect to purchases giving rise to nontaxable sales other than sales exempt because of exportation. Although somewhat troublesome for the administration and taxpayers, the proration of credits is not excessively difficult in the case of items currently expensed, the taxpayer merely being required to allocate his credits in the proportion that his sales and self-deliveries subject to the value-added tax or exported bear to his total sales.[100]

On the other hand, considerable complexity in administration and compliance has resulted from the need to prorate credits in the case of depreciable assets, that is, the proration over time. The problem consists

[99] Including services rendered for the individual or collective needs of managers and personnel as well as those concerned with noncompulsory services (Instruction no. 195 of June 30, 1955).

[100] His sales and self-deliveries are not reduced by any discounts. The numerator of the proration fraction also contains any sales on which the value-added tax has been "suspended" as well as sales of the taxpayer's waste products. Moreover, the taxable sales and self-deliveries, sales in suspension, and export sales are recorded tax included, which means that the effective rate of tax must be added to the sales in suspension and export sales. Since Jan. 1, 1959, a firm may use one proration fraction for all its activities, whereas before it was required to segregate those purchases relating to mixed activities from those definitely attached to taxable or nontaxable sales. However, the administration may permit or require a segregation when a firm clearly engages in various types of activities, the proration fraction being determined separately for each (C.G.I., Annexe III, art. 69A-3).

in the fact that the relative importance of nontaxable sales not entitled to the credits varies over time; and inequities would result while taxpayers would engage in adjusting their outlays to minimize tax, if the administration did not attempt to make corrections in the original proration ratio so as to make it conform with the situation in a given year.

The law therefore provides that an adjustment must be made in the original amount of credits granted, that is, the taxpayer must either repay part of the original credit or may obtain increased credits if the firm's activities in a given year during the five years following the purchase of an asset have shown a significant divergence from their situation in the year on which the proration ratio was based. (C.G.I., Annexe III, art. 69C.) Such adjustments are made if the firm's activities vary enough to cause a change in the original proration ratio by more than ten percentage points. When this occurs, the tax credits in a given year are modified to the extent of one fifth of the difference between the tax credits available under the new and original proration fractions.

For example, if the amount of the original credit was 70,000 NF and because of an increase in the proportion of the firm's taxable sales, the proration ratio in a given year equals 85 percent as compared with the original ratio—that is, the ratio in the year of acquisition—of 70 percent, the firm is entitled to increased credits of 3,000 NF or one fifth of the difference between 70,000 NF and 85,000 NF. If the proration ratio in a given year has declined 15 percentage points from the original, the concern would have had to repay 3,000 NF to the public treasury.[101]

In order that tax credits on depreciable assets may not provide an opportunity for tax avoidance, the French value-added tax requires repayment of some of the credits received on the original purchase of an investment good if the asset is sold, transferred, or destroyed or if the taxpayer discontinues business less than five years after the date of acquisition, the year of acquisition being counted as a full year. The amount of repayment equals one fifth of the original credits for each year remaining in the five-year period. Thus, if the asset is sold one year after the date of acquisition, three fifths of the credit must be repaid to the

---

[101] No adjustments are made in the firm's capital accounts as a result of these modifications in the amount of the original credit although at the time of purchase the assets were recorded in the capital accounts at cost exclusive of the amount of tax credits. Instead, the additional credits or repayments are merely entered in the firm's current accounts (Note no. 716 of Feb. 17, 1959).

government, with, however, permission to transfer the credit to the purchaser if the latter is a payer of the value-added tax.

SYSTEM A AND SYSTEM B FOR PARTIAL TAXPAYERS. Special arrangements to aid taxpayer compliance are necessary in the case of those concerns which combine sales subject to the value-added tax with distributive activities not subject to the value-added tax either because the taxpayer has elected payment of the local tax or because the distributive sales are exempt. These concerns, called "partial taxpayers" (*assujettis partiels*), are entitled to tax credits only on their purchases entering into sales subject to the value-added tax or into exports. However, as the concerns usually do not know the destination of their sales at the time when they make their purchases, the administration allows them a choice between two methods of provisional tax payments, with final regularization when the actual results are known. The systems concern only the so-called "physical deductions," that is, the credits allowed on ingredients and items disappearing on first use. Any tax credits arising from purchases utilized within the business, such as investment goods or general expenses, are prorated and taken independently of the two systems.[102]

System A, which assumes that most of the taxpaper's sales will not be liable for the value-added tax, delays tax credits until the moment of sale. At that time, credits are allowed on purchases relating to sales subjected to the value-added tax and on export sales. The creditable amount is computed by applying the tax rate to purchase prices estimated, if necessary, through reducing sales prices by estimated profit margins. Corrections must be made as soon as actual results are known.

System B assumes that most of the taxpayer's purchases are destined for sales subject to the value-added tax. Consequently, tax credits are taken without restriction but only provisionally, during the month following that of purchase; because the taxpayer is rightfully entitled to tax credits only on sales subject to the value-added tax or on exports, he must reimburse the government at the time of sale for any excess credits taken on purchases entering into nontaxable sales. The amount due is computed by applying the effective tax rate to the value of purchases estimated, if necessary, as in system A.

BUFFER RULE. As previously explained, the provision disallowing the reimbursement of excess tax credits except for exports (C.G.I., art.

[102] "Guides des taxes sur le chiffre d'affaires," *La revue fiduciaire*, No. 399, pp. 113–14.

273-1-1°) has been interpreted so as to interfere with the functioning of the tax-credit mechanism as applied to domestic sales when a payer of the value-added tax has derived the excess credits from his purchases of ingredients. This "buffer rule," which is maintained in the 1960 reform project, prevents any reimbursement when the amount of tax paid on the purchase of a given product exceeds that due on its sales.

In addition to cases where the credits are understandably denied because of a fraudulent understatement of sales,[103] there are a number of situations in which the buffer rule frequently takes effect. They are as follows: (1) sales taxed at a lower rate than purchases, (2) sales of buildings to which the 40 percent discount applies in computing the taxable sales, (3) sales at a loss, (4) unpaid sales, (5) stolen merchandise, and (6) retail sales to which a discount is applied in order to reduce retail to wholesale price.

As demonstrated in Chapter 1, when excess credits arise because sales have been taxed at a lower rate than purchases, the taxpayer should be reimbursed for such excess credits if the tax is intended as an indirect type of personal taxation. In other words, if the law says that certain ingredients of food products are to be taxed at 25 percent, it is necessary to reimburse the excess credits if the value of the food products at their final taxable stage is to be subjected to the 6.38 percent rate rather than a higher one. Yet this is not done under the French system unless, as in the case of book publishers, subjected to the reduced rate of 11.1 percent, the administration makes a special concession.[104]

As the discount of 40 percent applied in computing the taxable sales of building contractors is in effect a reduced rate, the buffer rule often prevents the full reimbursement of the tax credits to which the building contractors are entitled. This has had the unfortunate result of imposing a discrimination against prefabrication, a type of inequity and subsidy to inefficiency which was supposed to be eliminated when building construction was subjected to the value-added tax rather than the service tax.

Assume, for example, a building sold for 500,000 NF including 60,000 NF of value-added tax. If it is largely the product of construction services,

---

[103] The buffer rule would also operate in the case of nontaxable sales; but no credits are allowed in any event in such cases in view of the provision restricting credits to those subject to the value-added tax (C.G.I., art. 273–101°).

[104] The administration allows reimbursement of part of the tax as if the sales of books had been export transactions. See Lauré, *Au secours de la T.V.A.*, p. 70.

the buffer rule will not take effect, so that the tax will remain at 60,000 NF. On the other hand, if prefabricated supplies had been purchased to the extent of 400,000 NF including tax of 80,000 NF, 20,000 NF of tax credits will be disallowed, so that the actual tax on the building amounts to 80,000 NF instead of 60,000 NF.

The administration has prevented the rule from taking effect when building contractors sell to payers of value-added taxes entitled to tax credits because it allows the contractor to pay the tax on his total sales instead of using the discount. The fact that his tax is higher than it would be otherwise does not matter so long as it merely represents an advance of the amount due on his customer's sales.

If an item is sold for 1,000 NF including tax of 200 francs but was purchased at 2,000 NF including tax of 400 NF, no reimbursement is allowed for the excess credits of 200 NF. As the final value of the product as determined by the market is only 1,000 NF, the taxpayer is in principle entitled to the full amount of credit on his purchases and therefore a reimbursement of excess credits.

In the case of bad debts, the buffer rule has been applied so as to allow a reimbursement of the difference between the amount of tax paid by the vendor and the amount of tax incorporated in the related purchase. Thus, if an item sells for 1,000 NF including 200 NF of tax, while the raw materials from which it was manufactured were purchased at 400 NF including tax of 80 NF, the vendor is reimbursed on the unpaid sale for 120 NF of tax. This is a more debatable case than the others, for it can be argued that the government should not suffer a loss once a sale has been completed and, in fact, that there should be no reimbursement even of the amount paid by the vendor. However, it is customary to grant an allowance for bad debts under both income and sales taxes, in which event it can be argued that the total amount of tax, not merely the fraction paid by the vendor, should be allowed and that excess tax credits should therefore be reimbursed.

The buffer rule is applied to stolen articles. It is evidently reasoned that the government should not pay for this contingency. On the other hand, when commodities have been lost or destroyed and the taxpayer has been able to prove that this is the case, the rule is not applicable.[105]

---

[105] Complete destruction is required; the rule is applied when articles have merely deteriorated. See "Guide des taxes sur le chiffre d'affairs," *La revue fiduciaire,* No. 399, p. 85.

The application of the buffer rule to situations where tax credits exceed the amount of tax liability on sales because of the discount applied in reducing taxable to retail price occurs under the 20 percent discount when the firm's profit margins are less than 20 percent. Apparently visualized as a way of preventing an unduly low tax base in the case of certain methods of distribution, the rule also results in discriminating in favor of direct retail sales by manufacturers because a manufacturer, in contrast to retailers and even some wholesalers making direct retail sales, is unlikely to have a profit margin as low as 20 percent and therefore escapes the application of the buffer rule. It will also discriminate against ordinary retailers with low profit margins who compete with retailers assuming certain functions ordinarily undertaken in the taxable stages, whether such retailers use the 20 percent discount or gross-profit margins.

In addition to discriminating among business firms engaged in similar activities, the buffer rule obviously intensifies the problems of administration and compliance. Since it must be applied to a particular sale of a product, or in the case of building construction to a particular contract, the amount of record keeping occasioned by the rule must be enormous. If, for example, an item is purchased in June and sold at a loss in December, it is evident that detailed inventory accounting is required to enable the effective application of the rule. Similar accounting is required in the case of the retail discount, while building contractors are obliged to keep records according to each contract.[106]

Carryforward and Transfer of Credits

A carryforward of excess tax credits is allowed whenever the buffer rule does not apply, notably in the case of inventory accumulation and purchases of investment goods. Generally speaking, no refunds are granted other than in the case of exports or where a concern discontinues its activity entirely.

Inability to transfer credits or receive a refund has caused difficulty in the case of certain enterprises which have made heavy longterm investments but, lacking sufficient taxable transactions to which credits may

---

[106] Lauré recommends abolition of the buffer rule except in cases where evasion is suspected. See *Au secours de la T.V.A.,* p. 146.

be applied, find that any reimbursement will be postponed for a number of years. Such enterprises have tended to combine with other taxable enterprises in order to take advantage of the credit.[107]

A special arrangement has been introduced for enterprises which form a group making investments designed to increase their productivity and which will be used in common.[108] Before the group purchases lead to any taxable sales, the credits arising from the purchases may be transferred to individual members of the group. Authorization to transfer the credits must be obtained from the Ministry of Finance and Economics after consultation with the General Planning Commission.

Taxable Event and Invoicing System

The taxable event, that is, the occasion on which the tax becomes due, is delivery in the case of domestic sales of commodities and collections or customer payments in the case of sales of services, although service enterprises may be authorized to pay the tax at the time the invoice is rendered (C.G.I., art. 275). In practice, delivery has also been identified with invoicing, although it is legally defined as the transfer of an article into the control or possession of the buyer (Code Civil, art. 1604). In the case of buildings, the tax is in principle due on delivery of the work of construction, but taxpayers are permitted to pay the tax according to collections and the administration assumes that this will be the usual method except in the case of construction for a firm's own account.[109]

In order to implement the tax-credit system of collecting the value-added tax, the amount of value-added tax or service tax must be quoted on sales of creditable items to payers of the value-added tax. Actually, the law requires that the taxes be quoted on all invoices along with the price net of tax (C.G.I., art. 268); but the administration has assumed that the obligation under the value-added tax is limited to cases of sales to payers of the value-added tax and under the service tax to sales of

---

[107] See Lauré, *Au secours de la T.V.A.*, p. 73. Lauré notes the interesting case of the Atomic Energy Commission unable to combine with other taxable enterprises and therefore induced to avoid the value-added tax on its purchases as, for example, through work done by jobbers.

[108] Decree of Apr. 22, 1960 (no. 60–381, codified in C.G.I., Annexe III, art. 69).

[109] The option to pay the tax according to delivery is revocable, but once the option to pay according to collections has been chosen, it is irrevocable.

creditable items made to payers of the value-added tax.[110] If the tax is not quoted the purchaser is not entitled to any tax credits because the law specifies that only taxes mentioned on invoices are deductible (C.G.I., art, 273-1-1°).

International Transactions

The collection of the value-added tax on imports occurs at the time of importation, that is, when the product passes the customs barrier. The rates imposed are those which would be applicable to domestic sales of similar products except in the case of used articles which are taxed on importation even though the domestic sales are exempt (C.G.I., art. 279).[111]

Unlike the case of domestic sales, no attempt is made to assess the tax on the basis of wholesale value. Instead, it applies to values as declared at the customs, including any special excises applicable to the product, even if the value is retail value or a wholesale value which, in the case of competing domestic sales, has been subjected to the local tax rather than the value-added tax. On the other hand, imports are placed at an advantage because they cannot be subjected to the buffer rule. Thus a food import subject to a 6.38 percent rate may be favored over a similar domestic product taxed at the same rate but denied excess tax credits on ingredients taxed at 25 percent. Moreover, any imports entitled to an exemption may be favored over domestically exempt enterprises to the extent that the latter have been subjected to the value-added or service taxes imposed on their purchases of both currently expensed items and investment goods.

As explained above, when imports are sold on the French market by a firm related to a foreign enterprise, the tax is imposed on the importer's sales whatever his taxable status would have been otherwise. However, this is not the case if the foreign firm sells to independent French firms at the same price as it sells to the related enterprise.

Finally, the tax is imposed whenever a foreign firm or resident orders someone in France to purchase and resell products on the French market,

---

[110] "Guide des taxes sur le chiffre d'affaires," *La revue fiduciaire,* No. 399, pp. 78, 152.

[111] However, the administration allows the tax-free import of industrial waste materials, presumably on the ground that they will be taxed when they are used to make taxable products.

the tax being collected from whoever negotiates the transaction (C.G.I., art. 293). This provision is designed to reach the possible loophole occasioned when a nontaxpayer, such as an individual, executes the foreign orders, given the possibility that he might add some taxable value. However, there would seem to be few occasions when such an individual would escape classification as a French taxpayer.

Most French exports of goods and services are probably almost entirely exempt from sales taxes. In the first place, there is no restriction with respect to the reimbursement of value-added or service tax credits in the case of exports even though the export transaction is exempt. Secondly, the system of voluntary payment makes it possible for all distributors and service enterprises to enter the regime of the value-added tax if they are engaged in exportation and also facilitates the maintenance of an unbroken line of credits for all concerns engaged in activities directed toward the export stage.

Of course, the exports are burdened with any value-added or service tax applied to noncreditable categories of purchases. Also, the special excises are not creditable. Moreover, all activities excluded or exempt from the value-added and service taxes, whether or not subject to the special excises, are ineligible for the option of voluntary payment of the value-added tax so that they are placed at a disadvantage with respect to taxable activities, being unable to credit the taxes on either their current expenses or investment purchases.

In addition to exports, proper, various transactions are treated as if they were exports. Thus, "invisible exports," that is, items sold to foreign tourists which would normally be carried in their luggage, are treated as if they were exports.[112] Also, the customs administration has set up various sales counters near the customs offices from which foreign tourists can purchase articles free from tax.[113] Sales of items delivered to steamships and international airplanes and trains as well as those sold to foreign merchants in France during the exhibition season are considered exports. So are sales to international organizations.[114] The concessions to the export industry in the form of reduced rates on domestic sales of luxuries when business groups are committed to increase their sales abroad and in the form of an increased retail discount for certain luxury enterprises have already been noted.

[112] Administrative decision of April 24, 1950, *La revue fiduciaire, feuillets hebdomadaires d'information,* No. 190 (Nov. 22, 1950), p. 4.
[113] Customs circular no. 1978 of July 7, 1959.
[114] "Guide des taxes sur le chiffre d'affaires," *La revue fiduciaire,* No. 399, p. 186.

Sales to those undertaking exempt naval and aircraft construction have also been assimilated to exports. Thus, vendors who supply the ship contractors are entitled to tax credits on all their purchases, whereas if their sales had been exempt they would not have been entitled to such credits. On the other hand, the contractors themselves, conducting exempt activities, obtain no tax credits. However, they receive their supplies free of tax, supplies being interpreted to cover all equipment such as engines and machinery (C.G.I., Annexe III, art. 74).

Reimbursement of the excess credits arising from exports is effected in the first instance by applying the credits to any value-added tax due on domestic sales in the month following that of purchase. Of creditable sums in excess of the amounts imputed on domestic taxes, part is refunded in cash while the remainder is carried forward to subsequent months. The cash refund is limited to the amount of value-added tax computed fictitiously at the effective rate on the firm's export sales in the month following purchase.

In order to reduce the number of cases where a carryforward is required, the law allows exporters to purchase commodities destined for export in suspension of tax up to the amount of exports of taxable products during the preceding year, providing their suppliers with exemption certificates (C.G.I., arts. 266 and 269). This arrangement reduces the need for some of the refunds which would otherwise be required if those who supply exporters are likely to have more taxable domestic sales to which tax credits can be imputed. To discourage any evasion, all those receiving products in suspension of tax may be required to obtain a bond covering the taxes and penalties with which they might be charged (C.G.I., art. 269-3).

In order that exporters benefiting from the suspension system will not be unduly favored as contrasted with others, the administration requires that the cash refund of their tax credits be limited to the amount of value-added tax computed by applying the tax fictitiously at its effective rate to the gross profit margins derived from the export sales rather than to the total amount of sales. Meanwhile, in the special case of export agents and brokers who usually have no opportunity to apply their credits to domestic sales, the administration refunds their taxes in cash.[115]

[115] "Guides des taxes sur le chiffre d'affaires," *La revue fiduciaire*, No. 399, p. 189.

APPLICATION OF THE SERVICE TAX

Generally speaking, the service tax applies to all business activities other than sales of commodities and fixed construction (C.G.I., arts. 256-2, 270). Services are defined to encompass the sales of patents and copyrights as well as the renting of property or services. All types of commercial intermediaries are covered, including commission agents and brokers. Real estate dealers and developers, whether intermediaries or those who purchase for resale, are included.[116] Also, sales of collectors' items are treated as if they were sales of services rather than commodities subject to the value-added tax.

Artisans are specifically exempt from the service tax as well as the value-added tax.[117] Services rendered by enterprises classified as non-business occupations are, of course, excluded from the scope of the tax. Professional services are the outstanding category of exclusion from the service tax; and the administration is responsible for making the fine distinctions necessary to segregate such activities from similar activities which nevertheless are commercial and therefore taxable. It is reported to apply the criteria of whether the enterprise engages in speculation with respect to the work of others and whether the transactions are undertaken in the same manner as if by individuals working alone.[118]

Thus corporations are classified as inventors or research organizations exempt from the service tax provided that the technicians have undertaken their research for the corporation, at its expense and risk and under its control, rather than for themselves. The sales of such inventions or the sales or rentals of the patents are not taxable. However, the tax does apply if the inventor, whether an individual or legal person, exploits it or when any individual or legal person purchases inventions and patents

---

[116] The law of Mar. 15, 1963 (no. 63–254) has subjected to the value-added tax various real estate transfers to which the service tax was originally applied. Presumably under the service tax, such dealers adopted the position of intermediaries in order to limit the tax to their commissions; the new legislation supposedly ends the tax advantage given to intermediaries.

[117] They are allowed to enter the regime of the value-added tax voluntarily and, as explained below in the section on methods of payment, they may also elect payment of the service tax.

[118] "Guides des taxes sur le chiffre d'affaires," *La revue fiduciaire*, No. 399, pp. 123–24.

with a view to speculation. Similarly, author's rights are not taxed while editorial rights are taxable. Various noncommercial intermediaries are also exempt, including certain publicity agents, whose activities are limited to advising advertisers.

The rental of empty buildings is considered a nonbusiness activity regardless of the status of the renter and therefore escapes tax. However, the rentals of furnished lodgings and business establishments, that is, places equipped for business, are taxable.

Rates

The general rate of the service tax is 9.29 percent. A luxury rate of 13.64 percent is applicable to beauty parlors, collectors' items, and to those subject to the value-added tax at luxury rates who elect to pay the service tax rather than the value-addd tax under the arrangements for simplified payment explained below.

Exemption from the service tax is usually granted with respect to services relating to products excluded or exempt from the value-added tax. Thus, the commission, brokerage, and jobbing operations relating to products subject to special excises and exempt food products and publications are likewise exempt.

Commission and brokerage operations are exempt from the service tax when rendered with respect to products subjected to the value-added tax, whether the services have been rendered in the taxable stage or after the product has left the taxable stage. In the case of the exemption for commission and brokerage services rendered prior to the final taxable stage, the value of the services enters the tax base of the payer of the value-added tax. Commission agents and brokers are allowed to elect voluntary payment of the value-added tax when they sell to other value-added taxpayers or export. The 1960 reform project, which abolishes the service tax, subjects all commission agents and brokers to the value-added tax. Jobbing operations are exempt if rendered for those subject to the value-added tax or if the jobber exports the product directly.

The exemption under the value-added tax with respect to nonprofit organizations and medical and health establishments is repeated under the service tax. Likewise, there is an exemption for the social, cultural, educational, and travel services provided by local governments when they do not compete with private enterprises in the local communities in which they operate.

Transactions on the securities and commodities exchanges, the operations of insurance companies, and activities of certain savings societies are exempt from the service tax as well as the value-added tax. All such activities are subjected to special taxes and, in any event would in principle not be subjected to a sales tax to the extent that they merely represented an exchange of capital assets. Banks are exempt on their receipts from certain types of interbank operations.

Sales of collectors' items are exempt if sold at public auction, in order to avoid superposition with the registration taxes. Certain services are exempt because subject to the local tax, which in these instances is applied at the same rate as the service tax, that is, eating and drinking establishments, rental of furnished lodgings, and certain amusements.

Transportation services are in principle subject to the service tax. However, freight transportation and the rental of transportation vehicles used in freight transportation by road, rail, or inland waterway are specifically exempt, a replacement tax being imposed on vehicles used on highways and inland waterways. Freight transportation by sea and air is still subject to the service tax, as is transportation of passengers.

Computation of Tax Liability

Generally speaking, the service tax applies to the total sales of services including any accessory expenses and taxes, including the service tax itself imposed at the nominal rate. Intermediaries, however, including commission agents or brokers, are taxed only on their services as intermediaries, that is, they are allowed to subtract from their gross sales the outlays which they advance for their principal.[119] Although no credits are granted under the service tax, all service enterprises may elect the status of payers of value-added taxes.

Construction contractors undertaking installation and repairs of movable items rather than fixed construction are treated as combining the sales of commodities with services, the former being subjected to the

---

[119] Art. 274–1 of the Tax Code states that the tax is imposed on "the amount of brokerage fees, commissions, remittances, salaries, rental price, contracts, bills, invoices, interests, discounts, agios, and other profits finally acquired."

value-added tax and the latter to the service tax,[120] a situation which has given rise to numerous changes in methods of doing business in order to minimize tax. On the one hand, an effort is made to enlarge the service component at the expense of transactions subject to the much higher rate of the value-added tax. On the other hand, installers of costly materials may seek to pass as entrepreneurs of fixed construction so as to receive the 40 percent discount, while entrepreneurs of fixed construction often seek to pass as installers or even service enterprises.[121]

Taxable Event and Invoicing

The service tax is due upon collections or, if authorized by the administration, at the time of invoicing. As noted above, the tax must be invoiced in the same manner as the value-added tax when customers are entitled to tax credits.

International Transactions

Like the value-added tax, the service tax is imposed according to the destination principle, the tax being applicable "when the service rendered, the right transferred, or the object rented are utilized or exploited in France" (C.G.I., art. 259). Thus, in effect, imports of services are taxed while exports are exempt. However, the service tax is collected at the customs only in the case of collectors' items and industrial plans and designs. In the case of the importation of other services, the tax must be collected through a representative of the foreign enterprise.[122]

Exports of services escape tax by the rule that the tax is not applied when the services are to be utilized or exploited abroad. No credit for value-added or service taxes paid on the purchases of the service exporter are creditable under the regime of the service tax; but, of course, the

---

[120] The administration may allow the vendor to invoice separately his purchases burdened with the value-added tax, no further tax being due on these items.

[121] These examples are given in Lauré, *Au secours de la T.V.A.,* pp. 74–75.

[122] Any person not having an establishment in France and engaging in transactions subject to the French sales taxes must have a representative accredited by the French tax administration who lives in France and pays the taxes instead of the foreign individual. Otherwise, the taxes are due with penalties from the French customer (C.G.I., Annexe I, art. 26, *quinquiés*).

exporter may voluntarily enter the regime of the value-added tax. The export exemption is more difficult to administer in the case of services than in the case of commodities; and the taxpayer must prove that the service is being utilized or exploited outside of France (C.G.I., Annexe I, art. 26, *quater*).

APPLICATION OF THE LOCAL TAX

The scope of the local tax as defined in art. 1573 of the Tax Code has already been described. In brief, the local tax reaches all retail sales by business firms of commodities exempt or excluded from the value-added tax or subjected to the tax but benefiting from the retail discount, as well as wholesale sales of commodities subjected to the local tax rather than the value-added tax. In addition, it reaches the sales of services exempt or excluded from the service tax as, for example, commission and brokerage services relating to products subjected to the value-added tax. It encompasses the sales of artisans unless they have elected payment of the value-added or service taxes. Also, commercial representatives, whose activities are usually classified as nonbusiness, are specifically subjected to the tax.

Rates

The rates of the local tax are uniform in all the localities. The regular rate is 2.83 percent and the increased rate imposed on the rental of furnished lodgings, eating and drinking establishments, and entertainment is 9.29 percent, with a few specified types of entertainment subjected to half the increased rate.

A long list of consumer necessities and producers' goods which are exempt under the value-added and service taxes are also exempt from the local tax. These include products subjected to the petroleum taxes, meats, food products widely consumed, sales of seed, fertilizers, and insecticides, sales of water, electricity and compressed air by public concessions, sales of second-hand materials and industrial waste. The transactions of state monopolies including the tobacco and match monopolies are exempt. Newspapers, periodicals, phonograph records, and motion picture films as well as publications of charitable organizations are exempt as under the other sales taxes. So are items sold by medical and health establishments to their patients. Also, the departmental and local agencies undertaking social, cultural, educational, and tourist services not competing with private enterprise in the locality are exempt.

Computation of Tax Liability

The tax is imposed on the sales price. In the case of its application to sales other than for resale, the system of exemption certificates is used, the customer giving such certificates to his supplier if the purchase is destined for resale.

Taxable Event and Place of Payment

The tax is due when payment is received, regardless of whether sales of commodities or services are involved. The taxpayers may be authorized to pay the tax at the time of invoicing. The quotation of the local tax on invoices is not required but it is not prohibited and may be quoted at the effective rate.[123]

The tax is collected from the taxpayer's local establishment which undertakes the taxable transaction wherever the head office or place of delivery happens to be (C.G.I., art. 1576-3). Most of the proceeds are paid to the local community in which the sale occurs, but a small portion is allocated to the departments and to the national fund for equalizing the distribution of the proceeds among the localities (C.G.I., art. 1577-1).

International Transactions

Although imposed on the destination principle, the local tax is never collected at the customs frontiers. It is collected on all taxable sales of imported products made by concerns located in France or representatives

---

[123] See "Guide des taxes sur le chiffre d'affaires," *La revue fiduciaire,* Vol. II, No. 324 (Sept. 1955), p. 92.

of foreign concerns but apparently does not reach direct imports by ultimate users.

Meanwhile, there is a specific exemption for all direct exports of goods and services subject to the local tax. However, as there are no credits for value-added or service taxes paid on products purchased by exporters subject to the local tax, they succeed in escaping all general sales taxes only if they are qualified to elect the status of payer of the value-added tax, an option unavailable with respect to products exempt or excluded from the value-added or service taxes.

METHODS OF PAYMENT

Taxpayer Registration

Within fifteen days after commencing operations, all those liable for sales taxes must register with the appropriate collector's office in the place where their principal establishment or branch is located (C.G.I., art. 297-1). Registration consists in supplying certain information according to a form provided by the administration, including the surname and given name of the taxpayer and, in the case of a company, the firm name as well as certain information about its operations. Similarly, a statement of cessation of operations must be made when a taxpayer ceases his activity or sells his business.

Tax Payments

The tax payments are generally due monthly before the twenty-fifth of the month following sale if the director has not set a prior date (C.G.I., Annexe IV, art. 40-1). Unless the taxpayer has elected the estimate procedure for small taxpayers or the system of provisional accounts described below, the payments must be accompanied by a statement of the total amount of transactions and taxable transactions on a form prescribed by the administration (C.G.I., art. 296-1). Returns are required even when no tax is due ("negative return"), except for seasonal businesses during the months when they are not operating (C.G.I., Annexe IV, art. 402).

If payments amount to less than 200 NF a month, returns and pay' ments may be made quarterly (C.G.I., art. 296-1). Quarterly returns are also used for taxes on commissions, brokerage fees, and other receipts of agents and brokers through their contracts with insurance companies or savings and investment societies, such taxes being withheld at the source by the latter concerns (C.G.I., art. 1692, Annexe IV, art. 190).

As an enforcement device, all taxpayers are responsible for obtaining the information necessary to identify their customers on sales of 50 NF or more other than in the case of retail sales (C.G.I., art. 1649). Failure to do so incurs the penalty of half the amount of sales plus the penalties for evasion, notably four times the amount of tax (C.G.I., Annexe III, art. 344D). The taxpayer is absolved from this responsibility only if he obtains payment in such manner that the identity of his customer is indicated as by check or money order. Another alternative is that he obtain from his customer an order certificate (*bulletin de commande*), detached from a book provided by the administration and which identifies the customer. This certificate must be attached to a copy of the invoice or, in its absence, to some other accounting document, and must be kept for five years (C.G.I., Annexe III, art. 344F).

Forfait

For the relief of small taxpayers who were vigorously protesting the complexities of the sales tax system, the reform of 1955 introduced a simple estimate procedure, used largely by those liable for the service or local taxes. Unlike the *forfait* of the twenties, considerable record keeping is required of the taxpayer although generally less than in the case of the regular regimes. Actually, the chief advantage of the procedure for the taxpayer is the absence of any penalty other than a fine for lateness, even in the case of outright evasion. Those in the *forfait* regime may not invoice any taxes to their customers while their credits are fixed by the estimate.

Those eligible for the procedure are taxable enterprises selling commodities and fixed construction or offering furnished lodgings whose turnover, including items exempt or excluded from tax, during the two preceding years has not exceeded 400,000 NF per year and other taxable concerns whose aggregate annual turnover does not exceed 100,000 NF.

Those engaged in both categories of activities are eligible if neither of the two limits has been exceeded.[124]

Several groups are ineligible for the *forfait*. The three most important groups comprise persons subject to the corporate income tax, payers of value-added taxes who sell to other payers of value-added taxes, and exporters. Also excluded are new enterprises in existence for less than one year, certain amusements, real estate dealers, and brokers working for insurance companies and societies of capitalization or savings.

The elimination of most payers of value-added taxes is consistent with the provision that concerns using the estimate procedure may not quote taxes on their invoices, thereby depriving their customers of tax credits. Because the inability to mention the taxes paid may seriously interfere with the business of some small taxpayers, the law provides that an occasional sale to payers of value-added taxes may be made independently of the estimate and invoiced in the usual manner. Such occasional sales are to be grouped by the taxpayer and subjected to the usual rules of taxation including tax credits for deductible purchase. However, the "partial *forfait*" requires detailed records of transactions excluded from the estimate so that the taxpayer is better off if he remains under the regular regime.[125] Another disadvantage in the case of payers of value-added taxes is the impossibility of deducting actual outlays on investments or general expenses in excess of those made during the period on which the estimate is based.

As this simple estimate procedure is expected to be generally used by eligible taxpayers, the tax administration takes the initiative by sending them a printed form which has to be returned within twenty days with the following information:

1. Given name and surname of taxpayer or name of the firm; address; and type of business.
2. Location of the business establishment and of any secondary establishments in existence.
3. Annual receipts of the preceding calendar year and elapsed quarters of

---

[124] Instead of an estimate procedure, the 1960 reform project recommends an exemption system for very small firms, those with receipts under 25,000 NF. However, taxpayers with sales under 400,000 NF are to be allowed an estimate procedure with respect to their tax credits.

[125] "Les options fiscales des industriels et commerçants," *La revue fiduciaire*, No. 326 (Nov. 1955), p. 47.

the current year by type of activity and with taxable receipts distinguished from those exempt or excluded.

4. Amount of purchases during the preceding calendar year and elapsed quarters of the current year.

After the estimate is concluded on the basis of the above information and possibly after discussion with the taxpayer, the latter has twenty days in which to accept the estimate or suggest some changes, acceptance being assumed if there is no further communication. When the taxpayer suggests some changes, the administration notifies him of its acceptance or rejection. In the latter event, the taxpayer again has twenty days in which to denounce the estimate and be taxed on actual transactions or place the matter before a departmental commission. After receiving the commission's decision, he still has the privilege of rejecting the estimate within twenty days. If he accepts, the estimate is valid for two years unless new legislation significantly alters the scope of the tax or a change has occurred in the taxpayer's situation equivalent to the cessation of his business or the creation of a new activity. Upon actual payment of the tax up to the date of the cessation, the successors are permitted to request the extension of the pre-existing estimate. At the close of the two-year period, the estimate is automatically renewed unless denounced by the taxpayer within one month or by the administration within three months.

The taxpayer is required to denounce the estimate at the end of the two-year period when his purchases or gross receipts have varied over 20 percent from the amounts used in the estimate. The administration is instructed to denounce the estimate with a view to its revision each time that the taxpayer's activity has changed appreciably or when the economic situation is such as to involve an increase in taxable receipts.

Taxpayers are obliged to maintain the same records required for the estimate procedure of assessing the income tax on industrial and commercial profits. The records consist of an account book totaled annually and presenting the details of purchases supported by invoices and all other pieces of evidence. When the business involves transactions other than the sale of merchandise or refreshments—in other words, building construction and services—the taxpayer is required to maintain a daily journal kept up-to-date and stating the details of the sales. If these records are not kept or if the taxpayer is convicted of having entered deceptive or false statements, the renewal of the estimate may be refused for one year following the date of proof. A new estimate may be established, however, at the expiration of the year.

If the taxpayer has made false statements in the information on which the estimate is based, the administration is required to send a detailed report to the departmental office of the Director of Indirect Taxes. The departmental commission is then allowed to establish the tax on the basis of actual transactions, the only penalty being the fine for late payment.

Option to Elect Service Tax

Another method of assessment designed to simplify the situation of small firms is provided by the option granted to those subjected to the value-added tax to elect the regime of the service tax provided that their transactions subject to the value-added or service tax do not exceed 400,000 NF.[126] The option is available at the request of the taxpayer and is valid for one calendar year. Those subject to the simple estimate procedure are allowed to elect the service tax for all their transactions or merely for those declared outside the estimate.

The service tax paid as a result of the option may be quoted on invoices so that customers may obtain tax credits in the same manner as the regular application of the service tax. Those paying the service tax are, of course, not entitled to any credits themselves.

If those electing the option for the service tax have been subjected to the increased rates of the value-added tax, they must also pay the increased rates of the service tax. The optional service tax is imposed on all transactions, including a firm's deliveries of items to itself and exempt activities. Only wholesale transactions remain subject to local tax as do the services subject to the increased rates of the local tax. Thus, the situation of many taxpayers who engage in mixed activities is simplified, as, for example, operators of garages who manufacture articles and sell them at retail, thereby being liable for the value-added tax, local tax, and service tax.

Those wishing to elect the option are required to request it from the

---

[126] The transactions must be effectively subjected to the value-added tax, which means that sales are calculated after subtraction of the discounts on retail sales or construction.

administration, attaching the request to their annual return for the preceding year. Certain categories of taxpayers are ineligible for the option.
In addition to concerns in existence for less than one year, they comprise
real estate dealers and developers, salesmen and brokers working with
insurance companies and savings and investment societies, certain entertainment enterprises, and exporters—all categories excluded from the
simple estimate procedure. In addition, industrial enterprises in which
the essential raw material is not subject to the value-added tax may be
excluded;[127] and in accordance with this provision the administration has
excluded the manufacturers of wooden packages and articles made of
stone as well as stone and sand quarries.[128]

Provisional Accounts

A third estimate procedure, of minor importance, is employed in the
collection of the general sales taxes, namely, the "provisional payments"
(*acomptes provisionnels*). This system is available to all taxpayers regardless of size who have a permanent establishment (C.G.I., arts. 296-2
and 1693).

It consists in the payment through twelve equal monthly installments
(or quarterly installments when the monthly payments are below 200
NF) of an amount not less than the tax due on the business of the preceding year. Tax payments must be accompanied by a "payment certificate" (*bulletin d'échéance*), conforming to a model supplied by the
administration. The payments may be less than the taxes due in the preceding year only when there has been a change in the rates or the assessment of the tax.

Taxpayers are required to submit a statement by the first of February
of each year indicating the turnover in the preceding year and showing
distinctly the portion of this amount exempt or taxable at each rate of
tax. Any underpayment of taxes resulting from the use of the provisional-
payments method in the preceding year is to be paid by April 25. Any
excess payment is credited to taxes due subsequently or reimbursed if
the taxpayer is no longer subject to the tax.

[127] Law of Dec. 17, 1960, no. 60–1365, art. 9.
[128] "Guide des taxes sur le chiffre d'affaires," *La revue fiduciaire,* No. 399, p.
214.

An important disadvantage of this procedure is that, if the tax paid in the course of the year or in one of the elapsed quarters happens to be more than 20 percent below the amounts actually due, there is a penalty of 25 percent of the late payments in addition to the usual fine for lateness (C.G.I., art. 1756-2). This probably accounts for the fact that the procedure is seldom used. In 1961, out of 2,139,055 returns, only 4,577 were provisional, as compared with 666,632 returns using one of the estimate procedures and 1,467,846 based on actual accounting records.[129]

Taxpayers' Records

All taxpayers, except firms selling tangible articles and refreshments under the simple estimate procedure, are required to keep detailed records. The Tax Code specifies that if they do not regularly keep adequate records for determining their gross receipts, they must maintain a journal of their transactions listed on numbered pages with no blanks or erasures and showing clearly their taxable and nontaxable receipts (C.G.I., art. 297-2). The register is to show the items sold and the services rendered; the sales or purchase price; and the amount of brokerage fees, commissions, remittances, wages, rental price, interests, discounts, agios, or other proceeds. Transactions under 5,000 francs may be lumped at the end of the day. All transactions must be totaled at the end of the month. One of the records may be a "purchase stamp" (*bulletin de commande*), noted above.

All records, including purchase invoices and other papers indicating the operations of the taxpayer, have to be kept for three years from the date last recorded in the account or the date of the paper. Special information is required of certain enterprises, such as insurance companies and their representatives; real estate agents and developers; dependent enterprises; exporters; and those engaged in shipbuilding and aircraft construction.[130] The records required under the estimate procedures have been indicated above.

---

[129] Ministère des Finances, "Les impôts indirectes en 1961 et diverses reseignements statistiques." *Statistiques et études financières,* Supplément No. 165 (Sept. 1962), p. 1045.

[130] "Guides des taxes sur le chiffre d'affaires, *La revue fiduciaire,* No. 324, p. 65.

CONCLUSIONS

The French value-added tax as supplemented by the service tax has the distinction of being the first and thus far the only significant example of the practical application of an indirect spendings tax through the value-added procedure. Considerable progress has been achieved in the direction of a rational implementation of this principle. Moreover, the 1960 reform project as well as the 1963 changes in the methods of taxing residential construction indicate that the government is concerned with improving the system so as to eliminate discriminatory burdens on different taxable products and methods of doing business, that is, aside from any discrimination which may be inherent in a system which exempts investment goods from tax. Such differential taxation not only distorts the competitive relationships among various industries and firms within an industry but also leads to changes in business methods not intended by the tax, and, moreover, directs taxpayers efforts toward the nonproductive pursuit of tax avoidance.

The fact that the value-added tax does not extend beyond the wholesale stage while wholesalers have the option of electing payment of the local tax means that taxpayers must continuously spend time searching for the regime which will minimize their tax burden while the administration is handicapped by being unable to concentrate on the application of one type of tax. Moreover, firms can avoid the value-added tax by changes in their methods of doing business through enlarging the relative amount of value added in a stage not encompassed by the value-added tax. The application of the value-added tax to integrated distributors—that is, retailers who combine wholesale and retail sales—has been an ineffectual method of equalizing the tax burden among various channels of distribution. In the first place, such retailers are allowed to reduce their tax base through a fraction based on their profit margins, thereby making it possible to retain in the nontaxable stage values transferred from the taxable stages. Secondly, many large retailers capable of assuming functions otherwise undertaken in the taxable stages are not reached at all under the criteria used to identify taxable retailers, that is, wholesale sales equal to one third of turnover or the operation of more than four retail stores.

Under the 1960 reform project, the wholesalers' option to elect the local tax was discontinued. In addition, the value-added tax was applied to all retailers with sales exceeding 400,000 NF without any option to use gross profit margins in reducing retail price to the wholesale level, a uniform 20 percent discount being required. On the whole, this recommendation seems a quite satisfactory solution to the problem of establishing a uniform taxable price among different channels of distribution, assuming that for administrative or political reasons it is not yet feasible to extend the tax through the retail stage. However, it is worth noting that the project allowed the government to modify by decree the discount rate, provided that in a given business the uniform rate causes economic difficulty, especially with respect to the relative situation of different concerns. It is to be hoped that this provision will not be permitted to lead to the extensive system of constructive pricing which has characterized the British Purchase Tax in the effort to apply the tax to a standard price on wholesale sales defined as the price at which an independent wholesaler would sell to retailers in ordinary quantities.[131]

The separate service tax also creates the possibility of variation in the tax burden imposed on different products and methods of doing business. This has been especially evident in the case of the construction industry where taxpayers must often engage in adjusting their activities among the regimes of the value-added tax with the discount, the value-added tax without the discount, and the service tax. However, even if the value-added tax is extended to service enterprises, a reduced rate on services as recommended in the 1960 reform project will still make it worthwhile for taxpayers to rearrange activities to minimize the tax burden—that is, they would in certain cases be interested in having their activities classified as a service rather than manufacturing or wholesaling.

Apparently no change is being contemplated with respect to the differential treatment among products and enterprises caused by the disallowance of tax credits on purchases made by concerns exempt or excluded from the tax other than exporters. To eliminate the existing discriminations, either such activities must be subjected to the value-added tax or the taxpayers must be reimbursed for the value-added tax imposed on their purchases. Revenue considerations as well as the possibility of some administrative problems are apparently responsible for the disallowance of tax credits on such purchases. However, the adminis-

[131] For an analysis of this problem, see Due, *Sales Taxation,* pp. 210–16.

trative difficulties involved in the proration of credits as between taxable and nontaxable sales and especially with regard to the adjustments needed over time in the case of investment purchases are so great that reimbursement of credits to exempt enterprises would hardly seem to be more troublesome than the present arrangement.

The buffer rule undoubtedly constitutes the most serious defect in the application of the value-added tax; but its elimination does not seem to be contemplated; it is, for example, maintained in the reform project. Yet it should be abolished, except in cases of outright fraud, if the tax is to be equitably imposed among different methods of doing business because it is not compatible with the concept of indirect personal taxation, especially with respect to its restriction of tax credits when sales are made at reduced rates.

In accordance with the Mill-Fisher thesis, French authorities assume that a consumption type of value-added tax, that is, one that in effect exempts investment goods purchased by value-added taxpayers, is neutral as between different products and methods of doing business. However, a question may be raised concerning the relative positions of capital-intensive and labor-intensive industries and firms under the tax; and it is worth noting that a study by the German Ministry of Finance of the application of the French value-added tax in Saarland reached the conclusion that the exemption of investment goods severely discriminates in favor of capital-intensive enterprises as against those which are labor-intensive[132]

In any case, the consumption principle has been adopted in France in the interest of economic development so that even if the neutrality thesis is questioned, the tax may be supported as a method of encouraging investment; in other words, the tax represents a type of incentive taxation. The value of any tax incentive must be measured in terms of the investment which would not have occurred in its absence.[133]

---

[132] Der Bundeskanzler, *Überprüfung des Umsatzsteuerrechts* (Bonn, 1958), p. 32.

[133] The criteria to be used in weighing the success of an incentive is a matter of judgment. The incentive may be considered worthwhile, for example, if the amount of investment induced by the incentive net of any investment discouraged by it is as great as the revenues sacrificed on investment which would have occurred anyway, that is, autonomous investment, an allowance being made for any additional governmental expenditures occasioned by the induced investment. In other words, the incentive may be conceived as a substitute for direct public spending. One valuable study on incentives suggests use of the criterion of maximizing

An analysis of the effects of the value-added tax in stimulating investment outlays would require a separate treatise. It may be noted, however, that there have been periods following the adoption of the value-added tax when expansion in investment outlays has produced severe inflationary pressures,[134] suggesting that, if the tax encouraged investment, it was also paid at times through reduced savings rather than through a curb on consumption. Of course, wage and monetary policies also affected the situation.

The application of the French value-added tax is undoubtedly complicated and requires considerable effort on the part of administrators and taxpayers. Nevertheless, all general tax laws involve certain unavoidable complexities; and the application of a direct spendings tax would be much more difficult, especially in France where direct taxation has never been popular. Although admittedly the problems under the direct approach are the price paid for greater equity among individual consumers, this would not necessarily be the case if various pressure groups were able to obtain special concessions.

Whether the value-added procedure of implementing an indirect spendings tax is more or less efficient than the single-stage method is doubtful except for some advantage with respect to the exemption of small firms. On the whole, it would seem to be a case of six of one, half a dozen of the other, so long as the application of the tax is applied under the destination principle. Yet Lauré recommends the return to the suspensive system, in part because of certain types of evasion pos-

the difference between net induced investment and net revenue loss, given by the formula:

$$\frac{\text{change in total revenue loss}}{\text{change in total investment}} = \frac{\text{induced investment}}{\text{autonomous investment}}$$

See Jack Heller and Kenneth M. Kauffman, *Tax Incentives for Industry in Less Developed Countries* (Cambridge, Mass., 1963), Harvard Law School International Program in Taxation, p. 130. In the extreme and improbable situation in which the demand for investment goods is infinitely elastic, so that a tax would bring autonomous investment to zero, the above formula as well as the previously noted criterion would justify the exemption. However, that situation would raise the question of whether it would not be better to have the government undertake the investment anyway. Furthermore, such a situation is unlikely given the fact that much demand for investment goods is derived from demand for consumer goods.

[134] See, for example, United Nations Economic Commission for Europe, "Current Economic Developments in Europe," *Economic Bulletin for Europe*, IX (Aug. 1957), 14, and X (May, 1958), 23–24; also see United Nations Economic Commission for Europe, *Economic Survey of Europe in 1957* (Geneva, 1958), Chap. II, p. 16.

sible under the value-added but not the suspensive system and in part because of other considerations, mostly administrative.[135] The probability is, however, that for one type of evasion under the value-added procedure or one source of administrative difficulty there will be an equally aggravating one under the suspensive system. The most efficient administration under either system implies a general measure extending through the service and retail sectors with a minimum of rate differentiation, including exemptions.

A planned rate progression is, of course, impossible under any indirect method of taxing personal incomes or consumer outlays. Also, given the exemption of savings and investment, any progression in terms of aggregate income is unlikely as a general rule under either the direct or indirect spendings tax.

The indirect approach raises the further question of the extent to which progressive rates succeed in achieving any progression even with respect to consumer outlays, a problem which deserves more careful examination than it has received to date, since the progressive rates are an administrative nuisance. True, the exemption of certain consumer essentials eliminates the tax burden on the lowest income groups. However, the real question is how the tax burden is distributed among those above the lower level.

Consumer necessities are bought by all income groups; but it is probably reasonable to assume that they represent a decreasing proportion of consumer budgets as income levels rise so that rate concessions on such items under the French sales taxes effect some progression with respect to consumers at different income levels. Meanwhile, the taxation of residential construction may be somewhat progressive, especially under the system recently instituted of including the value of land in the tax base.

On the other hand, the purchase of commodities subjected to the luxury rates under the French tax for the most part probably do not represent an increasing proportion of consumer budgets as incomes rise. Thus, such items as washing machines, waxers, ventilators, lighting fixtures, cameras, phonographs, and most other categories are purchased by moderate as well as upper income groups although the latter may tend to buy higher priced articles and may purchase them somewhat more frequently. The higher rates are most useful as a discouragement to certain outlays, which is probably their major purpose.

[135] See Lauré, *Au secours de la T.V.A.*, pp. 89–112.

It is probable that more progression would be achieved under an indirect spendings tax by applying the general rate to services, including residential rents, than under a system of differentiated rates applied to commodities. This, however, would require the extension of the tax through the retail stage in order that purchases of commodities would not be favored by the application of the tax to wholesale prices.

Chapter 3

The Japanese Value–Added Tax

The value-added tax advocated in 1949 by the Shoup Mission for use in postwar Japan—a proposal which passed the Japanese legislature but was never put into effect—was largely formulated by tax experts from the United States, the names of those directly concerned being listed in the Shoup Mission's report. They were assisted by some members of the staff at General Headquarters as well as a number of Japanese tax economists and government officials.[1]

The Mission recommended the value-added tax as the major source of revenues for the prefectures, which were to receive the entire yield. It was to be substituted for the current enterprise tax collected by the prefectures and shared with the municipalities. The enterprise tax had in principle been imposed upon net profits as computed under the national income tax, except that no personal exemptions or dependency deductions had been allowed in the case of unincorporated firms.[2] However, in some prefectures, the enterprise tax had not been based upon taxpayer returns. Instead, it had been assessed, by an executive committee representing the municipalities, industry, trade, and other interests and appointed by the governor of the prefecture, on the basis of a "standard" rate of profit estimated for the various classes of taxable activity.[3] This

[1] Shoup Mission, *Report on Japanese Taxation* (4 vols., Tokyo, 1949), I, iii--iv.
[2] *Ibid.,* II, 197–98.
[3] *Ibid.,* pp. 199–200.

system resembles the tax on "potential profits" discussed in Germany and proposed for use in France as an "estimated business tax."[4]

In the general tax system designed by the Shoup Mission, the national government was to depend largely upon the income tax, personal and corporate, and upon tobacco and liquor excises.[5] An attempt was made to strengthen the power of the municipalities—i.e., cities, towns, and villages. Municipal revenues were to be increased by 40 billion yen and independent sources of revenues were to replace the existing system of taxes shared with the prefectures and so-called "voluntary contributions."[6] The municipal revenues were to consist of a property tax on land and depreciable assets; an "inhabitant's tax," which was a combination poll and income tax; and various special excises.[7] In addition to the value-added tax, the prefectures were to rely upon admissions and amusement taxes and upon other special excises.[8]

In the fiscal year 1950–51, the national government was to receive 646 billion yen in revenues, of which 165 billion yen were to be distributed to the localities—i.e., prefectures and municipalities. This compared with estimated budget receipts for the fiscal year 1949–50 of 705 billion yen for the national government, of which 143 billion yen consisted of grants to the localities. The local governments were to receive revenues amounting to 425 billion yen, including the national grant of 165 billion yen in fiscal 1950–51 as compared with budget estimates for fiscal 1949–50 of 376 billion yen, to which national grants contributed 143 billion yen.[9]

JUSTIFICATION OF THE VALUE-ADDED TAX

The Shoup Mission's deep concern with considerations of equity is revealed by the following quotation from the report:

[4] Günter Schmölders, "À propos de la réforme fiscale en allemagne, idées et propositions," *Revue de science et de législation financières*, XLV (Paris, 1953), 625–28; *La revue fiduciaire, feuillets hebdomadaires d'information*, No. 321 (Nov. 23, 1953), p. 6.

[5] Shoup Mission, *Report on Japanese Taxation*, I. II, Chaps. 4–9.

[6] *Ibid.*, I, 22–24. The voluntary contributions represented an informal type of taxation.

[7] *Ibid.*, II, 182–96, 209.

[8] *Ibid.*, I, 39; II, 201, 206, 209.

[9] *Ibid.*, I, 36–38.

A tax system can be successful only if it is equitable, and the taxpayers must realize that it is equitable. Tax equity is partly a matter of administration of taxes according to the law, and partly a matter of fairly drawn tax laws. The details of equity in administration we leave to the administrators, but the assurance that there is equity in the provisions of the tax law is one of the main objects of our work. We have often encountered surprise at the emphasis we place on the search for equity. But no one remains in the tax field for long without realizing that nothing he recommends will stand up unless it meets the test of fairness in the distribution of the tax burden. This means, first, that the system must be free of discrepancies in tax treatment that are obvious to anyone as being unjust—once they are pointed out. The difficulty is, of course, that many of these discrepancies are hidden below the surface. They are noticeable not by the public at large but only by those who are directly concerned. Sometimes even the latter do not clearly understand the issues. Equity also means that the tax system must satisfy the deep, widespread feelings of the people as to what is fair. Here, of course, it is much more difficult for the tax student to be sure that his recommendations are right. He must estimate what the prevailing feeling is with respect to the distribution of income, wealth, and economic opportunity, yet he cannot be expected to abandon completely whatever ideas of his own he may have on these subjects. In any event, it must be pointed out that without some ideas of equity as a guide, a tax mission is lost. . . .[10]

However, the report called attention to a "basic conflict between simplicity and equity."[11] It stated that an attempt had been made to balance these divergent criteria with more emphasis upon simplicity than refinement or equity, especially with respect to taxpayers who could not reasonably be expected to keep a full set of accounts.[12]

As noted in Chapter 1, the report sought to justify selection of the value-added measure on the ground that "Some kind of prefectural tax on enterprises is justifiable, in order that the businesses and their patrons shall help defray the cost of government services that are made necessary by the existence of the business and its employees in that local area. For instance, public health expenses are multiplied when a factory and its employees come into a certain area."[13] Thus the business-benefit thesis was used merely as a vague justification for the measure, which in effect was intended to implement the principle of indirect personal taxation.

Two reasons were given for replacing the existing enterprise tax with the value-added measure. One was the reduction of the tax burden

[10] *Ibid.*, pp. 16 f.
[11] *Ibid.*, p. 18.
[12] *Ibid.*
[13] *Ibid.*, II, 201.

on net profits which, being excessive, was likely to be shifted forward to consumers in a manner "more unequal and probably more inequitable than under a value-added tax."[14] The second was administrative simplification.[15] Furthermore, the report stated that the value-added measure had been chosen in preference to retail or manufacturers' sales. The administration of a retail sales tax would have been difficult because of the importance of small shops in Japan which could not have been exempted without removing too much of the tax base. A manufacturers' sales tax, on the other hand, would have involved multiple taxation unless refined by an excessive number of special provisions.[16]

Professor Hanya Ito of Hitotsubashi University, one of the Japanese advisers to the Shoup Mission, gave some consideration to the theory of business taxation as it relates to the value-added tax in two essays, published in 1950 and 1955.[17] In the first place, he maintained that business taxation, strictly speaking, presumed the continental view of business organization as an independent taxable personality—a concept strange to Anglo-Saxon countries but recognized in the writings of Professor Studenski.[18] In practice, it was represented in the southern license taxes in the United States which had been modeled on the French *patente* and in the British national defense contribution of 1938 and profits tax of 1947.[19]

According to this viewpoint, a distinction must be made among the terms "profits tax" (*Ertragsteuer*), "business tax" (*Gewerbsteuer*), and "sales tax" (*Umsatzsteuer*) or "transactions tax" (*Verkehrsteuer*). Ito regarded the value-added tax (*Nettoumsatzsteuer*) as a hybrid form of taxation which combined the elements of a business tax and a sales tax.[20] Although the value-added tax was intended to replace the "enterprise tax," which was a "business tax," Ito noted that the existing national

[14] *Ibid.*, p. 203. A combined marginal rate of 70% was possible even for a small business, *Ibid.*, p. 200.

[15] *Ibid.*, p. 201.

[16] *Ibid.*, p. 166.

[17] Hanya Ito, "The Value-Added Tax in Japan," *The Annals of the Hitotsubashi Academy*, No. 1 (Oct. 1950), pp, 43–59; "Theorie und Technik der Nettoumsatzsteuer in Japan," *Finanzarchiv*, XV, No. 3 (Tübingen, Germany, 1955), 447–78.

[18] Ito, "Theorie und Technik der Nettoumsatzsteuer in Japan," pp. 452–53. The concept has also been propounded by Adams and by Seligman. See Thomas S. Adams, "Fundamental Problems of Federal Income Taxation," *Quarterly Journal of Economics*, XXXV (Aug. 1921), 543; Edwin R. A. Seligman, *Essays in Taxation* (9th ed., rev., New York, 1921), p. 702.

[19] Ito, p. 452.

[20] *Ibid.*

transactions tax or turnover tax was also to be abolished.[21] He also pointed out that the first report of the Shoup Mission referred to the tax as an "enterprise tax" while the second used the term "sales tax."[22] It is true that the first report did refer to the value-added tax as an enterprise tax with an expanded base;[23] but the expansion of the tax base was designed to effect forward shifting of the tax. In other words, Ito's analysis reflects the confusion mentioned in Chapter One which has arisen concerning the character of the value-added tax and indeed of all sales taxes and which is still prevalent.

Ito held that general business taxation might be justified either by the ability or the benefit principle. The benefit principle consisted of two variants, the "objective value theory" and the "subjective value theory." The former, or cost of benefit, theory assumed that government benefits should be measured by their cost and allocated in proportion to the value of business activity. The latter took into consideration the utility of the government services received.[24]

According to Ito the ability principle justified taxes on net profits. On the other hand, the objective benefit theory, which is the only variant of the benefit thesis he considered applying, warranted taxation regardless of profits.[25] One application of the objective theory was the system of external signs as in the French *patente*; but it was unsatisfactory because the tax measure varied with individual trades and failed to cover all the sources of revenue on which the government had a just claim. It was also difficult to administer efficiently.[26]

In Ito's opinion, general turnover and value-added bases were simpler and more rational measures which accurately and conveniently measured business activity; but, actually, only the value-added base was capable of representing the business activity of an individual enterprise because it excluded the value created by other concerns.[27] It moreover possessed the advantage of avoiding multiple taxation and encouragement to in-

[21] *Ibid.*, p. 454.
[22] *Ibid.*, p. 451.
[23] Shoup Mission, *Report on Japanese Taxation*, II. 202.
[24] Ito, "The Value-Added Tax in Japan," *Annals of the Hitotsubashi Academy*, No. 1 (1950), pp. 45 f.
[25] Ito, "Theorie und Technik der Nettoumsatzsteuer in Japan," *Finanzarchiv*, XV, No. 3 (1955), 455.
[26] *Ibid.*, p. 456.
[27] *Ibid.*

tegrated enterprises.[28] A retail-sales base might also avoid multiple taxation provided that a true distinction could be made between retail and wholesale trade. However, this method of distributing the tax burden would be less equitable than the use of value added because the entire impact was on the retailer.[29]

Ito believed that the Japanese tax system as a whole required a balanced use of both the benefit and ability principles of business taxation. It was because the ability principle had been emphasized at the national and municipal levels that he favored the value-added base for the prefectures.[30]

SUBJECTS AND OBJECT OF THE TAX

According to the Japanese tax bill which, it should be noted, contained many details not covered in the 1949 report of the Shoup Mission, the value-added tax was to be imposed upon persons who engaged in any of three categories of business. The bill reads as follows: "The value added tax shall be imposed, for value added of the business of the first through third categories, with the amount of value added as the taxable basis, by the Do, Fu or prefecture where an office or place of work is located, on the persons who operate such business."[31] Therefore, according to economic terminology, the subjects of the tax are persons operating certain types of business and the object of the tax is the taxable business.

SCOPE OF THE TAX

The first category of taxable business comprised the sales and rentals of goods and the furnishing of various services, such as warehousing, publishing other than newspapers listed by cabinet order, hotels, the operations of agents and brokers, and financial business. The second category included livestock breeding and fisheries. The third category

[28] *Ibid.*
[29] *Ibid.,* p. 457.
[30] *Ibid.,* p. 455.
[31] Local Autonomy Agency and Local Finance Commission, *Local Tax Law, 1950,* art. 23(1), p. 12.

consisted of the professions and certain services, among which were newspapers excluded by cabinet order from the first category. Under each category, there was a provision for the taxation by cabinet order of business similar to the enumerated activities.[32]

Nonprofit activities of an educational, charitable, and religious nature were automatically excluded. Cooperatives, however, were taxed in the same way as other business, and the bill specifically mentioned the taxation of agricultural cooperatives, although agriculture was exempt,[33] on the assumption that the outlays of the cooperatives for nonprofit undertakings were financed from the profit of taxable activities.[34]

Firms engaged in the property rental business were also automatically excluded from the tax. This was primarily because rent payments, rather than rent receipts, were taxed. To the extent that some rentals escaped taxation, the exemption was reported to have been partially based upon the fact that such enterprises were heavily burdened by the newly imposed municipal property tax.[35]

Specific Exemptions

The specific exemptions were limited in number. They were granted to the following classes of business:

1. Business conducted by the national government or localities.
2. Business of the second and third categories conducted by legal persons who establish schools which conformed with certain school laws.
3. Business conducted by various public corporations such as the Japanese National Railways, the Japan Broadcasting Company, various public banks, and several others.
4. Agriculture.
5. Forestry.
6. Mining and placer mining.

[32] *Ibid.*, art. 23(2), (3), (4), pp. 13–14.
[33] *Ibid.*, art. 30(9), p. 19.
[34] M. Bronfenbrenner, "The Japanese Value-Added Sales Tax," *National Tax Journal*, III (Dec. 1950), 305 f.
[35] Ito, "Theorie und Technik der Nettoumsatzsteuer in Japan," *Finanzarchiv*, XV, No. 3 (1955), 458.

7. Business conducted mainly by self-labor and determined by cabinet order.[36]

In August and September, 1950, the Shoup Mission returned to Japan for the purpose of reviewing its various recommnedations. It suggested that the original value-added tax proposal be revised to eliminate the exemption of the Japanese National Railways for the purpose of equalizing the position of private and government railroads. The local Finance Commission was authorized to establish rules for computing the profits of the railway for assessment of the value-added tax. The Mission's report expressed the opinion that the railroads were responsible for certain government services and even received benefits from the building of roads which facilitated the transportation of freight and passengers between the railway terminals and their various destinations.[37]

Except for the case of mining, the exemptions were of a conventional type. The exemptions of schools and public corporations are customary in sales tax legislation. The exemption of agriculture and forestry was necessary because Japanese firms engaged in such activities were generally too small to warrant the application of the tax. Additional reasons for not taxing agriculture were the wish to exempt food in order to reduce the regressivity of the tax and the fact that property taxes had been substantially increased under the new tax system.[38] The exemption of self-labor or the self-employed was obviously designed for administrative convenience although it may also have reflected a wish to treat such business leniently.

The author has seen no explanation for the mining exemption. This is rather puzzling in view of the fact that quarrying was taxed.

The bill also granted an exemption for the sake of administrative convenience to concerns with value added less than 90,000 yen during the taxable year, and prefectures which needed the revenues were to be permitted to adopt a lower limit.[39] The exemption was not extended to all firms because Japanese authorities contended that the tax base would be excessively reduced.[40]

[36] *Local Tax Law*, art. 24, pp. 14–15.
[37] Shoup Mission, *Second Report on Japanese Taxation* (Tokyo, 1950), pp. 18 f.
[38] Bronfenbrenner, "The Japanese Value-Added Sales Tax," *National Tax Journal*, III (Dec. 1950), 308.
[39] *Local Tax Law*, art. 34, p. 20.
[40] Bronfenbrenner, "The Japanese Value-Added Sales Tax," *National Tax Journal*, III (Dec., 1950), 307 f.

TAX BASE

Subtraction Method

The sales subtraction method of computing a consumption-type tax base was adopted in the original version of the Japanese bill, which provided that "The amount of value added . . . shall be an amount obtained by deducting from the total amount of the sales . . . the amount of specific outlays."[41] Outlays in excess of sales were to be carried forward for a period of five years.[42]

Sales were defined as transactions in tangible property, including the capital assets of business firms, and in services.[43] The taxation of capital assets was presumably intended to prevent any possibility of tax avoidance through purchasing items as deductible business outlays and then discontinuing taxable activities or reselling the assets to purchasers not entitled to deductions.

Three reasons for adopting the consumption-type tax have been given by Professor Bronfenbrenner of the Cargenie Institute of Technology, who served as tax economist in Tokyo during the academic year 1949–50 and helped to implement the Mission's report. One was the intention of encouraging new and growing firms by allowing the deduction of capital outlays. Another was simplification in the computation of the base. A third was the aim of stabilizing the yield; for capital outlays would fall off when sales declined while depreciation would provide a fixed deduction.[44] This reasoning, of course, ignored any possible effects which the tax might have had in intensifying business cycles through the excessive stimulation of investment expenditures during periods of prosperity.

Rental receipts from land and house rents and receipts of interest and dividends, other than those of financial enterprises, were excluded.[45] This prevented the double counting of such items in view of the fact that payments were not deductible.

The specific outlays included all amounts paid to outsiders for the direct needs of the business even though the suppliers might have been

[41] *Local Tax Law,* art. 30(4), (5), p. 18.
[42] *Ibid.,* art. 31, pp. 19 f.
[43] *Ibid.,* art. 30(6), p. 18.
[44] Bronfenbrenner, "The Japanese Value-Added Sales Tax," *National Tax Journal,* III (Dec. 1950), 304.
[45] *Local Tax Law,* art. 30(6), p. 18.

exempt from the tax. The outlays comprised business purchases of raw materials, supplies, services, all capital outlays, and cost taxes.[46] Interest payments by financial institutions were deductible, a provision consistent with the inclusion of interest receipts in the tax base.

When taxable business was conducted by certain exempt groups, such as school corporations and other legal persons designated by cabinet order, the business was permitted to deduct outlays for "social works" or "other public utilities."[47] The deductible outlays of agricultural cooperatives, on the other hand, were expressly limited to those allowed other business firms.[48]

Various categories of deductible expenditures were enumerated in the law. They were as follows:

1. The purchases of land, houses, and other depreciable assets such as patents, trademarks, and rights.
2. Merchandise, semi-manufactured products, raw materials, supplementary materials, and all articles consumed.
3. Fees, storage charges, and rental charges other than land and house rents.
4. Interest payments by financial enterprises.
5. Damage insurance premiums, including reinsurance premiums.
6. Repairing and processing expenditures.
7. Advertising outlays.
8. Purchases of motive power, water, light, and heat.
9. Taxes and other government levies except the income tax, corporation tax, net worth tax, inhabitant's tax, and others listed by cabinet order.
10. Payments to the national treasury arising from profits created by price differentials under price-control legislation.
11. Similar outlays determined by cabinet order.[49]

No depreciation was allowed in the first version of the bill. Instead, as indicated above, total capital outlays were deductible. Strong opposition developed on the part of concerns with large investments made prior to the legislation.[50] Ito, who claimed that the discrimination against prior investment was particularly beneficial to very large firms in a position

---

[46] *Ibid.,* art. 30(7), pp. 18 f.
[47] *Ibid.,* art. 30(8), p. 19.
[48] *Ibid.,* art. 30(9), p. 19.
[49] *Ibid.,* art. 30(7), pp. 18 f.
[50] Bronfenbrenner, "The Japanese Value-Added Sales Tax," *National Tax Journal,* III (Dec. 1950), 304.

to undertake heavy expansion programs and injurious to small and average enterprises, advocated either of two solutions: (1) the deduction of the value of capital assets owned by a firm on the effective date of the law, and taxation of the assets when sold; (2) the exclusion from taxable receipts of sales of capital assets owned prior to the law.[51] Bronfenbrenner thought that it was probably desirable in the interest of equity to end the discrimination against previous investment through the allowance of depreciation on such property even though it might complicate the administration of the law;[52] and, when the Shoup Mission returned to Japan in 1950, it recommended that the problem be solved by allowing the depreciation of assets in existence prior to January 1, 1952,[53] the effective date of the law then scheduled. Of course, none of the solutions met the problem of the smaller firm in no position to undertake expansion programs—a problem inherent in the consumption type of value-added tax.

For the most part, the legislation succeeded in avoiding double counting and omissions in the tax base as a whole. Difficulty was encountered only in the case of financial enterprises and rental business.

In computing the value added of financial institutions—i.e., banks, trusts, insurance companies, and money-lenders—double counting occurred because their interest and dividend receipts were taxed while the same interest and dividends were components of the tax base of nonfinancial business. On the other hand, a gap in coverage occurred because the interest payments of financial enterprises were deductible but were not included in the tax base of nonfinancial concerns.[54]

The effort to avoid double counting in the rental business led to the exclusion of receipts of land and house rents from the tax base. Bronfenbrenner questioned this provision on the ground that it exempted the service charges of the property-management business.[55] Ito adopted a similar position. Although he indicated that the heavy property tax was a partial conmpensation for this omission, he would have preferred some

---

[51] Ito, "The Value-Added Tax in Japan," *Annals of the Hitotsubashi: Academy,* No. 1 (Oct. 1950), pp. 50, 58.

[52] Bronfenbrenner, "The Japanese Value-Added Sales Tax," *National Tax Journal,* Vol. III (Dec. 1950).

[53] Shoup Mission, *Second Report on Japanese Taxation,* p. 17.

[54] Ito, "Theorie und Technik der Nettoumsatzsteuer in Japan," *Finanzarchiv,* XV, No. 3 (1958), 457.

[55] Bronfenbrenner, "The Japanese Value-Added Sales Tax," *National Tax Journal,* III (Dec., 1950). 304

solution other than the exclusion of an entire field of business activity
from the value-added tax.[56] In the case of rental business other than
land and house rents, there was no problem; rental receipts were taxed
and rental charges were deductible.

Addition Method

One of the revisions in the original legislation recommended by the
Shoup Mission in 1950 was the option of using an addition procedure
in computing the tax base. This system summarized wages and salaries,
interest and rent payments, and net profits as derived for the national
income tax.[57]

Of course, net profit for income tax purposes diverged from the profit
concept utilized in value added as defined under the subtraction procedure, a fact recognized by the Shoup Mission. In the first place, net
income profits included capital outlays and inventory changes but allowed
depreciation. The amount of profit under the two procedures would have
been equal if the taxpaying firms made no net additions to their investments; but profit under the addition procedure would have exceeded that
under the subtraction procedure in the event that the firms were increasing their capital assets or accumulating inventories. Secondly, net income
profits comprised items extraneous to the concern's usual business operations, as, for example, interest receipts.[58] As Bronfenbrenner pointed out,
"The two methods give the same result—always on the proviso that
'profit' is defined appropriately."[59]

The Shoup Mission allowed the addition procedure because concerns
with elaborate systems of accounting contended that the method would
facilitate their computation of the tax.[60] The Mission would have been
justified in assuming that the tax base was likely to be either the same
or larger than if the subtraction procedure had been elected. Even in
the event of disinvestment the tax base would initially have been no less

[56] Ito, "The Value-Added Tax in Japan," *Annals of the Hitotsubashi Academy*,
No. 1 (Oct., 1950), p. 57.
[57] Shoup Mission, *Second Report on Japanese Taxation*, pp. 17–18.
[58] For an analysis which emphasizes the difference in results under the two
procedures, see Ito, "Theorie und Technik der Nettoumsatzsteuer in Japan,"
Finanzarchiv, XV, No. 3 (1955), 462–66.
[59] Bronfenbrenner, "The Japanese Value-Added Sales Tax," *National Tax
Journal*, III (Dec., 1950), 306.
[60] Shoup Mission, *Second Report on Japanese Taxation*, p. 17.

than under the subtraction procedure in view of the fact that the latter permitted a depreciation allowance on investments made prior to the introduction of the value-added tax.[61]

The addition procedure received the active support of the Japanese accounting profession on the ground that it conformed with conventional methods. It was also favored by many taxpayers to whom the explicit deduction of losses appealed. It was opposed by tax officials who wanted the information provided by the subtraction method as a means of checking evasion.[62]

Ito, who objected to the use of the option because of possible divergent results might have been expected to endorse the subtraction procedure unequivocally, given his general anlysis. Instead, although he recommended the subtraction procedure if the tax was to be imposed in the form of a "sales tax," he was sympathetically disposed toward the addition procedure which, on the assumption that it taxed net income profits, he described as a method of converting the "sales tax" into a "business tax" based upon external indices.[63] He therefore advocated the use of a tax base which consisted of two distinct components. The first component, which was supposed to apply the ability principle, comprised net profits. The second component, held to represent the benefit principle and, indirectly, taxable capacity (*Leistungsfähigkeit*), comprised the sum of payments of wages, rents, interest, and dividends; and he regarded it as a tax based upon external signs. In the case of the second component, he considered the desirability of differentiating the tax rates with industrial categories because he frankly questioned the equity of any value-added type of base. However, he warned against excessive differentiation because of administrative difficulties. His proposal was advanced as a solution to the problem of the taxation of financial institutions without double counting which, he claimed, inevitably characterized the subtraction procedure utilized by a "sales tax" base.[64] Actually, as ex-

[61] Initially, the tax base would have been less only in the event of inventory liquidations or sales of capital assets. After existing assets had been fully depreciated, it would have been less for a firm which was not replacing its depreciable assets.

[62] Bronfenbrenner, "The Japanese Value-Added Sales Tax," *National Tax Journal*, III (Dec., 1950), 306.

[63] Ito, "The Value-Added Tax in Japan," *Annals of the Hitotsubashi Academy*, No. 1 (Oct., 1950), p. 54.

[64] Ito, "Theorie und Technik der Nettoumsatzsteuer in Japan," *Finanzarchiv*, XV, No. 3 (1955), 470.

plained in Chapter 5, a formula can be devised to avoid such double taxation.

In 1953 the Japanese Diet revised the value-added levy in accordance with the above suggestions except that no rate differentiation by industrial category was adopted. Interest payments by banks were excluded for the erroneous reason that they differed in character from those paid by ordinary concerns. For the first year the rate of the tax imposed on profits was to be 10 percent, 12 percent having been the rate of the current enterprise tax, while the rate for the second component equaled 1 percent; ultimately the rates were to be 8 and 2 percent, respectively.[65]

This certainly constitutes an odd version of value-added taxation which, as Ito suggests, can be explained only as a type of *patente*, viewed as an impersonal tax on business not expected to be shifted forward but rather to rest primarily on business profits. It impairs the generality of the base apparently in an effort to introduce the ability principle into a measure which ignores this principle so far as the legal taxpayer is concerned. Presumably the dual rates are intended to allow for the fact that profits are measured on a net basis while the second component in a sense represents gross measures except in the case of dividends. The proposal does not solve the problem of double taxation even under the second component because dividends are partly made up of inter-firm receipts of interest, dividends, and rents; and, of course, there is double taxation between the two components. As interest payments by banks are excluded from the tax base, double taxation is avoided in this instance; but such interest is then unduly favored. The levy would certainly be much more difficult to compute than the deduction variant of the consumption type of value-added tax which Ito considers a sales tax, strictly speaking.

Special Base for Certain Businesses

In the case of financial enterprises, transportation, and warehousing, the original legislation permitted the calculation of value added for the first year of the tax by using a given percentage of sales.[66] Bronfenbrenner observed that in most cases the percentages were so low as to be a real

[65] *Ibid.*, pp. 470–71.
[66] *Local Tax Law,* art. 74, p. 48.

concession to the industries involved,[67] and their elimination was recommended by the Shoup Mission in 1950.[68]

Base for Inter-prefectural Transactions

When business was transacted in more than one prefecture, one half of the tax base was allocated according to the value of the fixed assets and one half according to payrolls in the case of manufacturing, the supply of gas and electricity, motor highways, canals, wharves, mooring, and cargo unloading. For other business, the total amount of value added was allocated to payrolls.[69]

The allocation formulas, which were based upon the origin principle, were intended to increase the revenues of rural prefectures in comparison with the yield of the enterprise tax. The proceeds of the enterprise tax were attributed to the place where the head office was located, and large firms were concentrated in the six largest cities—Tokyo, Osaka, Yokohama, Kobe, Kyoto, and Nagoya. For example, nation-wide industries in lumbering, fishing, and agriculture were carried on in the island of Hokkaido while the head offices were in Tokyo.[70]

TAX RATE AND YIELD

The standard rate of the tax according to the Local Tax Law was 4 percent of the value added for business in the first category and 3 percent for business in the second and third categories. Rates up to 8 percent and 6 percent, respectively, were to be permitted provided that the Local Finance Commission was notified and that the same rates were maintained for one fiscal year. The Mission anticipated that, after two years of experience, it would be possible to allow the prefectures to impose whatever rate they wished.[71]

In 1950 the Mission recommended that the differential rates be eli-

[67] Bronfenbrenner, "The Japanese Value-Added Sales Tax,"*National Tax Journal,* III (Dec., 1950), 312.
[68] Shoup Mission, *Second Report on Japanese Taxation,* p. 18.
[69] *Local Law Tax,* p. 37.
[70] Bronfenbrenner, "The Japanese Value-Added Sales Tax," *National Tax Journal,* III (Dec., 1950), 309.
[71] *Report on Japanese Taxation,* II, 204.

minated in view of the fact that the tax was intended to be shifted forward to consumers. It stated that there was no evidence that tax shifting was more difficult for those activities subject to the lower rate, such as livestock breeders, dentists, or tax consultants, than those subject to the higher rate, such as steel mills, retails shops, and pottery manufacturers.[72]

An average rate of around 4 to 6 percent was expected to yield annual receipts of around 44 billion yen. This compared with receipts from the current enterprise tax of around 50 billion yen.[73]

ADMINISTRATION OF THE TAX

The tax was to be administered by the governor of the prefecture where the office or place of work of the business was located. It was due semi-annually from legal persons and tri-annually from individuals by means of a system of approximate self-assessment in the manner of the French provisional payments on the basis of the value added in the preceding year. However, when the value added in the current year was likely to be less than half that of the preceding year, the estimate was to be based upon the current year's experience. The final return with any necessary additional payment was due two months after the close of the business year in the case of legal persons and by February 10 of the following year in the case of individuals.[74] Other administrative details may be found in the Local Tax Law of 1950, articles 35 through 73.

The localities were to be aided in the administration of the tax by two agencies of the central government, the Local Autonomy Agency and the Local Finance Commission. They were to act in an advisory capacity and were entrusted with the responsibility of protecting the independence of the localities.[75]

INCIDENCE AND EFFECTS OF THE TAX

The Japanese value-added tax was intended as a consumption tax. In reply to the contention that the tax discriminated against labor-intensive

[72] Shoup Mission, *Second Report on Japanese Taxation*, p. 18.
[73] *Report on Japanese Taxation,* II, 197.
[74] *Local Tax Law*, arts. 35–38, pp. 20–26.
[75] Bronfenbrenner, "The Japanese Value-Added Sales Tax," *National Tax Journal,* III (Dec., 1950), 302.

firms, the Shoup Mission made the following statement: "A common complaint is that the value-added tax, not being restricted to profits, will bear unfairly on those firms with a large labor element. But this complaint seems to assume that the value-added tax is supposed to be borne out of profits, like the present enterprise tax. Instead, the value-added tax is supposed to be passed on to purchasers in higher prices; it is a type of sales tax."[76]

During the discussion of the measure, the issue of discrimination against labor-intensive firms was raised by the Japanese labor and left-wing movements on the ground that payrolls comprised a large proportion of the tax measure.[77] Fear had developed that the tax would lead to mass unemployment, as had occurred under postwar programs for the rationalization of Japanese industry.[78] Bronfenbrenner agreed that the tax favored the substitution of machinery for labor but believed that its potentialities in this direction had been exaggerated for two reasons. One was that the concession to capital was partly offset by the new property tax, applicable to land and depreciable assets, which was estimated to be somewhat less than half the tax on payrolls. Secondly, the value-added tax was imposed upon investment goods along with other products so that the price of capital equipment might be expected to rise.[79] Actually, however, investments are in effect excluded from the tax base in the case of the consumption type of tax, as explained in Chapter One.

Business was unenthusiastic about the proposal because it felt no assurance that the tax could be shifted forward. Its attitude, largely the result of the unusual nature of the tax, was intensified by the general economic situation of the period when the measure was introduced.

The value-added tax appeared complicated in comparison with more usual forms of sales tax where the tax was clearly a given percentage of sales and could be readily added to prices. Bronfenbrenner stated that most firms did not know their own percentage of value added to sales, much less that of their rivals, and they feared that the tax would not be shifted or would even be evaded.[80] Actually, to the extent that there was no rate differentiation, the amount of tax to be shifted forward merely equaled sales times the tax rate. However, even the slight amount of rate differentiation did complicate the situation somewhat.

[76] Shoup Mission, *Second Report on Japanese Taxation,* p. 17.
[77] Bronfenbrenner, p. 311.
[78] *Ibid.*
[79] *Ibid.,* pp. 311–12.
[80] *Ibid.,* p. 310.

Fear that the tax could not be shifted forward was aggravated by the economic recession prevailing at the time the tax was being discussed. Business took it for granted that the shifting would be difficult under such circumstances, although Bronfenbrenner maintained that economic theory considered forward shifting possible, apparently on the debatable assumption that, in the absence of the tax, consumers would pay less for the products.[81] Another factor expected to impede shifting was the existence of price controls, despite official promises that the authorities would make an allowance for the tax.[82]

The Japanese newspapers adopted an especially antagonistic attitude. Along with certain other industries, they objected to the taxation of the expense accounts of employees which had been included with payrolls. Expense accounts were an accepted practice, and it was reasoned that they should have been regarded as direct purchases of services from outsiders. This had not been done because the system had been widely abused through the substitution of such allowances for wage increases under the income tax.[83]

Agricultural cooperatives were another group dissatisfied with the tax. They felt that they should have been classed with exempt agricultural firms.[84]

Finally, the bill was vigorously opposed by large enterprises in general, who thought that the impact of the new measure would be greater than their burden under the enterprise tax. Bronfenbrenner summarizes the situation as follows:

The shift [in the allocation of the tax burden] is in favor of firms making high profits with relatively low payrolls and much new capital. It is against firms making low profits (or losses), with high payrolls, or with large fixed capital investments if depreciation cannot be charged against value-added. Generally speaking we may say that the tax burden is shifted against big business, and in favor of medium and smaller enterprises, as the larger firms are the ones most heavily saddled with a payroll which Japanese customs render frequently supernumerary, and with old capital equipment which may remain ineligible for depreciation deductions. This would seem to be a point in favor of the tax in present-day Japan. However, the medium and small enterprises, being relatively unorganized, have remained almost silent, while the large firms have presented a most effective campaign of opposition.[85]

[81] *Ibid.,* p. 311.
[82] *Ibid.*
[83] *Ibid.,* p. 305.
[84] *Ibid.*
[85] *Ibid.,* p. 312.

Ito also attributed the unpopularity of the value-added tax to the fact that it imposed a heavier burden upon large firms than the enterprise tax. He claimed that a secondary consideration was the greater complexity of the value-added levy as compared with the enterprise tax.[86]

He undertook a statistical analysis in which he estimated the amount of the value-added tax for various industries during the year 1951 at the standard rate of 4 percent as compared with the enterprise tax of 12 percent. He noted that the statistics did not represent the situation of representative firms but that they indicated the truth of several generalizations.[87]

In the first place, small firms would have paid a smaller amount of value-added tax than enterprise tax because their value added consisted primarily of net profits taxed at 4 percent instead of the 12 percent rate of the enterprise tax. The other elements of value added were not likely to be taxable in the case of small firms which were largely family undertakings utilizing family assistance and residential property and making few payments to outsiders for wages, interest, and rents.[88]

The value-added tax also imposed a lighter burden when profits constituted a large proportion of the tax base. This was the case of the paper manufacturing industry and banks.[89]

The value-added tax was much heavier on labor-intensive firms than the enterprise tax. Examples of labor-intensive firms were vehicle manufacturing, construction, and hotels.[90]

The study also indicated that the use of the substraction procedure of computation resulted in a tax upon certain industries less than half that imposed by the addition method. This was the situation in steel manufacturing, cotton-yarn spinning, chemicals, and paper manufacturing. Ito surmised that the difference arose primarily because capital outlays were not deducted under the addition procedure.[91]

Ito also estimated the relative importance of the value-added and enterprise taxes as between incorporated and unincorporated firms for the year 1953. In the case of unincorporated firms, presumably smaller

[86] Ito, "Theorie und Technik der Nettoumsatzsteuer in Japan," *Finanzarchiv*, XV, No. 3 (1955), 473.
[87] *Ibid.*, pp. 473–75.
[88] *Ibid.*, p. 476.
[89] *Ibid.*
[90] *Ibid.*
[91] *Ibid.*

enterprises, the value-added tax was estimated at only 50 percent of the enterprise tax. For incorporated firms, the percentage was 148 percent. The average for both classes equaled 106 percent.[92]

In August, 1953, the Japan Tax Association, an organization parallel to the National Tax Association in the United States, sent its members a questionnaire which inquired whether they preferred the value-added tax or the existing enterprise tax with some modifications. Ten voted for the value-added tax and seventy-two for the enterprise tax.[93]

The unpopularity of the tax was reflected in the unwillingness of the government to put it into effect. Its application was postponed from one year to the next. It was subjected to a revision in 1953 which revolutionized its character, but the effective date continued to be postponed until it was finally repealed in May, 1954.[94]

APPRAISAL OF THE TAX

The value-added tax proposed by the Shoup Mission is part of a carefully planned national tax system and must be judged accordingly. It is intended as a consumption tax designed to provide funds which cannot be raised from taxes on personal incomes and wealth and which will provide the prefectures with an independent source of revenues.

The economic scene which confronted the Shoup Mission was one of extreme overpopulation in both rural and urban areas relative to available land and capital facilities. Therefore, a proposal to encourage the expansion of investment was an understandable measure. The value-added tax was considered superior to the enterprise tax because it would not overburden profits. The report of the Shoup Mission contains the following statement: "In comparison with the business tax on a pure net profits base, the value-added tax has the economic advantage that it does not discriminate against the use of capital, especially in the form of labor-saving machines. The net profits tax bears on value created in this manner and not on value created by the use of direct labor. This is an important point in Japan at the present time, where modernization of plant and equipment is one of the more urgent needs."[95] Furthermore, the Mission

[92] *Ibid.*, p. 477.
[93] *Ibid.*
[94] *Ibid.*, p. 471.
[95] Shoup Mission, *Report on Japanese Taxation*, II, 203.

believed that the profits taxes were being shifted forward in a less equitable manner than the value-added tax would be.

Abstracting for the moment from the issue raised by the choice between the subtraction and addition procedures, the Japanese proposal for value-added taxation in general adequately implements the principle of indirect personal taxation. It possesses the virtue of wide scope, being imposed on most products, whether goods or services, the chief exceptions being products of extractive industries and residential rents. Also, it extends through the retail stage. As a carryforward is allowed there is no restriction on the deductions to which a taxable enterprise is entitled because the taxable outlays exceed taxable receipts, other than any delay which might be occasioned by an absence of enough taxable receipts in the following period.

Given the fact that there are some exemptions, the tax-credit procedure or the disallowance of deductions in the case of purchases from exempt enterprises would ensure a more accurate implementation of the underlying principle. Also, like the French tax, exempt firms are not entitled to any deductions, so in effect they are obliged to pay the tax on their purchases of investment goods. Deductions would therefore have to be prorated when firms combined taxable and exempt activities, although in view of the more limited number of exemptions, the proration problem would not be anywhere near as troublesome as under the French legislation.

The definition of the tax base in the case of financial institutions leaves something to be desired in view of the resulting double tax on interest and dividends on the one hand, and the undertaxation of their interest payments on the other. Moreover, the proposal does not provide a satisfactory solution to the problem of taxing rents. While residential rents and the services of the property management business escape tax, business rents are taxed on a gross basis. Also, it remains to be seen whether it would have become necessary to restrict any of the deductions for investment purchases in view of the fact that some might have been diverted to personal use.

As previously explained, the use of the origin principle for taxing products traded across jurisdictional borders is not as appropriate to the concept of indirect personal taxation as is the destination principle. However, on the assumption of similar rates in all the prefectures, the use of the origin principle merely effects a different allocation of tax receipts than that which would have resulted from use of the destination principle.

Given the benefit of hindsight, it may be said that the only real mistake in the Japanese proposal is the option granted taxpayers to choose between the subtraction and addition procedures. While introduced merely to simplify the bookkeeping problem of large firms, it amounts to a choice between two principles of taxation. The subtraction procedure represents an indirect tax on consumer outlays while the addition procedure represents an income type of indirect taxation. It is this mixture of principles which finally caused so much confusion as to the character of the tax that it led to its being viewed as a *patente*. Apparently, it was assumed that the taxpayer would be quite unable to shift the income-type tax forward although no attempt seems to have been made to explain this position. In theory, the tax on purchases of investment goods should have ultimately entered into the prices of the products.

The value-added tax is the only measure proposed by the Shoup Mission which has never been put into effect. However, Ito reported that in the years following the departure of the Mission, Japanese public opinion rejected the spirit of the proposals and sought to reinstate the tax system previously in force. Furthermore, the slogan of economic reconstruction and need for capital accumulation was used to support excessive favors to big business, a tendency which Ito deplores.[96]

[96] Ito, "Theorie und Technik der Nettoumsatzsteuer in Japan," *Finanzarchiv*, XV, No. 3 (1955, 477-78; and Ito, "Direct Taxes in Japan and the Shoup Report," *Public Finance*, VIII (1953), 382–83.

Part II

Toward an Understanding of the Tax on Value Added

Chapter 4

The Theoretical Justification of the Tax on Value Added

A theory of tax justice is the general principle which guides the distribution of a nation's tax liabilities among individual taxpayers. If generally accepted, it becomes one of the most important standards for judging a tax measure or a system of taxes.

Almost all tax authorities have emphasized the criterion of justice. "Equality" comes first on the list of maxims enumerated by Adam Smith.[1] T. S. Adams feels that he stands alone in preferring "simplicity," "certainty," and "convenience" to "equity."[2] The Shoup Mission calls attention to the fact that "no one remains in the tax field for long without realizing that nothing he recommends will stand up unless it meets the test of fairness in the distribution of the tax burden," in the sense that it must seem equitable to the general public.[3]

According to Gerhard Colm, theories of tax justice formulated by economists or students of public finance must implement "the given general content of political justice" which delimits the sphere of governmental responsibility.[4] Although at first glance this injunction appears to restrict the province of the tax student, it really allows him considerable latitude; for "general content of political justice" means

[1] *An Inquiry into the Nature and Causes of the Wealth of Nations* (The Modern Library, New York, 1937), p. 777.

[2] "Fundamental Problems of Federal Income Taxation," *Quarterly Journal of Economics,* XXXV (Aug., 1921), 554.

[3] *Report on Japanese Taxation* (4 vols., Tokyo, 1949), I, 16.

[4] Colm, "The Ideal Tax System," *Essays in Public Finance and Fiscal Policy* (New York, 1955), p. 48.

governmental practice rather than express doctrine.[5] Hence, on the ground that many government services are in fact designed to aid business, Colm feels free to advocate recognition of the state as a "partner in production" in order to support business taxation at a time when the "social state" and the theory of personal ability to pay represent the only accepted concepts.[6] Furthermore, pointing out that the tax student may regard the tax system as an inappropriate method for carrying out government policies,[7] he wisely rejects the concept of tax justice implied by the "control type of state," which seeks to discriminate among various types of expenditures and economic activities[8] and issues the following warning:

Thus the control type of state lies on the boundary line of the capitalist system and sets a limit to the application of the criterion of political justice in the sphere of production. Only such a state, in assuming responsibility for the production process, may in all fairness raise this type of discrimination to the level of a general taxation principle. But since the modern state, except in Russia, does not assume full responsibility for production, these discriminations pass easily from a form of higher justice into a manifestation of rank injustice.[9]

Colm is apparently concerned with forestalling theories of tax justice which merely reflect the personal views of the tax economist with respect to political and economic justice—issues which, he claims, constitute the province of statesmen and social philosophers, respectively.[10] Yet history reveals some salutary violations of this injunction unless one reasons circuitously that, whenever an economist challenges accepted theory, he functions as a statesman or social philosopher. In the latter part of the Middle Ages, tax students began to advocate the principle of the universality and uniformity of taxation when the prevailing concepts favored the exemption of the secular and ecclesiastical nobility.[11] In the nineteenth century, when a narrow interpretation of the benefit theory threatened to obstruct necessary welfare expenditures, economists protested that ability to pay represented the only valid concept of tax

---

[5] *Ibid.,* p. 49.
[6] *Ibid.,* pp. 51–53.
[7] *Ibid.,* p. 48.
[8] *Ibid.,* pp. 55–56.
[9] *Ibid.,* p. 57.
[10] *Ibid.,* pp. 45 f.
[11] Edwin R. A. Seligman, *Essays in Taxation* (8th ed., New York, 1919), p. 8.

justice.[12] As Studenski indicates, they might have used the argument that the rich received more benefits than the poor except that it was less compatible with the views of the middle class, the dominant political group, who wanted a concept of the state as a cooperative commonwealth based upon social equality.[13]

Moreover, even granted the desirability of Colm's restrictions on the authority of tax students, how is one to tell whether a program merely represents prevailing concepts of political or economic justice or the student's own views on these subjects if governmental expenditure policies indicate the prevailing criterion of justice? For example, as noted above, Colm accepts the implications for tax policy of the partner state but not of the control state, apparently on the ground that the student may exercise his personal judgment concerning the desirability of modifying the distribution of the tax burden to reinforce public policy. With parallel logic, students may refuse to accept the implications for tax justice of the partner state; and, indeed, many students regard business taxes as unjust. In both instances, how is one to know whether or not the student is injecting his own political or social views? His attitude toward expenditures may indicate his position, a fact which raises the question of whether a tax student is forbidden to express his own ideas concerning the justification of expenditures. In any event, what if the expenditures are contingent upon the rejected tax measures?

In discussing the role of the tax student, the Shoup Mission emphasizes that "the tax system must satisfy the deep, widespread feelings of the people as to what is fair"[14]—a position equivalent to Colm's if one assumes that the government adequately represents the will of the people. However, it frankly and sensibly recognizes that the tax student is bound to have his personal views concerning the justice of the economic system and "cannot be expected to abandon completely whatever ideas of his own he may have."[15]

As Colm notes, one principle of justice has been recognized in every age, namely the doctrine that the law should treat persons in similar circumstances in the same way. It is the definition of similar circum-

[12] *Ibid.,* p. 73; Herbert D. Simpson, "The Changing Theory of Property Taxation," *The American Economic Review,* XXIX (Sept., 1939), 462.

[13] Paul Studenski, "Modern Fiscal Systems, Their Characteristics and Trends of Development," *The Annals of the American Academy of Political and Social Science,* CLXXXIII (Jan., 1936), 28–30.

[14] *Report on Japanese Taxation,* I, 17.

[15] *Ibid.*

stances—or, as Colm puts it, "the determination of which inequalities are to be politically relevant"—which varies from time to time.[16]

Principles of tax distribution inevitably involve assumptions concerning the incidence and effects of the fiscal measures through which they are applied;[17] and their significance depends upon the extent to which their assumptions conform with reality. During the depression of the thirties, for example, the incidence of the general net income tax could probably be considered more certain and equitable than that of *ad rem* taxes while the former undoubtedly had more favorable effects on output —thereby justifying the predominance of the ability-to-pay theory of tax justice. This situation has been changing during the postwar inflation because of growing uncertainty concerning the incidence of business net income taxes and the possibility that an excessively progressive rate structure may impair longrun productivity. Thus, the study of incidence and effects is as important as concepts of tax justice which are, in fact, judgments concerning the desirability of one group of incidence and effects as compared with another. There is, of course, some interdependence between the two issues for, in the words of Professor Groves of the University of Wisconsin, "the effects of a tax depend considerably upon the reasonableness of its imposition."[18]

THEORIES ADVANCED TO JUSTIFY THE VALUE-ADDED TAX

There is more than one concept of value added, and the theories or, rather, hypotheses used to justify the tax should be related to the type of measure employed, for it is logical to suppose that the incidence and effects of the levy will vary with the nature of the tax base. As explained in Part I, the first proponents of the tax and their followers have recommended types of value-added taxation which may be classified as "production taxes" in the sense of levies on the total value of a con-

---

[16] Colm, "The Ideal Tax System," *Essays in Public Finance and Fiscal Policy,* p. 47.

[17] "Incidence" may be defined as effects on the distribution of real incomes and "effects" as the resulting changes in output. See R. A. Musgrave, "On Incidence," *The Journal of Political Economy,* LXI (Aug., 1953), 307. "Incidence" has traditionally but less rigorously been defined as short-run changes in prices resulting from a tax and "effects" as other consequences.

[18] Harold M. Groves, *Postwar Taxation and Economic Progress* (New York, 1946), p. 20.

cern's product, with deductions limited to purchases on current account from outside enterprises and possibly depreciation. Using national-income terminology, the measure which disallows depreciation may be termed the "gross product" or "gross income" type of concept while the measure which deducts depreciation may be designated as the "net product" or "net income" type of concept. Hence, the tax would apply to the final output of both producers' and consumers' goods or, in other words, to items purchased by investors or savers as well as ultimate consumers. In fact, the aggregate tax base has been regarded as a rough approximation of that utilized by the general income tax although, of course, the gross product type base, under which the investment component represents gross rather than net investment, is far different from the net-income base. On the other hand, the more recent discussions of the tax envisage a measure equivalent to a proportional spending tax—a "consumption-type tax" or "sales tax," strictly speaking—so that the levy is imposed only on sales for ultimate consumption or, in other words, items purchased by ultimate consumers. Like the proportional spendings tax, it effects a regressive distribution of the tax burden, thus contrasting with the net income type tax, which is proportional to income. Meanwhile, the gross product type tax is probably quite progressive in view of the concentration of property ownership in upper income groups although the pattern of progression is not clear.[19]

The hypotheses used to justify the production-type measures may be classified according to Studenski's terminology as follows: (1) the "cost-of-service variant" of the "general-benefit theory," (2) the "general-welfare theory," and (3) the "social-expediency theory."[20] In justifying consumption-type measures, emphasis has been placed on the stimulation of investment and the neutrality of the tax with respect to various methods of production, especially the absence of discrimination against capital expenditures, sometimes as compared with net profits taxation and sometimes as compared with a no-tax situation. Under the older hypotheses the neutrality criterion represents a subdivision of the social expediency theory. The benefit doctrines have also been applied to consumption-type taxes; but, while they may afford some explanation of the production-type levies, they seem somewhat removed from the basic

[19] The distribution of the tax burden under the various concepts is further discussed in Chapter 7.

[20] Studenski, "Toward a Theory of Business Taxation," *Journal of Political Economy*, XLVIII (Oct., 1940), 630, 648, 649.

philosophy actually underlying the consumption taxes for reasons discussed later in this chapter. The cost-of-service version of the benefit principle is presented as a partial justification for the consumption-type Japanese value-added tax, but it is supplemented by the more accurate explanations of the need to encourage investment, the neutrality of the tax as compared with an ordinary turnover tax, the avoidance of discrimination against capital inherent in the net profits base, and a belief that the incidence of the net profits tax is inequitable.

HYPOTHESES DEVISED TO JUSTIFY PRODUCTION-TYPE MEASURES

Cost-of-Service Variant of the Benefit Principle

The cost-of-service version of the benefit doctrine used to support most early proposals for value-added taxation was first advanced by Adams in justification of general business taxation, and hence his proposal for value-added taxation. It has been elaborated by Colm and Studenski, who have sought to devise as strong a philosophical basis for general business cost taxes as has been provided by the ability-to-pay theory for direct personal taxation, Colm being especially concerned with the reluctance of American states to allow the federal government exclusive use of income and inheritance taxes partly because of the inferior moral status of the *ad rem* taxes on which they would be forced to depend.[21]

The hypothesis may be expressed as follows. In rendering services of general benefit to business enterprises, the government functions in the same way as private factors of production and should recover the cost of these services through business taxes. Value added by the individual firm provides an objective index of the concern's relative utilization of these services. Therefore, it is just to allocate such governmental costs according to value added.

As Studenski observes, the hypothesis combines the cost-of-service and value-of-service principles. Value added is supposed to indicate not only the amount of government services utilized but also the value to the firm

[21] Colm, "The Basis of Federal Fiscal Policy," *Taxes—The Tax Magazine,* XVII (June, 1939), 340.

of the opportunities provided by a market. Studenski cites Adams' statement that the volume of trade represents a firm's opportunity and is responsible for public expenditures,[22] while Colm states that a tax measured by value added "imposes an equal burden on every branch of industry" for government services "contributing to the more or less equal advantage of all branches of business."[23] Studenski supplements the hypothesis with his well-known contention that business taxes are imposed on the activities of a business organization as such rather than on the activities of individual businessmen or, for that matter, consumers, the levies being intended to reach a concern's "collective and impersonal productive powers"—"the result of the effective combining of men, machines, and materials and the collaboration of government and society as a whole."[24]

Colm refers to the concept of political justice which he uses in support of business taxation as the "partner state" or the state as a *partner in production*."[25] Studenski, on the other hand, designates his rule for business taxation as a "cost-of-service variant" of the "general-benefit theory" in opposition to the "partnership variant," the distinction being that the former but not the latter permits business taxation regardless of profits.[26] The National Tax Association has made the same distinction. It notes that there are two schools of thought regarding the relationship of government to business. One represents the concept of the state as an " 'agent in production' " under which both successful and unsuccessful concerns are taxed; the other represents the principle of the state as a "partner in production" under which only successful concerns are taxed.[27]

The cost-of-service variant of the benefit theory as formulated by Colm and Studenski is based on the following assumptions.

1. That the government operates as either a productive factor employed within an enterprise, analogous to labor and capital, or an external supplier of services resembling an independent business firm.

[22] Studenski, "Toward a Theory of Business Taxation," *Journal of Political Economy,* XLVIII (Oct., 1940), 646 f.
[23] Colm, "The Ideal Tax System," *Essays in Public Finance and Fiscal Policy,* p. 54.
[24] "Toward a Theory of Business Taxation," pp. 623–24.
[25] Colm, "The Ideal Tax System," pp. 53–54.
[26] Studenski, "Toward a Theory of Business Taxation," pp. 630 f.
[27] "Final Report of the Committee of the National Tax Association on Federal Taxation of Corporations," *Proceedings of the Thirty-Second Annual Conference on Taxation of the National Tax Association, 1939* (Columbia, S. C., 1940), p. 565.

2. That it is feasible to segregate general public services rendered to business from other categories of public outlays.

3. That it is reasonable to apportion the cost of such services according to a firm's value added.

4. That a tax may be regarded as a price paid for public services, chargeable to the business owner like other costs, thereby circumventing the problem of ascertaining the incidence of the tax among individuals.

In the following analyses of the assumptions, Studenski's argument that a business tax should be regarded as a levy on the activities of the business organization as such is discussed in connection with the assumption that a tax is a price paid by business for public services. However, the argument is also related to the concept of the government as a productive factor.

GOVERNMENT AS A PRODUCTIVE FACTOR.   Although Colm is the first tax economist to have utilized the analogy of government as a productive factor in support of business cost taxes, his approach is very like one previously employed by Antonio de Viti de Marco in developing a general-benefit theory to justify income taxation. De Viti de Marco adopts the view that "The position of the State does not differ in kind from that of the worker or any other agent of production."[28] He even goes so far as to identify general public services as capital or instrumental goods when utilized by private individuals "because the means of communication, the agencies for the maintenance of order, and so on, are forms of capital destined to assist in the production of private wealth."[29] Colm, being concerned with the justification of business cost taxes instead of an individual income tax, asks whether government functions as a productive factor internal or external to the business firm. He raises the issue while discussing the treatment of business cost taxes in the national income accounts rather than with reference to the value-added tax, but the issue involves the definition of the tax base as well as the contribution of business to national income.[30] Colm apparently prefers the view of government as an external factor, for he compares the services which it renders to business with "raw materials or fuel."[31] This approach is probably

---

[28] Antonio de Viti de Marco, *First Principles of Public Finance,* trans. by Edith Pavlo Marget (New York, 1936), p. 233.

[29] *Ibid.,* p. 58.

[30] Colm, "Public Revenue and Public Expenditure in National Income," *Studies in Income and Wealth,* Conference on Research in National Income and Wealth, I (National Bureau of Economic Research, New York, 1937), 205.

the more logical one, government presumably being less closely associated than internal factors with business management.

Colm's thesis of government as a business organization producing services utilized by business as well as those benefiting ultimate consumers bears a resemblance to the analogy employed by the national-income authority, Professor Simon Kuznets. In his estimates of national income under the auspices of the National Bureau of Economic Research, Kuznets treats the government as a vast producing organization selling its services for tax revenues to business enterprises and ultimate consumers.[32] Shoup also acknowledges the possibility of comparing the government to a giant enterprise, when he states that "the economy may first of all be divided into two great industries: government and private enterprise."[33] He adds that government is a vertically integrated concern and that the value-added technique might conceivably be applied to its internal operations if adequate data were available.[34]

Groves, who opposes the view that government resembles a private factor of production, reasons that the analogy is untenable because private factors are engaged voluntarily while the use of public services is compulsory; he writes as follows:" It is interesting that the factors of production—land, labor, capital, management, and government—are all, with the exception of the latter, employed voluntarily by the business man. The amount of government and the apportionment of its cost to business are determined by voting. However, in the voting process, business (directly at least) has a minority voice."[35]

Those who endeavor to meet this objection point correctly to the resemblance between government and the monopolistic owner of a private factor who may force business to employ the factor at a given price or withhold the supply.[36] They are also justified in calling attention to the great political influence exercised by business interests, one tax scholar having gone so far as to say that "In a capitalist State the government is of business, by business, and for business."[37]

Groves obviously fears a large shift from individual income taxes to

[31] *Ibid.*, p. 194.
[32] Simon Kuznets, "Discussion," *ibid.*, p. 237.
[33] Carl S. Shoup, *Principles of National Income Analysis* (Boston, 1947), p. 331.
[34] *Ibid.*, pp. 334–35.
[35] Groves, *Postwar Taxation*, p. 24.
[36] Clark Warburton, "Discussion," *Studies in Income and Wealth*, VI (1943), 30.
[37] Jens P. Jensen, *Government Finance* (New York, 1937), p. 148.

business cost taxes under the slogan of government as a factor of production. Assuming that the rendering of government services to business
constitutes the sole rationale of business cost taxes, the hypothesis might
indicate a reduction in the amount of such taxes currently levied, the
outcome depending upon the definition of such services. "The amount of
cost services," says Colm, "may be larger or smaller than business taxes;
under modern conditions all non-income taxes ar larger than the amount
spent on cost services."[38] Estimates by Colm and by Dr. Clark Warburton
of the Federal Deposit Insurance Corporation suggest that during the
thirties, when Colm began sponsoring his hypothesis of business taxation,
actual business cost taxes considerably exceeded government services to
business.[39] Likewise, Shoup, who is writing in the postwar period, states
that "There is some reason to believe, however, that such services do not
form a substantial part of total economic activity in the United States or
Great Britain, aside from subsidies."[40] As the discussion below makes
evident, however, services to business have frequently been defined so
as to justify Groves' concern.

FEASIBILITY OF IDENTIFYING GOVERNMENT SERVICES TO BUSINESS.
If the government is to charge business in general with the cost of services
rendered for the latter's benefit, it becomes necessary to identify the
services involved. This task is far from easy because, even when there
are grounds for regarding a service as one which particularly benefits
business, it is usually possible to argue that it provides indirect benefits
which accrue to the community as a whole. Unless generally accepted,
objective criteria were developed or the task were entrusted to an independent official authority, intense political controversy would be
inevitable.

Widely divergent classifications have been suggested by proponents of
the agent-of-production theory of business taxation who have sought to
distinguish between government services to business and those to ultimate
consumers. Moreover, Colm maintains that most government services to
business represent special benefits to particular industries rather than to
business as a whole.[41]

[38] "Public Revenue and Public Expenditure in National Income," *Studies in
Income and Wealth*, I (1937), 205.
[39] Colm, *ibid.*, pp. 210, 212; Clark Warburton, "Accounting Methodology in the
Measurement of National Income," *ibid.*, p. 87.
[40] Shoup, *Principles of National Income Analysis*, pp. 256 f.
[41] Colm, "The Ideal Tax System," *Essays in Public Finance and Fiscal Policy*,
p. 55.

Adams claims that a substantial portion of expenditures on the judiciary, police and fire departments, the army, and the navy may be attributed to business.[42] Colm divides general business services into the following three categories: (1) the establishment of business laws and their legal enforcement through the courts, (2) public education which provides the skill and efficiency required of labor, and (3) social costs which result from business operations, such as unemployment and the preservation of the ability to work.[43] He specifically mentions the following as general business services: industrial education, encouragement of technical research, economic and statistical reporting, recovery programs to reduce cyclical business risks, and various public improvements[44] —items which might be classified in either category (2) or (3) or both, except for the last one, which relates to all the categories. Apparently, Colm would exclude war expenditures although he does not mention this issue in connection with the agent-of-production theory. He merely notes that the older benefit theories provided no guide for the allocation of war expenditures among taxpayers because it is impossible to assign the benefits to each individual.[45] It may be noted that for purposes of estimating national income he assigns national defense to a special category described as "political services that are rendered for the political organization's own sake, for national prestige and power or for the protection of the social order."[46] Moreover, he classifies all educational expenditures as consumer services although he notes that they also operate as a " 'factor of production.' "[47]

Studenski, on the other hand, would attribute a portion of defense expenditures to business although no part of educational outlays. His list of general government services to business includes the establishment of laws; the safeguarding of property rights and contracts; the judiciary; the police; the army and navy; public roads (classified as a special service to the automobile industry by Colm); public improvements of harbors and waterways; and assistance in foreign markets (also designated as a

[42] "The Taxation of Business," *Proceedings of the Eleventh Annual Conference of the National Tax Association, 1917* (New Haven, Conn., 1918), p. 187.

[43] Colm, "Conflicting Theories of Corporate Income Taxation," *Law and Contemporary Problems,* VII (Spring, 1940), 283.

[44] Colm, "The Ideal Tax System," *Essays in Public Finance and Fiscal Policy,* p. 53.

[45] *Ibid.,* pp. 50 f.

[46] Colm, "Public Revenue and Public Expenditure in National Income," *Studies in Income and Wealth,* I (1937), 215.

[47] *Ibid.,* p. 216; p. 216, n. 46.

special service to business, i.e., the import and export industries, by Colm). He remarks that most government activities, such as protection to life and property, national defense, and highways, combine both producer and consumer services while expenditures on education, recreation, and control of public health are consumer services only.[48] The Shoup Mission, it will be recalled, regarded some public health expenditures as services to business.

The problem of separating government services to business from those to consumers is discussed extensively in the literature on national income accounting, where its significance lies in the need to identify the final output of the community. Most authorities acknowledge the theoretical desirability of segregating government services to business in order to prevent their being counted twice, once in the output of the private sector and a second time in the public product. Therefore, the discussion has focused upon the practicability of making the estimates and the methods employed. Meanwhile, suggested classifications have been even more diverse than those advanced for purposes of business taxation, the underlying philosophy ranging from the attitude that most public expenditures primarily benefit business to the position that it is most accurate to classify all public outlays as consumers' services.[49] In his estimates of national income, Kuznets has assumed that business taxes, defined as taxes for which business firms are legally liable, equal government services to business and that personal taxes equal government services to consumers. Once extremely skeptical of any attempts at a more accurate appraisal, he described public expenditures as "an indissoluble amalgam of efforts to preserve the business system (which may be classified as service to it) and to modify it for the benefit of non-business groups (which may be classified as service to individuals),"[50] and defended the assumption of equivalence between government service to business and taxes paid by business on the ground that it is more reasonable to assume this equivalence than to assume no relationship between taxes and governmental benefits.[51] The fact that taxes paid by business include special

[48] Studenski, "Government as a Producer," *The Annals of the American Academy of Political and Social Science,* CCIX (Nov., 1939), 23–30.

[49] Cf. Gottfried Haberler, "National Income, Saving and Investment," *Studies in Income and Wealth,* II (1938), 144, and John Lindeman, "Income Measurement as Affected by Government Operations," *Studies in Income and Wealth,* VI (1943), 18.

[50] Kuznets, "Discussion," *Studies in Income and Wealth,* I (1937), 235.

[51] *Ibid.,* p. 237.

excises, such as those on liquor and tobacco, which are clearly intended as levies on consumers and obviously do not coincide with services to business, constitutes the strongest argument against Kuznets' assumption.

Colm rejects the view that existing business taxes approximate the value of government services to business.[52] As indicated above, he holds that such services may be greater or smaller than the amount of actual taxes, probably the latter, so that direct estimates are essential.

A number of students have adopted the same position as Colm. One is Warburton, who wants a committee of economic experts to undertake direct estimates. He considers the direct approach less arbitrary than Kuznets' procedure or one endorsed by Mr. John Lindeman, when a government economist, that all government services be classified as consumers' goods. Warburton states that it would be no more arbitrary than the line of demarcation sometimes drawn by estimators of national income between intermediate and final output in the nongovernmental sectors of the economy. Medical services, for example, are treated as final output when paid for by the individual and intermediate output when provided by a business firm.[53] Likewise, Studenski implies that he would favor direct estimates when he recommends a deliberate attempt to bring about a closer correspondence between government services to business and business taxes.[54]

Shoup also believes that government services to business should probably be estimated on the basis of direct estimates because "the assumption that the amount of government services to business equals the amount of business taxes seems too wide of the mark to be acceptable."[55] Moreover, in his analysis of government expenditures, he establishes a third category of government activity, namely, "general-purpose services," which he defines as follows: "Such a service is not enjoyed by consumers for its own sake. And it cannot be conceived of, at the given time and place, as being produced by private enterprise; hence it cannot be said to supply business firms with a free substitute for some item of

[52] Colm, "Public Revenue and Public Expenditure," *Studies in Income and Wealth,* I (1937), 205.

[53] Clark Warburton, "Discussion," *Studies in Income and Wealth,* VI (1943), 24–25.

[54] Studenski, "Government as a Producer," *Annals of the American Academy,* CCIX (Nov., 1939), 29–30.

[55] Shoup, *Principles of National Income Analysis,* p. 263.

cost. . . ."[56] The category would include maintenance of the armed forces, the system of courts, and all other items which may be regarded more accurately as intermediate products of general benefit rather than final output, the list varying with circumstances.[57] A similar classification is now favored by Kuznets, who has changed his attitude toward the feasibility of distinguishing between intermediate and final public output and who emphasizes that final products must represent "net contributions to individuals' welfare."[58]

The most ambitious attempt at a direct estimate of government expenditures according to benefits was undertaken in 1938 for the Conference on Research in National Income and Wealth by two government economists, Mr. R. W. Nelson and Mr. Donald Jackson, who endeavored to divide government expenditures for the fiscal year 1936 between consumption services and aids to production.[59] When unable to decide upon the classification of a given type of expenditure, they divide it equally between the two categories, justifying this procedure as follows:

In defense of this position it may be argued that costs of this type are incurred in the interests of the entire body politic, regarded as an organic entity, and that each member stands on an equal footing with every other member in this social whole; and, further, that every person constitutes a dual personality with respect to his relations with the economic system—that is, he exists both as a consumer and as a producer. Even the infirm, the aged, and the children . . . are dependent for their real incomes upon the productive activities of others. . . .[60]

They add the qualification that the benefit from general services might have been distributed according to income, wealth, or some index rather than production and consumption. However, they regard their procedure as less likely to be challenged, apparently because it reflects a more neutral political attitude.[61]

Nelson and Jackson were handicapped by the absence of the three-fold classification recommended by Shoup and Kuznets. The equal division of general services between production and consumption recalls

[56] *Ibid.*, p. 266.

[57] *Ibid.*

[58] Kuznets, "On the Valuation of Social Income—Reflections on Professor Hicks' Article," Part I, *Economica*, XV (Feb., 1948), p. 9, n. 1.

[59] R. W. Nelson and Donald Jackson, "Allocation of Benefits from Government Expenditures," *Studies in Income and Wealth*, II (1938), 317–31.

[60] *Ibid.*, p. 323.

[61] *Ibid.*, p. 323, n. 9.

the comment by Groves that "For all the guidance we get from the benefit theory, we might resolve the problem by taxing all individuals twice on their personal income, once for the benefits enjoyed in production and once for benefits enjoyed as consumers."[62] This is, in fact, the approach which Adams considers reasonable.[63] It obviously supports a broader base for business taxation than that provided by direct services to business; and it resembles the approach of the "general-welfare theory," discussed later in this chapter, which seeks to tax the income of individuals both directly and indirectly.

VALUE ADDED AS AN INDEX OF RELATIVE UTILIZATION OF PUBLIC SERVICES BY BUSINESS CONCERNS. The hypothesis that business taxes represent charges for services rendered to business by the government as a factor of production or producing enterprise requires a formula which will allocate the cost of these services among the recipients in a manner similar to the accountant's distribution of overhead charges in a business concern. Studenski states that the selection of value added for this purpose rests on the assumption that a firm's relative input of government services is more or less correlated with its size and with its use of the market maintained by society as indicated by its volume of activity, thereby implying that value added measures the comparative size of business concerns and their volume of activity.[64] He further states that the recommendation of proportional rates reflects the intention of taxing in proportion to a firm's utilization of such services.[65] Therefore, the proportional rate must also reflect the assumption that the utilization of government services is in proportion to a firm's value added rather than progressive or regressive—a position which is implied by the premise that the public services involved are of general benefit to business. As Colm explains: "It follows that from the point of view of the partner state a tax on business incomes must be proportional, not progressive; the latter would imply discrimination, which is not in accord with the aims of the pure partner state."[66]

---

[62] Groves, *Postwar Taxation*, p. 25.

[63] Adams, "The Taxation of Business," *Proceedings, National Tax Association, 1917*, p. 239; Adams, "Fundamental Problems of Federal Income Taxation," *Quarterly Journal of Economics*, XXXV (Aug., 1921), 542.

[64] Studenski, "Toward a Theory of Business Taxation," *Journal of Political Economy*, XLVIII (Oct., 1940), 630, 646–48.

[65] *Ibid.*, p. 630.

[66] Colm, "The Ideal Tax System," *Essays in Public Finance and Fiscal Policy*, p. 54, n. 8.

Economists have used various measures to indicate the relative size of business enterprises, including sales, assets, number of employees, and profits, as well as value added.[67] There is no ideal measure; the appropriate one depends upon the problem concerned.

In selecting a measure of size suitable to a business tax on a firm's use of the market, the choice rests between sales or turnover and value added. Both employment and profits ignore a number of relevant factors, while the case against assets, as Adams states, is the possibility of "much property with little business or much business with little property."[68]

Gross turnover, a commonly accepted measure of a concern's amount of business or volume of activity, provides a logical index of its use of the market. The relationship between value added and gross turnover, however, is not consistent as between one concern and the next. Adams' endorsement of value added in preference to turnover is motivated by his wish to correct the multiple taxation of "cost of sales" so as to avoid a subsidy to integration.[69] Studenski, on the other hand, claims that value added constitutes not only "a fairer basis" for general business taxation than turnover but also "a far more accurate measure of the volume of activity of business enterprises,"[70] thus implying that the mere turnover of items entering into cost of sales does not involve use of the market although, of course, such is not the case.

Groves would deny that any index of the use of the market could measure benefits derived by business from government services. He challenges the validity of Adams' hypothesis on the grounds that everyone benefits from the maintenance of a community market and that the relative benefits are indeterminable.[71]

However, if one accepts the view that government services to business can be identified, then some forms of value added provide a more or less adequate index of their relative utilization; rather arbitrary allocation formulas are sometimes used by business accountants. As previously

[67] Herbert A. Simon and Charles P. Bonini, "The Size Distribution of Business Firms," *The American Economic Review*, XLVIII (Sept., 1958), 611.

[68] Adams, "The Taxation of Business," *Proceedings, National Tax Association, 1917*, p. 188.

[69] Adams, "Fundamental Problems of Federal Income Taxation," *Quarterly Journal of Economics*, XXXV (Aug., 1921), 553.

[70] Studenski, "Toward a Theory of Business Taxation," *Journal of Political Economy*, XLVIII (Oct., 1940), 648.

[71] Groves, *Postwar Taxation*, p. 23.

noted, the concept of value added ranges from the production-type bases which equal the value of a concern's contribution to society's total output (gross or net) to the consumption types which are intended as measures of output destined for ultimate consumption. The gross product type provides the closest approximation to a firm's volume of activity, for obviously use of the market occurs when capital is replaced. The net income variant includes only net investment; and a firm may undertake no new investment and yet make substantial use of the market in meeting its replacement needs. By excluding investment, the consumption-type bases omit important portions of activity and are therefore wholly inadequate indices of either the size of a concern or its use of the market.

If the measure of a concern's value added is to reflect the view of government as an external supplier of services to business, the charge for government services to business should be deductible in the same way as purchases from outside firms. However, this issue would presumably not be important except for the value-added tax itself. The treatment of indirect taxes in general is discussed in the following chapter.

CONCEPT OF A TAX AS A PRICE FOR PUBLIC SERVICES. The agent-of-production theory assumes that the government may follow a policy of charging a price or a fee to finance its general expenditures as if it were a private business, the only difference being that it anticipates no profit on the transaction. It is not clear whether the tax is expected to cover the total cost of the services. Studenski, for example, states that it may be desirable to partly finance them through taxes on personal incomes, property, or consumption.[72] Colm, on the other hand, who employs a narrower definition of public services to business than Studenski, seems to assume that, in addition to financing services which benefit business in general, the tax will cover a portion of the costs of services to particular industries which the government is unable or unwilling to cover through special charges.[73]

One of the weaknesses of the above hypothesis is the fact that it supports a tax without regard to the consequent distribution of tax payments among individuals. If a tax represents a just charge for services rendered to business, it is merely one of many business costs to be combined with

[72] Studenski, "Toward a Theory of Business Taxation," *Journal of Political Economy,* XLVIII (Oct., 1940), 629 f.

[73] Colm, "The Ideal Tax System," *Essays in Public Finance and Fiscal Policy,* p. 55.

them, thus neglecting the problem of incidence among individuals and effects. Groves calls attention to this issue, emphasizing that taxes are borne by individuals, not inanimate objects, and that the benefit thesis provides little assistance in allocating the tax burden among individuals.[74]

In view of the controversial nature of the subject of incidence and effects of direct as well as indirect taxation and the weaknesses of the subjective sacrifice doctrines, the ability theory also fails to provide an unequivocal guide for the distribution of the tax burden among individuals; but at least it affords no excuse for dodging the problem. Most advocates of a value-added tax as a charge for public services rendered to business appear to have been more concerned with its potentiality for raising revenues than economic repercussions. One exception is Adams, who explicitly indicates his wish to reduce the tax burden on upper income groups on the ground that it is overburdening savings and investment.[75] As explained in Part I, the Shoup Mission also reveals its concern with the incidence and effects of the Japanese value-added tax which, however, mainly utilizes a consumption-type base rather than the production-type levies being discussed in this section.

Following a line of thought suggested by Adams, Studenski attempts to reinforce the philosophy of a business tax which neglects incidence among individuals with his thesis that a business tax represents a levy on business organization as such rather than on individuals. He claims that a modern business enterprise represents a "group venture having an organic unity and collective personality of its own"[76] distinct from that of its owners. Moreover, he maintains that although individuals associated with a business are presumably rewarded according to their contribution to the concern's product, the enterprise possesses a "productive capacity which is impersonal in character" generated by an environment which encompasses various factors—"mechanical, governmental, social, natural, and fortuitous"—as well as by personal capabilities, and that a business tax seeks to reach these impersonal factors.[77]

It is true that the general environment created by the impersonal factors mentioned by Studenski favors certain types of business as op-

---

[74] Groves, *Postwar Taxation,* p. 24.

[75] Adams, "Fundamental Problems of Federal Income Taxation," *Quarterly Journal of Economics,* XXXV (Aug., 1921), 537.

[76] Studenski, "Toward a Theory of Business Taxation," *Journal of Political Economy,* XVLIII (Oct., 1940), 623.

[77] *Ibid.,* pp. 623–24.

posed to others. It is true that in a business organization the personality of the individual may be dominated by the psychology of the group or an individual personifying the psychology of the group, with either good or bad effects, depending upon the group values. However, Studenski does not make clear the implications of his philosophy for tax policy. One possible interpretation is that he is attempting to reach the total incomes of larger enterprises which he considers unduly favored by the environment, for he claims that the productive powers of a business depend upon its size as well as management and other factors. He may also be concerned with the large funds accumulated by business organizations which are not allocated to individuals, such as undistributed profits and various reserve funds. However, the incidence of business taxes, including the value-added tax, is upon the income of individuals as well as undistributed funds so that the business-entity hypothesis cannot represent a general standard of tax justice.

The concept of a tax as a price paid for public services characterizes all benefit doctrines and distinguishes them sharply from the principle of ability to pay. In the case of the cost-of-benefits-to-business thesis, the concept is more appropriate when public services to business are defined to exclude general-purpose services, for the tax is then closer to a fee. Its difference from the concept of a tax under the ability theory is discussed below in connection with the general-welfare doctrine.

General-Welfare Theory

A second philosophical approach to general business taxation has been taken through a version of the benefit doctrine which Studenski has named the "general-welfare theory." Studenski invokes this thesis to support a national defense tax of 4 percent in the form of a value-added tax.[78] Arant and Mr. Wadsworth W. Mount, a businessman who once proposed the adoption of value-added taxation by the United States federal government, also use this justification.[79]

[78] *Ibid.,* p. 650.
[79] Arant, "The Place of Business Taxation in the Revenue Systems of the States," *Taxes,* XV (April, 1957), 195; Wadsworth W. Mount, "A Re-examination of Taxation Fundamentals," *Financial Management Series,* No. 67 (American Management Association, New York, 1941), pp. 10 f., 12.

A thorough exposition of the general-welfare or general-benefit theory appears in the treatise, *First Principles of Public Finance,* by de Viti de Marco. His doctrine may be summarized as follows: Most public expenditures represent an inseparable mixture of benefits to producers and consumers. However, there is good reason to believe that the benefits may be allocated among individuals in proportion to their respective incomes. Hence, the cost of such services should be covered by a proportional tax on individual incomes. Furthermore, to be certain that no incomes escape assessment, both direct and indirect taxation should be employed. The quotation below from de Viti de Marco's work describes this dual approach:

In other words: income which escapes, in whole or in part, direct valuation at the moment of its production is watched for and seized in the successive moments in which its possessor spends it. The Treasury waits for him to acquire private goods—whether they are consumers' goods or producers' goods —in order that it may deduce from the value of these goods the total income spent or invested.[80]

De Viti de Marco's analysis reveals an interesting acquaintance with the concepts of value added; but, because of his inconsistent definitions of income, it is not clear whether he favors a production-type or consumption-type tax. On the one hand, he emphasizes the desirability of including savings in the base of an indirect tax as evidenced by the following quotation: "After the taxpayer has paid direct taxes on the incomes he has produced, he owes indirect taxes on the same income, to the extent that he in fact spends it either in the acquisition of direct goods, in order to satisfy present wants, or in the acquisition of instrumental goods, when he saves his income in order to satisfy future wants."[81] On the other hand, he sometimes defines income as consisting only of direct or consumption goods. For example, he states that *"The product or income of society consists of the quantity of goods of the first order annually produced and consumed."*[82] Moreover, when he utilizes a concept of value-added taxation in explaining the avoidance of double taxation under the direct income tax, he speaks in terms of the deduction variant of the consumption-type tax as follows:

[80] De Viti de Marco, *First Principles of Public Finance,* pp. 131 f.
[81] *Ibid.,* p. 309.
[82] *Ibid.,* p. 218.

Let us suppose that the State turns first to the manufacturer of ploughs—which we have considered as the enterprise with which the cycle of bread-production begins—and takes from him 20 per cent of the price of the ploughs sold to the grain-grower. It then turns to the grain-grower, to collect 20 per cent of the grain sold to the miller. The grain-grower, however, objects on the ground that from the value of the grain sold to the miller should be deducted the part that the manufacturer of ploughs has already paid, and the State allows this, because *it has already collected the tax on this part of the product*. And when it turns to the miller, from the flour or the price of the flour is deducted the part that the miller has paid the grain-grower (in which is also included the share of the plough-manufacturer) because the State has already collected the tax on it. And when the State turns to the baker, it deducts the part which the latter has already paid to the miller (in which is included the share belonging to the grain-grower, and a second time that belonging to the manufacturer of ploughs), and on which the State has already collected the tax.[83]

He adheres to a similar definition when he discusses the possibility of an indirect tax on all goods and services, although he is unable to visualize the value-added technique in the sphere of indirect taxation. In fact, he claims that such a tax is impossible partly because of the administrative difficulty of taxing services and partly because of the problem of preventing multiple taxation.[84] Instead of a general indirect tax, therefore, he advocates selective excises on articles of mass consumption which, however, may be considered nonessentials, such as coffee, tea, tobacco, liquors, etc.[85]

Thus, the most important assumptions of the general-welfare hypothesis are as follows:

1. That benefits from public services can be allocated among individuals.
2. That those who receive the benefits should be made to pay for them or, in other words, that a tax may be regarded as a price paid for public services.
3. That a dual approach to general taxation is more efficient than a single general tax.

ALLOCATION OF BENEFITS AMONG INDIVIDUALS. Allocating the benefits from public expenditures among individuals is undoubtedly much more difficult than the problem of identifying services to business. In

[83] *Ibid.*, p. 220.
[84] *Ibid.*, p. 313.
[85] *Ibid.*, p. 315.

fact, it is probably impossible to do so with any degree of objectivity either because, as in the case of education and public health expenditures, there are indirect as well as direct benefits, while in the case of war and national defense expenditures even direct benefits cannot be identified.

De Viti de Marco's hypothesis of a proportional relationship is merely an assertion unsupported by statistical evidence or adequate analysis. Furthermore, in the older benefit theories, numerous attempts to establish a *quid pro quo* between government services and individual taxpayers have arrived at positions ranging from the view that government benefits are regressive to mathematical demonstrations that they increase faster than property or income. The position of a proportional relationship is taken most frequently in contrast with the ability-to-pay doctrine, which has usually led to progression.[86]

A TAX AS THE PRICE OF GOVERNMENT SERVICES.   As noted above, the view of a tax as a price paid for public services characterizes all benefit doctrines and distinguishes them sharply from the principle of individual ability to pay. The latter emphasizes the contributory nature of the tax payment and implies that the benefits from most government expenditures, being of a general rather than a special nature, cannot be traced to individual recipients. Even if a public service appears to directly benefit certain individuals or groups, it is usually of indirect benefit to all as, for example, the case of educational or public health expenditures.

The originators of the benefit approach called attention to the exchange relationship between government and taxpayers in order to eliminate concessions to privileged groups and to combat the dictatorial policy of holding that a tax is due "by virtue of the personal domination of the subject by the sovereign."[87] In time, however, some of its advocates developed a narrow interpretation which held that no individual owed a tax unless there was a commensurate direct benefit.[88] For example, some argued that the taxation of property to finance public education was inequitable.[89] This position was incompatible with the development of

[86] Edwin R. A. Seligman, *Progressive Taxation in Theory and Practice*, Publications of the American Economic Association, Vol. IX, Nos. 1 and 2 (Baltimore, 1894), pp. 77–126, esp. 78.

[87] De Viti de Marco, *First Principles of Public Finance*, pp. 113, 184.

[88] Seligman, *Essays in Taxation*, p. 72.

[89] See William J. Shultz and G. Lowell Harriss, *American Public Finance* (6th ed., New York, 1954), p. 428.

modern societies where the growing interdependence among their members required recognition of the social benefits derived from government expenditures as contrasted with direct benefits to individuals, and it led to the widespread abandonment of the general benefit theories. In 1919 Seligman wrote that the thinkers of the past fifty years had discarded the general benefit doctrines[90] and that the benefit thesis was acceptable only in the limited number of cases where the government was justified in levying tolls, fees, and special assessments[91]—the special benefit doctrine. He described the general benefit approach as "a narrow and selfish doctrine" and asserted that we pay taxes not because we receive benefits but because it is our duty.[92]

One of the serious weaknesses of the concept of a tax as a price is the fact that it is difficult to reconcile with transfer expenditures and deficit spending. Such outlays might be regarded as a form of investment made for the general welfare—a rather far-fetched explanation, however. Also, this view of a tax does not usually jibe with the policy of designing a tax system which would automatically stabilize business fluctuations, for it generally does not support a progressive rate structure.

The current orthodox theory of tax justice is the principle of ability to pay. Most authorities maintain that the benefit principle is valid only for special government services where taxes bear a close resemblance to market prices as, for example, postal charges, street railways, and special assessments. They may extend the use of the special benefit doctrine to highway taxes and even social security taxes on the ground that direct benefits are readily discernible in these cases.[93] They may even tolerate the general benefit theory as a vague justification for taxation as a whole or as a limit to the scope of the taxing power of state and local units; but they do not accept it as a guide for allocating the general tax burden.[94]

Regardless of their limitations, the general benefit theories render service in calling attention to an issue neglected by the ability theory, namely, that the distribution of money incomes before tax may diverge

[90] Seligman, *Essays in Taxation,* p. 73.
[91] *Ibid.,* p. 72.
[92] *Ibid.*
[93] See Harold M. Groves, *Financing Government* (4th ed., New York, 1954), pp. 18–19; Shultz and Harriss, *American Public Finance,* pp. 192–95.
[94] See Groves, *Financing Government,* p. 19.

considerably from the distribution of real incomes after tax.[95] Thus, Professor Alfred G. Buehler of the University of Pennsylvania expresses the opinion that "As progressive taxation is pushed to its logical and practical limits and as society distributes income more equally, with the rise of a socializing Welfare State or a Liberal Capitalistic State, more weight may be given to cost and benefit factors."[96] Obviously, if public expenditures were primarily for the benefit of lower income groups and were financed by taxes on the middle and upper income groups, the burden imposed on the taxpayers would be greater than the amount indicated by taxes paid on the conventional assumption of a proportional distribution of benefits. In fact, some students consider public expenditures on social services a more effective means of alleviating income inequalities than taxation.[97]

De Viti de Marco's revival of the benefit theory is motivated not by his faith in a doctrine but by his opinion that the effects of a proportional tax system are preferable to those of a highly progressive one. Strictly speaking, therefore, the general-benefit hypothesis should be classified under Studenski's social-expediency theory. De Viti de Marco believes that "proportional taxation respects the natural play of the economic forces involved and remains neutral as between them" with the result that tax shifting would be minimized.[98] He says that the adoption of proportional taxation by the French Revolution reflected not only the political fear of excessive concessions to privileged groups but also the economic aim of removing obstacles to the indefinite growth of wealth or, "in other words, the problems of *production* prevailed over those of *distribution,* and found their natural expression in the system of proportional taxation.[99] Any number of authorities have pointed out the conflict between distributive justice and society's productivity; and Brown summarizes their view when he writes as follows:

If men received their incomes without effort or savings, so that there would be no discouragement to either from the denial of a proportionate reward and if there were no possible danger of over-population or of multiplication of the unfit from proportioning family incomes to family need, then perhaps wealth and income should be apportioned on the principle of maximizing

---

[95] See Shoup, *Principles of National Income Analysis,* pp. 239 f.
[96] "The Cost and Benefit Theories," *Tax Law Review,* V (1949–50), 17.
[97] Harold M. Groves, *Trouble Spots in Taxation* (Princeton, N. J., 1946), p. 14.
[98] De Viti de Marco, *First Principles of Public Finance,* p. 187.
[99] *Ibid.*

utilities. As it is, to maximize utilities in the present would very likely not conduce to their maximization in the long run.[100]

Because of current inflationary pressures on economies throughout the world, the issue of productivity has again come to the forefront of economic discussions[101] so that increasing attention is likely to be given the possibility of modifying tax systems in order to foster or at least not curtail economic growth. Unfortunately, it is extremely difficult to determine just when the progressivity of a tax system is unduly curbing the amount of savings, impairing incentives to save and invest, and discouraging work, particularly when there are significant loopholes in the tax statutes;[102] when the amount and quality of expenditures rather than the distribution of the tax burden may be at fault; or when nontax and even noneconomic factors are affecting the situation.

EFFICIENCY OF DUAL APPROACH. The use of the general benefit theory in support of business taxation implies that a dual approach to general taxation is more efficient than a single one. As previously noted, De Viti de Marco recommends this method, claiming that the direct income tax should be supplemented by an attempt to reach incomes through indirect taxation on expenditures for consumption and investment goods.[103] Adams endorses a similar approach when he suggests that individuals be taxed once as producers and a second time in their role as consumers.

While the dual approach by one level of government may succeed in reaching some incomes which would otherwise evade or avoid taxation, there is always the danger that the ease of raising revenues under this system will result in the toleration of unjust loopholes which might have been eliminated if major reliance had been placed on a single approach. Moreover, the supply of trained administrators may be inadequate to handle both levies. The system is more suitable for application at two different political levels as, for example, the use of the direct approach by the national government and the indirect approach by the local level.

France uses the dual approach to general taxation on the national

[100] Harry Gunnison Brown, *The Economics of Taxation* (Columbia, Mo., 1938), pp. 200 f.

[101] "Productivity—The Hot New Issue," *Business Week*, No. 1436 (Mar. 9, 1957), pp. 25–26.

[102] See J. Keith Butters, Lawrence E. Thompson, and Lynn L. Bollinger, *Effects of Taxation: Investment by Individuals* (Boston, 1953), p. 65.

[103] De Viti de Marco, *First Principles of Public Finance*, pp. 131 f.

level by combining a general income tax with a value-added levy. Meanwhile, the former has been described as "a hybrid, mutilated income tax system"; and its future status is uncertain.[104]

Social-Expediency Theory

Most early proponents of value-added taxation invoked considerations of expediency in support of their measure. Studenski groups such considerations within a general category which he designates as the "social-expediency theory" and subdivides into "fiscal," "political," and "economic" expediency.[105] The fiscal principle emphasizes the facility with which a tax produces revenue and its administrative convenience. The political principle supports taxes which seem least unpopular, such as hidden taxes. The economic principle is concerned with the neutrality of a tax measure in the sense of an absence of disturbance to business relationships or the distribution of income and wealth.

Because the attitude toward this criterion has ranged from the position that it represents a necessary principle of taxation to the view that it constitutes a deplorable violation of ethics, a close examination of its meaning is essential. The dictionary gives two definitions of the term "expedient": (1) "apt and suitable to the end in view" and (2) "conducive to special advantage rather than to what is universally right."[106] This double meaning makes the interpretation of the term very slippery and dependent upon its context.

Tax students invariably draw a distinction between theories of tax justice and other standards of taxation which are frequently designated as considerations of expediency. The latter are regarded as essential qualities of an adequate tax measure although there are differences of opinion with respect to their relative importance. Studenski apparently considers the "social-expediency theory" inferior to other justifications because he calls it "opportunistic" on the ground that it may be used to

---

[104] Shoup, "Taxation in France," *National Tax Journal,* VIII (Dec., 1955), 341.

[105] Studenski, "Toward a Theory of Business Taxation," *Journal of Political Economy,* XLVIII (Oct., 1940), 639–40.

[106] *Webster's New Collegiate Dictionary* (2d ed., Springfield, Mass., 1956), p. 290.

support different bases at different times.[107] Some students, on the other hand, have advanced the "neutrality doctrine" as a leading standard of taxation.[108]

Use of the term "expediency" in the sense of an unprincipled violation of justice appears when the "fiscal" and "political" criteria are thought to have been overemphasized. Under certain circumstances, it may be very difficult to determine what constitutes such overemphasis. Groves, for example, points out that "a bad tax, as a last resort, may, under certain circumstances, be better than none."[109] As he observes, the need for revenue to support certain necessary public expenditures, such as those which raise cultural standards, improve distribution, and promote production, might justify the adoption of a tax solely on the basis of the "practical canons."[110] Then, there is always the question of what to do where the alternative is no tax despite increased expenditures during an inflationary period. The decision between justifiable and unjustifiable expediency therefore depends upon the tax student's judgment concerning the economic, political, and social effects of a fiscal measure. Such judgments should, of course, be related to alternative fiscal measures.

HYPOTHESES DEVISED FOR CONSUMPTION-TYPE MEASURES

Benefit Theories

As previously observed, the benefit theories have sometimes been used to justify the consumption type of value-added tax; but as explained in Chapter 1, their usefulness for this purpose is limited to a general justification in support of indirect personal taxation on consumer spendings as in the case of the Japanese value-added tax. The benefit thesis, which regards a tax as a price paid for governmental services which directly benefit business, requires an income type of tax. This is certainly the

---

[107] Studenski, "Toward a Theory of Business Taxation," *Journal of Political Economy,* XLVIII (Oct., 1940), 640.
[108] Shultz and Harriss, *American Public Finance,* p. 197.
[109] Groves, *Trouble Spots in Taxation,* p. 97.
[110] *Ibid.*

case if the tax is not expected to be shifted forward to consumers in its entirety but expected to remain in part on the various factors participating in the production process, presumably in conformity with their enjoyment of the governmental benefits. It will also be the case even if the tax is expected to be shifted because a tax on individuals in their capacity as producers rather than consumers implies that savings as well as consumer outlays should be reached by the tax.

Encouragement of Productivity

The adoption of a general consumption type of value-added tax, which is practically equivalent to a proportional spendings tax, is likely to be motivated by the belief that the prevailing tax system is preventing a growth in national productivity by impairing the incentives to save, invest, and work. In France a gross product type of value-added tax was converted into a consumption-type levy because investment outlays were considered overtaxed. It is not clear whether the new tax was generally expected to be more regressive than its predecessor although Lauré implies that it would be; but his main concern was to eliminate the taxes on investment goods in order to remove any handicap to technological progress.[111] In Japan a consumption-type tax was recommended because the business income tax which would have been retained in its place would have overburdened net profits while the incidence of the consumption levy was expected to be more equitable than that resulting from the forward shifting of a net profits tax.

Use of a regressive tax on the national level merely to counteract the progression of a national personal income tax would be an underhanded procedure. This is especially true when the situation is one described by Groves:

In the opinion of many critics, Congress has left too many loopholes in the income and death tax statutes. Indeed, there is reason to believe that some of this failure to tighten the tax laws is deliberate. There are those in Congress who calculate, cynically, that high rates are a bone to throw to the demagogic masses and that these rates can and should be made ineffective by leaving holes in the tax fences. This is playing reckless politics with the tax laws and throwing concern for equity and rationality out the window. Usually

[111] See *La taxe sur la valeur ajoutée,* pp. 44–47.

it is very good strategy (except politically) to trade a reduction of rates for the closing of a loophole.[112]

In any event, if the need to increase productivity requires a less progressive tax system, a direct reduction in progression is preferable to an indirect one. Furthermore, primary attention should probably be given to nontax factors affecting productivity such as monopolistic practices and the social values produced by advertising.

There is more justification for use of a regressive tax by subordinate levels of government, which modifies the degree of progression in the national tax system in cases where the national government has exclusive use of the progressive system because subordinate political levels require steadier revenues or are unable to administer progressive taxes effectively. However, there is always the danger of an excessive burden on certain groups regardless of the degree of progression at the national level.[113]

The argument that the consumption-type tax will encourage investment is frequently supplemented by the contention that the tax is neutral in its treatment of labor and capital. This issue was emphasized by Lauré in his recommendation for a consumption-type tax in France. The report of the Shoup Mission only notes the fact that the tax is more neutral than a business tax confined to net profits.[114] The validity of the neutrality argument will be examined at some length in Chapter 7.

Miscellaneous Justifications

Any of the numerous arguments used in support of sales taxation are likely to be advanced in justification of the consumption-type of value-added tax.[115] One of the most appealing is the possibility that the tax might reach incomes which evade or avoid direct taxation, but not enough could be accomplished in this direction to provide the principal justification for the tax. General sales taxation has sometimes been suggested as a replacement for a conglomeration of special excises, particularly

[112] Groves, *Trouble Spots in Taxation*, p. 68.
[113] See William Vickery, *Agenda for Progressive Taxation* (New York, 1947), p. 306.
[114] *Report on Japanese Taxation*, II, 203.
[115] Due reviews all the arguments in his treatise, *Sales Taxation*, pp. 30–48, 249–52.

on the state level of government; on the national level, the amounts involved are significant in an absolute sense but too small as compared with the amounts raised by the personal and corporate income taxes to warrant the adoption of an additional major tax solely for this purpose. Finally, the tax may be advocated as a substitute for a single-stage sales tax for administrative reasons—an issue discussed in Chapter 6.

Chapter 5

The Definition and Nature of the Base for the Tax on Value Added

RELATIONSHIP OF TAX BASE TO SOCIAL DIVIDEND

The base of the value-added tax was originally derived by Thomas S. Adams and Wilhelm von Siemens from accounts of the individual firm in order to eliminate the multiple taxation of items entering into cost of sales which characterize the general turnover tax. The relationship of the base to the social dividend was first recognized in the Brookings report on the Alabama tax system, which observed that the tax would be distributed according to a firm's share of the total income earned within the state.[1] The report recommends a base which is described as approximating "net value added by manufacture" as estimated by the United States Bureau of the Census.[2]

"Value added by manufacture" measures the difference between the value of an industry's shipments and its purchases from outside firms of materials, factory supplies, containers, fuel, purchased electrical energy, and contract work.[3] It is an inaccurate measure of a firm's contribution to the social product because it excludes products which a firm manufactures for itself while it includes services, other than contract work,

[1] Brookings Institution, *Report on a Survey of the Organization and Administration of the State and County Governments of Alabama* (Montgomery, Ala., 1932), IV, 340.

[2] *Ibid.*, p. 339.

[3] U.S. Bureau of the Census, *1949 Annual Survey of Manufactures,* Series MAS–49–3 (Aug. 17, 1951), p. 1.

purchased from outside firms and minor items, such as office supplies. It also includes depreciation and certain indirect taxes which are deducted in computing national income, proper. However, it roughly approximates the tax base proposed by the Brookings Institution, which limits the scope of the tax to manufacturing, trade, construction, and mining and allows a deduction for purchases of taxable raw materials and supplies.[4] Colm also relates the tax base to "value added by manufacture," but he would deduct expenditures on repairs and possibly depreciation as well as purchases of raw materials.[5] Furthermore, he indicates that the tax should be imposed on both goods and services, in which event, purchases of the latter would presumably be an additional deduction.[6] Actually, Colm's concept of value added by manufacture amounts to value added by production in the sense of a firm's contribution to national product or national income.

The concepts of national income and product, which have been developed extensively since the early thirties, have now entirely replaced value added by manufacture as a guide to the tax base. They provide an indispensable tool for understanding the nature of the tax base and are helpful in drafting tax legislation. However, as they have not been specifically designed for tax purposes, actual tax measures have never reflected and should not reflect a rigid application of their principles, sometimes because of administrative requirements and sometimes because the principles themselves are controversial.

The national accounts measure the value of a nation's income and product during a given period, generally a year. They cover all activities involved in the market economy regardless of ethical quality except that they customarily exclude illegal activities.

Most students of national income have emphasized the significance of the absence of ethical criteria. Kuznets, for example, makes the following observation: "It would be of great value to have national income estimates that would remove from the total the elements which, from the standpoint of a more enlightened social philosophy than that of an

---

[4] Brookings Institution, *Report on a Survey of the Organization and Administration of the State and County Governments of Alabama*, p. 358.

[5] Gerhard Colm, "Methods of Financing Unemployment Compensation," *Social Research*, II (May, 1935), 161, and 161, n. 1.

[6] Colm, "The Ideal Tax System," *Essays in Public Finance and Fiscal Policy* (New York, 1955), p. 54; and "The Basis of Federal Fiscal Policy," *Taxes*, XVII (June, 1939), 369.

acquisitive society. represent dis-service rather than service. . . ."[7] While this limitation must be borne in mind when interpreting the statistics, it does not concern tax measures, which, on the contrary, should reach even illegal activities.

The national income accounts utilize three concepts which are related to bases suggested for the value-added tax. They are national income, proper, personal consumption expenditures, and gross national product. The corresponding tax bases are the net income type base, the consumption-type base, and the gross product type of base, respectively.

Three Concepts of National Income and Product

The national income concepts originate in an accounting system which adopts a dual approach to the computation of aggregate income and product through the use of credit and debit entries whose totals balance. The credit entries, which are listed on the right side of the account, summarize the market value of the final output produced during the period. The debit entries, on the left side of the account, represent the costs incurred in producing the final output and consist largely of returns to the current factors of production. The product approach yields a measure designated as gross national product while national income, proper, is derived from the cost approach.[8] The United States Department of Commerce offers the following explanation of its procedure:

A fundamental distinction relevant to the measurement of economic production so delimited is suggested by observation of the operations of a typical business firm. On the one hand, such a firm produces and sells a flow of product values. On the other hand, it pays out (or retains) incomes that accrue in the course of its operations. This double aspect of the activities of the single business firm suggests that the measurement of national output can be approached in a two-fold manner, either by summing product values or by summing income flows. It will be seen that the measure of national output in terms of product flows which is obtained by pursuing this approach is

[7] Simon Kuznets, "Discussion," *Studies in Income and Wealth,* I (New York, 1937), 37. Also, see M. A. Copeland, "Concepts of National Income," *ibid.,* pp. 3–13; Warburton, "Discussion," *ibid.,* pp. 45–46; Henry C. Simons, *Personal Income Taxation* (Chicago, 1938), pp. 11–18; Shoup, *Principles of National Income Analysis* (Boston, 1947), pp. 111–12.

[8] U.S. Department of Commerce, *National Income, 1954 Edition* (Washington, 1954), pp. 1, 30–31.

the gross national product and that the corresponding measure in terms of income flows is the national income.[9]

This dual approach corresponds to a distinction made by de Viti de Marco when he discusses the relation between a tax on product and a tax on income in the following quotation:

Now, there are taxes on product and taxes on income. What is the difference?

The product consists of goods in kind, considered in relation to the enterprise from which they come and before they are distributed among those who take part in their production. In a primitive economy, the tax is a percentage of the product; this was the case for example, with the tithe, which was deducted in kind on the threshing-floor, and fell on the enterprise itself. In the concept of income, on the other hand, there is a personal element that is lacking in the case of the 'product.' Whereas the latter has reference to the enterprise as such, the former has reference to the person to whom the product belongs. In ordinary speech, we make no distinction between the statement that a piece of land produces 1000 gallons of wine and the statement that it yields $1000, although this second formulation already suggests the idea of a proprietor. But the difference becomes evident if we have regard to the moment at which the product is divided among those who have taken part in its production; because then one does not speak of 'the product of the proprietor' and 'the product of the labourer,' but rather of 'the income of the proprietor' and 'the income of the labourer.' Usually one speaks, correctly, of the 'product of industry' and the 'income of a person.'[10]

As previously noted, the product approach has been found more suitable for computing gross national product and the income approach for arriving at national income, proper, although either method may be used to measure any concept of national income. National income and gross national product are the predominant concepts while personal consumption expenditures appear as a subcategory of gross national product.

National income, proper, differs from gross national product primarily because it excludes certain charges which are not considered returns to current factors of production but which, being regarded as costs, are included in the market value of final output. A further difference is the inclusion of subsidies as factor incomes and their deduction in computing gross national product.

The costs which are excluded from national income but not gross

[9] *Ibid.,* p. 30.

[10] Antonio de Viti de Marco, *First Principles of Public Finance,* trans. by Edith Pavlo Marget (New York, 1936), p. 212.

national product are designated as "nonincome charges or nonfactor charges."[11] Depreciation and indirect business taxes are the largest components. The minor items consist of capital outlays charged to current account and accidental damage to fixed business capital; nontax liabilities mostly representing charges for government products and services not rendered by government enterprises, including rents and royalties, fines, and penalties; the surplus from government enterprises less subsidies; business transfer payments, chiefly corporate gifts to nonprofit institutions and allowances for consumer bad debts. There is also a balancing item called "statistical discrepancies."[12]

Both concepts include the value of net additions to inventory after correction for changes resulting from variations in prices. The product approach places inventories in gross private domestic investment, after having deducted the adjustment for price changes, while the corresponding factor costs are registered among various components of national income, the price adjustment being subtracted from corporate and noncorporate business profits. In other words, inventory gains and losses are regarded as akin to capital gains and losses and must therefore be excluded from estimates of current production or income.

NET INCOME OR NET PRODUCT TYPE OF BASE.   Most countries, including the United States, regard national income, proper, as the basic concept of the social product.[13] This is the concept which Shoup utilizes in his definition of the "income type of value added."[14] On the assumption that the product concept is defined so as to equal national income, he concludes that "The value-added tax is, then, either a tax on product or a tax on income, depending from which angle we choose to look at it."[15]

The net income or net product type of concept was adopted as one of two alternative measures in the Japanese proposal.[16] The National Tax Association Committee on Personal Property Taxation indicates a preference for this concept when it advocates the deduction of depreciation

[11] U.S. Department of Commerce, *National Income, 1954 Edition*, pp. 31, 41.

[12] *Ibid.*, pp. 33; 41–42; 170, n. 6; 171, n. 13.

[13] See *ibid.*, p. 31; United Nations, *National Income Statistics* (New York, 1948), p. 17.

[14] Shoup, "Theory and Background of the Value-Added Tax," *Proceedings of the Forty-Eighth Annual Conference of the National Tax Association, 1955* (Sacramento, Calif., 1956), p. 9.

[15] *Ibid.*, p. 7.

[16] Shoup Mission, *Second Report on Japanese Taxation* (Tokyo, 1950), pp. 17 f.

rather than total capital outlays.[17] As previously noted, there has been an upward trend in the number of students of the value-added tax who assume that depreciation at least, if not additional capital outlays, should be deductible.

Little attention has been paid in theoretical discussion of the tax base to "nonfactor charges" other than depreciation. To the extent that they have been considered, there seems to be general agreement that indirect taxes, nontax charges, and bad debts should be excluded from the tax base, solutions which are consistent with the net income type measure. The question of contributions to nonprofit institutions has been ignored, although such contributions made by corporations are classified as business transfer payments in the national accounts and therefore excluded from national income. Outlays on capital items charged to current expense would presumably be deductible along with other current purchases from outside firms. However, in the French law of fractional payments which, as a gross product type of tax, also encountered this problem, some of these items called "products rapidly consumed" were placed in a special category lying between current expenditures and capital outlays and were deductible at only 50 percent of their value, a system which proved excessively cumbersome. The treatment of subsidies has also been ignored although they should be included in the net income type base if the principles of national income accounting are followed. Apparently some subsidies were incorporated in the income-type base of the Japanese bill because profits under the addition procedure were the same as profits subject to the income tax, and the latter included certain subsidies.[18]

Except for a brief discussion by Shoup, no consideration has been given in this country to the problem of taxing a firm's production for its own use and the personal consumption of the owner under the value-added tax although state sales taxes often apply to such values. Under the Japanese income-type tax, the definition of a concern's value added automatically includes the cost of production on force account and the owner's personal consumption. Likewise, the French law of fractional payments and value-added tax have always taxed the manufacture of

---

[17] "Report of the Committee on Personal Property Taxation on Possible Substitutes for Ad Valorem Taxation of Tangible Personal Property Used in Business," *Proceedings of the Forty-Sixth Annual Conference on Taxation of the National Tax Association, 1953* (Sacramento, Calif., 1954), p. 390.

[18] Letter from Professor Hanya Ito (Oct. 7, 1953).

products on force account when comparable market transactions are taxable.

The value of additions to inventory after adjustments for inventory profits and losses arising from changes in the price level should also be included in the income-type base if the principles of national income accounting are to be observed. However, aside from Shoup, proponents of value-added taxation have generally assumed cash accounting, which allows the deduction of all purchases regardless of whether they are sold or added to inventories. Shoup describes the inventory accounting for the net income type base as follows:

Under the income type of value-added concept, an increment in inventory for the economy as a whole represents a value added that must be taken into account. The way to take it into account is to stipulate that each firm must use the following formula to compute the income type of the value-added concept: sales, plus excess of closing over opening inventory, less purchases from other firms. Alternatively, if the "addition method" is employed, it is enough to follow the usual rule for computation of profit that includes in cost of goods sold the excess of the initial inventory over the final inventory.[19]

For example, the addition procedure under the Japanese tax bill, which utilized the net income type base, allowed for inventory accumulation by computing net profits according to income tax rules.

The extent to which inventories are taken into consideration will vary with the accounting practices of the individual firm. The value of inventories at the end of the period may be limited to the invoice cost of materials and direct production costs or it may include general, administrative, and even selling expenditures.[20] Whether inventory profits or losses arising from changes in the price level are removed from the tax base will also depend upon the accounting practices adopted by the individual firms and permitted by the tax administration.[21] Given the method of inventory valuation, the larger the value of final inventory, the greater the amount of profits included in the tax base.

[19] Shoup, "Theory and Background of the Value-Added Tax," *Proceedings, National Tax Association, 1955,* p. 15. Under the subtraction formula the deductible purchases would have to be limited to those which did not enter inventories.

[20] W. A. Paton, "The Cost Approach to Inventories," *Journal of Accountancy,* LXII (Oct., 1941), 300.

[21] See J. Keith Butters, *Effects of Taxation: Inventory Accounting and Policies* (Boston, 1949), *passim.*

CONSUMPTION-TYPE BASE. A second concept which may be used to define the base of the value-added tax is one which Shoup has designated as the "consumption type of value-added."[22] This concept may utilize either of two formulas, "the *deduction variant*" or "the *interest-exclusion variant*."[23] The first allows the deduction of all outlays on capital investment and inventories while the second uses the net income type base less a deduction for interest. They are alternative measures because "it comes to the same thing whether deduction of the purchase price in the first year is allowed, or whether it is disallowed, and, in exchange, the taxpayer is allowed to deduct in later years both depreciation and the return earned on the investment."[24] This type of measure conforms with the income concept developed by Fisher and is designed to approximate a "true retail sales tax"[25] or a spendings tax levied directly. The deduction variant limits the tax base to sales to ultimate consumers or retail sales, proper. It resembles a subcategory in the product approach of the national income accounts, "personal consumption expenditures," although, as indicated below, it is not the same item.

As in the case of the income-type measure, nonfactor charges other than capital allowances have not been considered despite the fact that the treatment of indirect taxes and subsidies is an important issue. Because the consumption-type measure is derived from the net income type, indirect taxes are presumably deductible; and they were deductible in the Japanese bill. However, they are part of "personal consumption expenditures," and whether or not they should be included in a substitute for retail sales taxation is a debatable issue discussed in a later section of this chapter.

GROSS PRODUCT OR GROSS INCOME TYPE OF BASE. Adams recommends a base which suggests the concept of gross national product rather than national income or consumption. He describes his proposal as a "sales tax with a credit or refund for taxes paid by the producer or dealer (as purchaser) on goods bought for resale or for necessary use in the production of goods for sale."[26] Thus, the base includes deprecia-

---

[22] Shoup, "Theory and Background of the Value-Added Tax," *Proceedings, National Tax Association, 1955*, p. 9.

[23] *Ibid.*, p. 12.

[24] *Ibid.*

[25] *Ibid.*, p. 8.

[26] Adams, "Fundamental Problems of Federal Income Taxation," *Quarterly Journal of Economics*, XXXV (Aug., 1921), 553. Von Siemens adopted a similar tax base except that he deducted outlays rather than taxes.

tion and possibly some or all of the other nonfactor charges listed by the Department of Commerce although Adams explicitly mentions only depreciation. His treatment of services is not clear; he may have intended to tax them and allow a deduction when they were purchased or to exempt them and allow no deduction. The Department of Commerce has adopted "a working definition of final product as a purchase that is not resold, and of intermediate product as one that is resold," which is very similar to Adams' definition of the tax base.[27] It also advances an alternative definition of a final product as "a purchase that is not charged to current cost whereas an intermediate product is one that is so charged."[28] It gives the following explanation of how these definitions lead to the measure of gross national product:

The total value of final products can thus be broken down into elements consisting of the total product of each producing unit less its purchases of intermediate products. However, for each producing unit the difference between the value of its product and its intermediate purchases consists of the incomes that accrue in the course of production (wages and salaries, interest, profits, etc.) plus certain "nonincome" charges against the value of its production, the most important of which are taxes (such as property, excise, and sales taxes) and depreciation charges for the wear and tear and obsolescence of fixed capital.

Thus, since (1) the value of the final product of the economy equals the sum of the total product of each producing entity less its purchases of intermediate products, and (2) for each producing entity, product less intermediate purchases equals income plus nonincome charges against the value of production, it follows that (3) for the economy as a whole the total value of final product equals the sum of incomes accruing in production plus nonincome charges against the value of production.[29]

Adams' definition is apparently utilized in the tax bill sponsored by Smoot and is quoted by Arant for his own definition of value added.[30] In the tax proposal for the State of New York, the base is to be computed by deducting the cost of materials and supplies that enter into sales rather than taxes while services are clearly exempt; and a similar defi-

[27] U.S. Department of Commerce, *National Income, 1954 Edition*, p. 31.

[28] *Ibid.*

[29] *Ibid.*

[30] H. R. 8245, Title IX, Sec. 900(3), *Congressional Record* (Nov. 4, 1921), 7295; Arant, "The Place of Business Taxation in the Revenue Systems of the States," *Taxes*, XV (Apr., 1957), 199.

nition is used by the Brookings Institution.[31] Studenski, who favors the net income concept but considers the inclusion of depreciation for reasons of expediency, would allow the deduction of indirect taxes in either case.[32] Mount includes depreciation but deducts all taxes paid by business firms.[33] As previously noted, cash accounting is generally assumed so that inventory accumulation escapes the tax base in the current period.

The French law of fractional payments, in force from 1948 until 1953, when a 50 percent deduction for certain capital outlays was introduced, was a gross product type of tax which included both depreciation and indirect taxes in the base. It also used cash accounting for inventories.

Situs of Tax Base

The national accounts measure income and product derived from productive factors owned by residents of the United States rather than income originating in factors physically located within its geographical boundaries. International transactions appear on the product side of the accounts as net foreign investment which includes net exports of goods and services; net gifts received from abroad; and net receipts of wages and salaries, interest, dividends, and branch profits.[34] They should also include net receipts of rents and royalties and net equity in all undistributed profits; but, because of inadequate data, they do not.[35]

The implications of the above procedure for the value-added tax is that the base should include factor incomes received by residents from abroad and exclude factor incomes belonging to foreign claimants. However, being collected only from business firms, sales taxes are not a convenient method for implementing the residence principle. Thus, the value-added tax has usually been conceived as a tax on income origi-

---

[31] *Proceedings of the Twenty-Second Annual Conference of the National Tax Association, 1929,* p. 126; Brookings Institution, *Report on a Survey of the Organization and Administration of the State and County Governments of Alabama,* p. 338.

[32] Studenski, The Place of a "Value-Added" Tax in a War Time Fiscal Program (Preliminary Memorandum, mimeo., Apr. 6, 1942), pp. 23–24, 26.

[33] Mount, "A Re-examination of Taxation Fundamentals," *American Management Series,* No. 67 (New York, 1941), pp. 11, 13, 18.

[34] U.S. Department of Commerce, *National Income, 1954 Edition,* p. 35.

[35] Shoup, *Principles of National Income Analysis,* pp. 185–86.

nating from factors employed within a given geographical area. In conformity with this concept, income produced within the area would remain in the tax base, even though received by nonresidents, while income received by residents from factors located abroad would be excluded. Meanwhile, use of the destination principle as in France reflects a concept of national consumption as it were, while use of the destination principle under an income principle of sales taxation would reflect a concept of national expenditure, including outlays for investment as well as consumption.

Scope of the Tax

The advocates of value-added taxation have generally assumed that the scope of the tax would be limited to business enterprise. Business as defined in the national accounts contributes around four fifths of the total national income and product.[36]

Probably the most difficult problem in designing a value-added tax is the question of what to include in the definition of business. The United States Department of Commerce classifies all producing units, both business and nonbusiness, according to the following categories: manufacturing; agriculture, forestry, and fisheries; mining; contract construction; wholesale and retail trade; finance, insurance, and real estate; transportation; communication and public utilities; services; general government and government enterprises; and the rest of the world, which might be allocated among the other groups.[37] Except for general government and the part of the service industry represented by households and personal nonprofit organizations, these activities also belong to the business sector, proper. The latter comprises "all organizations which produce goods and services for sale at a price intended at least to approximate costs of production."[38] It encompasses all private profit-

[36] National income and product approximates the measure underlying the federal direct income tax, the major difference being the exclusion of all interest paid by the federal government from the national accounts. An example of estimates of the federal income tax base derived from national income statistics appears in Groves, *Postwar Taxation and Economic Progress* (New York, 1946), pp. 166–70.

[37] U.S. Department of Commerce, *National Income, 1954 Edition*, p. 66.

[38] *Ibid.*, p. 40.

making enterprises, mutual financial institutions, cooperatives, and nonprofit organizations servicing business.[39]

The value-added tax might include all the above business activities. However, exclusions and exemptions of certain activities are often envisaged either because of varying concepts of business activity or the difficulty of defining the tax base for a particular industry. Agriculture, professional occupations, and all nonprofit institutions are sometimes excluded for the first reason while financial institutions have sometimes been excluded for the second. The base may also be reduced by exemptions for the benefit of special industries and by administrative exemptions. Finally, in the United States, the tax may not be applied to certain transactions because of constitutional restrictions. The Federal Constitution, for example, prevents a tax on exports. Moreover, the extent to which the courts would uphold a tax on instrumentalities of subordinate levels of government is uncertain.[40] On the state level, the Federal Constitution limits the application of taxes with respect to interstate commerce and federal instrumentalities while individual state constitutions may impose additional restrictions.

Most Controversial Issues in Definition of Aggregate Tax Base

Depreciation, indirect taxes, subsidies, and imputations are the most controversial aspects in the definition of the tax base.

DEPRECIATION.   The deduction of depreciation on fixed capital in computing national income, proper, is based on the assumption that replacement of such capital is necessary before income is available for other uses. The Department of Commerce has questioned the significance of the definition of final product which does not deduct capital replacement.[41] It attributes its own use of the gross concept to the difficulties of defining net capital and the lack of statistical data which prevents the computation of capital consumption allowances in terms of current prices.[42]

The deduction of depreciation on physical capital, only, is consistent

---

[39] Ibid.
[40] Letter from Professor C. Lowell Harriss, Columbia University, May 1, 1959.
[41] U.S. Department of Commerce, National Income, 1954 Edition, p. 38.
[42] Ibid., p. 43.

with the views of most classical economists.[43] Ricardo, however, defines the net revenue or produce of a country as the difference between the value of the total output and the sum required to maintain the working population as well as physical capital. He distinguishes between net and gross product for the economy as a whole in the following quotation:

It is of importance to distinguish clearly between gross revenue and net revenue, for it is from the net revenue of a society that all taxes must be paid. Suppose that all the commodities in the country, all the corn, raw produce, manufactured goods, etc. which could be brought to market in the course of the year, were of the value of 20 millions, and that in order to obtain this value, the labour of a certain number of men was necessary, and that the absolute necessaries of these labourers required an expenditure of 10 millions. I should say that the gross revenue of such society was 20 millions, and its net revenue 10 millions. It does not follow from this supposition, that the labourers should receive only 10 millions for their labour; they might receive 12, 14, or 15 millions, and in that case they would have 2, 4, or 5 millions of the net income. The rest would be divided between landlords and capitalists; but the whole net income would not exceed 10 millions. . . .[44]

It should be noted that he defines gross revenue as being net of depreciation on physical capital.[45]

An interesting memorandum relevant to this issue has been found in a copy of Ricardo's *Principles* at the library of his residence at Gatcombe Park. It is inserted at the close of the chapter entitled "Taxes on Raw Produce," and describes the laborer as an individual business firm which, the author implies, must also replace its capital. The inscription reads as follows:

The labourer is in the same situation which any other manufacturer is in. He gives his labours, and the food and necessaries which are actually necessary to support him is [sic] the price of that labour, while the additional luxuries and comforts which he can obtain are the profits upon his capital, the labour of his body. Then if we could by any means distinguish these two

---

[43] See Adam Smith, *An Inquiry into the Nature and Causes of the Wealth of Nations* (The Modern Library, New York, 1937), pp. 271–72; Alfred Marshall, *Principles of Economics* (8th ed., London, 1938), pp. 79–82.

[44] Piero Sraffa (ed.), with the collaboration of M. H. Dobb, *The Works and Correspondence of David Ricardo* (Royal Economic Society, Cambridge, Eng., 1951), I, 421 f.

[45] *Ibid.*, p. 388.

sums, *viz.* the price given him for labour and his profit upon it, the price given him for labour would be a standard measure of value. . . .[46]

The editor, J. H. Hollander, claims that the inscription is in Ricardo's handwriting. However, the recent Sraffa edition of Ricardo's works, which refers to the memorandum without reproducing it, reports that although the handwriting resembles Ricardo's, it is probably not his.[47] As the preceding quotation from Ricardo indicates, the first part of the observation is consistent with Ricardo's thinking; but the measure-of-value theory is not, for Ricardo would point out that the cost of production of the necessities would vary.

A number of economists have applied the term "capital" to human resources. Jean-Baptiste Say remarks that "Thus, the productive means of this description [human faculties of mind and body], which yield to an artisan the wages of 3 *fr.* a day, or of 1000 *fr.* a year, may be reckoned equivalent to a vested capital yielding an equal annual revenue."[48] Marshall writes that "the carpenter's skill is as direct a means of enabling him to satisfy other people's material wants, and therefore indirectly his own, as are the tools in his work-basket"; and he refers to the "investment of capital in the rearing and early training of the workers of England."[49] However, he believes that a failure to distinguish sharply between personal and material capital or wealth would cause confusion and that the terms "capital and wealth" should apply to external resources, only, when used without modifying adjectives.[50]

Some students of national income have considered the possibility of deducting depreciation on the human being. The allowances would be based on expenditures necessary for maintaining efficiency rather than the capitalization of earnings, the latter being an undesirable procedure in view of the fact that it would treat human beings as slaves.

Professor Kuznets, for example, calls attention to the inconsistency of the conventional methods of estimating national income which add the net return from capital to the gross return from labor, no attempt being

---

[46] J. H. Hollander (ed.), *Letters of David Ricardo to John Ramsay McCulloch, 1816–1823,* Publications of the American Economic Association, X., Nos. 5 and 6 (New York, 1896), 60.

[47] Sraffa, *Works and Correspondence of Ricardo,* VIII, 173, n. 2.

[48] Jean-Baptiste Say, *A Treatise on Political Economy,* trans. by C. R. Prinsep (3d American edition, Philadelphia, 1827), Book II, p. 246.

[49] Marshall, *Principles of Economics,* pp. 57, 561.

[50] *Ibid.,* pp. 58, 81.

made to provide allowances for depreciation or obsolescence with respect to "human capacity."[51] He suggests the possibility of classifying every wage and salary earner, entrepreneur, and holder of managerial and executive positions as independent enterprises and defining their net income as the difference between their compensation and the cost of maintaining and reproducing their capacity for service. He adds that even property income might be granted an allowance for the abstinence and foresight necessary for savings and investment. However, he points out that with this approach net national product or national income would become an "exceedingly minor magnitude."[52] Moreover, he reasons that the conventional procedure is the preferable one because men should work to consume rather than vice versa. He writes as follows:

We do not look upon human beings as enterprises, as units for the production of other goods; consequently, we do not view the raising and education of the younger generation or the sustenance of the working population as intermediate consumption destined to produce or sustain so many machines for performing labor, management, entrepreneurial, or capital-saving functions. It is this idea of economic goods existing for men, rather than men for economic goods, that gives point to the concept of ultimate consumption and special interest to national income as usually defined.[53]

The deduction of allowances for the maintenance of human capital would, of course, seriously undermine the base of a general income tax unless there were a very limited definition of human depreciation. For example, Professor Walter Lotz has favored the following deductions from the base of the income tax in addition to those for the minimum of subsistence of a worker and his family: reserves for inability to work and for unemployment; interest and amortization on educational and training expenditures; provision for survivors and cost of burial; an allowance for the unproductive period of old age if there is no pension system; the outlays on equipment and working space if not supplied by an employer; and, finally, travel expenses to and from work.[54]

In commenting on Lotz's views, Professor Henry Simons reaches a conclusion similar to Kuznets. He suggests that it is better to note the limitations of the conventional concept of income than to destroy it.

[51] Simon Kuznets, *National Income and Its Composition* (New York, 1941), I, 38.
[52] *Ibid.*, p. 37.
[53] *Ibid.*, pp. 37 f.
[54] From a quotation in Henry C. Simons, *Personal Income Taxation*, p. 73.

Many of these deductions would be necessary in order to place recipients of personal-service incomes on a parity with those living from property. Even from this point of view, however, Lotz goes much too far. One may, with Schanz, inquire whether laborers live in order to work or work in order to live! It is necessary to distinguish between consumption and expense; one cannot include particular outlays under both heads. Furthermore, this is simply not a world in which laborers are dealt in and valued as property. While this imposes limitations on the income concept, for some purposes, it is presumably best to recognize and accept these limitations, instead of destroying the concept in trying to remove them.[55]

This statement is equally applicable to the base of the value-added tax. It is wiser to accept the conventional concept of national income while acknowledging any differential treatment of physical capital than to risk undermining the tax base through replacement allowances for human capital. However, in an era when heavy taxation imposed under conventional concepts favors intermediate consumption financed by organizations over expenditures for similar purposes financed by employees as individuals and stimulates evasion through disguising personal consumption expenditures as business outlays, tax students might do well to investigate the implications of a new concept of enterprise which regards the individual employee as a business concern.

INDIRECT BUSINESS TAXES AND SUBSIDIES.   In computations of total national income, the treatment of indirect taxes and subsidies is concerned with the problem of how to correct fictitious changes in national income caused by the use of shifted taxes to finance services to consumers or nonshifted taxes to finance services or subsidies to business.[56] It requires adjustments by price indexes—an impracticable procedure for defining the base of the value-added tax.

The national income problem which is relevant to the value-added tax is how to measure a firm's contribution to national income as measured in current prices. In this connection, Shoup points out that there are "two meanings in which an industry (or a firm) can be said to share in the production of national income."[57] If interest centers on the relative amounts which consumers are willing to spend on various products, the taxes should be included. If, on the other hand, the measure is supposed

---

[55] *Ibid.*, p. 74.
[56] See Shoup, *Principles of National Income Analysis,* pp. 265–66, 277.
[57] *Ibid.*, p. 240.

to reveal the amounts available to factor owners in the business enterprise, the taxes should be deducted.

In line with this approach, if the value-added tax is viewed as an indirect personal tax or even a charge for the payment of public services to business, it seems reasonable to assume that other indirect taxes should as a rule be included in the tax base. They would, for example, be automatically included under a direct spendings tax. If they are deducted, they reduce the relative tax burden on the products concerned; and a direct reduction of the other indirect taxes seems preferable to an indirect one.

Under the unusual concepts in which the value-added tax is not expected to be shifted forward, there might be some justification in allowing the deduction of indirect taxes. The measures would then be intended to reflect the amounts available to factor owners in the business enterprises.

Even if it were decided to include indirect taxes in the tax base it would be logical to deduct any indirect taxes considered a price for governmental services to business on the ground that the government is analogous to an independent supplier. As previously noted, this is presumably a minor consideration except for the value-added tax itself.

A much deeper study of the problems raised by indirect taxes in defining value added for tax purposes is required than has been undertaken here. Also, there are the further problems, not considered in this book, of whether subsidies should be treated as negative indirect taxes and of the extent to which a value-added tax should be allowed as a deduction in computing the tax base of a business firm under a simultaneously imposed direct income tax.

IMPUTATIONS. In addition to the imputations involved in estimating changes in inventories and fixed capital, the official measures of national income and product include the following items which do not take the form of monetary transactions and thus require imputations: wages and salaries in kind; food and fuel produced and consumed on farms; the rental value of owner-occupied homes; and interest imputed to financial intermediaries.

In principle, the base of the value-added tax should also include income and salaries in kind and food and fuel produced and consumed on farms. These items may be omitted on the ground of administrative convenience; and the National Tax Association has recommended that imputations be avoided in the interest of certainty.[58] Nevertheless, if the tax is heavy, considerations of equity and economic effects militate against their exclusion, especially in view of the growing importance of fringe benefits.[59]

The imputations in the national income accounts are based upon an estimation of the market value of similar goods and services, a difficult procedure in the case of wages and salaries in kind. In the case of food and fuel produced and consumed on farms, prices received by farmers for similar products are more easily ascertained.[60] Several American states, like Wisconsin, have endeavored to apply their income tax to farmers' consumption of their own products; and Groves believes that equity requires some provision of this nature, even if arbitrary.[61]

Rental and interest imputations involve theoretical as well as administrative problems. These issues are discussed below in connection with the computation of value added for the individual firm.

ALLOCATION OF AGGREGATE TAX BASE AMONG INDIVIDUAL FIRMS

After having decided upon the nature and scope of the tax base, it is necessary to apportion the total among taxpaying enterprises. The problem of allocation consists in distributing the base so that no portion escapes taxation and none is taxed more than once. De Viti de Marco calls this procedure "the depuration of incomes," which he applies to the direct income tax and describes as follows:

To sum up: the translation of gross income into net income, or what we shall call the 'depuration of incomes,' is merely a technical accounting procedure, by means of which the total quantity of direct goods produced annually in a country and the corresponding total tax-burden are divided among those engaged in production and among the taxpayers. No part of so-called gross or total income escapes taxes on income. The deduction

---

[58] "Report of the Committee on Personal Property Taxation on Possible Substitutes for Ad Valorem Taxation of Tangible Personal Property Used in Business," *Proceedings, National Tax Association, 1953,* p. 390.

[59] See Hugh Holleman Macaulay, Jr., *Fringe Benefits and their Federal Tax Treatment* (New York, 1959).

[60] U.S. Department of Commerce, *National Income, 1954 Edition,* p. 46.

[61] Groves, *Postwar Taxation and Economic Progress,* pp. 238–39.

of expenses of production, as revealed by the budget of each individual business, prevents any part of income from being taxed more than once.[62]

His statement is applicable to the value-added tax as well as the income tax. The difference between the two approaches lies in the way income is "depurated" among individual taxpayers. The base of the income tax is allocated among individual income recipients, and the base of the value-added tax is distributed among business units. The former constitutes a direct and personal approach while the latter is indirect and either less personal or wholly impersonal.

Whether the base of the value-added tax is the net income type, the consumption type, or the gross product type, it may be computed either through the income or product approach. Items are usually added under the income approach while the product approach involves a subtraction procedure for the most part. In measuring national output, the addition procedure is more suitable for income flows and the subtraction procedure for product flows. Similarly, the addition method seems appropriate for the net income type base and the interest-exclusion variant of the consumption-type base. The subtraction method is more readily applicable to the deduction variant of the consumption-type base and to the gross product type.

Net Income Type Base: Income Approach or Addition Procedure

The net income type base for the individual firm may be computed by adding its wages and salaries; interest paid to individuals; and value-added profits which should include an estimated profit on the owner's personal consumption of the firm's products.[63] Each component must be defined to exclude value added by other firms and by the nonbusiness sectors. This procedure is patterned on the approach used in measuring national income, proper; but there are significant modifications in the method of measuring interest payments to individuals and in the treatment of rents.

WAGES AND SALARIES. The wage and salary component in the national accounts comprises the compensation of employees, whether in

---

[62] De Viti de Marco, *First Principles of Public Finance*, p. 221.

[63] Also, see Shoup, "Theory and Background of the Value-Added Tax," *Proceedings, National Tax Association, 1955*, p. 11.

money or in kind, and supplements to wages and salaries. The compensation of employees includes employee contributions to social insurance while employer contributions are part of supplementary compensation, which also covers such items as pension funds and compensation for injuries.[64] In principle, all the above items belong in the tax base even though not all are taxable under the federal income tax.

As in the case of the direct income tax, expense accounts are likely to create difficulty because they may either represent outlays which are deductible as current account purchases from other firms or they may be a form of supplementary compensation which should be part of the firm's tax base. Expense accounts are omitted in national income statistics as the data on wages and salaries are obtained from social security records of business payrolls which exclude expense accounts. During the discussions on the Japanese value-added tax, Japanese administrators favored treating all expense accounts as wages in order to prevent tax evasion, thus requiring firms to make direct payments when they had legitimate expenses;[65] and this is probably the best solution.

INTEREST PAID TO INDIVIDUALS. The direct measurement of interest paid to individuals in calculating the tax base differs from the procedure used in the United States national income accounts. Because of inadequate data, the Department of Commerce approximates interest paid to individuals by subtracting interest receipts from interest payments in the case of corporations.[66] The same principle is applicable to unincorporated firms; but, again, because of inadequate data, the Department of Commerce only counts their interest payments, interest receipts being treated as if received by individuals.[67] The approach suggested is preferable in calculating the tax base because following the procedure used by the Department of Commerce would require a special definition of value added for financial enterprises—an issue discussed later in this chapter.

One result of the procedure suggested is to tax interest received by business concerns on a basis net of certain expenses while interest received by individuals is taxed on a gross basis. However, the inequity

---

[64] U.S. Department of Commerce, *National Income, 1954 Edition*, p. 41.

[65] Bronfenbrenner, "The Japanese Value-Added Sales Tax," *National Tax Journal*, III (Dec., 1950), 305. The evaluation of other fringe benefits, which should be included, will also cause difficulty.

[66] U.S. Department of Commerce, *National Income, 1954 Edition*, p. 41.

[67] Shoup, *Principles of National Income Analysis*, p. 340.

is probably not important enough to warrant correction, which would have to be made by treating individual interest recipients as independent business firms engaged in the business of lending money and would therefore considerably complicate the administration.

Another result of this procedure is that receipts of interest from United States governments (federal, state, and local) are included in value added by business unless special provision is made for their deduction. Although this is not in conformity with principles of national income accounting, it may be logically maintained that business concerns function as financial enterprises when they receive interest.

PROFITS.   In order to compute value-added profits, certain adjustments must be applied to the figure computed for purposes of the income tax. In the first place, dividends received from other firms must be subtracted in order to prevent double counting. This procedure is used in national income accounting except that, as in the case of interest, dividends received by unincorporated firms are attributed directly to persons because of lack of data.[68] Furthermore, if the principles of national income accounting are followed, adjustments must be made to remove the effect on profits of capital gains and losses, which are not considered part of current production.[69] Depletion is added because the national accounts do not treat discoveries as capital formation or increased profits.[70] Also, state and local income taxes should be added because they are deducted for income-tax purposes while only indirect business taxes are deductible in the national accounts. In short, value-added profits approximate a firm's operating profits except that interest payments have been deducted. Whether, as in the Japanese consumption-type tax, a concern's receipts from sales of its own capital assets should be included in the tax base depends upon whether their omission would constitute a significant loophole. Indirect taxes and subsidies will not be taken into consideration here because of complex theoretical issues involved in this area which have not yet received adequate analysis.

PROFIT ON OWNER'S PERSONAL CONSUMPTION OF FIRM'S PRODUCTS. In principle the personal consumption by an owner of the firm's products should also be included in the tax base. Presumably the costs, exclusive of profits, of this consumption have already been integrated with

<hr />

[68] *Ibid.*
[69] U. S. Department of Commerce, *National Income, 1954 Edition*, pp. 41, 92.
[70] *Ibid.*

other components; but, if such consumption is to be treated equally with products sold on the market, an imputation should be made for estimated profits.

RENTS. Under the suggested formula for computing the tax base, rents from real property (or royalties), like other rental income, are treated as representing receipts from the supply of services rather than a type of factor income. Thus, the individual recipient of rents is regarded as a business concern in the rental business and computes his value added in the same way as a business organization.

In the national income accounts, on the other hand, the "rental income of persons" is classified as a type of factor income. It comprises only net rents from real property in the sense of net income from rents received by individuals who are not professional real estate operators,[71] the remaining elements of value added being merged with other items in the national accounts. Similarly, the rents received by unincorporated firms, including farmers, are partly recorded as "income of unincorporated enterprises," a net profit figure, and partly merged with other components of value added or with current costs. In the industrial classification, however, all the components of value added by individual landlords and concerns mainly engaged in the real estate business are placed in the real estate industry, a subcategory of the classification, "finance, insurance, and real estate."[72] In the case of concerns whose rental business is subordinate to other activities, rent receipts are part of general gross income and become merged with the various elements which make up the concern's value added and current costs.

The national income accounts include an imputation for rental incomes from owner-occupied dwellings; and, in principle, an imputation should be made in calculating the base of the value-added tax. No imputation is necessary for owner-occupied business premises, such rents being reflected in other elements of a firm's value added and purchases on current account.

Rental imputations may be based upon information on rents arising from similar property in the same neighborhood or the application of a rate of interest or profit to the estimated value of the property.[73] Despite administrative complexities, the inclusion in the tax base of imputed

---

[71] *Ibid.*, pp. 10, 42.
[72] *Ibid.*, p. 176, n. 1.
[73] *Ibid.*, p. 91; Shoup, *Principles of National Income Analysis*, p. 96.

rents on owner-occupied dwellings is desirable in the interest of equity. In 1962 imputed gross rents on owner-occupied nonfarm dwellings were estimated at around $12,399,000,000.[74] The figure for value added would, of course, be less by the amount of depreciation and other deductible expenses.

Net Income Type Base: Product Approach or Subtraction Procedure

The net income type base may also be computed through a subtraction procedure. The subtraction method applies the product approach under which certain outlays are deducted from certain receipts. The French system of deducting value-added taxes paid on deductible outlays from value-added taxes due on taxable turnover may also be used; and, as explained in Chapter 1, it is preferable, given rate differentiation.

The subtraction formula may be expressed as follows: receipts from sales (net of returns, cancellations, cash discounts, and bad debts), and from interest, rents, or the supply of other services *minus* current account purchases of goods and services from other firms, including all rental payments and interest payments to other firms, and depreciation *plus* personal consumption by the owner of a firm's products, capital investment on force account, and net additions to inventory.

OWNER'S PERSONAL CONSUMPTION OF FIRM'S PRODUCTS. The personal consumption by an owner of the firm's own products may be evaluated on the basis of market sales of similar products. In principle, retail sales should be used when the value-added tax is imposed through the retail stage although this might excessively complicate the administration. In the absence of similar market products, the imputation must be based upon cost.

CAPITAL INVESTMENT ON FORCE ACCOUNT. A firm's construction of plant and equipment for its own use may be measured at cost or, where practicable, at the market value of similar products. Shoup recommends the former method, which is undoubtedly the easier one to administer.[75] The French use market value when comparable products are sold on the market; otherwise, they estimate the cost.

[74] U.S. Department of Commerce, Office of Business Economics, *Survey of Current Business*, XLIII (July, 1963), Table 72, p. 39.
[75] Shoup, "Theory and Background of the Value-Added Tax," *Proceedings, National Tax Association, 1955*, p. 14.

INVENTORY ACCUMULATION.   Under the product approach it is necessary to take special account of inventory accumulation. This imputation may be made by computing the difference between the values of the opening and closing inventories, with no deductions allowed for purchases entering into inventories.

Summary of Net Income Type Formulas

The rules for computing the net income type base of the individual firm under the income approach or addition procedure and under the product approach or subtraction procedure are summarized in Table 2.

TABLE 2. Formulas for Computing the Net Income Type Base of the Individual Firm

Income Approach or Addition Procedure	Product Approach or Subtraction Procedure
Wages and salaries Interest paid to individuals Value-added profits[b]	Receipts from net sales,[a] from the supply of services including rentals, and from interest Investment on force account Inventory accumulation Owner's personal consumption of firm's products *Minus* current account purchases of goods and services from other firms[c] *Minus* depreciation

[a] Net of returns, cancellations, cash discounts, and bad debts.
[b] Profits should include estimated profits on the owner's personal consumption of the firm's products; but the imputation may be omitted for administrative reasons.
[c] Including outlays on interest paid to other businesses and on rents.

In order to visualize how the tax would be applied in the case of a particular firm, imagine a concern, the Woodland Furniture Company, which manufactures home furnishings. Then assume that in a given month the firm has taxable sales of $195,000; spends $72,500 on materials and supplies of which $25,000 is added to inventories, $2,000 for fees to a furniture designer; $500 for interest paid on a bank loan, and $5,000 for a new machine. Its payroll equals $85,000 excluding $15,000 of wages paid to its own workers to construct a new building, which are capitalized rather than expensed. The monthly depreciation charges on its existing capital is $10,000. Its operating profits during the month amount to $65,500 of which $5,000 is paid out to individual bondholders. Then its net income type of base would equal $150,000 computed as follows under the addition and subtraction procedures:

Addition Procedure		Substraction Procedure		
Payroll	$ 85,000	Taxable sales		$195,000
Interest paid to		Building by own force[a]		15,000
individuals	5,000	Deductible outlays		
Net profits	60,000	Materials and supplies[b]	$47,500	
		Fees to designer	2,000	
		Interest paid to bank	500	
		Depreciation[c]	10,000	
				−60,000
Value added	$150,000			$150,000

[a] Strictly speaking, there should also be an allowance for overhead costs but it would have needlessly complicated the exposition.

[b] Material and supplies of $72,000 less $25,000 of inventories.

[c] As the $5,000 new machine is capitalized, its purchase does not affect the tax base until it is depreciated.

Comparison of Above Formulas with Income-type Base in Japanese Bill

In certain respects the procedure for arriving at value added suggested above differs considerably from the definition of the net income type base in the Japanese tax bill which requires the summation of profits as computed for the national income tax, net payments of interest and rent, and payrolls. According to the Japanese bill, therefore, profits coincide with ordinary net profits rather than value-added profits, strictly speaking. Furthermore, "net" with respect to payments of interest and rent means a concern's payments less its receipts, a method which follows the national-income procedure of handling interest and dividends.

While, in the case of general business, the rule for computing value added in the Japanese bill is adminstratively superior to the formulas suggested above, it suffers from certain important disadvantages which, in fact, also characterize the bill's consumption-type tax computed under the subtraction procedure. For one thing, rents are taxed on a gross rather than a net basis. Its chief defect, however, lies in the special definitions of value added required for property-management and financial enterprises.

Firms engaged solely in managing real estate create a problem in defining the tax base. As part of the business sector, they should be taxed on their contribution to value added by business. However, they should be allowed to deduct their rent receipts which have been previously taxed in the hands of the payers. If all their receipts were from business real estate, they would be entitled to complete exemption. Actually, they might even have a negative value added because, as business firms, they are entitled to a deduction for purchases of intermediate goods and services on current account and for depreciation, items which have presumably been part of gross rents taxed to the payers. The Japanese bill exempts the property-management business in its entirety; but this removes from the aggregate tax base the portion of value added arising from service charges from the management of property used in non-business sectors.[76]

A problem similar to the one created in the rent component by property-management concerns is engendered in the rent, interest, and profit components by financial enterprises. The general rule for computing value added in the Japanese bill breaks down when applied to financial intermediaries where it reduces value added to a negligible or even a negative amount.

In order to circumvent this type of difficulty in the national income accounts, the Department of Commerce has introduced nonmonetary income and product flows which are designed to account for transactions implicit in the dealings of financial institutions but which are not expressed in monetary terms. For example, on the income side of the accounts of financial concerns, other than life insurance and all mutual companies, monetary interest payments are increased by the addition of "imputed interest payments" equal to income from property (dividends, interest, and sometimes net rents) less monetary interest paid. The difference between interest receipts and interest payments (monetary and imputed) is therefore reduced to zero. On the product side of the accounts an item, "imputed service charge receipts," equal to imputed interest payments is added to monetary service charge receipts.[77] It is as if depositors, policyholders, or security holders receive all property income earned by the financial institutions and hire these institutions to

---

[76] Bronfenbrenner, "The Japanese Value-Added Sales Tax," *National Tax Journal*, III (Dec., 1950), 301.

[77] U.S. Department of Commerce, *National Income, 1954 Edition*, pp. 46–47.

manage their funds or perform other financial services, paying them through monetary and imputed service charges.

The Department of Commerce gives a rough illustration of its computation of value added for commercial banks, which is reproduced in Table 3. In the interest of simplicity, dividends are ignored; and the calculation is in terms of gross product, no provision being made for depreciation or indirect taxes.

TABLE 3. Income and Product Account of a Commercial Bank,
Monetary and Imputed Transactions
(*Thousands of dollars*)

Income Account		*Product Account*	
Wages paid	50	Service charge receipts	105
Net interest paid	0	Monetary	10
Monetary interest paid on deposits	5	Imputed	95
Imputed interest paid on deposits	95	*Less* current account	
Less monetary interest received	100	purchases from other firms	25
Profit	30		
Income originating	80	Product originating	80

Source: U.S. Department of Commerce, *National Income, 1954 Edition* (Washington, D.C., 1954), p. 47.

As a result of the interest imputation, net interest paid by nonfinancial enterprises is reduced to the extent of their imputed interest receipts from commercial banks estimated according to the former's ownership of deposits. This partially offsets the corresponding increase in value added by the commercial banks. Also, because of the imputed interest payments, total interest paid to individuals and governments by all business including commercial banks (the "net interest" component in the national accounts) is increased by the difference between the imputed interest payments and the imputed interest receipts of nonfinancial business.[78] The addition of dividends received by commercial banks would increase the items "monetary interest received" and "imputed interest payments" of banks as well as the imputed interest receipts of nonfinancial business, of governments, and of persons.[79]

On the product side of the accounts of commercial banks, value added is increased through imputed service charge receipts. This is partially offset by a reduction in the value added of nonfinancial business through

[78] *Ibid.*, p. 47.
[79] *Ibid.*, and p. 100.

an increase in its current account purchases from other firms equal to imputed service charges paid to banks which are in turn equal to imputed interest received from banks.[80]

Except for commercial banks, imputed interest receipts are allocated entirely to persons rather than business because of inadequate data.[81] In the case of life insurance companies, for example, all receipts of interest and dividends are attributed to individual policyholders. Premiums and claims are assumed to cancel each other and are therefore treated as transfers among persons. Consequently, value added by life insurance companies consists of operating expenses–which are financed through imputed service charges paid by policyholders–exclusive of purchases on current account.[82]

The above procedures have not received complete acceptance. The Department of Commerce makes the following comment with respect to the banking imputations:

The above description of the measurement of imputed flows in banking is only a brief summary of a complex subject which is still the subject of lively discussion among technicians in the field. The procedure has been criticized in general as unduly complex and, more specifically, as based on certain assumptions of doubtful validity. Particular exception has been taken to the assumption that all banking services not explicitly charged for are rendered to depositors and that the borrowers of bank loans are not involved, as well as to the assumption that these services are distributed in proportion to the ownership of the volume of deposits irrespective of turnover.[83]

If the above procedures are controversial for purposes of national income accounting, they would be even more so if applied in the definition of a tax base. In the Japanese bill, which contains the only practical application of the value-added tax to banking, imputations are wisely avoided. Instead, a special definition has been devised for all financial intermediaries. The formula for the consumption-type tax is as follows: total receipts inclusive of rent, interest, and dividends less rental receipts, *interest payments*, purchases of goods and services from other firms, and other business taxes.[84] Under the net income type tax, the formula must have been payrolls, rent paid, and profits as computed for the income

[80] *Ibid.,* p. 47.
[81] *Ibid.,* p. 102.
[82] *See ibid.,* p. 48.
[83] *Ibid.,* p. 47.
[84] Bronfenbrenner, "The Japanese Value-Added Sales Tax," *National Tax Journal,* III (Dec., 1950), 307, Table I, B.

tax. In principle, the effect of these procedures on nonfinancial business should have been a decrease in their net interest payments and taxable profits equal, respectively, to the interest and dividends paid to banks or, in other words, a commensurate increase in their current account purchases from other firms. Actually, the Japanese bill does not modify the formula for nonfinancial enterprises so that the interest and dividends involved are subjected to a double tax.

Consumption-Type Base

FORMULA FOR DEDUCTION VARIANT. The deduction variant of the consumption type of value added is the base most easily computed. It approximates retail sales to ultimate consumers and differs from the income-type base in the generosity of its capital allowances, permitting deductions for total capital outlays and for inventory accumulation rather than only depreciation.[85]

The formula may be stated as follows: receipts from net sales, from the supply of services including rentals, and from interest *minus* purchases of all goods and services from other firms (including interest paid to other concerns, and rental payments), whether on current or capital account. Inventory accumulation and investment outlays are therefore automatically excluded from the tax base. Deliveries for the personal use of the owner should be taxed in principle. They are not taxed in the consumption-type base of the Japanese bill to the extent that value has been added by the taxpaying concern, probably because of an oversight. Also, in the Japanese bill, the consumption-type base includes receipts from the sales of capital assets.[86] Although this is consistent neither with the concept of the base as sales to ultimate consumers nor with national income concepts, it is probably necessary to avoid a loophole. The problems of situs are the same as those in the income-type formulas.

Like the definition suggested for the net income type base, it avoids a separate definition for property-management and financial businesses.

[85] See Shoup, "Theory and Background of the Value-Added Tax," *Proceedings, National Tax Association, 1955*, p. 11.

[86] Bronfenbrenner, "The Japanese Value-Added Sales Tax," *National Tax Journal*, III (Dec., 1950), 304; Local Autonomy Agency and Local Finance Commission, *Local Tax Law, 1950*, art. 30(6).

However, there is a new consideration arising from the fact that the deduction of capital outlays and inventory accumulation create the possibility of a negative value added for any one period which must be offset against the value added in other periods. The Japanese bill allows a five-year carryforward.[87] A carryforward possesses the administrative advantage of avoiding refunds of taxes previously paid. One possible disadvantage is the fact that when a firm's value added is negative, a carryforward creates uncertainty as to the amount of its ultimate tax bill. A carryback would let the firm know where it stands. On the other hand, when value added is positive, a carryback creates uncertainty because the value added in the current year may be reduced by capital outlays of subsequent years. A carryfoward would avoid this problem because future capital outlays would not affect the current tax bill.[88] If, as seems likely, uncertainty during a period of expansion is less injurious than at other times, a carryforward is preferable.

The computation of the deduction variant may also be made through the income approach. Depreciation is added to the addition formula for the net income type base while capital outlays and net additions to inventory are subtracted.[89] The formulas are summarized in Table 4.

TABLE 4. Formulas for Computing the Deduction Variant of the Consumption-Type Base of the Individual Firm

Income Approach or Addition Procedure	*Product Approach or Subtraction Procedure*
Wages and salaries	Receipts from net sales,[a] from supply of services including rents, and from interest
Interest paid to individuals	
Income type of value-added profits[b]	
Depreciation	Owner's personal consumption of firm's products
Sales of capital assets	
Minus capital outlays	*Minus* all purchases from other firms[c]
Minus net additions to inventories	

  [a] Net of returns, cancellations, cash discounts, and bad debts, and including sales of capital assets.
  [b] Profits should include estimated profits on the owner's personal consumption of the firm's products; but the imputation may be omitted for administrative reasons.
  [c] Including outlays on interest paid to other businesses and on rents.

[87] *Local Tax Law, 1950,* art. 31.
[88] Also, see Shoup, "Some Considerations on the Incidence of the Corporation Income Tax," *The Journal of Finance,* VI (June, 1951), 195–96.
[89] Shoup, "Theory and Background of the Value-Added Tax," *Proceedings, National Tax Association, 1955,* p. 11.

In the case of the Woodland Furniture Company, the consumption type of base would amount to $115,000, computed as follows under the addition and subtraction procedures:

Addition Procedure		*Subtraction Procedure*		
Payroll	$ 85,000	Taxable sales		$195,000
Interest paid to		Deductible outlays		
individuals	5,000	Materials and		
Net profits	60,000	supplies	$72,500	
Depreciation	10,000	Fees to designer	2,000	
Minus building	−15,000	Interest paid		
machine	− 5,000	to bank	500	
inventories	−25,000	Machine	5,000	
				−80,000
Value added	$115,000			$115,000

INTEREST-EXCLUSION VARIANT.   The interest-exclusion variant of the consumption-type base is computed by subtracting interest on investment from the income-type base.[90] Either the addition or subtraction procedure may be used, interest being deducted from both the income and product sides of the account.

Gross Product Type of Base

The gross product or gross income type of base is most readily computed through the product approach and hence the subtraction procedure. In principle, the formula should be stated as follows: gross receipts from sales, from the supply of services including rentals, and from interest *minus* purchases of goods and services from other firms on current account (including interest paid to other concerns and rents paid), *plus* the value of capital investment on force account, inventory accumulation, and deliveries for owner's personal consumption. However, net rather than gross sales might be used. Moreover, every proponent of value-added taxation who has considered the issue has assumed the deduction of all purchases on current account including those accumulated in inventories even if depreciation is to be included in the tax base. One possible formula for this concept is given in Table 5.

As in the case of the other formulas, the base is defined so as to

[90] *Ibid.*, p. 12.

TABLE 5. Formulas for Computing the Gross Product Type of Base of
the Individual Firm

Income Approach or Addition Procedure	Product Approach or Subtraction Procedure

Wages and salaries
Interest paid to individuals
Income type of value-added
    profits excluding subsidies[b]
Depreciation
	Net receipts from sales,[a] from the
	    supply of services including rents,
	    and from interest
	Capital investment on force account
	Inventory accumulation
	Owner's personal consumption of
	    firm's products
	Minus purchases of goods and services
	    from other firms on current account[c]

[a] Net of returns, cancellations, cash discounts, and bad debts.

[b] Profits should include estimated profits on the owner's personal consumption of the firm's products; but this imputation may be omitted for administrative reasons.

[c] Including outlays on interest paid to other businesses and on rents.

avoid the problem of separate definitions for property management and financial enterprises. The absence of capital allowances constitutes the only departure from the other concepts; and the differential effects anticipated from the respective provisions concerning investment goods should be the dominant reason for selecting a particular base. A gross product type of base was utilized in the French law of fractional payments; and as explained in the following chapter it has generally been used for the ordinary type of retail sales tax.

The gross product type of tax base for the Woodland Furniture Company would be $160,000. Depreciation of $10,000 would have been added to the addition side of the formula while there would have been no deduction for depreciation on the subtraction side.

International Transactions

There is neither time nor space in this study to enter into a detailed discussion of the definition of the tax base of an individual firm when products are bought and sold over the boundaries of the taxing jurisdiction. Generally speaking, if the origin principle is applied, the tax base must include the value of exports deemed to have arisen in the taxing jurisdiction while purchases of imports are deductible up to their import value. In order to attribute values to the proper jurisdiction, it is necessary to apply either a system of source rules or allocation formulas such as the one used in the Japanese value-added tax.[91] In the case of the destination principle, imports of deductible purchases may be subtracted in computing the tax base for the individual firm in the same way as purchases from domestic firms while the export transaction must be exempt from tax and the exporter reimbursed for any value-added tax incorporated in the prices of the products which he purchased.

[91] For a brief analysis of this issue, see Clara K. Sullivan, *The Search for Tax Principles in the European Economic Community* (Chicago, 1963), pp. 47–48.

Chapter 6

The Administration of
the Tax on Value Added

Many proponents of value-added taxation have believed that the measure offers the advantage of administrative simplicity as compared with other general taxes for which it is a likely substitute. In fact, Adams favors a business tax on " 'modified gross income' " or " 'approximate net income' " largely on the grounds that the administrative and compliance problems would be much less than those of a net income tax which, in turn, would be easier to administer than a tax on gross turnover with differentiated rates.[1] In a brief analysis, Studenski indicates his agreement with Adams, and, in addition, suggests that the value-added tax would probably be easier to administer than a single-stage manufacturers' or retailers' sales tax although he observes that these single-stage taxes are administratively superior to the value-added tax in some respects.[2] The Brookings Institution, Arant, and Mount are among others who have emphasized the administrative simplicity of the tax as compared with one on business net income. Finally, Bronfenbrenner has stated that the value-added tax is superior to the single-stage retail sales tax chiefly because of its "ease of collection."[3] Obviously, there-

---

[1] Adams, "Fundamental Problems of Federal Income Taxation," *Quarterly Journal of Economics*, XXXV (Aug., 1921), 552; and "The Taxation of Business," *Proceedings of the Eleventh Annual Conference of the National Tax Association, 1917* (New Haven, Conn., 1918), p. 190.

[2] Studenski, The Place of a "Value-Added" Tax in a War Time Fiscal Program (Preliminary Memorandum, mimeo., Apr. 6, 1942), pp. 15–19, 27.

[3] Bronfenbrenner, "The Japanese Value-Added Sales Tax," *National Tax Journal*, III (Dec., 1950), 299 f.

fore, an appraisal of the administrative efficiency of the value-added tax as compared with the general measures which it may replace is an important consideration. In this study, it will be compared with other general taxes on current receipts.

The administrative and compliance problems involved in any tax will vary with the number of taxpayers, the frequency of returns, the rate of tax, the difficulty of identifying taxable persons, the problems encountered in computing the tax base, and, not least important, the attitude of taxpayers toward the tax. Consequently, it is necessary to consider the situation of the value-added tax with respect to the above variables.

NUMBER OF TAXPAYERS

The United States Treasury Department has observed that the number of taxpayers is a factor responsible for a considerable portion of administrative and compliance costs.[4] On this count, the value-added tax applied through the retail stage has a great advantage over taxes assessed directly on individual incomes, notably, the personal income tax or the spendings tax; some advantage over a retail sales tax because the value-added technique facilitates the exemption of small concerns; and probably no advantage over a general turnover tax; while it ranks below the corporate income tax viewed as an independent business tax. As in the case of a tax through the retail stage, the value-added method of collecting a manufacturers' or wholesalers' sales tax offers an advantage over the single-stage method with respect to an exemption for small concerns.

Comparison of Value-Added Tax with Taxes Assessed
Directly on Individual Income

Excluding agriculture and the professions, there are almost 5 million business firms in the United States.[5] The addition of agriculture and the

---

[4] U.S. Treasury Department, "Considerations Respecting a Federal Retail Sales Tax," *Hearings before the Committee on Ways and Means, House of Representatives, on Revenue Revision of 1943,* 78th Congress, 1st Session (Washington, D.C., 1943), p. 1119.

[5] U.S. Department of Commerce, Office of Business Economics, *Business Statistics: 1963* (Washington, D.C., 1963), p. 10.

professions would greatly increase the number. However, even the most comprehensive value-added tax would involve a much smaller number of taxpayers than the personal income tax. Individual returns under the United States Federal law currently amount to over 60 million.[6] A spendings tax of like scope would involve an equal number of taxpayers.

Moreover, the number of those paying the value-added tax would be reduced to a greater or less degree by a minimum administrative exemption. In 1942, when business firms other than agriculture and the professions amounted to around 3,000,000, Studenski estimated that the number of taxpayers could be kept down to 725,000 with a measure excluding agriculture and the professions and providing minimum exemptions based on gross receipts which varied from $20,000 to $50,000 according to industrial classification.[7] The most inclusive measure which he recommended covered 2,105,000 taxpayers. It applied to agriculture and the professions and allowed administrative exemptions of $5,000 to $10,000.[8] These figures are quoted merely to give some indication of the relative magnitudes involved. Basing exemptions on gross receipts rather than value added and varying exemptions with industrial classification provides administrative convenience at the expense of equity.

Comparison of Value-Added Tax with Other Sales Taxes

Studenski claims that a retail sales tax would have to cover twice as many taxpayers as a value-added tax of equivalent scope and revenue productivity because a large administrative exemption for smaller taxpayers would sacrifice too much revenue and would give an excessive competitive advantage to exempt firms.[9] The United States Treasury Department also reached the conclusion that the exemption of small firms under a retail sales tax was not feasible because of "competitive disturbances and discrimination."[10] As previously noted, the Shoup Mission

---

[6] U.S. Department of Commerce, Bureau of the Census, *Statistical Abstract of the United States: 1963*, 84th ed. (Washington, D.C., 1963), p. 397.

[7] Studenski, The Place of a "Value-Added" Tax in a War Time Fiscal Program (Preliminary Memorandum, mimeo., Apr. 6, 1942), p. 10.

[8] *Ibid.*

[9] *Ibid.*, pp. 18–19.

[10] U.S. Treasury Department, "Considerations Respecting a Federal Retail Sales Tax," *Hearings, Revenue Revision of 1943*, p. 1119.

decided that a retail sales tax was impracticable for Japan because small retail shops, which kept inadequate records or none at all, could not be exempt without eliminating a large part of the tax base.[11]

The advantage of the value-added technique in this respect lies in the fact that the tax is imposed upon all sales of business firms as contrasted with the system used by the retail sales tax of suspending the tax on sales for resale and imposing the tax on sales for final consumption or business use. An administrative exemption for small firms under the value-added tax would eliminate only the value added by the small firms. Under the retail sales tax, on the other hand, the exemption would include the total value of sales made by small firms.

It would be possible to restrict the administrative exemption under the retail sales tax to value added by small firms if the sales to such firms could be treated as final sales and therefore subject to tax. The original French manufacturers' sales tax used this system but abandoned it less than two years after its adoption when small producers were integrated with the suspensive regime.[12] In his treatise on the production tax, Larguier mentions no official reason for this step although his criticisms of the exemption indicate that he considers it excessive and therefore discriminatory.[13] Perhaps its abolition was to some extent the result of administrative difficulties like those encountered in Finland's manufacturers' sales tax where "determination of the firms exempt from the licensing requirements because of their small size is troublesome, partly because the status of some firms changes frequently."[14] The Canadian manufacturers' sales tax is applied on sales to small enterprises exempt from tax, but the exemptions are determined by administrative rulings and have apparently been quite restricted.[15] Likewise, the Swiss wholesalers' sales tax exempts concerns with sales of 35,000 francs (about $9,000) or less;[16] but, in view of current price levels, this limit is much below the original French exemption of a similar amount. In any event, the value-added technique is undoubtedly more efficient in this respect.

---

[11] Shoup Mission, *Report on Japanese Taxation* (4 vols., Tokyo, 1949), II, 166; Bronfenbrenner, "The Japanese Value-Added Sales Tax," *National Tax Journal,* III (Dec., 1950), 300.

[12] Émile Larguier, *Traité des taxes à la production* (Paris, 1939), pp. 34, 48, 563.

[13] *Ibid.,* p. 26.

[14] John F. Due, *Sales Taxation* (Urbana, Ill., 1957), p. 168.

[15] *Ibid.,* p. 152.

[16] *Ibid.,* p. 175.

The value-added tax would probably offer no advantage over a general turnover tax of equal scope with respect to the number of taxpayers. The greater base provided by the multiple counting under the latter measure might make it possible to grant a larger administrative exemption. However, it is difficult to compare the base of a general turnover tax with either a value-added or single-stage measure. On the one hand, the general turnover tax imposes a relatively light burden on investment goods as compared with an income-type base under the noncumulative taxes while, on the other hand, it taxes investment goods which would be exempt if the consumption-type base were used for the noncumulative taxes.

The manufacturers' sales tax, whether collected through the value-added or single-stage procedure, would involve a smaller number of taxpayers than any of the above measures, and most of the taxpayers would keep adequate records. The United States Treasury Department once estimated that there would be seventeen times as many taxpayers under a single-stage retail sales tax as under a single-stage manufacturers' sales tax and nine times as many as in the case of a wholesalers' sales tax on the assumption that the last two taxes would permit an administrative exemption of $5,000 and that there would be no exemption under the retail sales tax.[17] The proportions would have been 8.6 and 4.6, respectively, if an exemption of $5,000 had been allowed under the retail sales tax.

In estimating the number of taxpayers, it must be borne in mind that the sales tax is not restricted to the type of firm indicated by the name of the tax. A manufacturers' sales tax, for example, would apply not only to manufacturers and importers but also to wholesalers and retailers undertaking some manufacturing. A wholesalers' sales tax would apply to all who sell at wholesale, including manufacturers and some retailers, and to importers. A retail sales tax would apply to manufacturers, wholesalers, and importers who make retail sales as well as retail outlets, strictly speaking.[18]

---

[17] U.S. Treasury Department, Division of Tax Research, "Federal Manufacturers' Wholesale and Retail Sales Taxes," Memorandum Submitted by Randolph Paul, *Hearings before the Ways and Means Committee, House of Representatives, on Revenue Revision of 1942,* 77th Congress, 2d Session (Washington, D.C., 1942), I, 350.

[18] See ibid., p. 346.

Comparison of Value-Added Tax with Corporate Income Tax

Even if its scope be greatly limited through exclusions and administrative exemptions, the value-added tax may be expected to cover a larger number of taxpayers than the corporate income tax. Returns under the United States federal corporate income tax currently number around 1,191 million.[19]

NUMBER OF RETURNS

Taxes collected directly from individuals and corporate net income taxes require annual returns. Tax payments, however, are made at more frequent intervals under withholding systems—quarterly, in the case of employers' withholding of tax on wages and salaries for the United States federal income tax.

Value-Added Tax and Other Sales Taxes

Sales tax laws, on the other hand, usually require monthly or quarterly returns and payments. Monthly returns increase administrative and compliance costs but present the advantage of a close check on taxpayers. Professor Jacoby makes the following observation with respect to this issue:

The proper period for which sales tax returns should be made is a subject of debate among administrators. Unquestionably a technical advantage inheres in the monthly return in dealing with transient or seasonal vendors, for a more frequent indication is afforded of whether taxes are being paid, and if not, action can be promptly taken. Yet monthly returns triple the amount of paper work of receiving, opening, checking remittances, auditing and filing necessary in the case of quarterly returns. The extra cost can be justified if better enforcement results from the more frequent collection, and less evasion occurs on the part of seasonal and transient merchants. This advantage can, of course, be realized to some extent if administrators are empowered to make jeopardy assessments or to require bonds or returns at

[19] U.S. Department of Commerce, *Statistical Abstract of the United States: 1963*, p. 401.

their discretion. California's apparently good record with quarterly returns and these administrative powers indicates that the extra costs of monthly returns may be unnecessary, though no positive conclusion is possible.[20]

The United States Treasury Department favored quarterly returns under a retail sales tax because of administrative convenience. It reasoned that with quarterly returns it could complete its checking and clear delinquencies for one period before beginning work on the returns of the following period. However, it suggested more frequent returns for financially unstable and seasonal business.[21]

The French value-added tax and the other French sales taxes have required monthly returns and payments unless the payments were very small—at present, when they average less than 200 NF a month. Payments are due by the twenty-fifth of the month following sales except that the Departmental Director has the authority to establish earlier dates according to categories of taxpayers. In the district of Paris, the taxpayers are arranged alphabetically. For example, those having names beginning with A or B must make their returns by the fifth of the month; those having names beginning with C or D make their returns by the sixth or seventh of the month, and so on.[22] Even taxpayers who use the system of provisional accounts and those assessed under the estimate procedure for small taxpayers make monthly payments.

The Michigan Business Activities Tax requires quarterly returns and payments as a general rule. They are due by the end of the month following the last month in the quarter except that the payment for the final quarter is due within four calendar months after the close of the tax year.[23] The Michigan statute also provides a simplified procedure whereby a taxpayer may make only an annual return if he is willing to pay in advance at the beginning of the year a sum equal to the taxes due in the preceding year. Those engaged in agriculture might be authorized to make annual returns without any payment in advance.[24]

The Japanese tax bill employs a system of annual statements with more frequent payments by "approximate self-assessment" based upon value

[20] Neil Herman Jacoby, *Retail Sales Taxation* (Chicago, 1938), p. 271.

[21] U.S. Treasury Department, "Considerations Respecting a Federal Retail Sales Tax," *Hearings, Revenue Revision of 1943*, pp. 1159–60.

[22] "Guide des taxes sur le chiffre d'affaires," *La revue fiduciaire*, II, No. 324 (Sept., 1955), 59–60.

[23] Michigan Department of Revenue, "Michigan Business Activities Tax," *Public Act No. 150, Public Acts of 1953, as Amended*, Sec. 5, par. 1.

[24] *Ibid.*

added in the preceding year. If the taxpayer is able to submit evidence which indicates that the value added in the current year would be less than half that of the previous year, the payments are to be based on the probable value added of the current year. Unincorporated firms are to make payments three times a year and corporations or other legal persons semi-annually. Any discrepancies between the amounts due and the amounts paid are to be adjusted at the time of the annual statement.[25]

When taxes are paid provisionally on the basis of the previous year's liabilities, they will be either more or less than the amounts actually due. A lag in collections is detrimental to the treasury; and, in any event, there is discrimination among taxpayers. Under the deduction variant of the consumption-type tax, expanding concerns may advance much more than the amounts owed because of deductions in value added caused by heavy investment outlays in the current year. This is presumably why the French law permits the deduction of current outlays in its system of provisional accounts and why the Japanese value-added tax allows the use of probable value added for the current year.

Under other forms of value-added taxation, the amounts paid by expanding firms may be less than their ultimate tax liability while the amounts paid by contracting businesses may be more. In this case, a rough solution may be provided by applying the previous year's ratio between value added and gross receipts to the gross receipts of the current period, any discrepancy from amounts actually due being corrected at the end of the year.[26]

TAX RATE

The tax base which makes possible a relatively low effective tax rate has an administrative advantage over one which requires a higher effective tax rate. The United States Treasury Department has noted that high rates create an incentive to evasion and intensify competitive inequalities, especially when a tax is new.[27] Generally speaking, this means that, for

[25] Local Autonomy Agency and Local Finance Commission, *Local Tax Law, 1950*, arts. 35–38.

[26] See Studenski, The Place of a "Value-Added" Tax in a War Time Fiscal Program (Preliminary Memorandum, mimeo., Apr. 6, 1942), p. 6.

[27] U.S. Treasury Department, "Federal Manufacturers' Wholesale and Retail Sales Taxes," *Hearings, Revenue Revision of 1942*, I, 349.

a given revenue yield, a tax which utilizes a measure of wide scope and thereby permits a lower effective rate on each taxpaying unit is preferable to one imposed on a limited base. For instance, other things being equal, a sales tax through the retail stage and imposed on products taking the form of services as well as commodities is preferable to one limited to manufacturers' sales of commodities.

Comparison of Value-Added Tax with Taxes Assessed on Individual Incomes

With respect to the rate required to raise an equal amount of revenue, the income type of value-added tax applied through the retail stage is on a par with a personal income tax of equivalent scope. Both taxes utilize the same aggregate base, which is allocated among business enterprises in case of the value-added tax, and among individuals in the case of the personal income tax. However, the rate required to raise a given amount of revenue under the personal income tax may be superimposed upon a rate which is already high. This may create more administrative problems than the same rate imposed under a new measure.

The deduction variant of the consumption type of value-added tax applied through the retail stage is on a par with a spendings tax of equal scope, both measures utilizing approximately the same base. Under the former measure, the base is allocated among business firms while, under the latter, it is distributed among individuals.

Comparison of Value-Added Tax with Other Sales Taxes

In comparing the general turnover tax with the retailers', wholesalers', and manufacturers' sales taxes, Shoup has stated that "The only major advantage of the turnover tax is that for a given amount of revenue a smaller rate is needed, and consequently the inducement to evasion of the tax at any one point is somewhat smaller."[28] This is the case only if the general turnover tax encompasses more products or more stages of distribution than the other taxes. As in the case of a sales tax imposed

---

[28] Shoup, "Taxes Available to Avert Inflation," in Carl S. Shoup, Milton Friedman, and Ruth P. Mack, *Taxing to Prevent Inflation* (New York, 1943), p. 87.

on all products and through the retail stage, use of the general turnover system of collection would frequently result in the same effective tax rate on each taxpaying unit, the lower statutory rate being offset by the higher base resulting from the cumulative nature of the general turnover tax. However, as observed above, it is difficult to visualize a general turnover tax equivalent to a noncumulative tax because of the manner in which the general turnover tax is applied to investment goods.

The deduction variant of the consumption type of value-added tax applied through the retail stage would in principle require the same rate of tax as that of a single-stage retail sales tax with equal scope because both taxes utilize the same base. The only difference is that the value-added technique distributes the base among business firms at various stages of production and distribution while the base of the single-stage retail sales tax is in effect concentrated at the final stage of distribution. In practice, however, the difficulty of applying either tax to small firms may necessitate an administrative exemption which removes more of the tax base under the retail sales tax than under the value-added tax. In such circumstances, the latter tax would permit a lower rate.

The gross-product type of value-added tax employs the same base as a single-stage retail sales tax imposed on sales for final business use as well as for consumption. As in the preceding case, it would allow a lower rate in the event of an administrative exemption.

No concept in retail sales taxation is equivalent to the interest-exclusion variant of the consumption type of value-added tax. However, the base of the interest-exclusion variant is close to that used by the deduction variant and would therefore require similar rates.

A value-added tax imposed through the retail stage and the retail sales tax would make possible lower effective rates than the wholesalers' and manufacturers' sales taxes. The United States Treasury Department estimated that for the fiscal year 1943, a 10 percent tax on retail sales could be made to produce a maximum of $4,632,000,000 and that the maximum yield for the wholesalers' and manufacturers' sales taxes would be $3,059,000,000 and $2,382,000,000, respectively.[29] Therefore, the rate of the wholesalers' sales tax would have to be one and one half times and the rate of the manufacturers' sales tax about twice that of the retail sales tax in order to produce the same yield. The Treasury

[29] U.S. Treasury Department, "Federal Manufacturers' Wholesale and Retail Sales Taxes," *Hearings, Revenue Revision of 1942,* I, 347.

Department observed that the superior revenue productivity of the retail sales tax was partly the result of applying the tax to retailers' distributive margins and partly the result of including more activities.[30]

Comparison of Value-Added Tax with Corporate Income Tax

The value-added tax in any form would require a much lower rate than the corporate income tax. This is because of its broader scope and because the net-profits base is much smaller than value added. To the extent that the lower rate merely reflects the fact that the corporate tax is applied to a narrower base, the effective rates are the same under both taxes.

INDENTIFICATION OF TAXPAYERS

Problem of Defining Taxable Activity

The identification of taxpayers under any tax on current receipts requires a definition of taxable economic activity which involves such troublesome issues as the casual sale; the status of nonprofit organizations and their unrelated activities; and the passive receipt of income as, for example, rental payments to holding company lessors. Unlike net income taxation, however, sales taxes have usually been characterized by numerous exclusions and special exemptions which complicate the problem of identifying taxpayers. In the French sales taxes, for instance, the exclusion of agriculture and the professions has engendered extensive litigation over the taxability of borderline firms, and special exemptions have created similar difficulties. Although these problems are eventually resolved by court decisions, the process may take many years during which administration and compliance are upset by the uncertain status of some activities.

The identification of taxpayers under sales taxes customarily rests on a definition of business. Business may be defined broadly, or specific types of business may be enumerated. The French sales taxes, the Michigan Business Activities Tax, and the Japanese value-added tax

---

[30] U.S. Treasury Department, "Considerations Respecting a Federal Retail Sales Tax," *Hearings, Revenue Revision of 1943*, p. 1117.

utilize a broad definition of business. The Japanese bill lists taxable activities but achieves broadness through a provision which is a catchall. As Firmin indicates in his study of the Michigan Business Activities Tax, a broad definition of business places a burden of interpretation on the administrative authorities and the courts; but it is preferable to a statutory enumeration of taxable activities which might prove inflexible.[31]

Problem of Taxing Services

The identification of taxpayers is in some respects simpler under sales taxes which apply to services than under taxes largely restricted to sales of tangible property. In the latter case, questions arise as to the taxable status of those who combine a "sale" in the legal sense with exempt services, a problem which is described in the next section. Furthermore, sales may be disguised as other forms of transfers such as rentals and lease agreements which would be covered if rentals were taxed. In fact, some American states have found it necessary to extend sales taxes to rentals in order to protect revenues.[32]

In principle, the general turnover tax and the value-added tax should be imposed on services. In practice, the general turnover tax has usually included services but has then become entangled in the administrative problem of taxing commission merchants. If the tax is applicable to their gross turnover, middlemen are eliminated while, if applied only to commissions, it is commonly evaded by ordinary dealers who pose as commission merchants. There has not been much practice in value-added taxation. The Michigan law, which is imposed at a very low rate, is being applied to services; but the taxation of services under the French legislation continues on a gross-turnover rather than a value-added basis except that the tax on services rendered to business is deductible by value-added taxpayers and service enterprises may elect entrance into the regime of the value-added tax.

Probably most tax students would hold that the principle of retail sales taxation also justifies the inclusion of services. However, the United

[31] Peter A. Firmin, *The Michigan Business Receipts Tax* (Ann Arbor, Mich., 1953), p. 14.

[32] Denzel C. Cline, "Expanding Scope of Sales Taxes," *Proceedings of the Forty-Third Annual Conference of the National Tax Association, 1950* (Sacramento, Calif., 1951), p. 298.

States Treasury Department has indicated a possible theoretical reason for exempting services in the following quotation:

A retail sales tax is frequently regarded as a tax applying only to sales of goods and not to the rendering of services. Perhaps the reason for this conception is the recognition of substantial differences in the nature of most transactions involving the rendering of services as compared with the nature of those involving the sale of goods. A great many services are not rendered by established commercial enterprises on a buyer-seller basis, but rather by individuals hiring themselves to business concerns or individuals on an employee-employer basis. Even in the case of many of those services rendered to the public at large, as for example, professional services, the methods of conducting business and the relationships between the customer and the person rendering the service differ from those of the usual sales transaction.[33]

According to Due, the argument that a tax on services is a tax on labor is one reason for the failure to extend the retail sales tax to services; and, as he observes, the contention is untenable because "the burden of the tax must be considered in terms of the persons who bear it, not in terms of the goods and services the sale of which serves as the base of the tax."[34] It should be added that the exemption of services discriminates in favor of labor rendered in conjunction with such services as compared with labor rendered in the production of commodities.

A much more substantial reason than the above for the exemption of services is the administrative difficulty of taxing them, a fact noted by Jacoby, who has attributed the customary exemption to this factor and to the political opposition of professional groups and real estate interests.[35] The United States Treasury Department also emphasized the difficulty of effectively administering the retail sales tax on services not rendered by regularly established business firms, observing that the tax would be applicable to many small taxpayers who were hard to locate and liable for small amounts of tax.[36] In view of this difficulty and its opinion that the taxation of many services would involve a discriminative double taxation of sales to business, obviously on the assumption that the suspensive system would not apply to services, the Treasury Department

[33] U.S. Treasury Department, "Considerations Respecting a Federal Retail Sales Tax," *Hearings, Revenue Revision of 1943*, p. 1137.

[34] John F. Due, "Retail Sales Taxation in Theory and Practice," *National Tax Journal,* III (Dec., 1950), 320.

[35] Jacoby, *Retail Sales Taxation*, p. 106.

[36] U.S. Treasury Department, "Considerations Respecting a Federal Retail Sales Tax," *Hearings, Revenue Revision of 1943*, pp. 1139 f.

concluded that most services should be exempt. Under the usual type of retail sales tax, which reached purchases for final business use, producer expenditures for services would thereby have been favored over their purchases of producers' goods. However, this possible loophole as well as other avenues of tax avoidance were largely eliminated by the recommendation that the tax be applied to a few categories of services in order to improve the administration of the tax on tangible personal property, as follows:

1. The repair and fabrication of taxable articles.
2. The rental of taxable tangible personal property.
3. Laundry service and dry cleaning.
4. Barber shop and beauty parlor services.[37]

The application of a value-added tax to services would encounter the same difficulties involved in their taxation under the retail sales tax. On the other hand, the fact that the value-added approach facilitates an administrative exemption which would exclude the smallest enterprises is an important advantage. A comparison of the possible treatment of services under the two forms of taxation will be undertaken below in discussing the computation of the tax base.

Finally, all taxes which apply through the retail stage avoid the troublesome problem of identifying taxpayers presented by taxes limited to prior stages. Under the manufacturers' sales tax, litigation is fostered because of the difficulty of distinguishing manufacturing from certain types of distributive activity such as packaging and bottling, especially when trademarks and private brands are involved.[38] As these functions may be performed at the retail stage, the wholesalers' sales tax presents a similar problem to a lesser degree.

DETERMINATION OF THE TAX BASE

The determination of the tax base is responsible for some of the heaviest burdens in administration and compliance, whatever the form of taxation. Where general taxes on current receipts are concerned, the most difficult questions in tax accounting arise from the evaluation of deprecia-

[37] *Ibid.*, pp. 1137 f.
[38] *See ibid.*, pp. 1120 f., and Due, *Sales Taxation*, p. 152.

tion and inventories, fringe benefits, the derivation of a uniform price base, the prevention of multiple taxation of turnover, and exclusions and exemptions.

Depreciation and Inventory Accounting

Depreciation and inventory accounting, which are major problems in net income taxation, are also required for computing the base of the net income type of value-added tax and the interest-exclusion variant of the consumption-type tax. Strictly speaking, only the deduction variant of the consumption type of value-added tax avoids both problems. Yet Adams and others have attributed this virtue to the gross product type which in principle disallows depreciation but not inventory accounting. However, as Studenski suggests, cash accounting may be used as a matter of convenience. In fact, he states that purchases might be deducted regardless of inventory accumulation even in the case of a base which allows depreciation and depletion.[39]

Neither the spendings tax nor the general turnover tax require depreciation and inventory accounting although the spendings tax encounters similar problems if an attempt is made to spread outlays on consumer durables over a number of years. The single-stage sales taxes have also avoided these complications, although single-stage levies designed to reach all final products whether for personal consumption or business use employ a gross-product base which should theoretically be imposed on inventory accumulation.

Fringe Benefits

The value-added tax does not escape the difficulty of how to handle fringe benefits, which have provided opportunities for evasion and avoidance under net income taxation. In the case of expense accounts, the recommendation of the Japanese tax administrators that such expenditures be treated as supplementary compensation to the extent that the expenditures are made through employees rather than as direct business

[39] Studenski, The Place of a "Value-Added" Tax in a War Time Fiscal Program (Preliminary Memorandum, mimeo., Apr. 6, 1942), p. 5.

outlays of the employer[40] offers a partial solution insofar as it entails a closer supervision of such expenditures by business owners or managers. Nevertheless, excessive expenditures of this type are still possible. A similar problem exists under single-stage taxes when such outlays are made in suspension of tax in the name of the employer. In fact, the question raised by all fringe benefits is the same under any "national-income tax." Are they business purchases of goods and services from outside suppliers or supplements to wages and salaries?

Establishment of a Uniform Price Basis

The deduction variant of the consumption type of value-added tax imposed through the retail stage and a single-stage retail sales tax on sales to ultimate consumers, only, avoid two groups of pricing problems which are inherent in other forms of value-added and single-stage taxes. One group concerns the adjustment of prices to the level appropriate for a given stage of distribution. The other involves the establishment of a price basis when transactions are between dependent enterprises. Furthermore, taxes which include all services escape questions with respect to the taxability of charges for services beyond the scope of the tax if performed by specialized concerns and the question of the taxability of transactions which combine a sale of goods with the supply of services. As noted above, manufacturers', wholesalers', and retailers' sales taxes have in practice seldom included more than a few selected services although the extension of the single-stage retail sales tax to most services is as feasible as in the case of the value-added method of collection; and a tax on services applied at a reduced rate may be incorporated with manufacturers' or wholesalers' sales taxes regardless of whether the value-added or single-stage method is used.

PRICE ADJUSTMENTS REQUIRED FOR SALES MADE AT VARYING STAGES OF DISTRIBUTION. Whenever a sales tax is restricted to a single stage of production or distribution, the tax base should be defined in terms of the price level appropriate to that stage. If vendors' prices are not adjusted when they sell at other stages, relative tax liability will vary with the

[40] Bronfenbrenner, "The Japanese Value-Added Sales Tax," *National Tax Journal,* III (Dec., 1950), 305.

differing proportions of producers' or distributors' margins included in the tax base; and methods of doing business will be affected.

Apparently, the problem is often considered especially troublesome in the case of the manufacturers' sales tax where the appropriate price is the one used for manufacturers' sales to unrelated wholesalers and industrial concerns which do not assume any of the functions usually undertaken by manufacturers. The 1955–56 Sales Tax Committee in Canada recommended the conversion of the Canadian manufacturers' sales tax into a wholesalers' sales tax in the belief that "the use of the wholesale level would permit the application of the tax to the actual selling prices in a much larger number of cases, and thus the use of constructive selling prices would be reduced."[41] The United States Treasury Department took a similar position in 1942.[42] However, both groups ignored the problems raised by direct sales of manufacturers to retailers under the wholesalers' sales tax when the retailer assumes distributive or even some manufacturing functions. The need for "uplifts" is likely to be greater under the wholesalers' sales tax; and "uplifts" involve more administrative complexities than "discounts."[43]

To equalize the tax burden among varying channels of distribution, a manufacturers' sales tax should, on the one hand, allow a discount for direct retail sales and direct sales to retailers. On the other hand, there should be an upward adjustment for functions assumed by distributors which are generally undertaken by manufacturers. For example, as in the case of the wholesalers' sales tax, large retailers who make direct purchases from manufacturers may assume certain wholesale or even manufacturing functions. If the manufacturer is allowed to apply a standard discount to such sales, the purchases of the large retailers will be taxed on a smaller base than comparable purchases of smaller retailers.

Under a wholesalers' sales tax, a discount is needed only on direct sales to consumers. However, as noted above, there remains the problem of an upward adjustment on both wholesalers' sales and direct sales by manufacturers to large retailers who perform wholesaling functions or

[41] Due, *Sales Taxation*, p. 162. Also see John F. Due, "Report of the Sales Tax Committee: One Year in Retrospect," *Canadian Tax Journal*, V (Mar., 1957), 88–105, for an excellent analysis of the issues involved in determining taxable price.

[42] U.S. Treasury Department, Division of Tax Research, "Federal Manufacturers' Wholesale and Retail Sales Taxes," *Hearings, Revenue Revision of 1942*, I, 350.

[43] Due, *Sales Taxation*, p. 364.

create values customarily added at the manufacturing stage, especially through brands or trade marks.

The ordinary retail sales tax which utilizes the physical-ingredient rule and is therefore imposed on sales of finished articles to industrial users in principle also requires adjustments on such sales made at prices containing varying amounts of production and distributive charges.[44] The problem is avoided only by the pure retail sales tax, one restricted to sales for ultimate consumption, and its counterpart, the deduction variant of the consumption type of value-added tax applied through the retail stage. It remains under other forms of value-added taxation insofar as they are imposed on sales for business use.

A vigorous effort to equalize the tax burden among varying distributive channels distinguishes the Canadian manufacturers' sales tax and especially the British Purchase Tax, a wholesalers' sales tax levied primarily on consumers' goods at highly differentiated rates. As Due indicates, however, the administrative problems are considerable and, at best, only rough justice is achieved, a completely satisfactory solution being provided only by a retail sales tax.[45] He makes the following observation with reference to the Canadian tax:

On the whole, the question of determination of the taxable sale price is an inherent difficulty with the manufacturers' sales tax, one for which there can be no solution which is both completely equitable and adminstratively feasible. The extent to which various manufacturing and distribution functions are divided among manufacturers and their customers varies tremendously, even in the case of particular manufacturers, and no type of adjustment can insure that the base of the tax includes the charges for precisely the same functions in all cases. . . . No standard discount formula can handle all cases equitably, and any attempt to treat each firm individually would encounter hopeless administrative complications, require secrecy, and create fears of favoritism. The problem is basically unsolvable; all that can be done is to minimize the gross inequities. This, the Canadian system has done reasonably well. . . .[46]

For many years the British Purchase Tax made excessive use of constructive prices under the misguided philosophy of trying to equalize the

---

[44] U.S. Treasury Department, Division of Tax Research, "Federal Manufacturers' Wholesale and Retail Sales Taxes," *Hearings, Revenue Revision of 1942*, I, 351. In practice, such sales are usually assumed to have been made at a manufacturer's or wholesaler's price, and no adjustment is made.

[45] *Sales Taxation*, pp. 157, 161.

[46] *Ibid.*, p. 157.

absolute amount of tax imposed on a particular product regardless of differences in cost of production as well as in channels of distribution.[47] Its price adjustments are now limited to a discount for direct sales to consumers arrived at through agreement between the Administration and trade associations and to an "uplift" which seeks to eliminate the advantages enjoyed by large retailers from assuming wholesale functions and from quantity discounts—the economies from quantity discounts not being passed on to consumers because of price-maintenance laws.[48] As Due emphasizes, only a retail sales tax can solve the "uplift" problem.

The taxation of the actual purchase price paid by retailers in all cases is definitely discriminatory in favor of those retailers performing substantial wholesaling functions, and may be regarded as discriminatory in favor of those receiving large quantity discounts. But any attempt to "uplift" the lower prices leads to tremendous complications and strenuous complaints from various groups of firms. There can be no entirely satisfactory solution to this problem unless the tax is imposed on the retail sale.[49]

In the case of the French manufacturers' sales tax and its successor in value-added form, the attempt to equalize the tax burden among varying channels of distribution has been restricted to corrections for direct retail sales although, under current French legislation, the discrimination against small retailers is slightly reduced because certain large retailers are required to pay the value-added tax. The French legislation provides that prices used in retail sales should be reduced to the wholesale level by means of a discount (currently 20 percent) or, alternatively, by a a reduction equal to a certain proportion (currently two thirds, as a general rule) of the average gross profit margin realized on sales in the preceding year, the method chosen being applicable to all sales in the current year.[50]

In applying the adjustments, it has been necessary to identify retail sales; and this problem has seriously complicated the administration of the tax. Retail sales are currently defined as those made at retail prices relating to quantities not exceeding the normal private needs of an individual consumer. Additional limitations concerning sales which may never be considered retail have the effect of largely restricting the de-

[47] *Ibid.*, p. 214.
[48] *Ibid.*, pp. 215–16.
[49] *Ibid.*, p. 232.
[50] "Guide des taxes sur le chiffre d'affaires," *La revue fiduciaire*, I, No. 321 (June, 1955), 35.

finition of a retail sale to those made to ultimate consumers. The additional limitations are as follows:

1. Sales of objects which by their nature or employment are not generally used by individual consumers.

2. Sales at identical prices whether at retail or wholesale. (In this case, the fact that a sale has been made in retail quantities does not signify a retail price provided that the concern charges the same prices to other firms as to ultimate consumers.)

3. Sales of products destined for resale, regardless of quantity.[51]

TRANSACTIONS BETWEEN DEPENDENT ENTERPRISES. The United States Treasury Department has stated that valuation problems are more difficult for a manufacturers' and wholesalers' sales tax than for a retailers' sales tax primarily because of the prevalence of common ownership or affiliation among buying and selling enterprises.[52] When transactions are not conducted at arm's length, prices are likely to be below those established by independent enterprises in order to avoid the tax. The problem concerns final sales of products to other taxable related firms and all sales to nontaxable related firms. For example, under a manufacturers' sales tax, a parent company may produce machines and sell them at reduced prices, and hence reduced tax, to an affiliate which uses them in its business. Also, it may sell its entire output at reduced prices, and hence reduced tax, to distributive affiliates who resell the products at the regular wholesale price without being subject to tax. A similar problem exists in retail sales taxation when the tax is imposed on sales for business use, the manufacturer being able to sell its product to an affiliate at a lower taxable price than it charges to independent concerns. However, the proportion of related sales is less in the case of the retail sales tax than in the case of the other single-stage taxes.[53]

The issue is avoided by a single-stage retail sales tax which exempts sales to business firms and by the deduction variant of the consumption type of value-added tax applied through the retail stage except to the extent that there are no tax refunds on sales to exempt concerns and sales are made to nontaxable related concerns. It would exist to some extent under the other versions of the value-added tax where the tax is imposed on sales for business use; for example, a parent company would be able

---

[51] *Ibid.*

[52] U.S. Treasury Department, "Considerations Respecting a Federal Retail Sales Tax," *Hearings, Revenue Revision of 1943*, p. 1120.

[53] *Ibid.*

to sell machinery to its affiliate at reduced taxable prices for use in the latter's business.

The United States Treasury Department was of the opinion that the problem would have to be handled through administrative discretion.[54] The 1932 proposal for a manufacturers' sales tax provided that when dealings were not at arm's length the fair manufacturers' price would be the selling price of articles by producers or manufacturers in the ordinary course of trade as determined by the Commissioner of Internal Revenue.[55]

The French value-added tax and its predecessors have provided that when selling and buying enterprises are related, the tax is applicable to the selling price of the purchasing concern. The law of April 10, 1954, substituted a definition of dependence based upon the degree of economic control for a definition in terms of the legal concept of affiliation, which was limited to companies.

SERVICES BEYOND SCOPE OF TAX WHEN PERFORMED BY SPECIALIZED FIRMS. The United States Treasury Department emphasized the difficulty of arriving at a uniform price basis in the case of the manufacturers' sales tax because manufacturing enterprises differ in the extent to which they undertake certain distributive functions such as packaging, selling, and advertising.[56] It maintained that such expenditures should be excluded in order to approximate the f.o.b. price either by deducting them from market prices or by estimating the cost of the unfinished articles and adding a markup for profits; and in its 1932 proposal for a manufacturers' sales tax, it recommended that administrative officials confer with industry representatives in order to reach an agreement on methods.[57] The French manufacturers' sales tax, on the other hand, has used a system which includes distributive expenditures in taxable receipts but which attempts to define manufacturing so as to reach distributors specializing in these operations.

Packaging, selling, and advertising expenditures may cause somewhat less difficulty in the case of the wholesalers' sales tax. The Treasury De-

[54] *Ibid.*

[55] U.S. Treasury Department, "Proposed Manufacturers' Excise Tax, Revenue Bill of 1932. Ways and Means Committee Report," *Hearings before the Ways and Means Committee, House of Representatives, on Revenue Revision of 1942,* 77th Congress, 2d Session (Washington, D.C., 1942), I, 434.

[56] U.S. Treasury Department, "Federal Manufacturers' Wholesale and Retail Sales Taxes," *ibid.,* p. 352.

[57] U.S. Treasury Department, "Proposed Manufacturers' Excise Tax, Revenue Bill of 1932. Ways and Means Committee Report," *ibid.,* p. 434.

partment once recommended that such charges should not be deductible from wholesalers' prices even though the tax were limited to sales of tangible personal property.[58] Presumably, it would have recommended their inclusion without question in a retailers' sales tax.

However, the problem of deriving a uniform price basis is complicated by the customary exclusion of general services from the scope of all three single-stage sales taxes. The taxable receipts of some vendors may include charges for services which a customer can obtain on his own account from tax-free sources.

Charges for services which the customer might obtain from nontaxable vendors involve such items as transportation, delivery, insurance, finance, warranty, and installation costs as well as various types of advertising. In its study of retail sales taxation, the Treasury Department stated that the measure of a retail sales tax should not include the price of these services if they were not taxable when rendered independently of the sale. It recommended that the law require a separate statement of deductible charges in order to prevent their overstatement and to facilitate administrative control.[59]

The Treasury Department's 1932 proposal for a United States Federal manufacturers' sales tax allowed a deduction of "transportation, delivery, insurance and like charges," provided that the invoices or other records of the vendor indicate the amount to the satisfaction of the commissioner.[60] The French manufacturers' sales tax and its value-added successor have applied to all accessory expenditures even when separately stated except that transportation expenditures are deductible when the purchaser assumes responsibility for transportation.

TAXABLE STATUS OF TRANSACTIONS COMBINING SALE OF GOODS WITH SUPPLY OF SERVICES. Closely related to the above problem because the service element can often be separated from the sale of goods so as to minimize tax liability is the question of the taxable status of the transaction which combines a sale of goods with the rendering of a service— sometimes designated as a "contract for labor and materials" rather than

[58] U.S. Treasury Department, "Federal Manufacturers' Wholesale and Retail Sales Taxes," *ibid.*, pp. 345, 352.

[59] U.S. Treasury Department, "Considerations Respecting a Federal Retail Sales Tax," *Hearings, Revenue Revision of 1943*, pp. 1151, 1153.

[60] U.S. Treasury Department, "Federal Manufacturers' Wholesale and Retail Sales Taxes," *Hearings, Revenue Revision of 1942*, I, 433.

a "sale."[61] A plumber, for example, may report that he has sold certain equipment on which he pays the sales tax and later install the equipment as a tax-free service. Also, methods of doing business may be modified, sales being made by one group of concerns and services rendered by another.

Arbitrary rules have been utilized in handling such transactions. In the sales taxes of the American states, when the service element is clearly dominant, the concern is allowed to segregate its sales of goods, which are taxable, from its supply of tax-free services, while the sales tax is incorporated in the purchase price of goods which it uses in rendering services.[62] Even when the distinction between the service and sales element is blurred, the concern may be allowed to establish separate invoices for the two types of activities or its receipts may be allocated according to a formula designed for its business.[63]

Arbitrary rules are bound to cause some competitive inequities which, given a high degree of differentiation between a tax on sales and a tax on services, will become excessive. Under the French manufacturers' sales tax, for example, treatment of receipts of building contractors as a combination of sales and services severely penalized prefabrication. The contractors' services were subject to the relatively low-rate service tax, the sales tax being imposed only on their acquisition of taxable products utilized in the construction. Prefabricators, on the other hand, were subject to the full rate of the manufacturers' sales tax. The discrimination was finally terminated in principle, although because of the buffer rule not always in practice, with the adoption of the reform of April 10, 1954, which applied the value-added regime to all building contractors while, at the same time, allowing them a discount of 35 percent of gross receipts in computing their tax base—in effect, a rate concession partly to make the shift from the previous regime more palatable and partly to favor construction.

Installations which are not accessory to fixed construction are not required to pay the value-added tax and so continue to be taxed as a combination of a sale and service. Because the administration has found it extremely difficult to draw the line between accessory installations and others, it has established a borderline category which allows the taxpayer

---

[61] Carl S. Shoup, *The Sales Tax in the American States* (New York, 1934), p. 561.

[62] Due, *Sales Taxation*, p. 297.

[63] *Ibid.*

a choice between the application of the value-added tax with the discount privilege and the former dual regime.

That it is sometimes difficult to decide whether a given transaction should be classified as a combined sale and service rather than a sale is indicated by the French experience with a group of taxpayers designated as transformers (*transformateurs*). The category includes orthopedists, tailors, dressmakers, milliners, shirtmakers, bookbinders, and makers of picture frames. Under the original production tax, they purchased supplies tax-paid while their total receipts were classified as services which were subject to the lower-rate service tax. However, the law of fractional payments ended their exceptional status and integrated them with the regime of the manufacturers' sales tax.[64] In addition to certain types of construction activity, various enterprises are still treated as a combination of sales and services as, for example, hairdressing and sales of drugs and medicines by sanitariums.[65]

MISCELLANEOUS PROBLEMS.   There are several other problems of more or less importance which are related to the definition of a uniform price base. Some of them are present in all taxes on current receipts while others are peculiar to one or another form of taxation.

The most important is the question of taxing products which a firm manufactures for its own use or for the personal consumption of the owner and which the French designate as a "delivery to oneself" (*livraison à soi-même*). No special provision is required to reach such transactions under the net income tax nor under the addition method of computing the value-added tax, with the possible exception of an imputation for profits on items destined for the personal consumption of the owner. The problem is circumvented by the general turnover tax, which is in principle applied only when there is a market transaction.

One might expect that the deduction variant of the value-added tax, which is intended to tax only ultimate consumption, would require no imputations of this nature other than for the personal consumption of the owner. However, except in the case of exporters, the French version imposes the tax on a concern's delivery to itself of products used within the business when the firm is excluded or exempt from the value-added tax or when it uses the producer's goods for the joint production of taxable

[64] Patouillet, "Aperçu sur les modifications apportées aux taxes sur le chiffre d'affaires," *Receuil Dalloz: Chronique, 1948* (Paris, 1949), p. 110.

[65] "Guide des taxes sur le chiffre d'affaires," *La revue fiduciaire*, I (June, 1955), 29.

and nontaxable items. The tax is necessarily imposed on a firm's delivery to itself of producers' goods to which the deduction privilege is not extended.

When items which are deductible if used to produce taxable goods are not deductible when employed in the production of tax-exempt articles, the law implies that the utilization of these items in the manufacture of exempt products represents a final rather than an intermediate use. Such is not the case, of course; and, in principle, a reimbursement of taxes paid on goods purchased to produce tax-free products should be allowed. The same reasoning applies to single-stage sales taxes; and some sales tax laws exempt items used to produce tax-exempt goods while some others grant refunds to producers of exempt goods for taxes paid on their purchases.[66] Under Canadian legislation, however, exemptions have been granted only on certain materials used to produce tax-exempt goods; and the regulations governing the matter are exceedingly complex—the reluctance to free such articles from taxation in all cases suggesting a fear of evasion. Unlike the French legislation, the Canadian tax allows firms producing exempt commodities and small manufacturers excluded from the tax to purchase in suspension of tax machinery used directly in production; but the exemption is not extended to enterprises producing nontaxable services.[67] Measures of value-added taxation other than the consumption type require a tax on a firm's production for business use; all measures require a tax on the owner's personal consumption.

Another important issue in defining the tax base and one which concerns all taxes on current receipts is the problem of how to treat credit sales. One question is whether to apply the tax when the sale is made or only when collections are made. The United States Treasury Department expressed a preference for the former procedure when it was reviewing problems in retail sales taxation, chiefly because collections might not be allocated to particular items, thereby causing difficulty when some articles were exempt. It also observed that the administration was simpler when there were rate changes and that there was an advantage for the government in earlier collections and in avoidance of a loss of revenue on unpaid sales, the vendor having collected the tax with the first installment.[68]

[66] Due, *Sales Taxation*, pp. 178, 199.

[67] *Ibid.*, p. 153.

[68] U.S. Treasury Department, "Considerations Respecting a Federal Retail Sales Tax," *Hearings, Revenue Revision of 1943*, p. 1152.

The French law uses the system of collecting the value-added tax and its predecessor at the time of delivery except that, since the adoption of the value-added tax, all construction contractors have been allowed to pay upon collections. The Michigan Business Activities Tax defines "sales" as the transfer of possession or ownership.[69] The Japanese bill on the value-added tax does not appear to deal with this issue.

A second question in connection with credit sales is whether to allow a deduction for bad debts. The United States Treasury Department recalled that this type of allowance has created administrative problems in the case of the federal income tax and that sales taxes present the additional problem of allocating bad debts between taxable and exempt items. However, it conceded that such allowances increase the goodwill of the taxpayers.[70] In the United States, some states which impose their sales taxes on gross sales allow deductions for unpaid sales.[71]

The French value-added tax and its predecessor have allowed the taxes paid on unpaid sales to be deducted from the taxes due. Since the law of fractional payments, however, the allowance has been limited to the tax actually paid or the difference between the tax on sales and the tax due on purchases. The Michigan Business Activities Tax does not specifically mention bad debts; but the tax administration has interpreted the deductions allowed for amounts paid to other businesses as permitting this adjustment.[72] The Japanese bill does not deal with the issue.

Under principles of national-income accounting the net income type of value-added tax requires an allowance for bad debts, and probably the consumption type does also. The allowance is theoretically unnecessary in the case of the gross product variant.

Taxes on current receipts usually allow deductions for trade and cash discounts. The taxpayer could easily avoid any disallowance by reducing his bills and charging a penalty for delayed payments.[73] The French sales taxes have always permitted such adjustments; and the Michigan value-added tax does likewise. The Japanese bill does not mention the problem.

[69] Michigan Department of Revenue, "Michigan Business Activities Tax," *Act No. 150, Public Acts of 1953, as Amended*, Sec. 1(h).

[70] U.S. Treasury Department, "Considerations Respecting a Federal Retail Sales Tax," *Hearings, Revenue Revision of 1943*, p. 1154.

[71] *Ibid.*, p. 1222.

[72] Michigan Department of Revenue, "Michigan Business Activities Tax," *Act No. 150, Public Acts of 1953, as Amended, Rules and Regulations* (1959), p. 13.

[73] Shoup, *Sales Tax in the American States*, p. 640.

Allowances are also customary in the case of refunds and returned merchandise, although repossessed articles under conditional sales contracts may or may not be treated as returned goods.[74] The French value-added tax grants such allowances. The Michigan Business Activities Tax contains a provision which allows a deduction from taxable receipts when the sale price is refunded or equivalent credit granted.[75]

Finally, trade-ins have created administrative problems in the sales taxes of the American states. The United States Treasury Department reported that some states deduct the value of trade-ins from taxable sales but tax the trade-ins when sold, while others allow no deduction but exempt the sales of trade-ins, in which event any value added to the trade-in is also exempt. It emphasized the need for care in preventing excessive deductions on trade-ins when they were allowed to reduce taxable sales.[76] The French value-added tax and its predecessors have contained the provision that taxable receipts consist of the amount of sales or the value of objects remitted in payment. The problem exists in all sales taxes but is greatest in the case of the retail sales tax.[77]

Avoidance of Multiple Taxation

The techniques employed to avoid multiple taxation of the same income or product are responsible for some of the most complicated administrative and compliance problems in taxes based on current receipts. Depreciation allowances, which represent one of these techniques, are considered the major difficulty in administering the net income tax. The spendings tax would avoid depreciation accounting but would probably run into equal difficulty in its application to outlays on consumer durables. Depreciation allowances would be necessary under the net income type of value-added tax and the interest-exclusion variant of the consumption type.

Depreciation accounting is unnecessary under the gross product type

[74] U.S. Treasury Department, Division of Tax Research, "Considerations Respecting a Federal Retail Sales Tax," *Hearings, Revenue Revision of 1942*, pp. 1219–20.

[75] Michigan Department of Revenue, "Michigan Business Activities Tax," *Act No. 150, Public Acts of 1953*, Sec. 1(j)(4).

[76] U.S. Treasury Department, "Federal Manufacturers' Wholesale and Retail Sales Taxes," *Hearings, Revenue Revision of 1942*, I, 353.

[77] Shoup, "Taxes Available to Avert Inflation," *Taxing to Prevent Inflation*, p. 89.

of measure and the deduction variant of the consumption type of measure. Moreover, the methods used to modify or eliminate the multiple taxation of the same product which characterizes the general turnover tax involve almost equally troublesome questions. In handling the problem of multiple taxation, the single-stage sales taxes employ the method of suspending the tax on sales destined for certain uses. The value-added technique reverses this procedure and taxes all sales while allowing the deduction of purchases destined for certain uses.

"PHYSICAL-INGREDIENT RULE" IN SINGLE-STAGE SALES TAXES. Under the single-stage sales taxes, the customary procedure for modifying multiple taxation consists in the exemption of "sales for resale" defined in terms of the "physical-ingredient rule." This rule stipulates that the product must either be resold in the same form or enter physically into the product which is resold.

For example, in the case of the manufacturers' sales tax, manufacturers are usually licensed or registered and permitted to sell "tax free" or "in suspension of tax" to other licensed manufacturers provided that the materials are destined for resale as defined by the physical-ingredient principle. The tax is applied when the products receive any other destination, except that exports are generally exempt. As a result, it is imposed not only on all sales to nonmanufacturers and on sales destined for the personal consumption of manufacturers but also on sales for use in manufacturing business. The avoidance of multiple taxation in the manufacturing sphere is therefore limited to materials which become physical components of consumers' goods. Business supplies and capital facilities which are merely financially integrated in the price of consumers' goods are taxed at least twice, once when sold to the manufacturer for business use and a second time when the cost of supplies and depreciation costs are embodied in the final sale of the finished products.

As previously explained, the original French manufacturers' sales tax allowed manufacturers to make sales for resale in suspension of tax when they sold to other manufacturers who were listed in a directory of producers compiled by the General Administration of Indirect Taxes or who provided a resale certificate endorsed by the Office of Indirect Taxes. If materials received untaxed were later used for a purpose not warranting the suspension, the vendee was obliged to pay the tax on the purchase price including tax. Manufacturers' accounts were required to contain evidence of the use or destination of products received by them.

The definition of a sale for resale was based upon the physical-ingredient rule, the tax being suspended on "raw materials or products entering wholly or for a part of their elements into the composition of products ultimately subject to the tax."[78] The requirement that the products should be ultimately subject to the tax meant that the tax was imposed on sales to enterprises which were excluded or specifically exempt with the stated exception of exports and a few activities which were treated like exports, notably naval construction.

The criterion of a sale for resale based on the physical-ingredient rule has also been the predominant method of limiting multiple taxation in the case of the wholesalers' and retailers' sales taxes. Under the wholesalers' sales tax, the tax is imposed unless a licensed wholesaler makes a sale for resale to another licensed wholesaler. Similarly, the retail sales tax is imposed on sales not destined for resale.

In the sales taxes of the American states, the physical-ingredient principle is universally employed. Due states that because the rule was administratively practicable, "it was widely copied, and came to be regarded, particularly by tax administrators and lawyers, as a logical dividing line."[79] He expresses his objection to the criterion as follows:

From the standpoint of economics, the rule makes no sense at all; the reason materials are excluded is not because they actually become physical ingredients, but because their costs enter into the prices of the finished products, and taxation of them produces multiple taxation of the final product. Exactly the same reasoning applies to fuel, machinery, supplies, etc. But the states have been very slow to recognize this logic, or fear the administrative problems and revenue loss from extending the exclusion of producers' goods. Producers' goods typically yield from 20 to 25 per cent of total sales tax revenue. . . .[80]

As indicated by the quotation below, Jacoby takes a similar position:

Significant it is that *no* statute makes use of that definition of "retail sale" which alone is economically consistent: namely, a sale to a consumer who enjoys and derives utility from the use or possession of that which he acquires, and does not employ it in a business or occupation. In view of the oft-expressed popular aversion to "double" taxation, the failure to avoid this condition by use of such a definition must be explained either by a belief

[78] *Code général des Impôts,* 1st ed., art. 267 (a). This quotation is extracted from the law of fractional payments but the wording is the same as under the original statute.

[79] *Sales Taxation,* p. 298.

[80] *Ibid.,* pp. 298 f.

in its administrative impracticability, by legislative ignorance of, or indifference to, elementary economics, or by pressure to produce a maximum of revenue from a "retail" sales tax.[81]

He concludes, however, that the probable explanation is administrative convenience:

Why then, have state legislatures made use of it [the physical-ingredient rule]? Aside from the unconsidered copying of legislation in other states that certainly determined the form of many sales taxes, the answer is probably its relative simplicity in conception and administration. Normally it is easier to decide whether or not any article becomes a physical ingredient of goods sold by the purchaser, than it is to say whether or not property is sold to a "consumer" in the economic sense. . . .[82]

EXTENSION OF PHYSICAL-INGREDIENT RULE. Although the physical-ingredient rule may be comparatively simple, its application often involves disputes, especially with regard to articles which, being destroyed in production, are closely related to physical ingredients, and articles which under some methods of production become physical ingredients and under others are destroyed. The solution of the problem frequently presupposes scientific knowledge.[83]

Consequently, it is not surprising that in considering a manufacturers' sales tax, the United States Treasury Department mentioned the possibility of allowing a suspension of tax on all "direct expenses," which, moreover, is the logical procedure for implementing either the consumption or income measures of sales taxation.[84] The State of Connecticut has attempted to use the criterion of direct expenses in its retail sales tax. A statutory exemption of materials and tools consumed or used directly in agricultural production or industrial plant has been interpreted in the administrative rulings to allow an exemption for materials, tools, and similar items used directly in processing if their normal life of usefulness is less than one year and their cost is allowed as ordinary and necessary deductible expenses in the federal income tax.[85] The provision is

[81] Jacoby, *Retail Sales Taxation*, pp. 129 f.

[82] *Ibid.*, pp. 133 f.

[83] Shoup, *Sales Tax in the American States*, p. 585.

[84] U.S. Treasury Department, Division of Tax Research, "Federal Manufacturers' Wholesale and Retail Sales Taxes," *Hearings, Revenue Revision of 1942*, I, 353.

[85] Denzel C. Cline, "Sales Tax Exemption of Producer Goods," *Proceedings of the Forty-Fifth Annual Conference of the National Tax Association, 1952* (Sacramento, Calif., 1953), p. 622.

reported to be troublesome because of its dependence on the federal income tax, taxpayers often deducting items later disallowed by the federal auditors.[86] Aside from this, it seems to be a simpler method than the physical-ingredient rule, especially when the latter is extended to special categories of products customarily charged to current account.

Under the French manufacturers' sales tax, for example, the suspensive regime was extended to certain categories of products other than physical ingredients. The first consisted of "raw materials or products not constituting equipment which normally and without entering the finished product are destroyed or lose their specific qualities in the course of a single manufacturing operation."[87] This category involves such materials as oxygen, steam, and gas used to heat ovens; electricity as a motor or chemical force; sulphuric acid for cleaning metals; explosives; calcium carbide; acetylene; and electrodes. A similar extension of the physical-ingredient rule has also been used in many sales taxes of the American states and has been designated as the "directly consumed rule."[88] As in the case of physical ingredients, identification of these materials requires scientific knowledge; and fine-drawn distinctions are involved because the use rather than the nature of the product determines its classification. The French statute referred disputes concerning both categories of articles to a committee of experts responsible for determining the nature and value of goods declared at the customs, except that a tax official and an expert selected by the General Tax Administration replaced the Director of Customs and the expert appointed by the Customs Administration.[89]

The French law also allowed a reduction from taxable gross receipts equaling 50 percent of the taxable value of "products rapidly consumed" or, in other words, a tax reduction of 50 percent.[90] They were listed by decree and included such items as foundry sand for running through a mold or cutting marble, abrasives, polishing products, magnesia, dolomite, refractory bricks for ovens, molasses for foundry crucibles and ingot molds, molders' points and cold nails, molds used in the glass and porcelain industry, electrodes for electrical ovens, cutting and soluble oils, grease for metal work, wire drawing and stretching, cutting products used

---

[86] *Ibid.*

[87] *Code général des Impôts,* 1st ed., art. 267(a).

[88] Cline, "Sales Tax Exemption of Producer Goods," *Proceedings, National Tax Association, 1952,* p. 621.

[89] *Code général des Impôts,* 1st ed., art. 267(a).

[90] *Ibid.,* art. 273–5.

in metallurgy, and animal charcoals. As in the case of the former categories, scientific problems were involved. The Council of State declared that it was illegal to designate electrodes for ovens as a product rapidly consumed regardless of the process used and that, in the particular instance, the electrodes were entitled to be sold in suspension of tax as a product which was destroyed or lost its specific qualities in a single operation.[91]

To alleviate further the burden on producers' goods, the French tax administration also granted concessions when manufacturers produced certain tools which were only useful for a specific job as, for example, engraving plates. Instead of taxing the plates as a firm's delivery for its own use, the administration collected the tax on the materials purchased from other firms and used in their manufacture, treating the remainder of the value added as services.[92]

Moreover, by administrative tolerance, certain producers' goods were not taxed although, strictly speaking, the law was applicable. For example, a producer might manufacture a final product which consisted of components which were usable in themselves, as in the manufacture of machinery which involved chains, leather straps, and motors. These so-called "internal manufactures" or "partial fabrications" were not taxed if the producer delivered them for his own use, whether business or personal, provided that the producer did not alter the nature of his business.[93] Another example is the case of samples without market value, where the administration allowed the materials concerned to be purchased in suspension of tax although, strictly speaking, they were not resold.[94]

Some American states have also extended the exemption of sales for business use beyond the categories of physical ingredients and products directly consumed. For example, the original Michigan retail sales tax which limited sales for resale to physical ingredients was amended in 1935 to include in "sales for resale" sales to manufacturers and processors of

[91] Re "Affaire Compagnie Universelle d'Acétylène et de Métallurgie," *Recueil des arrêts du Conseil d'État, Tables, 1948* (Paris, 1948), pp. 151 f.

[92] "Note Administrative No. 3.793, 2/1 du 27 septembre 1948," *Bulletin officiel de l'Administration des Contributions Indirectes*, No. 45 (Oct. 5, 1948), p. 715; Lauré, *La taxe sur la valeur ajoutée*, pp. 19–20.

[93] Patouillet, "La suppression du régime de la suspension de taxe en matière de taxe à la production," *Recueil Dalloz: Chronique, 1949*, p. 13.

[94] "La notion de livraison à soi-même," *Le revue fiduciaire*, No. 298 (June, 1953), p. 49.

machinery, power, tools, and other items *directly* used in processing.[95] However, an amendment in 1939 provided that the exemption was not applicable to tangible personal property which became attached to real estate.[96] Ohio was even more generous and added to the exemption provided by the physical-ingredient rule sales to purchasers who "use or consume the thing transferred *directly* (italics added) in the production of tangible personal property for sale by manufacturing, processing, refining, mining, production of crude oil or gas, farming, horticulture, or floriculture, or *directly* in making retail sales or *directly* in the rendition of a public utility service. . . ."[97] This exempted not only various types of machinery but also such items as showcases and fixtures sold to retailers. The administration of this type of provision is complicated because fine distinctions are required to identify articles directly used or consumed in production or in making retail sales. Considerable litigation has occurred in the case of the Ohio provision. For example, in 1950, the Ohio Supreme Court reversed the Board of Tax Appeals by deciding that certain boom and bucket cranes were taxable because they only conveyed ingredients to a place of processing while, in a later case, it held that such apparatus was used directly in processing and was therefore exempt. The Court stated that every case had to be decided on its own merits.[98]

Other states which have extended the physical-ingredient rule have used exemptions which depend largely on the nature of the product rather than its use. Thus, Florida exempts unconditionally a large number of products including seeds, feeds, fertilizers, insecticides and fungicides for application on crops and groves, cheesecloth for shading tobacco, motor vehicles, gasoline, kerosene, lubricating oils, diesel oil, crude oil, fuel oil, coal, coke, cordwood, electricity, water, and machinery on which the tax exceeds $300 or, with a tax rate of 3 percent, machinery selling for over $10,000.[99]

In his article on retail sales taxation, Due states that it is administratively practicable to exclude the majority of business purchases through the exemption of certain classes of products generally utilized for produc-

[95] Jacoby, *Retail Sales Taxation*, p. 131.

[96] Cline, "Sales Tax Exemption of Producer Goods," *Proceedings, National Tax Association, 1952*, p. 627.

[97] Jacoby, *Retail Sales Taxation*, p. 132, n. 38. Second and third italics mine.

[98] Cline, "Sales Tax Exemption of Producer Goods," *Proceedings, National Tax Association, 1952*, pp. 625 f.

[99] *Ibid.*, p. 624.

tion purposes such as industrial, agricultural, and commercial machinery and equipment; building materials for industrial construction; feed, seed, and fertilizers.[100] Although he accepts the principle of restricting the tax to sales for ultimate consumption, he warns that the exemption of all sales to business firms or even certain types of products would cause an excessive amount of evasion, annoyance to retailers, and auditing problems because of the extent to which articles were used by ultimate consumers as well as producers.[101]

His position approximates the one taken by the United States Treasury Department in its 1943 study of retail sales taxation. The Treasury Department also held that, in theory, the retail sales tax should be imposed only on sales to ultimate consumers but that, in practice, it would be necessary to rely upon the physical-ingredient rule because of the extent to which articles were purchased by consumers as well as producers so that many articles purchased for business use would be taxed. It reasoned that the exemption of all sales to business firms regardless of the nature of the product would create an excessive loophole for the personal consumption of business owners and their friends while exemptions based upon the nature of products used by business would sacrifice too much revenue because of the wide variety of items used by business. It conceded that an exemption limited to sales for business use would theoretically solve the problem but that this type of exemption would be impossible to administer primarily because the records of most retailers were not sufficiently complete to effect a distinction between sales for production and consumption purposes. In addition, it maintained that vendors would be unable to determine the use of articles at the time of sale; that, because of the large number of small transactions, the administration would be unable to check their ultimate use; and, finally, that many articles were used jointly for production and consumption as in the case of a grocer who rents a building containing his store and home.[102]

The Treasury Department concluded that exemptions for the purpose of modifying the double taxation of producers' goods should be restricted to a few clearly definable classes of products used primarily by business

[100] Due, "Retail Sales Taxation in Theory and Practice," *National Tax Journal,* III (Dec., 1950), 323.

[101] *Ibid.,* pp. 322–23.

[102] U.S. Treasury Department, Division of Tax Research, "Considerations Respecting a Federal Retail Sales Tax," *Hearings, Revenue Revision of 1943,* pp. 1129–30.

enterprises, accounting for a significant portion of business costs, and sold in large amounts by relatively specialized concerns which kept satisfactory records.[103] In the light of these considerations, it recommended the possible exemption of feed, seed, fertilizers, fuel, and industrial, commercial, and agricultural machinery.[104] It noted that fuel was used in large amounts by consumers as well as producers but that limiting the exemption to purchases by business firms would be inadvisable in view of the problem of determining destination.[105] Finally, it raised the question of whether to extend the exemption to the following classes of articles:

1. Durable equipment other than machinery such as tools, desks, tables, filing cabinets, and show cases.

2. Livestock for breeding purposes, work animals, dairy cows, and poultry for laying purposes.

3. Consumable articles (other than fuel) such as returnable containers, lubricants, abrasives and polishing agents, and chemicals (other than those becoming physical ingredients).

4. Miscellaneous supplies, such as cleaning materials, stationery, and light bulbs.

5. Building materials.

With the exception of containers, it rejected the idea of exempting these articles on the ground that each category consisted of a wide variety of individual products, requiring separate enumeration, and that many of the articles were used by consumers as well as producers.[106]

COMPARABLE TECHNIQUES UNDER SUBTRACTION METHOD OF COMPUTING VALUE ADDED. The value-added tax replaces the system which allows sales destined for certain uses (and possibly sales of certain products) to be made in suspension of tax with the method of taxing all sales and allowing the deduction of purchases destined for certain uses (and possibly purchases of certain products). Instead of being primarily concerned with the disposition of purchases by the vendee, it focuses attention on the use of purchases by the vendor. The question arises whether it thereby gains in administrative efficiency by making evasion more difficult. The answer appears to be in the negative.

[103] *Ibid.*
[104] *Ibid.*, p. 1131.
[105] *Ibid.*, p. 1133.
[106] *Ibid.*, pp. 1135–37.

As we have seen, the value-added technique offers two administrative advantages over the suspensive system. In the first place, it facilitates the exemption of small taxpayers with less impairment of the total tax base. Secondly, it does not require the licensing of taxpayers or resale certificates, thereby reducing the formalities of compliance. Otherwise, it seems not to be administratively superior to the suspensive system, at least with respect to intrajurisdictional transactions,[107] although it has frequently been credited with curbing the evasion possible under the latter method. Thus, in 1929, the National Industrial Conference Board expressed the opinion that, under a retail sales tax, the exemption of all sales to business would cause evasion and suggested as an alternative the taxation of all final sales, including those made to business, but with a deduction from tax liabilities of taxes paid on purchases destined for business use.[108]

Two of the official reasons for the replacement of the French tax of fractional payments by the suspensive system of collecting the manufacturers' sales tax involved administrative considerations. It was expected that evasion and avoidance would be reduced and that the formalities of administration and compliance would be simplified.

The reason why the collection of the tax by fractional payments rather than through a suspension system was expected to check evasion was the fact that it was to the manufacturer's self-interest to obtain purchase invoices indicating that his suppliers had paid the tax. If he failed to do so, he was entitled to no deduction.[109] Actually, this merely reversed the previous system under which it had been to the manufacturer's self-interest to obtain proof of destination from his customers. He might have required a resale certificate in which case he was absolved from further responsibility. However, if he had depended on the listing of his customers in the producer's directory, he was jointly responsible with the customer and subject to penalties in the event that any neglect of the legal formalities and rules had impaired the operation of the system.[110]

[107] Interjurisdictional transactions introduce additional considerations. The origin principle, although not the destination principle, implies use of the value-added procedure.

[108] National Industrial Conference Board, *General Sales or Turnover Taxation* (New York, 1929), pp. 95 f. Apparently the suspensive system was to be retained with respect to sales destined for resale.

[109] Patouillet, "La suppression du régime de la suspension de taxe en matière de taxe à la production," *Recueil Dalloz: Chronique, 1949,* p. 16.

[110] Larguier, *Traité des Taxes,* p. 78.

Whereas, under the suspensive system, the vendor was jointly responsible with the vendee for the destination of sales, the new system made the vendee jointly responsible with the vendor for the establishment of proper invoices.[111] If, under the old system, customers often made false statements concerning the destination of products, under the new system suppliers often misrepresented their tax situation. The new system increased the legal responsibilities of taxpayers only to the extent that they had previously used resale certificates through which the tax administration had shared some of the responsibility.

In any event, the hope that the new system would check evasion proved overoptimistic because of the use of false invoices. Consequently, the Budget Law of April 14, 1952 (no. 52-401, art. 51) imposed heavy penalties on vendors when invoices were incorrect unless payment was made through a check; money order; or, by administrative tolerance, a draft drawn directly upon the customer and held at acceptable institutions, provided that these documents indicated the buyer's identity or location. Lacking such evidence, the vendor was also absolved from responsibility if he obtained an order certificate (*bulletin de commande*) supplied by the General Tax Administration which gave the necessary information.[112] This measure is reported to have been a very effective means of curbing fraud.[113] However, a similar system might have been used under the former regime.

The expectation that the method of fractional payments would reduce avoidance was based on the fact that excessive inventories were being accumulated by merchant-producers who combined the sale of products to manufacturers with resales to nontaxpayers of products in the same form as when purchased, that is, distributive sales. These enterprises had been permitted to accumulate inventories in suspension of tax regardless of destination and were not required to pay the tax on the purchase price of articles resold in the same form to nontaxpayers until the sales were actually made.[114] Thereafter, however, the merchant-producers were permitted to deduct taxes paid on inventory purchases and delay payment of

[111] *Code général des Impôts*, 1st ed., art. 1756, par. 4.

[112] "Obligations des vendeurs, utilisations des bulletins de commande," *La revue fiduciaire: monographies*, No. 45 (June 2, 1953), pp. 1–10.

[113] Ministère des Finances, "Situation des recettes budgétaires de l'État," *Statistiques et études financières*, No. 61 (Jan., 1954), p. 62.

[114] "Nouveau régime de la taxe à la production," *Bulletin fiduciaire*, No. 246 (Jan., 1949), p. 16.

the tax due on the purchase price of distributive sales to nontaxpayers just as before.[115] The administration disallowed this procedure only when such sales represented at least half of the taxpayer's turnover and it was evident that he was trying to avoid the tax.[116]

The elimination of the producers' directory and resale certificates reduced administrative formalities. The administration was freed from the tasks of keeping a directory up-to-date and handling resale certificates. However, as these procedures had presumably been adopted in order to lighten the administrative burden of checking taxpayers' sales and purchases, the new system would appear to have required a more intensive checking. In the last analysis, therefore, improved control under the deductive value-added technique as compared with the suspensive system depends on whether it is easier to trace the disposition of purchases by a vendor rather than by a vendee; and there seems to be no reason why this should be the case. What difference does it make whether a firm as a vendee obtains certain purchases in suspension of tax or receives the same purchases burdened with tax and is then allowed to reduce its tax liability by the taxes paid on such purchases?

Although the French law of fractional payments may not have relieved the burdens of administration, it did reduce the compliance problems of the taxpayer. Voluntary payment of the tax when business concerns sold to manufacturers or for export merely involved paying and invoicing the tax in order to deduct the taxes paid on purchases. As this procedure is more flexible than the former system, it facilitates the avoidance of double taxation when products reenter the manufacturing sphere after having been previously taxed in a less finished form when transferred by a manufacturer to an enterprise in a nontaxable stage.

Under the former system, the tax administration allowed manufacturers to make occasional purchases in suspension of tax from an ordinary merchant. However, this tolerance only applied when a merchant was situated between two manufacturers and not when a second merchant intervened. Under the system of fractional payments, merchants were not only allowed to pay and invoice the tax when they were situated between two manufacturers but were able to request that a merchant-supplier pay

---

[115] Actually, no new revenues were obtained from use of the value-added procedure as such.

[116] "Les options fiscales des industriels et commerçants," *La revue fiduciaire*, No. 326 (Nov., 1955), p. 58.

the tax in order to avoid an interruption of the manufacturing circuit.[117] The problem of double taxation of products which reenter a taxable sphere as physical ingredients is characteristic of taxes limited to the manufacturing or wholesaling sphere whether or not the value-added technique is used; and both techniques may employ the system of voluntary payment to eliminate most multiple taxation.

The value-added method can avoid the type of double taxation which occurs under any form of single-stage sales tax when a firm in the suspensive system purchases materials tax-paid on the assumption that it will use them as final products and later resells them. Suspensive systems usually make no provision for a refund in such cases. However, under the French legislation which limits deductions to the invoices of the month preceding sales, this type of double taxation must still exist. Presumably, a purchase is assumed to be destined for resale or other deductible use where there is any doubt concerning its eventual status.

To ensure that the total base of a value-added tax is the same as the total base of a single-stage sales tax of equal scope, it is necessary to provide a carryover of excess credits arising under the value-added tax when deductions exceed taxable receipts. As previously explained, in certain special situations, the French law has prevented this equivalence through its rule of nonreimbursement or buffer rule (*règle du butoir*).

In summary, it may be stated that the system of suspending taxes due on sales and the technique of deducting taxable purchases from taxable sales are essentially the same. A sales tax which limits suspension of the tax to physical ingredients and products disappearing on first use presents the same type of problems as a tax which allows the deduction of similar taxable products from taxable sales.

If the suspensive method is applied to all materials which are considered direct expenses, the same problems would arise as under a procedure which deducts a concern's direct expenses from sales. As the suspensive system is extended to various types of investment goods, it approaches the consumption type of value-added tax.

It is possible to conceive of a retail sales tax which is imposed only on goods and services purchased by ultimate consumers. The tax would be suspended on all sales of goods and services delivered for business use. It is then equivalent to the deduction variant of the consumption type of

[117] "Paiement volontaire de la taxe à la production," *Le revue fiduciaire*, No. 270 (Jan., 1951). p. 48.

value-added tax which taxes gross receipts from sales of goods and services and deducts a firm's outlays on goods or services used in business.

If it is administratively difficult to include most services within the scope of a retail sales tax, it would be equally difficult to subject them to the value-added tax. The only advantage offered by the latter is its facility in exempting small taxpayers.

The failure in retail sales taxation to suspend the tax on all sales to business firms is attributable in part to probable avoidance or evasion; and there is no reason to believe that the deduction of all purchases for business use under the value-added tax woud improve the situation. The difficulties under the suspensive system arising from a concern's liability for the destination of its customers' sales is paralleled by its responsibility under the value-added method for seeing that the tax is paid by its suppliers. The French value-added tax limits the deductibility of goods and services purchased for business use partly in order to restrict tax credits to items necessary for an immediate increase in industrial production; but, as previously explained, the limitations probably primarily reflect the opinion that the limitations may prevent tax avoidance through the purchase of items diverted to personal consumption.

Exclusions and Exemptions

Certain exclusions and exemptions facilitate the administration of a tax. This is true of exemptions for small taxpayers. Furthermore, administrative considerations are often partly responsible for the exclusion of agriculture, the professions, and service enterprises.

Excessive exclusions and exemptions, however, complicate administrative and compliance problems because of the difficulty of distinguishing taxable from nontaxable transactions and the opportunities provided for evasion and avoidance. Moreover, the reduction in the tax base raises the necessary tax rate, thereby intensifying administrative problems and any inequities among the remaining taxpayers.

Excessive exclusions and exemptions have been a more outstanding feature of modern sales tax laws than of net income taxation probably for two reasons. In the first place, unlike the net income tax, a sales tax makes it possible to exempt specified products. Secondly, sales taxes are universally recognized as business costs so that taxpaying concerns are very conscious of inequalities arising from concessions made to either competing products or vendors and soon demand similar favors.

All tax concessions originate in more or less justifiable ethical, social, political, and economic considerations and are often the result of mixed motivations. It is the fact that they always have a plausible explanation that causes their inordinate use.

EXEMPTION OF PRODUCTS IN SALES TAXATION. Most students of sales taxation have favored the exemption of certain basic necessities. Jacoby, who questions the grounds for most exemptions, recommends a limited number justified by considerations of equity. He makes the following observation:

Exemptions have always been the bane of sales tax administrators. By making it necessary to separate taxable from non-taxable transactions, they add immeasurably to cost of administration and opportunities for evasion. Where exemptions find no equitable justification they are, of course, to be doubly condemned. Yet inefficiency is sometimes the price of equity in taxation, and some administrative difficulty should be tolerated if exemptions, such as primary foods, make a sales tax more equitable in its operation. Equitable exemptions should be confined to a *few, well-defined* articles, so that segregation between taxable and exempt sales is not too difficult. . . .[118]

Due approves of exemptions for food and medicine and, if services are taxed, for doctors, dental fees, and rental payments, the latter on the ground that the tax would discriminate against tenants as compared with homeowners.[119] In estimating the yield of a manufacturers' sales tax, Shoup allowed for a food exemption because of considerations of equity and the fact that there would be more interest in that type of tax[120] The United States Treasury Department, on the other hand, opposed the exemption of food and medicine in its plan for a possible federal retail sales tax, reasoning that most of these products were sold to upper as well as lower income groups and that many were luxury items.[121] It noted that very few American states have exempted food or medicine because of administrative problems.[122] The French value-added tax, on the other

[118] Jacoby, *Retail Sales Taxation*, p. 277.

[119] Due, "Retail Sales Taxation in Theory and Practice," *National Tax Journal*, III (Dec., 1950), 317.

[120] Carl S. Shoup, *Federal Finances in the Coming Decade* (New York, 1941), p. 58.

[121] U.S. Treasury Department, Division of Tax Research, "Considerations Respecting a Federal Retail Sales Tax," *Hearings, Revenue Revision of 1943*, pp. 1142–43.

[122] *Ibid.*, p. 1214.

hand, is encumbered by numerous exemptions and reduced rates for food products.

Although a food exemption may improve the distributional effects of a sales tax, it has the disadvantage of removing a large proportion of the tax base.[123] Due states that a food exemption would remove one fifth of the tax revenue of a retail sales tax, and Shoup has estimated that it would decrease the base of a manufacturers' sales tax by one fourth.[124]

Another type of exemption important in sales taxation concerns products subject to a special excise. This reason accounts for several exemptions in the French law and is generally assumed to justify exemption in the sales taxes of the American states. Jacoby objects to the exemption of sales subject to motor fuel taxes on the ground that the latter are for special benefits; but he considers it just to exempt sales subject to other heavy special excises.[125] However, it would be preferable to reduce the special excises rather than interfere with the application of a general law. In its study of retail sales taxation, the United States Treasury Department recommended the inclusion of vendors subject to special excises and repeal or reduction of the excises if the burden on producers or consumers was considered excessive.[126] Due holds that the exemption in state retail sales taxes of commodities subject to special excises—i.e., gasoline, liquor, and tobacco—is the most frequent and least justifiable type of exemption. He reasons that the introduction of a sales tax does not warrant a reduction in the relative tax burden on items subject to these special excises.[127]

Sales tax statutes sometimes provide for the exclusion or exemption of receipts which represent other taxes collected by the vendor who is regarded as merely an agent of the taxing authority in this respect. The Michigan Business Activities Tax, for example, excludes amounts received by "trustees of taxes received or collected from others under direction of the laws of the Federal government or of any state or local

---

[123] For a discussion of the reduction in regressivity effected by a food exemption, see J. W. McGrew, "Effects of a Food Exemption on the Incidence of a Retail Sales Tax," *National Tax Journal*, II (Dec., 1949), 362–67.

[124] Due, "Retail Sales Taxation in Theory and Practice," *National Tax Journal*, III (Dec., 1950), 317; Shoup, *Federal Finances in the Coming Decade*, p. 58.

[125] Jacoby, *Retail Sales Taxation*, pp. 108–13.

[126] U.S. Treasury Department, Division of Tax Research, "Considerations Respecting a Federal Retail Sales Tax," *Hearings, Revenue Revision of 1943*, p. 1148,

[127] Due, "Retail Sales Taxation in Theory and Practice," *National Tax Journal*, III (Dec., 1950), 323.

government" and allows a deduction from taxable receipts of all other taxes except those on net income.[128] In the computation of the tax base, the Japanese consumption type of value-added tax allows a deduction of taxes other than the net income tax, the net worth tax, and the inhabitant's tax (a combined income and poll tax). On the other hand, under the French value-added tax and its predecessor, the tax base has included all taxes, even the value-added tax itself. Failure to allow the subtraction of indirect taxes does, of course, increase the relative tax burden on the products involved; but, as previously noted, the treatment of other indirect taxes in sales tax measures requires a deeper analysis than has been given in this study.

A special exemption may be granted to any commodity; and the French sales taxes furnish numerous examples. In addition to the exclusion from the value-added and service taxes for items reached by replacement taxes and the exemptions relating to various specified food products, to agricultural producers' goods, and to naval and aircraft construction, there are exemptions concerned with newspapers and monthly periodicals conforming to certain requirements as well as the publications of nonprofit organizations and even reviews edited by organizations for family gardens, meals served by nonprofit student restaurants, and war memorials. Because they can easily be rationalized in terms of social desirability, they have powerful political appeal even though capable of abuse.

EXEMPTIONS OF CERTAIN GROUPS OF PERSONS IN SALES TAXATION. Political considerations are responsible for the excessive exemption of certain groups of taxpayers. In French legislation, Lauré has condemned the recently suppressed exemption of agricultural cooperatives and the exemption of artisans, regulated public utilities, and certain government enterprises.

Jacoby emphasizes the undesirability of exempting municipally owned utilities in state sales taxes because competing enterprises should be subjected to equal taxation.[129] For the same reason, Lauré objects to the exemption of certain French government enterprises. The United States Treasury Department favored the application of a retail sales tax

---

[128] Michigan Department of Revenue, "Michigan Business Activities Tax," *Act No. 150, Public Acts of 1953, as Amended*, Sec. 1 (j-5), (1-1).

[129] Jacoby, *Retail Sales Taxation*, p. 117.

to government activities of a proprietary or commercial nature.[130] In the American states, however, federal and state constitutional restrictions prevent the uniform application of sales taxes to government instrumentalities.

Under a value-added approach which uses the French system of computing tax liability, sales by and to government enterprises should be taxed in order not to interfere with the deduction process. In France, the chain of deductions has been broken by exempting the sales of some public industries. For example, the gunpowder monopoly often sells sulphuric acid to the private sector. Because the sale is exempt, no deduction is allowed for the taxes paid on the materials purchased by the government monopoly in order to manufacture the sulphuric acid. Meanwhile, private firms purchasing the sulphuric acid are in principle entitled to no deduction. Consequently, there is some double taxation of the value added prior to the governmental manufacturing stage, a situation which the administration tries to alleviate by allowing the private concerns a tax credit of a specified percentage of the purchase price of the sulphuric acid. The percentage varies with the nature of the product manufactured by the private concerns,[131] presumably because of the varying amounts of sulphuric acid incorporated in the final product. If sales to the government enterprise were exempt, there would, of course, be only a single tax; but the benefit of any intended subsidy to private concerns utilizing the government product would be lost.

Another problem is whether to tax sales to a general government agency within the limits of federal and state constitutional restrictions. Jacoby maintains that a state should exempt sales to itself because it would merely pay the tax to itself on the assumption that the tax is borne by the purchaser.[132] He observes that the exemption of sales to political subdivisions may be considered as a form of grant-in-aid; but he reasons further that all sales to government may warrant exemption because they are really "intermediate goods" used to produce government services which are the real final product.[133] However, to the extent that the output of free government services is not subjected to sales taxation, the exemption of government purchases would entirely free much final

---

[130] U.S. Treasury Department, Division of Tax Research, "Considerations Respecting a Federal Retail Sales Tax," *Hearings, Revenue Revision of 1943*, p. 1148.

[131] Lauré, *La taxe sur la valeur ajoutée*, p. 74.

[132] Jacoby, *Retail Sales Taxation*, pp. 117 f.

[133] *Ibid.*, p. 118.

product from taxation. It is the fact that, if government purchases are taxed, the government is in a position to shift the tax to taxpayers which may justify the exemption of these transactions. An important consideration in favor of taxing government purchases is that of administrative convenience, for the problem of distinguishing exempt from taxable sales is eliminated. The French sales taxes have always been imposed on government purchases.

The United States Treasury Department reasoned that exemption of all sales to government under a retail sales tax would so complicate the administration in order to forestall evasion that, if any exemption were allowed, it should be restricted to certain types of contracts, to sales above a certain amount, or to particular types of articles. It pointed out two disadvantages in taxing such sales. One was the fact that the gross tax yield would appear greater than the net and might therefore confuse policy decisions in regard to the tax; but this result would only be temporary. Secondly, it commented that the taxation of sales to states, which was constitutionally possible if the tax was legally imposed on the vendor, would violate the principle of taxing only the ultimate consumer. It added that the states and local governments would be obliged to shift the tax to their own taxpayers and would, therefore, probably tax sales to the federal government.[134] However, even on the basis of this philosophy a case can be made for taxing government purchases insofar as they are used to produce consumers' goods.

The issues raised by the exemption of nonprofit institutions somewhat resemble those presented by the exemption of government agencies. Because, in principle, nonprofit institutions provide socially important services which would otherwise have to be supplied by government, they have a logical claim to an exemption for their nonprofit activities.

Unfortunately, as in the case of the direct taxes,[135] the exemption of nonprofit institutions creates opportunities for avoidance and evasion and for building up tax-free economic and political power. Furthermore, even when the motives for establishing such enterprises are unimpeachable, the fact that the tax exemption constitutes an indirect subsidy means that the general taxpayer is supporting many enterprises over which his government exercises no direct supervision.

[134] U.S. Treasury Department, Division of Tax Research, "Considerations Respecting a Federal Retail Sales Tax," *Hearings, Revenue Revision of 1943*, pp. 1145–46.

[135] See "Why Business is Finding More Uses for Foundations," *Business Week*, No. 1294 (June 19, 1954), pp. 167–69.

The use of direct subsidies rather than tax exemptions constitutes an alternative approach to the problem and makes possible direct public control. Yet, if it is feasible to establish a highly responsible nonpartisan body capable of wisely administering direct subsidies, it should be equally practicable to establish and apply adequate standards for qualifying as a tax-exempt institution; and the exemption system offers the advantage of being more likely to foster independent and imaginative projects than the use of direct subsidies. A minimum requirement should be an absence of political activities and of commercial techniques such as high-pressure advertising. Obviously, it is not easy to devise and apply this type of standard, and an excellent article on foundations in *Business Week* states that "Removing exemptions is a drastic penalty that the government uses only rarely against a foundation that engages in propaganda, lobbying, or subversive activities."[136]

Whether purchases of nonprofit institutions for use in their exempt activities should also be exempt from tax, a reimbursement being allowed if necessary, is a controversial issue. When their exempt services represent a type of final product which is taxable to other purchasers, their taxation is necessary to avoid favoring collective purchasing. On the other hand, if they service poor consumers, there is a strong ethical and political case for their exemption. If the purchases are destined for an activity utilized by business, their treatment should presumably be related to the concept underlying the sales taxes.

Any business activities of nonprofit institutions which directly compete with independent business concerns should be taxed. The United States Revenue Act of 1950 apparently made some headway in closing this type of loophole.[137] It taxed " 'unrelated' income" in an effort to prevent "leaseback deals." It also prohibited "unreasonable" accumulation of income—a clause directed at the type of foundation which is regarded as a tax-free source of venture capital for the business enterprise by which it is established; but apparently this provision has been difficult to interpret. Similar to this issue, of course, is the question of the potential role of large funds as suppliers of venture capital to business.

In the study of retail sales taxation, the United States Treasury Department emphasized the administrative problem of administering exemptions because of the difficulty of distinguishing bona fide nonprofit

---

[136] *Ibid.*, p. 176.
[137] *Ibid.*, p. 169.

organizations from those performing only incidental nonprofit activities.[138] It also pointed out the competitive inequities arising from the exemption of sales by nonprofit institutions other than charitable and religious groups,[139] although, of course, exemption of sales by charitable and religious groups may also involve competitive inequities.

In the French and Japanese value-added taxes and the Michigan Business Activities Tax, nonprofit activities and related business are exempt. The Michigan legislation extends the exemption to unrelated business undertakings of religious organizations which support educational or religious programs while the Japanese tax extends the exemption to certain unrelated business enterprises. The Michigan and Japanese taxes, but not the French, also allow the deduction from taxable receipts of business purchases made from exempt institutions; and the Michigan administration classifies contributions to nonprofit institutions as deductible business expenditures.

The reasons for the exclusion or exemption of services from sales tax laws have been discussed above. In principle, they should be taxed. In practice, however, they have usually been exempt by single-stage sales taxes because of the administrative difficulty of applying the tax to the small enterprises involved and because many services are rendered to business firms. It may be more feasible to include them under a value-added tax than under a retail sales tax because of the former's advantage with respect to an administrative exemption.

COMPARATIVE TREATMENT OF EXEMPT ACTIVITIES UNDER VALUE-ADDED AND SUSPENSIVE METHODS. In principle, exemptions should produce the same results whether the suspensive or value-added techniques are used. If under the former system the tax is eliminated on sales of physical ingredients, including sales made to concerns producing exempt products or engaging in certain other exempt activities, then the value-added approach should allow a reimbursement of taxes paid on purchases of physical ingredients by such concerns. On the other hand, if under the suspensive method the tax is imposed on sales to all exempt concerns, then under the value-added approach the tax must likewise be imposed on all sales to exempt concerns with no provision for re-

---

[138] U.S. Treasury Department, Division of Tax Research, "Considerations Respecting a Federal Retail Sales Tax," *Hearings, Revenue Revision of 1943*, pp. 1147–48.

[139] *Ibid.*

imbursement; and the French, Michigan, and Japanese value-added taxes are imposed in this manner.

When sales to exempt concerns are taxable and a taxpayer engages in both taxable and exempt activities, his joint costs must be allocated between the two uses in order to compute his tax credits under the value-added approach. A comparable proration is necessary under the suspensive method.

In the French tax, export exemptions are an exception to the general rule of nonreimbursement. Deductions are allowed under the value-added tax even though exports are exempt, and there is a somewhat limited refund plus an indefinite carryforward of excess tax credits. Thus, the situation is roughly the same as under a suspensive system in which the tax is never collected on products entering into export sales.

CONCLUSION

As compared with a net income tax or a spendings tax of similar scope, a general value-added tax possesses the important administrative advantage of being collected from a smaller number of taxpayers. The concentration of the base in fewer hands enables a more thorough check on the accuracy of returns. Moreover, in contrast to the personal income tax, the taxation of income before its distribution to ultimate recipients makes it possible to reach undistributed profits without a special levy. In other respects, the versions of the value-added tax which require depreciation and inventory accounting would be as difficult to administer. Even those which avoid inventory and depreciation accounting would be troublesome in view of the difficulty of determining allowable deductions.

As compared with a retail sales tax of equal scope, the value-added technique would undoubtedly be easier to administer because it facilitates an administrative exemption of small taxpayers. For the same reason, it is probably somewhat superior to a manufacturers' or wholesalers' sales tax of equal scope. The value-added method seems to offer no other administrative advantages, given an equally intensive administration. It is sometimes said to possess the advantage of spreading the initial impact of the tax over a larger number of taxpayers than one collected at a single stage; but this is not so to the extent that the tax is expected to be shifted forward, in view of the fact that the taxpayer at the last stage must advance the tax incorporated in the purchase price of the products which he uses in his business.

Finally, in the case of interjurisdictional transactions, the value-added procedure seems the appropriate one to use in applying the origin principle of sales taxation.[140] On the other hand, the destination principle may be applied as readily through the single-stage procedure as through a value-added method, while the general turnover method is most unsatisfactory.[141]

Of course, both a retail sales tax and a value-added tax through the retail stage largely avoid many of the troublesome problems of determining the tax base involved in taxes limited to earlier stages and also permit a lower tax rate. In some ways, the general turnover tax without rate differentiation appears at first glance easier to administer than any of the above levies; but the problems involved in applying it to commission merchants and international transactions are formidable. Moreover, the obvious inequity to unintegrated enterprises prevents the application of the tax in its pure form when substantial amounts of revenue have to be raised.

[140] See Sullivan, *The Search for Tax Principles in the European Economic Community*, pp. 48 f.

[141] See *ibid.*, pp. 26–34, for a discussion of some of the administrative difficulties involved in applying the destination principle through various methods of collection.

Chapter 7

Some Observations on the
Incidence and Effects of the
Tax on Value Added

CONVENTIONAL HYPOTHESIS OF INCIDENCE

According to conventional doctrine, a general ad valorem tax on sales, and hence the value-added tax, is assumed to be shifted forward to the ultimate consumer through a rise in the prices of consumption goods[1] Thus, if the tax is imposed through the retail stage, it is expected to be the equivalent of a proportional spendings tax collected directly from individuals on the basis of their consumption outlays.

Forward Shifting to Consumer

Assuming full employment and the collection of the tax by the government before spending the money, the procedure of financing government expenditures through such taxation is apparently supposed to operate in the following manner. Under a purely competitive economic system, the tax will raise the marginal costs of private concerns, making some production unprofitable at current prices. To restore profits, the entrepreneur reduces output, thus freeing resources for government use. Given the employment of these resources by the government and, therefore, probably the same aggregate demand for consumers' goods despite

[1] E. Cary Brown, "Analysis of Consumption Taxes in Terms of the Theory of Income Determination," *The American Economic Review*, XL (Mar., 1950), 74.

a smaller output, the average price level of consumers' goods will rise by the amount of the tax. Appropriate adjustments in the velocity of money or, if necessary, its supply are also assumed. Under imperfect competition, similar results are achieved through direct action by taxable vendors who, with the use of average cost techniques, are expected to raise prices by the amount of the tax.[2] As Shoup observes, "the business firms do have to part with some of the money received from sales, for a while, until it comes back to them in government purchases"; but "it may be doubted that this pressure on working capital is strong enough to break down the initial effort of the business firms to add the tax to price."[3]

Possible modifications in relative factor prices because of shifts in quantities demanded are treated as effects rather than incidence.[4] Although a good case can be made for regarding any burdens on factor incomes as part of incidence and, in any event, such burdens should be taken into account, tax theory has thus far been unable to identify them. There have been a few interesting inquiries into the effects of sales taxes on relative factor prices through the combined use of partial equilibrium analysis and static macroeconomic models in an effort to overcome the well-known limitations of such techniques when used separately. Studies utilizing this approach have been made by Professor Earl R. Rolph of the University of California, Dr. J. A. Stockfisch, and Professor Richard A. Musgrave of Princeton University.[5] With respect to the incidence of a sales tax imposed exclusively on consumers goods, the analyses reach similar conclusions, the tax being expected to raise the relative if not absolute prices of the taxed products. Given pure competition and the condition that the consumers' goods industry is neither labor intensive nor capital intensive, they largely substantiate the conventional position that the incidence is on the ultimate con-

---

[2] See John F. Due, *Sales Taxation* (Urbana, Ill., 1957), p. 12.

[3] Carl S. Shoup, "Discussion," *The American Economic Review,* XLII (May, 1952), 162.

[4] See Due, *Sales Taxation,* p. 10.

[5] See, for example, Rolph, "A Proposed Revision of Excise-Tax Theory," *The Journal of Political Economy,* LX (Apr., 1952), 102–17; Stockfisch, "The Capitalization and Investment Aspects of Excise Taxes under Competition," *The American Economic Review,* XLIV (June, 1954), 287–300; Musgrave, "On Incidence," *The Journal of Political Economy,* LXI (Aug., 1953), 306–23; and Musgrave, *The Theory of Public Finance: A Study in Public Finance* (New York, 1959), Chaps. 15 and 16.

sumer.[6] However, Musgrave and Stockfisch arrive at divergent positions concerning the price effects of a sales tax restricted to investment goods. The former holds that it will be directly shifted to suppliers of investment funds, the prices of investment goods remaining unchanged.[7,8] Meanwhile, Stockfisch reasons on the basis of what appears to be the more logical analysis that the tax will cause a relative rise and even some absolute rise in the prices of investment goods,[9] a conclusion with which Rolph would presumably agree.[10]

In the absence of full employment, any tax but one on hoards may be expected to aggravate the situation by freeing private factor payments for governmental use when many factors are already idle. A direct income tax which reduces savings is less harmful during such periods because a tax which applies to savings is more likely to reach hoards; but tax reductions are preferable.

Regressivity of Tax Burden

Granted the hypothesis that the incidence of a general proportional sales tax rests with the ultimate consumer in proportion to his consumption outlays, the tax burden is regressive because consumer expenditures typically represent a decreasing proportion of individual or family income as income levels rise. The regression is alleviated but not eliminated by exemptions of products which rank high in the budgets of the lower income groups, e.g., food and clothing, but is intensified by the exemption of products consumed mainly by the wealthy, notably services, including imputed net rents from owner-occupied homes. Exemptions will also favor certain groups of consumers over others with equal incomes. Finally, to the extent that organized labor is able to obtain higher incomes because of the tax, it shifts its share to profits, a situation which may result in a wage-price spiral under conditions of full employment.

[6] Cf. Musgrave, Theory of Public Finance, pp. 379–81; Stockfisch, p. 294; Rolph, p. 114.
[7] Musgrave, "On Incidence," p. 321, and Theory of Public Finance, pp. 377–79.
[8] See Professor Due's comment on this issue in "Sale Taxation and the Consumer," The American Economic Review, LIII (Dec., 1963), 1082–83.
[9] Stockfisch, p. 296.
[10] Rolph, pp. 109–13.

Distortions in Relative Prices of Consumer Goods

Due emphasizes the phenomenon of "pyramiding," which consists in a rise in the price of consumer goods in excess of the amount of tax when a sales tax is collected prior to the retail stage under conditions of imperfect competition.[11] Pyramiding occurs when concerns apply a constant markup to costs, including tax, and frictions are such that the excessive price increase will be sustained. The degree of pyramiding will be greater the higher the percentage of markup. Thus, a tax collected at the manufacturing stage will result in more pyramiding than one collected at the wholesale stage. Pyramiding can be limited to some extent under the value-added tax by the requirement that inventories be recorded in the firm's accounts exclusive of tax. However, only a tax collected on sales to the ultimate consumer would seem to avoid this problem altogether.

A tax restricted to the stages of production and distribution prior to the retail stage will affect the relative prices of consumer goods to the extent that the tax base excludes varying percentages of profit margins. The burden is heavier on "low-margin" goods although this is offset somewhat by a smaller degree of pyramiding.[12]

Effect on Consumer Prices of Interest Charges
Required to Advance Tax

According to Jean-Baptiste Say, taxes collected at an early rather than a late stage of production, and thus to some extent the value-added tax through the retail stage as well as manufacturers' and wholesalers' sales taxes, have two disadvantages resulting from the capital required to advance the tax: (1) they cause serious inconvenience to concerns with limited capital resources or access to credit, (2) the interest charges on the additional capital must be passed on to consumers in higher prices, an extra charge from which the treasury derives no benefit.[13]

---

[11] *Sales Taxation*, pp. 20–21.

[12] See Due, *Sales Taxation*, p. 21.

[13] Straffa (ed.), *The Works and Correspondence of David Ricardo* (Cambridge, Eng., 1951), I, 379. The issue raised by Say should be distinguished from that of "pyramiding" discussed in the preceding section. The interest charge occurs even

While acknowledging the correctness of the first proposition, Ricardo points out an error in the second. The interest charge in itself may involve no extra cost because collecting a tax at the manufacturing level, for example, means that the manufacturer advances the tax for the consumer who, in the meanwhile, has the advantage of the use of the funds. It is the same as if the government collected the tax immediately from the consumer or as if the government postponed collecting the tax during the period of manufacture and borrowed the funds at the market rate of interest. However, Ricardo concedes that the manufacturer may charge a higher rate of interest than the government would have to pay "so that the manufacturer and Government together gain, or save, precisely the sum which the consumer pays."[14] It should be noted that the manufacturer may be obliged to charge a higher rate of interest than the government because his credit resources are more limited.

HYPOTHESES OF INCIDENCE HELD BY STUDENTS OF VALUE-ADDED TAXATION

Most recent students of value-added taxation seem to have accepted the conventional thesis of incidence although, like Bronfenbrenner and Due, some may believe that the shifting process will be slower than in the case of other forms of sales taxation.[15] They differ in this respect from the early proponents of the tax and their current followers who have envisaged a measure which will only partially rest on ultimate consumers.

To understand the difference between the two positions, views on incidence must be related to the structure of the tax base—a fact which Studenski and Ito seem to recognize but which they do not clearly explain. The original proponents of the value-added tax recommended a gross product type of base while their contemporary followers recommend either a gross product or net income type of base. The most

---

if prices are not based on a constant percentage of markup applied to purchase prices and even if competition is perfect. It would, of course, be a charge in addition to the tax, thereby increasing the purchase price to which any constant markup percentage is applied.

[14] *Ibid.*, p. 380.

[15] Bronfenbrenner, "The Japanese Value-Added Sales Tax," *National Tax Journal,* III (Dec., 1950), 310; Due, *Sales Taxation,* p. 366.

recent advocates of value-added taxation, on the other hand, have been primarily interested in a consumption-type base, the tax being imposed only on sales destined for ultimate consumption or the equivalent of a pure retail sales tax.

Some of the advocates of the consumption-type levy have also endorsed the net income-type tax, but they seem to assume that the incidence of both measures will be identical. Thus, in the *Second Report on Japanese Taxation*, the Shoup Mission speaks of a forward shifting of the tax to consumers.[16] Likewise, in his recent treatise on sales taxation, Due indicates that whether a measure is limited to sales destined for ultimate consumption or imposed on both consumption and investment goods, the tax will be shifted forward to the consumer, the inclusion of investment goods in the base merely making the tax more regressive.[17] In his analysis of French sales taxation, Lauré implies a similar conclusion when he claims that, in the case of an ad valorem tax on all products including investment goods, entrepreneurs will shift the entire tax to consumers.[18]

Studenski and Ito, however, are apparently aware of a fundamental difference between the incidence of taxes limited to consumers' goods and taxes which are also applied to investment goods when they emphasize the distinction between a "sales tax" or a "consumption tax," on the one hand, and a "business tax," on the other.[19] The fact is that the consumption-type base supports an indirect spendings tax, conventionally regarded as a sales tax, strictly speaking. On the other hand, the net income and gross-product measures implement an indirect tax on income defined to include savings as well as consumer outlays—a type of levy which may be designated as a business tax since it applies to income produced. In national income terminology, the net income and gross product types of levies may be termed "income or production taxes" as contrasted with consumption taxes, as explained in Chapter 1.

Just as under direct taxation, which is more regressive if savings

[16] Pp. 17, 18.
[17] *Sales Taxation*, pp. 160, 181.
[18] *La taxe sur la valeur ajoutée* (Paris, 1952), p. 46.
[19] See Studenski, "Characteristics, Developments, and Present Status of Consumption Taxes," *Law and Contemporary Problems* VIII (Summer, 1941), 417–422; Studenski, "Modern Fiscal Systems, Their Characteristics and Trends of Development," *Annals of the American Academy of Political and Social Science,* CCIX (Nov., 1939), 34; Ito, "Theorie und Technik der Nettoumsatzsteuer in Japan," *Finanzarchiv,* XV, No. 3 (1955), 452, 466 f.; Ito, "The Value-Added Tax in Japan," *Annals of the Hitotsubashi Academy,* No. 1 (Oct., 1950), pp. 45, 54.

are excluded, a levy which is imposed at proportional rates on consumption expenditures, only, will be more regressive than one which includes expenditures on investment or producers' goods. As Professor Pigou observes, "net saving is itself a form of spending, namely, spending upon the purchase of machines and other new capital objects."[20] Although he refers to "indirect" sacrifices[21] imposed on lower income groups when taxes on savings reduce the accumulation of capital and hence the ultimate rewards of wage earners, he concludes that "to remit taxation upon saved income would, as has been shown, confer a considerable bounty upon the rich."[22,23]

Those who assume that a tax on sales of consumption goods, only, is less regressive than one which includes investment goods overlook the probability that the tax on investment goods will first be shifted forward to purchasers of investment goods or savers rather than directly to ultimate consumers. This is presumably why T. S. Adams regarded a value-added tax of the gross product type as a substitute for the general proportional income tax, the personal and corporate rates being at about the same level. He also advocated a progressive spendings tax and reasoned that his proposal would not alter the basic philosophy of prevailing methods of income taxation under which the progressive surtaxes represented the taxation of the individual in his capacity as a consumer while the remaining elements of the general income tax represented the taxation of the individual in his capacity as a producer.[24] His choice of a gross product type of base rather than the net income type results from considerations of administrative expediency rather than any economic or philosophical predilections. In his opinion, the administrative and compliance problems presented by inventory accounting and by the estimation of depreciation, depletion, or amortization constitute the primary objection to a net income tax.[25]

Adams undertakes no discussion of the incidence of the value-added

---

[20] A. C. Pigou, *A Study in Public Finance* (3d ed., rev., London, 1956), p. 118.

[21] *Ibid.*, p. 58.

[22] *Ibid.*, p. 131.

[23] Pigou estimated that, as of 1938, the exemption of current savings in England from a 15% tax would require a 1% increase in the tax on other incomes while the exemption of investment earnings from tax, whether saved or invested, would require a 7½% increase in the tax on other incomes. *Ibid.*, p. 130.

[24] Adams, "Fundamental Problems of Federal Income Taxation," *Quarterly Journal of Economics*, XXXV (Aug., 1921), 553, 557.

[25] *Ibid.*, pp. 539, 552.

tax. He merely notes that a tax collected from business on a gross basis is more readily shifted than one restricted to net profits.[26] Adams' followers seem quite uncertain of the probable incidence of the tax except for Arant, who asserts without supporting analysis the extremely unorthodox position that a general value-added tax of the gross product type will be equivalent to a proportional tax on factor incomes by being shifted backward.[27] Firmin, who, in his study, *The Michigan Business Receipts Tax*, undertakes an inquiry into the incidence of a gross product type of levy, concludes "that no sweeping generalizations can be stated concerning the shiftability of the value-added tax as a general tax on business activity," and "that in the long run the tax will be shifted to many segments of the market and of the production process," while "even this conclusion will be challenged by some."[28]

Although it seems reasonable to assume that a tax on consumption goods will be largely shifted forward to consumers through a rise in product prices and that a tax on investment goods will be similarly shifted forward to purchasers of investment goods, some economists have recently been contending that, when the government imposes a sales tax, it may actually obtain its revenues from reductions in factor incomes or backward shifting rather than increases in product prices. If the levy takes the form of a partial tax, the purchaser may still be said to bear the tax in a certain sense because of a relative or even some absolute rise in the prices of the taxed products;[29] but, in any event, the incidence is traced through effects on factor incomes rather than product prices.[30] Due calls attention to the probability that, under actual conditions, this hypothesis can only be valid if the monetary authorities curb price in-

[26] *Ibid.*, p. 552.

[27] Arant, "The Place of Business Taxation in the Revenue Systems of the States," *Taxes*, XV (Apr., 1957), 199, 242.

[28] Pp. 129–30.

[29] See Rolph, "A Proposed Revision of Excise Tax Theory," *Journal of Political Economy*, LX (Apr., 1952), 109, 116; Musgrave, "On Incidence," *Journal of Political Economy*, LXI (Aug., 1953), 318–19; Stockfisch, "The Capitalization and Investment Aspects of Excise Taxes under Competition," *American Economic Review*, XLIV (June, 1954), 294, n. 15.

[30] In *The Theory of Public Finance*, pp. 355–61, Musgrave undertakes an exceedingly interesting analysis which attempts to trace changes in both relative factor prices and relative product prices caused by general and discriminatory taxes on incomes or products. As he indicates, the analysis "suggests an approach and poses problems for empirical investigation, but it does not provide a conclusive answer" (p. 357).

creases.[31] He concedes that, if the government sterilizes the proceeds—a case envisaged by Rolph—the deflationary effects of the tax will be greater than if the revenues are spent; but, as he points out, the results of Rolph's analysis which depend upon assumptions of perfect competition are useless for practical purposes.[32] The rigidities in modern labor markets would cause unemployment when there is backward shifting rather than diffusion of the tax burden among income recipients in proportion to factor incomes. The monetary authorities would therefore be likely to take action to offset this effect if it went very far. However, some temporary unemployment is presumably to be expected with any taxes which reduce private spending or cause shifts in relative demand for various products. Whether a tax is imposed directly on factor incomes or indirectly through increases in product prices, it will have further repercussions on factor incomes and employment.

ANTICIPATED EFFECTS ON ALLOCATION OF RESOURCES

A "neutral" tax may be defined as one which has no effect on the allocation of an economy's resources. A completely neutral levy has yet to be devised, even hypothetically; but every tax measure should be examined for its influence on the choices confronting the owners of the economy's resources. This consideration is vitally important whether a tax student believes that "neutrality" should be a guiding principle in taxation or favors a deliberate attempt to modify patterns of resource use.

Effects on Choice Between Work and Leisure

One way in which a tax modifies the allocation of resources is through its effects on the incentive to work or, in other words, its influence on the taxpayer's choice between work and leisure. This influence operates through the "income" effect, on the one hand, and the "substitution" or "price" effect, on the other.[33] The income effect, or the reduction of

[31] *Sales Taxation*, p. 14.
[32] *Ibid.*, n. 2.
[33] David Walker, "The Direct-Indirect Tax Problem: Fifteen Years of Controversy," *Public Finance*, I, No. 2 (1955), 158.

an individual's disposable money income through a tax, increases the incentive to work by lowering the marginal utility of "leisure"—a good complementary[34] to products purchased out of money income—and thereby lowering the marginal disutility of work relative to the marginal utility of money income. The substitution or price effect operates through a reduction in the reward for each marginal unit of work. In contrast to the income effect, it works in the direction of reducing the incentive to work by lowering the marginal utility of additional income. The income effect is supposedly the more important.[35]

A regressive tax, and hence a consumption-type sales tax, must by definition have a regressive income effect. The stimulus to work will be greater, the lower the income level; but this result may be short-lived if expenditures regarded as essential by the income recipients have to be cut and if there is resentment because distribution of the tax burden is considered inequitable. Meanwhile, the substitution effect will depress work to a smaller degree at all income levels than in the case of a proportional income tax and especially a progressive income tax.

The effect of the net income type of value-added tax on incentives to work will approximate that of a proportional income tax. The substitution effect will discourage work more than in the case of a regressive tax but less than in the case of a progressive levy. The gross product type of tax is probably a progressive levy, the degree of progression being uncertain but substantial, granted the concentration of property ownership in upper income groups. The income effect would therefore increase the incentive to work, as compared with a proportional levy, only at the higher income levels while the substitution effect would reduce the incentive to work at all income levels.

Whether the incentive to work provided by a tax results in a significant increase in effort depends upon the elasticity of the supply curve of labor which is affected by institutional and psychological factors as well as by monetary incentives. "Psychology will ultimately have to provide the basic analysis," writes Professor Paul J. Strayer of Princeton

[34] More than one approach has been employed by income-leisure studies, and the analysis might readily be made in terms of leisure as a rival product rather than a complementary one. However, the various approaches arrive at the same conclusion.

[35] An interesting analysis which relates the direction of change of income and price elasticities of demand for leisure to income levels has been undertaken by Michael E. Levy in *Income Tax Exemptions: An Analysis of the Effects of Personal Exemptions on the Income Tax Structure* (Amsterdam, 1960), Chap. IV.

University.[36] Meanwhile, one serious obstacle to meaningful conclusions in this field of inquiry is presented by the problem of defining leisure, which encounters the troublesome issues involved in distinguishing intermediate from final product. For example, leisure necessary in order to work represents intermediate product rather than a form of ultimate consumption or income, while some time spent on a job may be such a mixture of social and business pursuits as to defy separation.[37] Finally, the theoretical analyses would have to be supplemented by considerable statistical investigation before providing a basis for macroeconomic generalizations.

Effects on Choice Between Present and Postponed Consumption

Another very important question with respect to the effects of a general tax concerns its influence on the choice between consumption, on the one hand, and savings or investment, on the other—a choice which affects the degree to which production takes place through the use of capital equipment or indirect labor rather than direct labor. In "Theory and Background of the Value-Added Tax," Shoup demonstrates that even a proportional tax which applies to savings or investment goods as well as "true" consumer outlays or "true" consumer goods may be held to favor present over deferred consumption.[38] The analysis is in line with the hypothesis of Irving Fisher that there is a discriminative double tax on postponed consumption. Under an income-type concept, savings are taxed twice, once when the savings are made and a second time when interest is earned. Shoup is not convinced that the discrimination also applies to profit, for he says: "The role of profit, as contrasted with interest, in this connection remains somewhat unclear."[39] Mill, however, definitely includes profit in his presentation of the thesis quoted below:

[36] "An Appraisal of Current Fiscal Theory," *The American Economic Review,* XLII (May, 1952), 144.

[37] Possible criteria for identifying intermediate and final product are discussed in the following section of this study, which is concerned with distinguishng savings and investment from consumption expenditures.

[38] *Proceedings of the Forty-Eighth Annual Conference of the National Tax Association, 1955* (Sacramento, Calif., 1956), pp. 13–14, 16–18.

[39] *Ibid.,* p. 14.

If, indeed, reliance could be placed on the conscience of the contributors, or sufficient security taken for the correctness of their statements by collateral precautions, the proper mode of assessing an income tax would be to tax only the part of income devoted to expenditure, exempting that which is saved. For when saved and invested (and all savings, speaking generally, are invested) it thenceforth pays income tax on the interest or profit which it brings, notwithstanding that it has already been taxed on the principle. . . .[40]

In like manner, a tax which is imposed on the output of both true consumption and true investment goods is held to overtax the latter because the investment good is taxed twice, once upon the sale of the investment good and a second time when the yield from the investment good is incorporated in the consumers' goods which it helps to produce. Under the income-type concept, only depreciation on investment goods avoids the double tax. Under the gross product type of concept, depreciation is also double taxed, a fact emphasized by Lauré and Campet in their criticism of the French tax of fractional payments.[41] On the other hand, the consumption-type concept imposed only on pure consumer goods avoids this type of discrimination, which, as noted above, is said to favor the use of direct as opposed to indirect labor. Of course, if there is a question concerning the role of profit, the limitation of a tax to consumers' goods may result in some discrimination against direct labor.[42]

APPLICATION OF DOUBLE-TAXATION THESIS TO ACTUAL LEGISLATION. As previously noted, the above thesis has been utilized in France as an argument in favor of the consumption type of value-added tax as opposed to the tax of fractional payments or gross product type of tax. It was also employed by Mill as an argument in favor of a direct tax on

[40] John Stuart Mill, *Principles of Political Economy* (5th ed., New York, 1891), II, 406 f. Mill's emphasis throughout his discussion of taxation of the desirability of encouraging savings suggests that he would continue to support his policy of exempting savings and imposing heavy inheritance taxes even if the double-taxation thesis were invalid.

[41] See Lauré, *La taxe sur la valeur ajoutée,* p. 61, and Campet, *The Influence of Sales Taxes on Productivity* (Paris, 1958), p. 58.

[42] It may, of course, be contended that in a certain sense there is no double tax if a tax applies to savings and investment as well as the income therefrom aside from the element of depreciation. Thus, if the value of a machine is taxed in period one, when it is produced, and a tax is also imposed on the products which it turns out, in period two, the machine is double taxed only to the extent of depreciation. Similarly under the income tax, savings would be double taxed only if there were no allowance for replacing the investment good which yielded the income. If, on the other hand, a wage earner is taxed on his wages of $100 in period one under the income tax it is the income from his wages which are taxed. If he saves $50 and earns an interest of $5 in the following year, the $5 does not represent wage income but interest income.

consumer expenditures as opposed to the usual type of income tax. However, its application to actual national income taxes, whether direct or indirect, as they have been devised thus far is invalid, for conventional definitions of consumption and savings or investment do not coincide with definitions of true consumption or final product and true intermediate product whether in the form of current expenditures or investment outlays.

In the case of the United States national-income accounts where the definition of final product includes investment goods as well as consumption goods, the United States Department of Commerce calls attention to the limitations imposed by conventional accounting which assumes that, on the one hand, only business enterprises make intermediate purchases and that, on the other hand, business expenditures on current account invariably constitute intermediate outlays:

No precise line can be drawn between final and intermediate products from mere observation of the nature of the products or the uses to which they are put. It would be easy, for example, if all consumer purchases were for goods like Sunday clothes and holiday dinners, which are obvious elements of the good life, and if all business purchases were raw materials for further processing, which are obvious intermediate goods. Between these two extremes, however, there is a wide range of purchases for which neither the motivation nor the use is so clear-cut and which must be placed in one category or the other by somewhat arbitrary rules.

For this reason any measure of total production must be somewhat conventional. For instance, it must overlook the fact that the expenditures of individuals in their business capacity are influenced by their standards as consumers, and that expenditures of consumers are influenced by their activities as producers. It must overlook also the fact that the conditions under which work is performed have an important bearing on the welfare of individuals. These conditions are affected by business expenditures on goods and services that are classified as intermediate just because there is no satisfactory way to take account of their benefits in a quantitive measure of final output.[43]

Moreover, in his *Principles of National Income Analysis*, Shoup emphasizes the difficulty of identifying final product in the sense of ultimate consumption. For example, certain consumer purchases consist of durable products which, except for houses, are treated as consumption rather than investment when actually only the using up of the article over

---

[43] U.S. Department of Commerce, *National Income, 1954 Edition*, p. 38.

the course of its lifetime constitutes consumption.[44] An even more important consideration is the question of what criterion to use in classifying consumption expenditures.[45] This issue concerns both the extent to which consumers, as ordinarily defined, make expenditures which are akin to business outlays and the extent to which business makes expenditures which are akin to consumption outlays or, in other words, "mixed consumer goods."[46]

Shoup presents three possible criteria for identifying consumption expenditures—namely, purpose or intent of the outlay, presence of personal gratification, and effect on productivity. However, none of them provides an unequivocal guide.

The purpose or intent behind an outlay probably underlies customary methods of accounting; but, by convention, it is applied only to expenditures made through business concerns, not to those undertaken by individuals as such. Educational, medical, and recreational facilities or similar fringe benefits undertaken by a business firm for the benefit of its employees are classified as intermediate product because intended to increase output. Consequently, there is discrimination against individuals who prefer or are obliged to purchase such services on their own account. A similar problem occurs in the case of the services of radio and television industries which are treated as intermediate business outlays, thereby favoring individuals who prefer entertainment of this sort rather than amusements requiring individual consumption outlays, such as readings one's own books or attending the theater. It may even be contended that, if an individiual working in an industrialized community purchases a home in a suburban area because he believes that the surroundings will enable him to work better, the benefits from the home are as much an intermediate product as the benefits derived from comfortable working facilities. Whatever the present discrimination, however, the application of this concept to individuals as well as business would probably only multiply current inequities.

The use of the criterion of personal gratification creates equally formidable problems. If it is interpreted so as to classify as consumption goods all items which contain any element of personal satisfaction, it would encompass almost all output including business investment. If, on

[44] Shoup, *Principles of National Income Analysis*, p. 147.
[45] See *ibid.*, pp. 147–54.
[46] *Ibid.*, p. 149.

the other hand, it is applied only to items which contain no element but personal satisfaction, the amount of consumers' goods would be insignificant.

The criterion of effects on productivity, presumably anticipated rather than actual effects, is the one most appropriate for current tax legislation because of the prevailing concern with increasing output. As in the case of the preceding criteria, it is in principle applicable to both business and consumer expenditures. A business concern may undertake certain outlays which resemble pure consumption, such as the construction of sumptuous buildings or extravagant expenditures for business meetings. Meanwhile, as Shoup points out, "Food, clothing, and shelter may be more effective intermediate goods than electric generators or locomotives."[47] Naturally, the more essential an expenditure, the closer it is to a type of business outlay; and, because of its regressivity, the conventional type of consumption tax is more likely to curtail such expenditures than a proportional or progressive tax on income including savings or than a progressive spendings tax. Also, given the same income levels, consumer expenditures in urban communities are more likely to consist of mixed than pure consumer goods.

In practice, the productivity criterion seems to have been employed to some extent in sales taxation in order to limit the exemption of producers' goods; but it is apparently never used for exemptions of consumers' goods. In the French value-added tax, for example, it may be read into the denial of tax credits to fixed investment not destined solely for industrial use, and some administrative comments support this view; and the Canadian manufactures' sales tax restricts machinery exemptions to machines used directly in the process of manufacturing or production of goods. Both the French and Canadian laws also disallow exemption of producers' goods which might provide loopholes for personal consumption expenditures. Exemption of consumers' goods, on the other hand, are attributable to considerations of equity. Some of the sales taxes in the American states reflect a similar philosophy.

If true consumption or the least essential mixed consumers' goods could be identified through the use of the productivity criterion, the individual income recipient would be treated as a type of business concern; and the principle that investment outlays should be expensed rather than capitalized and depreciated would apply. Both individual income

[47] *Ibid.*, p. 152.

recipients and regular business concerns would be entitled to deduct outlays necessary for productivity in the year of acquisition, any excess deduction being carried forward, rather than to capitalize some of the expenditures and deduct depreciation from income in subsequent periods. Obviously, this new approach would severely reduce the aggregate tax base unless the reduction in consumption outlays by individuals were matched by an increase in purchases of business concerns classified as final products.

If, instead of the above concepts, the conventional definitions of consumption, savings, and investment are retained, the consumption-type tax cannot be considered neutral as between consumption and investment. Rather, it favors business investment and, in fact, all business expenditures. Thus, it not only favors certain consumers over others, but it also imposes a lighter burden on property incomes or capital as contrasted with personal service incomes or direct labor. As Simons and Kuznets have observed, the conventional income-type concept discriminates in favor of property incomes to the extent that it fails to provide an allowance for human capital or, in other words, the consumption outlays made by individuals in order to preserve their ability to work whether those outlays are of the type which may be classified as current or investment expenditures. Moreover, if one adheres to the possible position presented above that double taxation concerns only the element of depreciation, then a consumption-type tax favors savings and investment in any case.

Under the gross product type of base, there is certainly a double tax on business investment and the yield from this investment. However, there is also a double tax on all goods consumed by labor which is as essential to productivity as regular business outlays.

Conventional accounting assumes that all business purchases of goods and services are more productive than individual purchases. The extent to which this is the case will vary with circumstances and, moreover, involves subjective value judgements. The issues raised are those discussed by the classical economists under the headings of productive vs. unproductive labor and productive vs. unproductive consumption. As Mill explains, they center on the question of "what wealth is," to which Mill gives the answer "material wealth," while the current French answer is evidently "industrial production."[48]

[48] Mill, *Principles of Political Economy*, I, 73, 71–82.

EQUALIZING THE TREATMENT OF PRESENT AND POSTPONED CONSUMP-
TION UNDER ACTUAL SALES TAX LEGISLATION.   In designing a sales tax,
one might settle for the conventional concept of consumption, allow an
exemption for investment goods, and then seek some approach toward
neutrality by generous exemptions of consumer necessities. This approach
is suggested by the British Purchase Tax and the Australian and New
Zealand wholesalers' sales taxes. However, such measures are closer to
a collection of special excises than a general sales tax, strictly speaking,
as Due indicates.[49] Moreover, the yield of the British tax is only around
8 percent of total tax revenues and the figures for the Australian and New
Zealand levies are about 11 percent and 10 percent, respectively.[50]
In addtion to the administrative problems resulting from widespread
exemptions, this approach is likely to create competitive inequities among
producers, on the one hand, and discriminate among consumers, on the
other.

Going to the opposite extreme and adopting the gross product type of
concept is another possibility on the chance that a double tax on both
labor and capital might entail the least discrimination. However, this
solution, which may tend to favor labor incomes, will probably not
appeal to most contemporary students; and Kuznets has indicated
that regarding the individual income recipient as a business enterprise
will increase interest in national income, proper, rather than any other
concept.[51] Consequently, the conventional income-type concept seems to
be the best compromise.

Effects on Channels of Production and Distribution

INTEGRATED VS. UNINTEGRATED CONCERNS.   An outstanding merit of
all concepts of value-added taxation is the fact that they avoid the subsidy to integration afforded by the general turnover tax.[52] Because the

[49] *Sales Taxation*, pp. 184, 199, 202.
[50] *Ibid.*, p. 6.
[51] Kuznets, *National Income and Its Composition, 1919–1938* (2 vols., New
York, 1941), I, 37.
[52] It may be argued that the consumption type of sales tax may also favor the
combination of independent enterprises on the ground that it favors investment
outlays which are often so expensive that they can be afforded only by larger
firms. Even in this case, however, it is superior to the general turnover tax because at least its subsidy is limited to the growing enterprise. Finally, the carry-

general turnover tax is applicable only when there is a market transaction, firms which are able to supply their own materials, services, and
equipment are given a competitive advantage over those purchasing
such items from outsiders. Commission merchants, for example, would
be driven out of business if the tax were not limited to their commissions.
Even horizontal integration may be encouraged to some extent. When
jobbers, for example, are hired to do some of a concern's work, tax
liability would be reduced if the firms combined. Also, firms which are
able to lower the cost of their purchases by buying in large quantities
reduce their tax liability. However, a similar inducement to mass purchasing exists under single-stage or value-added taxes which are not
imposed through the retail stage; and any correction through an "uplift"
will, as in the case of the British Purchase Tax, eliminate the real economies of mass purchasing as well as the benefits of monopolistic power.

VARYING DISTRIBUTIVE MARGINS.   As discussed in the previous chapter, all taxes, including the value-added tax, which do not extend through
the retail stage are confronted with the problem of how to equalize the
tax burden on various methods of doing business when distributive margins vary. The manufacturers' sales tax and its value-added equivalent
require discounts on direct sales to consumers. On direct sales to retailers,
there is need for either a discount, an uplift, or both; for some manufacturers will assume the wholesaling function while others will transfer
them to retailers. A tax extending through the wholesale stage requires
a discount on direct sales to consumers and an uplift when retailers
assume wholesaling or manufacturing functions whether they purchase
from other wholesalers or from manufacturers.

COUNTERCYCLICAL EFFECTS

The built-in stabilizers which characterize the progressive personal
income and spendings taxes because of rate structures and personal
exemptions are lacking in indirect taxes including the value-added tax.
Indirect taxes may, of course, provide some equivalent of personal
allowances through exemptions of consumer necessities, but the rate

---

forward of excess credits or investment outlays may encourage some integration
under a value-added tax in order that the deductions may be applied to taxable
activities.

structure is the more important consideration. "The necessity of having a tax system that automatically contributes in these ways to economic stability," writes the Shoup Mission, "is one of the reasons for our recommendation that a sharply progressive personal income tax continue to play an important role in the Japanese tax system, and that the scope of indirect taxation be narrowed where possible."[53] However, as Shoup has observed, it is conceivable that the yield of a regressive tax will respond more quickly than that of a progressive one if changes in income are concentrated in the lower income groups.[54] Also, variations in tax rates may be substituted for the built-in stabilizers; but, as in the case of changes in credit policy, the problem of timing presents a troublesome though not insuperable difficulty. A major count against the system of varying the rates of indirect taxes to effect anti-cyclical policy is the fact that such variation invokes perverse reaction on the part of purchasers. If the rates are expected to be increased in order to depress buying, purchasers will rush to buy before the increases are put into effect and vice versa.

ANTI-INFLATIONARY EFFECTS

Although most tax students justly agree that any tax measure is likely to curb inflation more effectively than borrowing, there is no consensus on the comparative merits of alternative forms of taxation. To curb inflation, a tax must reduce aggregate demand to a greater extent than the aggregate supply of goods and services, and do so within a fairly short period of time.[55]

A consumption tax may be more deflationary than an income tax if, as Due suggests, it impedes consumption expenditures more than an income tax and, in the short run, even curbs investment spending to a greater degree because of its indirect discouragement to investment.[56] Of course, a curtailment of investment limits future supply; but projects which are expected to bear fruit only in the long run are as inflationary as outlays for immediate consumption. On the other hand, some tax students believe

[53] *Report on Japanese Taxation* (4 vols., Tokyo, 1949), I, 19.
[54] Shoup, "Discussion," *The American Economic Review,* XLII (May, 1952), 161.
[55] See Richard Goode, "Anti-Inflationary Implications of Alternative Forms of Taxation," *The American Economic Review,* XLII (May, 1952), 148 f.
[56] *Sales Taxation,* p. 38.

that income taxes may be more deflationary on the grounds that there is little difference between an income tax, even a progressive one, and a regressive tax in their short-run effect on consumer spending while income taxes, especially highly progressive ones, may reduce investment expenditures to a much greater extent than consumption taxes.[57]

Despite the number of careful explanations that taxes levied on commodities and services are not equivalent to inflation though, in contrast to direct income taxes, they raise prices,[58] the view that they are seems to persist.[59] They resemble inflation only to the extent that they have secondary repercussions on factor incomes or if they do not succeed in adequately reducing the quantity of products demanded relative to the supply. They may cause a rise in farm incomes, for example, by raising a farm parity-price index, thereby fostering further increases in the prices of agricultural products. Also, wage increases may result because of cost-of-living clauses in wage contracts; and union leaders may be more inclined to demand wage increases because of a tax-induced rise in product prices than because of a reduction in take-home pay under a direct income tax, thus possibly stimulating a wage-price spiral.[60]

If inflationary pressures are so great that prices rise by the amount of the tax and the same quantities are sold as before while supply has not increased to any extent, the tax has, of course, failed. This is most likely to occur because of excessively liberal credit policies which have the effect of raising the tax through inflationary borrowing.

Finally, if a tax is to be an anti-inflationary device, it must not seriously reduce the supply of labor by decreasing the ability or willingness of workers to produce. As Dr. Richard Goode indicates, taxes which reduce the labor supply may be inflationary because the drop in production is likely to be immediate while, the marginal propensity to spend being less than one, demand will fall off less than supply.[61] In other words, the decline in spending will be less than the reduction in disposable incomes resulting from the reduced labor supply to the extent that purchases are made out of past savings. The appraisal of alternative tax measures on the basis of this criterion is even more difficult than determining their effects on aggregate demand. If the reason for the reduced supply of

[57] Goode, "Anti-Inflationary Implications of Taxation," pp. 150–51.
[58] For example, Due, Sale Taxation, p. 43.
[59] See Campet, The Influence of Sales Taxes on Productivity, p. 46.
[60] Goode, "Anti-Inflationary Implications of Taxation," p. 157.
[61] Ibid., p. 149.

labor is a preference for leisure, then the substitution of a regressive or proportional tax system for a progressive one may increase the supply of labor provided that the taxes do not cause extreme resentment. On the other hand, if the problem lies in the inability of workers to work harder whether because of institutional or psychological factors, reducing progression will not have the desired effect. If the inability arises from inadequate consumption, then a more regressive distribution of the tax burden will intensify the situation; and a regressive system will be the least desirable for this purpose of the various alternatives.

In any event, the relative anti-inflationary power of a tax is never as important a consideration as its equity in distributing the tax burden. If two taxes are capable of raising the same amount of revenue, the more equitable one is preferable even if less deflationary per dollar of revenue.[62] This suggests that increased attention be given to curbing or redirecting governmental expenditures.

[62] See Shoup, "Discussion," *American Economic Review,* XLII (May, 1952), 163.

Chapter 8

Summary and Conclusions

Value-added taxation represents a new technique for collecting taxes on the output of economic enterprises. Like income or sales taxation, it is a generic term applicable to more than one type of measure; and the measure may be either general or partial in nature.

By and large, students of value-added taxation have been interested in general measures which would encompass a society's total economic output or at least the total output of those enterprises which are classified as business firms. Because output or product is merely an alternative view of the nation's income, value added may also be regarded as society's aggregate income. Value-added taxation is therefore closely related to direct income taxation, differing from the latter only by its impersonal character and its method of allocating the base among taxpayers. It is even more closely related to retail sales taxation, which is likewise impersonal and which utilizes a very similar mode of assessment.

The various types of measures recommended for value-added taxation reflect divergent concepts of aggregate income or product. There are at least three concepts, of which one or the other also underlies the various forms of personal income and retail sales taxation: (1) the consumption concept derived from the theories of Mill and Fisher; (2) net national income, which is the orthodox concept; and (3) gross national product. The essential difference among the various concepts lies in the treatment accorded business investment. Under the consumption concept, either capital outlays or returns to capital are exempt; under the net income concept, capital allowances are limited to depreciation; under the gross product concept, even depreciation is disallowed.

The consumption concept supports the consumption type of value-added base, which may be defined by either of two formulas—the deduction variant or the interest-exclusion variant. It is designed to reach the sales of goods and services for ultimate consumption which also represent the base of a retail sales tax, strictly speaking, and the direct spendings tax.

The deduction variant of the consumption-type base was recommended by the Shoup Mission for postwar Japan and is utilized in the current French value-added tax, although the French tax is a partial rather than a general measure not extending beyond the wholesale stage, excluding services as well as all activities not classified as commercial, and taxing certain producers' goods. The interest-exclusion variant has not yet been applied in actual legislation, although it approaches a payroll tax.

The orthodox concept of national income leads to the net income type of value-added tax. It also provides the foundation for the usual type of general income tax but has no practical equivalent in retail sales taxation. The base derived from this concept is adopted as an optional alternative to the consumption-type base in the Japanese proposal and is employed in an anomalous form by the Michigan Business Activities Tax. It is the base apparently intended by Colm, recommended by Studenski for peace-time value-added taxation, and preferred by the National Tax Association.

Finally, there is the gross product concept. This concept underlies the ordinary form of retail sales taxation which limits the exemption of producers' goods to sales for resale and closely related items, although its use has probably resulted from considerations of expediency rather than principle and although its application is partial, services invariably being excluded. A gross product type of value-added tax was recommended by Thomas S. Adams and, as a war measure, by Studenski for reasons of administrative expediency. Studenski, however, believes that there may be some logical justification for not deducting depreciation; and Mount apparently disallows depreciation as a matter of principle. The base derived from this concept is roughly approximated by the first version of the Michigan Business Activities Tax and was utilized in partial form by the French tax of fractional payments on manufacturers' sales.

Because output may be visualized as either product or factor payments, it is possible to compute value added through two alternative methods, the product approach and the income approach, which are designated as the subtraction procedure and addition procedure, respectively, according to the predominant nature of the calculation. Although any form of value-added base may be computed through either method, the product approach or subtraction procedure is the more natural one for the deduction variant of the consumption-type base and for the gross product type base, while the income approach or addition procedure is more suitable for the net income type and the interest-exclusion variant of the consumption type. Nevertheless, the former method has been assumed by Studenski in the case of the net income type measure; and the Michigan Business Activities Tax, which employs a base approximating the net income type, uses that method.

The general formula for the base of the consumption-type tax, deduction variant, may be stated as follows: sales net of returns, cancellations, cash discounts, and bad debts *plus* receipts from services including rent and from interest *minus* purchases of all goods and services from outside concerns destined for use in the business including total outlays on investment goods, all rental payments, and interest paid to other concerns. By regarding all rents as receipts from services rather than a type of factor payment and therefore taxing the payee rather than the payer, and by also taxing interest received by business firms, this formula avoids the need for a special definition of value added in the case of the property-management and financial businesses which caused difficulty in the Japanese bill.

The gross product type of tax restricts deductions to purchases of goods and services on current account. In theory, it requires an imputation for inventory accumulation as well as investment on force account. However, proponents of this measure have generally assumed that there would be no inventory accounting, and none was used in the French tax of fractional payments.

The net income type of value-added base may be computed by the individual firm through the addition of payrolls, interest paid to individuals, and value-added profits, which differ from profits as computed for purposes of the federal income tax primarily by the deduction of dividends received from other firms, by adjustments to eliminate the gains or losses from capital transactions, and by the inclusion of depletion and state income taxes. Inventory accumulation and investment on force account are automatically included by this procedure.

The consumption-type base, interest-exclusion variant, is derived from the net income type measure. It differs only by allowing a deduction from the value added thus computed of interest returns on investments received subsequent to the year of purchase.

The deduction variant of the consumption-type tax is administratively superior to the interest-exclusion variant and the net income type tax because it avoids inventory and depreciation accounting, although cash accounting for inventories has been suggested for the income-type tax as a means of simplification. As compared with the gross product type of base, it possesses the important administrative advantage of avoiding the distinction between purchases on current and capital account and requiring imputations only in the case of products destined for the owner's personal consumption. However, in practice, it is by no means free of administrative complexity. The French have evidently considered it necessary to disallow the deduction of some business purchases which may not increase industrial productivity or which afford loopholes for personal consumption. Hence, imputations are still required for certain items which a concern produces for use within the business. Also, the proration of deductions between exempt and taxable products is troublesome. Moreover, the French tax is not applied to service enterprises, although it would probably have been feasible to include them, given an administrative exemption and the elimination of unnecessary complexities in the law.

The value-added technique is superior to that used in retail sales taxation because it facilitates an administrative exemption. Also, it is the appropriate type of tax for the implementation of the origin principle as applied to interjurisdictional trade. Both forms of taxation are administratively superior to an income or spendings tax because equal aggregate tax bases are distributed among a smaller number of taxpayers.

The original proponents of value-added taxation and their followers have advocated a gross product or net income type of base, the income type being generally assumed by contemporary members of this group. Hence, they favor a measure which includes investment (net rather than gross investment in the case of the net income type tax) as well as consumption expenditures, or, in other words, a "business" or "production" tax. They have frequently sought to justify their proposals either on the ground that government should charge business concerns for the cost of services rendered to business or the closely related general-welfare doctrine. The former thesis provides an excuse for collecting heavy taxes through business enterprises without facing the problem of who actually bears the tax while the latter doctrine supports the simultaneous use of direct and indirect taxation as a matter of administrative efficiency. Hence, the justifications obviously reflect considerations of fiscal and political expediency—a fact indicated in discussions of the proposals by their advocates. Of course, this use of the expediency criterion has not been the result of irresponsibility but rather of a belief that the expedient would be more just than alternatives as, for example, the use of highly progressive direct taxes while permitting excessive loopholes and inadequate enforcement; allowing inflation to go unchecked; utilizing a mass of uncoordinated special excises which are inevitably arbitrary and inequitable; or adopting a general turnover tax with its undesirable subsidy to integration. Also, as explained in Chapter 1, the benefits-to-business thesis reflects to some extent uncertainty with regard to the incidence of sales taxes and the assumption that incidence will be related to the distribution of benefits.

The value-added levy has sometimes been proposed as a supplement to the personal income tax when the latter has been exploited to its psychological and political limits and additional revenues are needed. In this case, of course, it is of first importance to study the possibility of closing loopholes and correcting administrative inefficiencies in direct taxes before introducing a general indirect tax. The measure has also been suggested as a mainstay of the revenue systems of subordinate political units because of the need for steadier revenues than are available under progressive taxation or because of the policy which favors exclusive use of direct taxation by the national government. Adams and the National Tax Association have suggested its use under the origin principle as a supplementary tax for political subdivisions unable to satisfy their just claims on nonresident factors of production through property or direct income taxation; and the National Tax Association has also suggested it as a possible substitute for ad valorem taxation of tangible personal property used in business.

In contrast to the above group, many recent advocates of value-added taxation have focused their attention on the consumption type of value-added tax or a sales tax, strictly speaking. Because this tax treats business investment more favorably than the other value-added concepts, it especially interests underdeveloped economies and countries like France which have been seeking a rapid increase in productivity and are trying to design tax laws to support this policy.

On the basis of Mill's and Fisher's arguments, it is generally held that a tax imposed on both consumption and investment goods overtaxes the latter, thereby favoring the use of direct rather than indirect labor and impairing the growth of productivity. This argument is convincing provided that true consumption and true investment can be identified. However, because conventional definitions of consumption and investment ignore the fact that many consumer outlays are akin to business expenditures while many business outlays are akin to consumption expenditures, the consumption-type base, as conventionally defined, favors expenditures made through business concerns and hence property incomes as contrasted with personal-service incomes. While avoiding a double tax on business outlays, it imposes a double tax on personal investment and current outlays necessary for the employee's productivity. In principle, a neutral concept might be devised through treating all individual income recipients as business concerns and applying the productivity criterion for allowable deductions; but the practical difficulties of this procedure are so great that, given a decision to use the consumption-type concept, it seems preferable to retain the conventional version while recognizing its limitations and perhaps making some relatively minor adjustments.

This solution was apparently adopted for the French value-added tax when deductions were disallowed on business investment expenditures unlikely to increase industrial productivity to any extent or likely to provide loopholes for personal consumption. In the case of consumer expenditures, the French law does not tax certain necessities, chiefly house rents and unprocessed foods, while it imposes reduced rates on other slightly processed foods and on items widely consumed. The exclusion of rents and unprocessed food sold by farmers results from the nature of the activity; for agriculture and the renting of real estate to individuals are regarded as noncommercial activities and therefore nontaxable, although the agricultural exclusion may be partly based on a wish to exempt food. The other concessions to consumer necessities have resulted from considerations of equity except that, recently, some have been introduced in order to control the cost-of-living index to which minimum wages are tied. The application of the productivity criterion would, of course, lead to similar concessions. While, at first glance, French experience with a value-added tax of the consumption type as a major source of revenue seems to support the hypothesis that the levy stimulates industrial productivity, it has been far from reassuring because a substantial inflation has at times accompanied an admittedly rapid growth in industrial production and the volume of gross national product.

The consumption type of value-added tax may, of course, be regarded merely as a means of balancing a tax system which would be unduly progressive. On the national level, it would be more ethical to reduce the progression directly. However, under federal systems, it may be desirable for the national government to have exclusive use of a highly progressive tax for reasons of administrative efficiency and anti-cyclical considerations while the subordinate levels utilize taxes which provide a steadier revenue yield—a philosophy which underlies the Shoup Mission's proposal for a value-added levy in postwar Japan.

In this connection, it should be recalled that an erroneous assumption is usually made that all output taxes are regressive because shifted forward to the ultimate consumer, a tax on investment goods being assumed to increase the regressivity. However, only the consumption-type measure is essentially regressive. An indirect tax on investment as well as consumption goods would presumably be no more regressive than a direct tax on gross savings as well as consumer expenditures.

Appendix A

The Potential Yield of the
Tax on Value Added

As previously demonstrated, the base and hence the yield of two versions of the general value-added tax—the consumption-type tax, deduction variant, and the gross product type tax—are in principle the same as under a retail sales tax with equivalent scope and specific exemptions. The essential difference between the two forms of taxation is that the value-added tax is collected in fractional amounts according to a firm's contribution to the value of a society's aggregate final product, while, under the retail sales tax, the total tax due on each product is collected from the firm which makes the final sale. Estimates which have indicated that the value-added tax is more productive have assumed that it must necessarily be imposed on a broader base than the retail sales tax. Except for the effect of administrative exemptions, this assumption is unjustified and results from the fact that general practice in retail sales taxation has been compared with the theoretical application of the value-added tax, the latter being applied to services, for example.

The "consolidated business income and product account" in the national income statistics for the United States may be used to provide some indication of the tax bases available under the various concepts of value added; and, in any case, they reveal the possible fluctuations in relative yield. "Business sales to consumers less indirect taxes," "income originating in business," and "busines gross product" approximate the aggregate base of the consumption-type, net income type, and gross product type of taxes respectively. The only essential difference among the three bases is the treatment accorded business fixed investment. All investment outlays are exempt under the consumption-type base; investment allowances are limited to depreciation under the net income type base; and there are no investment allowances under the gross product type base. Also, there is inventory accounting under the net income and gross product concepts although cash accounting might be utilized in a tax law. Finally, as in the national income accounts, the gross product type base includes indirect taxes which, on the one hand, might have been deducted from this measure or, on the other hand, included in the consumption-type and net income type bases. Indirect taxes have either increased or exhibited a smaller decline than general economic activity when business has fallen off so that their inclusion reduces declines in the tax base. Subsidies are treated as negative indirect taxes, but they are a minor item in the total income accounts for the United States. Because the figures cover every kind of business activity, including agriculture, firms of all sizes, and some imputations not likely to be utilized in tax legislation, they are considerably larger than the bases available under any actual tax measures.

Table 6 presents 'the dollar amounts of the three income series from 1929 through 1956.[1] Table 7 presents the dollar amounts of the components accounting for most of the excess of business gross product over income originating in business. The five series given in Tables 6 and 7 are depicted in graph form on page 295.

These statistics reveal considerable fluctuation in all three income series. However, business sales to consumers have been steadier than the other two, and business gross product has generally shown somewhat more cyclical stability than income originating in business.

Business sales to consumers less indirect taxes were at their lowest level in 1933, about 45 percent less than their 1929 volume. By 1937, they were around 49 percent above their 1933 position but were still some 18 percent below 1929. After a decline of about 4 percent between 1937 and 1938, they rose steadily until, in 1956, they were around 3¼ times their 1929 level.

---

[1] No attempt has been made to bring the statistics up to date. For one thing, they have been used merely for purposes of illustrating underlying principles. For another, the series on business sales to consumers has not been published since the discontinuance of the accounts on the institutional origins of gross national product. For an explanation of the discontinuance of these accounts, see U.S. Department of Commerce, *U.S. Income and Output* (Washington, D. C., 1958), p. 51.

TABLE 6. Potential Tax Bases under Three Concepts of Value Added:
Consumption, Net Income, and Gross Product

(In billions of dollars)

Year	Business Sales to Consumers Less Indirect Taxes	Income Originating in Business	Business Gross Product
1929	66.5	78.2	94.8
1930	59.2	66.8	82.2
1931	50.7	51.5	68.0
1932	39.5	35.2	51.1
1933	36.6	32.9	48.7
1934	41.3	40.7	56.7
1935	45.1	48.3	63.7
1936	50.6	54.6	72.4
1937	54.4	63.3	80.5
1938	52.0	56.6	74.3
1939	54.6	61.7	80.1
1940	58.1	70.1	89.1
1941	66.6	91.4	112.5
1942	73.8	118.5	139.9
1943	83.3	140.6	162.8
1944	90.3	145.8	174.5
1945	100.1	141.1	173.4
1946	123.1	153.1	182.8
1947	139.3	173.6	208.6
1948	149.2	196.4	232.1
1949	150.3	188.4	229.5
1950	160.6	209.6	254.7
1951	172.1	239.1	290.3
1952	178.6	248.0	303.2
1953	187.3	258.1	319.2
1954	192.8	253.5	315.8
1955	206.4	275.4	343.1
1956	215.5	291.4	362.5

Sources: U.S. Department of Commerce, *National Income, 1954 Edition* (Washington, D.C., 1954), pp. 168–69, Table 7; U.S. Department of Commerce, Office of Business Economics, *Survey of Current Business*, XXXVII (July, 1957), 13, Table 7.

In 1933, income originating in business had reached its lowest point, which was about 58 percent under the 1929 level. In 1937, it was approximately 92 percent higher than in 1933 although still around 19 percent under 1929. It declined about 12 percent between 1937 and 1938. By 1956, it had risen to almost 3¾ times the 1929 level, having experienced minor setbacks from the previous year amounting to about 3 percent in 1945, 4 percent in 1949, and 2 percent in 1954.

TABLE 7. Components of Value Included in Gross Product Concept of Value
Added but Excluded from Net Income Concept

(In billions of dollars)

Year	Capital Consumption Allowances	Indirect Business Tax and Nontax Liability
1929	8.6	7.0
1930	8.5	7.2
1931	8.2	6.9
1932	7.6	6.8
1933	7.2	7.1
1934	7.1	7.8
1935	7.2	8.2
1936	7.5	8.7
1937	7.7	9.2
1938	7.8	9.2
1939	7.8	9.4
1940	8.1	10.0
1941	9.0	11.3
1942	10.2	11.8
1943	10.9	12.7
1944	12.0	14.1
1945	12.5	15.5
1946	11.7	17.3
1947	14.1	18.7
1948	16.5	20.4
1949	18.4	21.6
1950	20.5	23.7
1951	23.5	25.6
1952	23.9	28.1
1953	26.5	30.2
1954	28.9	30.1
1955	31.6	32.9
1956	34.3	35.0

Sources: U.S. Department of Commerce, *National Income, 1954 Edition* (Washington, D.C., 1954), pp. 168–69, Table 7; U.S. Department of Commerce, Office of Business Economics, *Survey of Current Business,* XXXVII (July, 1957), 13, Table 7.

Business gross product declined about 49 percent between 1929 and 1933. By 1937, it was around 65 percent above its level in 1933 but still about 15 percent below 1929. It declined some 8 percent between 1937 and 1938. By 1956, it was more than 3¾ times its 1929 level after having suffered negligible declines in 1945, 1949, and 1954.

Capital consumption allowances and indirect business taxes account for almost all of the excess of business gross product over income originating in business and for the difference in variation between the two series. Because some proposals for value-added taxation, even those based on

Graph of potential tax bases under three concepts of value added:
consumption, net income, and gross product.

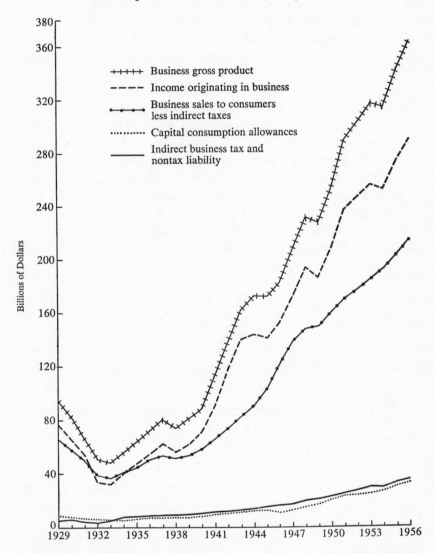

Sources: U.S. Department of Commerce, *National Income, 1954 Edition* (Washington, D.C., 1954), pp. 168–69, Table 7; U.S. Department of Commerce, Office
of Business Economics, *Survey of Current Business*, XXXVII (July, 1957), 13,
Table 7.

the gross product concept, have assumed the deduction of indirect business taxes, the effect on the base of capital consumption allowances is the more important issue.

Capital consumption allowances declined only about 18 percent between 1929 and their low point in 1934. By 1937, they had registered an 11 percent recovery from 1934 and were around 90 percent of their 1929 level. They rose thereafter without any setback other than a 6 percent decline in 1954; and, in 1956, they were almost 400 percent of the 1929 level. In the same year, business gross product was about 384 percent of its 1929 level and income originating in business was around 373 percent of its 1929 level.

Indirect business tax and nontax liability declined only about 5 percent from its high in 1930 to its low point in 1932. By 1937, it was some 31 percent above its 1929 level, having increased around 35 percent from its low point. It experienced no decline between 1937 and 1938. Since 1938 it has risen steadily, except for a negligible drop in 1954, and, in 1956, was 500 percent of its 1929 level.

Equivalent Nominal and Effective Rates

Rates of Sales Taxes when Tax Itself Is Included in Tax Base
Expressed in Terms of Equivalent Nominal and Effective Rates
(Rates Applicable to Prices Including Tax and Prices
Excluding Tax Respectively)

(In percentages)

Nominal Rates	Effective Rates	Nominal Rates	Effective Rates
0.10	0.1001	8.00	8.6957
0.25	0.2506	8.50	9.2896
1.00	1.0101	10.00	11.1111
1.01	1.0203	10.74	12.0323
1.10	1.1122	11.90	13.5074
1.50	1.5228	12.00	13.6364
1.75	1.7812	13.00	14.9425
1.80	1.8330	15.00	17.6471
2.00	2.0408	15.35	18.1334
2.65	2.7221	16.85	20.2646
2.75	2.8278	19.50	24.2236
2.80	2.8807	20.00	25.0000
3.00	3.0928	22.00	28.2051
3.50	3.6269	22.50	29.0323
4.00	4.1667	23.00	29.8701
5.80	6.1571	25.00	33.3331
6.00	6.3830	26.00	35.1351
6.35	6.7806	27.00	36.9863
7.50	8.1081		

The Michigan Business Activities Tax

On May 20, 1953, Michigan adopted a tax inspired by the value-added concept and officially designated as the Michigan Business Activities Tax.[1] Intended merely as a temporary expedient, it was scheduled to take effect on July 1, 1953, and expire on March 15, 1955. However, at the later date its expiration was postponed to the end of the year; and in June 1955 (Act 282, P. A. 1955, Sec. 25) it was made a permanent part of the tax system.

The tax is collected from business enterprises on the basis of their "adjusted receipts," or value added as defined in the Michigan statute. It is imposed at the nominal rate of 7¾ mills or 0.775 percent, except in the case of public utilities, which are subjected to a reduced rate of 2 mills or 0.2 percent. The yield of some $77,900,000 in the fiscal year July 1962–July 1963 accounted for only around 3.8 percent of combined state and local taxes.[2] However, because all the receipts from this tax enter the General Fund instead of being earmarked for specific purposes, it has become a major contributor to the financial resources which may be spent at the discretion of the state legislature, accounting for around one fifth of the General Fund's tax revenues in fiscal 1962–63,[3] and

[1] See Michigan Department of Revenue, *Michigan Business Activities Tax: Rules and Regulations* (October 1, 1953), and Michigan Department of Revenue, Michigan Business Activities Tax," *Act No. 150, Public Acts of 1953, as Amended* (State of Michigan, 1957).

[2] See Michigan Department of Revenue, *Twenty-Second Annual Report, 1962–63* (Lansing, 1963), p. 17.

[3] Estimated from statistics in Michigan Department of Revenue, *Twenty-Second Annual Report, 1962–63*, p. 15, p. 17.

ranking second only to the retail sales tax as a source of revenues for the fund.[4]

JUSTIFICATION OF THE TAX

An urgent need for revenue which might be spent at the discretion of the state legislature motivated the adoption of the Business Activities Tax. The annual deficits in the General Fund, which had been accumulating at an alarming rate, were expected to continue unless action was taken.[5]

A study financed by a group of fifty private citizens of Michigan, given legislative authorization to investigate the problem, concluded that a fiscal dilemma had arisen because, while aggregate revenues were adequate, an excessive use of earmarking had deprived the state legislature of the necessary control over the use of funds. The study recommended that a solution be found through eliminating the provision in the state constitution[6] which diverted the proceeds of the retail sales tax to the use of local governments and substituting a system of grants-in-aid to the localities.[7]

Meanwhile, immediate revenues were needed pending the implementation of the long-term program. The House of Representatives passed a bill providing for a 1-percent net income tax on individuals and corporations; but in the Senate the personal income tax component was dropped and the corporate income tax was transformed into the Business Activities Tax,[8] which was then enacted with "blitzkrieg celerity."[9]

The anticipated long-term reform never materialized. By constitutional amendment the rate of the retail sales tax was increased from 3 percent

[4] *Ibid.*, p. 62.

[5] See Allen L. Gornick, *Basic Discussion of the Michigan Business Receipts Tax —Its Bases and Economic Theory,* address delivered at the University of Michigan Law School Institute (July 30, 1953), p. 1.

[6] Art. X, Sec. 23, of the Michigan constitution of 1908 as amended in 1948 stipulated that ½¢ of the 3-cent sales tax should be allocated to local governments and 2¢ to the School Aid Fund. In other words, only one sixth of the proceeds from the sales tax was available for the General Fund.

[7] See discussion of report by Dr. James S. Sly and Associates of Princeton, N.J., in Gornick, *Basic Discussion,* pp. 2–6.

[8] Gornick, *Basic Discussion,* pp. 7–8.

[9] See Clarence W. Lock (then Deputy Commissioner, now Commissioner, Michigan Department of Revenue), "Administrative History of Michigan's Business Activities Tax," in *Proceedings of the Forty-Eighth Annual Conference on Taxation of the National Tax Association, 1955* (Sacramento, Calif., 1956), p. 20.

to 4 percent as of June 1, 1962, so that, given the constitutional provision with respect to earmarking, the proportion of receipts available
to the General Fund has been increased to three eighths.[10] Nevertheless,
about 56 percent of the state's total revenues and 70 percent of its tax
revenues remain earmarked for the use of localities and schools.[11]

The Business Activities Tax is apparently intended to implement the
principle of value-added taxation suggested by Adams, that is, a tax
paid by a business firm which is measured by its contribution to the
value of aggregate product or income originating in the taxing jurisdiction
and which is justified as payment for public services to business.[12] There
is even the suggestion of the Adams' formula of a combination value-
added tax and progressive spendings tax, for the state's retail sales tax
may be regarded as an indirect spendings tax, albeit it lacks the planned
rate progression of the direct spendings tax recommended by Adams.
The benefit to business thesis implied by the Michigan tax involves no
estimate of the cost of public services to business. The benefit principle
is used merely as a vague justification for a tax payable by business firms
regardless of type of organization or absence of net profits.

As originally enacted, the Business Activities Tax utilized Adams'
gross product concept for its definition of the tax base, which has since
been modified in the direction of a net income concept through depreciation allowances on business investment in real property. In accordance
with Adams' suggestion, the tax has applied the origin principle for
allocating value derived from business conducted across the state border.
However, it has been patterned after later developments of the concept
to the extent that it has been applied to sales of services as well as

[10] A report of the Michigan Department of Revenue contains the comment that
one of the advantages of earmarking is that voters are more likely to approve a
tax specifically dedicated to certain uses. See Michigan Department of Revenue,
Nineteenth Annual Report, 1959–60 (Lansing, 1961), p. 17.

[11] See statistics in Michigan Department of Revenue, *Twenty-Second Annual
Report, 1962–63,* pp. 14–15.

The General Fund continued to be plagued with deficits through fiscal 1962. In
fiscal 1963, however, there was a surplus of some $62,800,000, making it possible
to hold the accumulated deficit to $22,834,662 because of additional revenues,
which were obtained primarily through increases in the cigarette and liquor excises
and the corporate franchise tax and the adoption of a 4 percent tax on communication services. See Michigan Department of Revenue, *Twenty-First Annual
Report, 1961–62* (Lansing, 1962), p. 9, and *Twenty-Second Annual Report,
1962–63,* p. 7.

[12] See James A. Papke, "Michigan's Value-Added Tax after Seven Years,"
National Tax Journal. XIII (December 1960), p. 351.

commodities and has utilized the cost subtraction or sales procedure rather than the tax credit method of computing the tax base.

From the start, however, the tax contained provisions which seriously compromised its character as a value-added tax. Moreover, with the passage of time new distortions of the value-added principle have been introduced while none have been removed.

One significant divergence from a satisfactory implementation of a value-added tax is the statutory provision which allows firms whose "adjusted receipts" (value added), derived from itemized deductions, exceed 50 percent of "gross receipts" to arbitrarily reduce their tax base through a minimum deduction of 50 percent of gross receipts [Sec. 1(1)(3)]. This provision is said to have resulted from concern over the situation of service industries and professional occupations.[13] The 50 percent allowance apparently reflects an estimated average deduction of 45–55 percent of gross receipts for manufacturing firms.[14] In effect, however, it distorts the value-added tax in the direction of a general turnover or cumulative type of levy favoring firms with large amounts of value added relative to sales, resulting from vertical integration. The fact that no tax is applied to a firm's construction of real property through its own labor force also suggests a general turnover tax. The nondeductibility of construction payrolls in computing adjusted receipts does not eliminate this loophole, for the value of the construction does not enter gross receipts.

By a 1955 amendment to the law, firms using the 50 percent minimum deduction are also entitled to an additional deduction in the computation of adjusted receipts when their payrolls exceed 50 percent of gross receipts [Sec. 1(1)(3)]. This additional deduction is equal to 10 percent of gross receipts or one half of the excess of payrolls over 50 percent of gross receipts, whichever is smaller. For example, if a firm with annual gross receipts of $100,000 uses the minimum deduction of 50 percent and has an annual payroll of $50,000, its tax base will equal $50,000. If, however, it adds $8,000 to its annual payroll, it will be allowed to reduce its tax base by $4,000 or 8 percent. Explained as a means of relieving the burden on laundries, dry cleaners, and installers of hard-surfaced floor coverings, it makes little sense in terms of a tax intended

[13] Michigan Department of Revenue, *Seventeenth Annual Report, 1957–58* (Lansing, 1958), p. 66.
[14] Gornick, *Basic Discussion,* pp. 18–19.

as a nondiscriminatory levy and has been particularly criticized for the extent to which it favors specialty firms over department stores where high payrolls in one department are offset by low payrolls in others.[15]

Further distortions, present since the original act, reflect a policy of modifying the tax in an effort to take account of burdens imposed by other tax laws deemed to impose a discriminatory burden on certain elements of value or branches of economic activity. However, instead of fostering neutrality, this approach can readily lead to the subversion of any general principle of taxation unless restricted to very special situations.

The most serious impairment of the value-added principle resulting from the philosophy of replacement taxation has been the exclusion from gross receipts subject to the Business Activities Tax of receipts other than royalties subject to the Intangibles Tax Act (a tax on intangible personal property applicable to gross interest and dividend income) [Sec. 4(g)]. Meanwhile, interest payments, but not dividend payments, are deductible from gross receipts in computing adjusted receipts. Consequently, the interest component of value escapes the Business Activities Tax altogether; and, since dividend payments are not deductible, the law favors debt over equity financing.

Replacement taxation also explains the exemption of banks, insurance companies, firms engaged in pari-mutuel betting, and in part the reduced rate applied to public utilities. The exemption of banks has been attributed to the fact that federal law restricts the taxation of national banks to certain types of taxes, which do not include a value-added tax, and the Michigan legislature was reluctant to subject state banks to a tax which it would not be allowed to apply to national banks.[16] In any event, any attempt to apply general tax principles to financial institutions has usually given rise to difficulties, sometimes because of definitional problems in defining their tax base and sometimes because of political opposition by the potential taxpayers.[17]

Another serious distortion has arisen from the treatment of investment assets purchased by taxpaying businesses. While originally no deprecia-

[15] See E. C. Stephenson, "The Michigan Business Activities Tax: A Retailer's Viewpoint," in *Proceedings of the Forty-Eighth Annual Conference on Taxation of the National Tax Association, 1955*, p. 30.

[16] Peter A. Firmin, *The Michigan Business Receipts Tax*, Michigan Business Report No. 24 (Bureau of Business Research, School of Business Administration, University of Michigan, Ann Arbor, 1953), p. 23.

[17] *Ibid.*

tion was allowed on either real or personal property in the computation of adjusted receipts, a 1955 amendment permitted depreciation on investment in real property but not personal property. The allowance has been granted on the ground that the law otherwise favors the rental of real property over its purchase in view of the fact that rental payments are deductible in computing the tax base. However, businesses frequently rent assets classified as personal property. Furthermore, the tax is imposed on rental receipts so that, given the assumption of forward shifting to those renting the property, the claimed discrimination is nonexistent in the first place.[18]

Thus, the limitation of depreciation to real property can justly be termed a discrimination against personal property. The Department of Revenue has been protesting both the inequity and administrative complexity of the present provision and recommends that depreciation allowances be either extended to personal property or abolished.[19]

Finally, a significant impairment of the value-added principle was introduced as of July 1, 1959, in the form of a credit against tax liability under the Business Activities Tax [Sec. 2(c)]. The credit, which is limited to 25 percent of tax liability, is computed by applying to the amount of tax otherwise due the ratio between 1 percent of adjusted receipts and net income, with net income defined in the statute so as to largely coincide with that of the federal income tax. The credit apparently represents an effort to appease opponents of the tax, who have been objecting to its application in the absence of net income and, in their view, ability to pay[20]—a position which probably reflects the assumption that the tax is not shifted forward.

[18] See Richard W. Lindholm, "The Business Activities Tax," in *Michigan Tax Study Staff Papers* (Lansing, 1958), p. 267.

[19] Michigan Department of Revenue, *Seventeenth Annual Report, 1957–58,* p. 66.

[20] The Department of Revenue observes that most tax programs proposed in recent years have recommended the repeal of the tax and that opposition to the tax comes largely from those favoring net profits taxation. Michigan Department of Revenue, *Twenty-Second Annual Report, 1962–63,* p. 62.

Some estimates of the distribution of benefits from the credit among firms classified according to the ratio between their net income and adjusted receipts are presented in Papke, "Michigan's Value-Added Tax after Seven Years," p. 362, Table V. The table indicates that the greatest benefit from the credit accrues to firms with net income equal to less than 10 percent of adjusted receipts, the average amount of credit being 21 percent for this group. It also indicates that some credit is available even for firms with a very high ratio of net income to the tax base.

The irrational features in the law noted above account for the diversity of classifications applied to the tax. It is sometimes designated as a gross receipts business tax,[21] presumably in the sense of a tax representing an impersonal rental charge on the owners of the business, which in view of the nominal rates may well be the case. The hypothesis has also been advanced that a portion of the tax on adjusted receipts from business conducted over the state border is shifted back to wage receipts to the extent that taxable transactions are determined by the payroll factor of the allocation formula.[22] Although the prevailing opinion seems to assume forward shifting as under a sales tax,[23] there is justification for describing the tax as "a curious compromise of a net income, business receipts, and value-added tax"[24] or as "basically a gross receipts tax and in some respects a net income and sales tax."[25]

The Michigan tax authorities insist that the tax be legally classified as an income tax.[26] As the Business Activities Tax passed the legislature as a substitute for a general income tax, there was a risk that it would be declared unconstitutional if it failed to qualify as an income tax. Also, the Department of Revenue is of the opinion that the tax's qualification as an income tax will ensure more freedom in the taxation of adjusted receipts derived from business conducted across the state border.

SCOPE OF THE TAX

The Michigan Business Activities Tax applies to "persons engaging in business in Michigan" (Sec. 2). Business is defined as "all activities engaged in or caused to be engaged in within this state, whether in

[21] As noted by Theodore A. Andersen, "Recommended Changes in Michigan's Tax Structure," in Paul W. McCracken, ed., *Taxes and Economic Growth in Michigan* (Kalamazoo: W. E. Upjohn Institute for Employment Research, 1960), p. 20.

[22] See Richard A. Musgrave and Darwin W. Daicoff, "Who Pays the Michigan Taxes?" in *Michigan Tax Study Staff Papers*, p. 178.

[23] See Andersen, "Recommended Changes in Michigan's Tax Structure," p. 20.

[24] Alfred G. Buehler, "The State and Local Tax Structure and Economic Development," in McCracken, ed., *Taxes and Economic Growth in Michigan*, p. 41.

[25] See *Michigan State Tax Reporter*, Vol. I (Chicago: Commerce Clearing House, 1964), p. 6574.

[26] See Lock, "Administrative History of Michigan's Business Activities Tax," p. 21. Commissioner Lock emphasizes that the statute describes the tax as "certain specific taxes on income" and that the imposition section (Sec. 2) identifies the tax as "a specific tax on income."

intrastate, interstate, or in foreign commerce, with the object of gain, benefit or advantage, whether direct or indirect to the taxpayer or to another or others" [Sec. 1(2)].

Generally speaking, therefore, the tax encompasses all business firms whether selling commodities or services, and it applies to all branches of business activity, including agriculture and the professions. Moreover, it extends through the retail stage, for "adjusted receipts" are defined so as to include any distributive margins.

Businesses exempt from the tax because of replacement taxation have already been noted. They include all types of financial intermediaries and firms engaged in pari-mutuel betting. As previously stated, the reduced rate applicable to public utilities may also be explained by the philosophy of replacement taxation, the in lieu tax in this instance being a state ad valorem tax on utility property.[27] Also, the statute specifically exempts trusts exempt from the federal income tax [Sec. 4(j)], an exemption which assumes an absence of profit-making activities and which includes pension trusts.

"Any corporation or association organized and operating exclusively for religious, charitable, scientific, literary or education purposes and not for profit, and nonprofit associations and corporations organized and operating under sections 117 to 132, inclusive, of Act No. 327 of the Public Acts of 1931, as amended" are not subject to the Business Activities Tax provided that "no part of the adjusted receipts of such corporations or associations either directly or indirectly inures to the benefit of any private shareholder or individual" [Sec. 4(c)].[28] The exemption extends to related business activities but not unrelated business activities so that income-producing activities, such as eating or drinking establishments operated by nonprofit institutions, are taxed.[29] There is

[27] The statute once explained the concession to public utilities as the result of their especially high ratio of value added to gross receipts and the fact that they were subject to rate regulation [Act No. 150, Public Acts of 1953, Sec. 1(m)], but this section has since been deleted from the law. In any case, the reference to excessively high value added was apparently not supported by statistical evidence (see Firmin, *The Michigan Business Receipts Tax*, p. 248). Moreover, while it is rational to question the validity of a principle, it is irrational to accept it but undermine it with special concessions based on subjective judgments. (Also see Firmin, *ibid.*, p. 134.)

[28] The organizations mentioned in Act No. 327 of Public Acts of 1931 include clubs, business associations, and even political organizations. For a detailed list, see *Michigan State Tax Reporter*, Vol. I, p. 6590.

[29] *Ibid.*

an exemption for unrelated business activity granted to religious organizations, but this is limited to activities which are "part of the educational or religious program" and concerns such undertakings as athletic contests, church fairs, and bazaars.[30]

The tax does not apply to governments or their agencies and instrumentalities [Sec. 4(b)(d)]. Thus, any enterprises operated by federal, state, or local governments are exempt regardless of their degree of competition with private industry.

COMPUTATION OF TAX LIABILITY

The amount of tax liability is computed by applying the tax rate to the tax base, adjusted receipts, and subtracting the net income credit. Adjusted receipts are derived by subtracting various outlays from the "gross receipts" of the taxpaying business, with gross receipts defined as "the amount received or to be received in money, credits, property or other money's worth."[31] When firms conduct activities across the state border, the tax is applicable only to adjusted receipts which have their source in the state of Michigan. Thus, as contrasted with Michigan's retail sales tax, which is imposed in accordance with the jurisdictional principle of destination, the Business Activities Tax allocates values according to the jurisdictional principle of origin.

"Gross receipts" are further defined as "the entire receipts of the taxpayer" exclusive of certain items enumerated in the statute [Sec. 1(j)(1–5)]. They do not encompass the proceeds derived from the sale of the firm's capital assets and repayment of debts. They are net of any discounts or allowances on returned merchandise. Also, they exclude any amounts received by agents on behalf of their principals. Finally, there may be added to the list of exclusions income received from intangible personal property exempt by Section 4(g) of the statute because of the Intangibles Tax Act, that is, interest and dividend receipts.[32] The amount of gross receipts includes receipts from sales of goods and services and

---

[30] See Firmin, *The Michigan Business Receipts Tax,* p. 20.

[31] See Michigan Department of Revenue, *Michigan Business Activities Tax, Act No. 150, Public Acts of 1953, as Amended: Rules and Regulations* (State of Michigan, 1959), Rule 10, p. 11.

[32] The regulations have transferred this item from the exemption section to the exclusion section. *Ibid.*

receipts of rents and royalties. It also includes any sales to governments, the taxation of sales to the federal government being allowed under the tax because legal liability rests with the vendors.[33]

In conformity with the cost subtraction procedure of computing value added, the taxpaying business firms deduct various outlays from their gross receipts to arrive at value added as defined in the Michigan statute, that is, adjusted receipts [Sec. 1(h)(1–3)]. Because the tax utilizes an income rather than a consumption concept of value added, the deduction for goods and services purchased from other business firms consists of items which are expensed, with any capital allowances being limited to depreciation. Purchases of capital assets are thus included in the tax base although, as previously noted, any assets produced within the enterprise escape the tax. Expensed purchases may be deducted whether the items have been purchased from other taxable firms or from those excluded or exempt from the tax. As explained in the first chapter of this book, this procedure will reduce the effective tax rate on the final product as compared with the tax credit method, which automatically includes in the tax base any purchases from exempt firms.

The Department of Revenue allows deductions for dues and payments to business associations, contributions to charitable associations, payments to trusts exempt from federal taxes, and bad debts.[34] Taxes and fees paid to governments other than net income taxes are deductible unless they have been excluded from gross receipts, except for special assessments under local property taxes, which are regarded as outlays for capital assets.[35]

As previously explained, the taxpayer may deduct interest payments even though interest receipts are excluded. However, from the standpoint of the value-added principle, this concession to interest represents an excessive application of the policy of replacement taxation, and it obviously discriminates against dividend payments.[36]

The restriction of depreciation allowances to real property has also been mentioned. It is logical to treat real and personal property in an

---

[33] See Firmin, *The Michigan Business Receipts Tax*, pp. 18–19.

[34] Michigan Department of Revenue, *Michigan Business Activities Tax, Act No. 150, Public Acts of 1953, as Amended: Rules and Regulations*, Rule 10, p. 11.

[35] *Ibid.*, Rule 11, p. 12.

[36] Shoup recommends that interest and rentals be allowed as deductions in computing adjusted receipts only if paid to taxable recipients. See Carl S. Shoup, "Suggested Changes in the State and Local Tax System of Michigan," in McCracken, ed., *Taxes and Economic Growth in Michigan*, p. 162.

identical manner, and there is general recognition of the need to revise the law in this respect. The Michigan Department of Revenue has expressed indifference to the choice between no depreciation allowances and allowances to both real and personal property.[37] The Citizens' Advisory Committee has recommended the abolition of depreciation allowances, thereby restoring the gross product concept used in the original version of the statute,[38] while Shoup has recommended that depreciation be allowed in both cases,[39] which would reflect a net income concept of value added.

The minimum deduction of 50 percent of gross receipts allowed if itemized deductions are less than this amount and the additional allowance when payrolls exceed 50 percent of gross receipts have likewise been mentioned. In addition, the statute allows a general minimum deduction of $12,500 per taxable person regardless of the number of businesses conducted. Combined with the 50 percent minimum deduction, this means that all firms with gross receipts below $25,000 are exempt, probably including most professional activities and a large portion of service enterprises. The exemption is excessively high from the standpoint of maintaining competitive neutrality, but by considerably reducing the number of taxpayers it minimizes administrative tasks.[40]

Adjusted receipts derived from transactions across the state border are allocated between Michigan and out-of-state sources by means of a three-factor (sales, payrolls, and property) formula. For adjusted receipts derived from sales of goods and services other than transportation, the allocation fraction is the average of three ratios, separately computed: (1) receipts from sales of tangible personal property within the state, services rendered within the state, and rentals from property located within the state or royalties from the use of patents or copyrights

[37] Michigan Department of Revenue, *Seventeenth Annual Report, 1957–58*, p. 66.

[38] See *Report of the Citizens' Advisory Committee of the Michigan Tax Study, 1958, to the Special Legislative Committee on Taxation, House of Representatives* (Lansing: Speaker-Hines and Thomas, 1959), p. 21.

[39] Shoup, "Suggested Changes in the State and Local Tax System of Michigan," p. 162.

[40] About fifty-five taxpayers with tax payments in excess of $100,000 account for some 45 percent of the tax. See Michigan Department of Revenue, *Twenty-Second Annual Report, 1962–63*, p. 66.

within the state to gross receipts from all sources, (2) payrolls within the state to aggregate payrolls, and (3) value of real and tangible personal property within the state to total value of real and tangible personal property [Sec. 3(b)].[41] The allocation ratio thus computed is applied to the taxpayer's entire adjusted receipts in order to arrive at his tax base. Separate accounting may be used but only after permission is obtained from the Commissioner of the Department of Revenue [Sec. 3(b)].

Once the taxpayer has obtained the figure for "adjusted receipts" or value added in Michigan and subtracted the minimum exemption, he computes his tax liability by applying to the amount of his taxable value added the tax rate of 0.775 percent or, in the case of public utilities, 0.2 percent. He is then entitled to a tax credit equal to the amount of his tax liability times the ratio between 1 percent of his adjusted receipts and net income as defined in the statute, with the maximum credit of 25 percent allowed if the ratio is 25 percent or higher.

METHODS OF COLLECTION

The tax is due quarterly with returns which may be computed on either the cash or accrual basis (Sec. 5). The statutory exemption of $12,500 may be prorated in quarterly amounts. The Department of Revenue will allow returns for fiscal rather than calendar years provided that the fiscal year is the one used for the federal income tax.

An annual return is due four calendar months after the close of the tax year. At this time the taxpayer will pay any additional tax required or, if his payments are in excess of the amount due, may obtain a refund or credit the tax against future liabilities (Sec. 6).

With the approval of the Department of Revenue, the taxpayer is permitted to anticipate his tax liability if, when he makes his annual return for the previous year, he advances an amount equal to the tax liability of the previous year. He is then required to file only an annual return (Sec. 5). The Department of Revenue may also allow annual returns in the case of agriculture or seasonal business.

---

[41] Special formulas are used for transportation services and for the conveyance of oil and gas through pipelines [Sec. 3(c)].

SUMMARY AND CONCLUSION

As explained here, the Business Activities Tax apparently reflects the benefit to business principle of value-added taxation as conceived by Adams, with the benefit thesis used merely to justify the taxation of business firms regardless of form of organization or absence of net profits. Acceptance of this principle means that the value-added measure, or the contribution of the taxpayer to product or income originating in Michigan, must be assumed to provide an equitable tax base which, given proportional rates, will not distort the competitive relationships among producers in different branches of economic activity or among firms within a given branch.

However, the structure of the Michigan tax seems to reflect considerable lack of confidence in the equity of the value-added measure. From the beginning, the principle of the tax was seriously impaired by the 50 percent minimum deduction from gross receipts on the ground that value added in certain activities seemed excessive. This provision, combined with the absence of a tax on a firm's production of capital assets for its own use, modifies the tax in the direction of a general turnover tax, with the latter's inherent subsidy to integrated firms.

The extra deduction for labor intensive firms and the net income credit reflect a distrust of the value-added principle and a preference for net profits taxation. These modifications, which effect a discriminatory definition of value added, should be abrogated. In addition, the consequences for competitive neutrality of unlimited deductions for charitable contributions and deductions for club dues warrant further study if the tax is ever imposed at significant rates.

The policy of replacement taxation has also been employed so as to seriously impair the neutrality of the value-added measure. This is especially the case with regard to the exclusion of all interest from the tax base because subject to the Intangibles Tax. Moreover, the exemption of all financial institutions because of in lieu taxation seems excessive, although this difficulty arises because of the federal restriction with respect to the taxation of national banks. The low rate on public utilities, which also reflects the policy of replacement taxation, is likewise open to serious question. In no instance can the substitute taxes be assumed to effect a tax burden equal to that which would have been imposed under the value-added measure. As a rule, given a conflict between a general tax and a special levy, it is the latter which should give way.

The inconsistency with respect to capital allowances is completely unjustifiable. It confuses the net income and gross product concepts of value added and represents a wholly irrational type of discrimination within the context of a supposedly neutral imposition.

Given the foregoing distortions of the value-added principle, it is by no means clear that the Business Activities Tax represents an advance over general turnover taxation, a virtue sometimes attributed to it.[42] It can, of course, be argued that it constitutes a first step in the achievement of a rational tax.[43] At the moment, however, this position seems untenable in view of the fact that the trend has been in the direction of adding new distortions rather than removing those in the original act.

The Governor and the House Taxation Committee have recommended the abolition of the Business Activities Tax as part of a tax-reform program which would introduce a general income tax.[44] On the other hand, the Senate Taxation Committee has opposed this approach and favors the retention of the Business Activities Tax in preference to income taxation.[45]

As the law now stands, it does not provide a source of revenues elastic to changes in rates. The fact that it has not given rise to excessive administrative problems is undoubtedly the result of the nominal rates, the high exemptions which minimize the number of taxpayers, and the concentration of tax liability in a small number of large enterprises. Any significant increase in the rates would probably make the tax unbearable.

[42] See Harold M. Groves, "Michigan Taxes and Economic Growth," in McCracken, ed., *Taxes and Economic Growth in Michigan*, p. 92.
[43] *Ibid.*
[44] See Michigan Department of Revenue, *Twenty-First Annual Report, 1961–62*, pp. 8–9.
[45] *Ibid.*, p. 9.

Bibliography

Adams, Thomas S. "Fundamental Problems of Federal Income Taxation," *Quarterly Journal of Economics,* XXV (August, 1921), 527–56.

———— Statement. Hearings before the U.S. Congress, Ways and Means Committee, House of Representatives, on Revenue Revision of 1932. 72d Congress, 1st Session. Washington, D.C., 1932. Pp. 252–62.

———— "The Taxation of Business," in Proceedings of the Eleventh Annual Conference on Taxation of the National Tax Association, 1917. New Haven, Conn., 1918, pp. 185–94.

Arant, Roscoe. "The Place of Business Taxation in the Revenue Systems of the States," *Taxes—The Tax Magazine* (April, 1957), pp. 191–99, 242.

Assemblée nationale, deuxième législature, année 1952. Projet de loi portant réforme fiscale, No. 4579. Paris, Imprimerie Nationale, 1952.

Balassa, Bela. The Theory of Economic Integration. Homewood, Ill., Richard D. Irwin, 1961.

Bates, Stewart. "Classificatory Note on the Theory of Public Finance," *The Canadian Journal of Economics and Political Science,* III (May, 1937), 163–80.

Bonnefous, Georges. La taxe sur le chiffre d'affaires en Autriche. Ph.D. dissertation. Paris, Jouve, 1950.

Break, George F. "Excise Tax Burdens and Benefits," *The American Economic Review,* XLVII (September, 1957), 531–49.

Bronfenbrenner, M. "The Japanese Value-Added Sales Tax," *National Tax Journal,* III (December, 1950), 298–313.

———— "Second Thoughts on Value-Added Taxation," *Finanzarchiv,* XVI, No. 2 (1955), 310–12.

———— and Kiichiro Kogiku. "The Aftermath of the Shoup Tax Reform, Parts I and II," *National Tax Journal,* X (September and December, 1957), 236–54, 345–60.

Brookings Institution. Report on a Survey of Administration in Iowa: The Revenue System. Des Moines, Iowa, State of Iowa, 1933.

———— Report on a Survey of the Organization and Administration of the

State and County Governments of Alabama. Montgomery, Wilson Printing Co., 1932. Vol. IV, Pt. III.

Brown, E. Cary. "Analysis of Consumption Taxes in Terms of the Theory of Income Determination," *The American Economic Review,* XL (March, 1950), 75–89.

Brown, Harry Gunnison. The Economics of Taxation. Columbia, Mo., Lucas Bros., 1938.

———— "The Incidence of a General Output or a General Sales Tax," *The Journal of Political Economy,* XLVII (April, 1939), 254–62.

Buehler, Alfred G. "The Cost and Benefit Theories," *Tax Law Review,* V (1949–50), 17–34.

———— General Sales Taxation. New York, The Business Bourse, 1932.

———— "Sales Tax," in Encyclopaedia of the Social Sciences. Vol. VII (New York, 1934), pp. 516–18.

———— "The Taxation of Business Enterprises—Its Theory and Practice," *The Annals of the American Academy of Political and Social Science,* CLXXXIII (January, 1936), 96–103.

———— "Taxing Consumer Spending," *The Bulletin of the National Tax Association,* XXVII (January, 1943), 123–28.

Bulletin officiel de l'Administration des Contributions indirectes. No. 45 (October 5, 1948).

Bundeskanzler, Der, Bundesrepublik Deutschland. Überprüfung des Umsatzsteuerrechtes. Bonn, Bonner Universitäts-Buchdruckerei, December, 1958.

Butters, J. Keith, assisted by Powell Niland. Effects of Taxation: Inventory Accounting and Policies. Boston, Harvard University, Graduate School of Business Administration, Division of Research, 1941. *Passim.*

Butters, J. Keith, Lawrence E. Thompson, and Lynn L. Bollinger. Effects of Taxation: Investment by Individuals. Boston, Harvard University, Graduate School of Business Administration, Division of Research, 1953. *Passim.*

Campet, Charles. The Influence of Sales Taxes on Productivity. Report for the European Productivity Agency of the Organisation for European Economic Co-operation. Project No. 315. Paris, the European Productivity Agency, 1958.

———— "Quelques aspects économiques de la taxe française sur la valeur ajoutée," *Public Finance,* XII, No. 1 (1957), 22–33.

Chrétien, Maxime. "Les divers problèmes fiscaux des trois Communautés Européennes," in Les problèms juridiques et économiques du Marché Commun. Université de Lille. Paris, Libraires techniques, 1960. pp. 255–301.

———— Réforme fiscale. Paris, Juris-Classeurs, 1949.

Cline, Denzel C. "Expanding Scope of Sales Taxes," in Proceedings of the Forty-Third Annual Conference on Taxation of the National Tax Association, 1950. Sacramento, Calif. 1951, pp. 296–301.

———— "Sales Tax Exemption of Producer Goods," in Proceedings of the

Forty-Fifth Annual Conference on Taxation of the National Tax Association, 1952. Sacramento, Calif. 1953, pp. 618–31.

Clough, Shepard B. "Economic Planning in a Capitalist Society: France from Monnet to Hirsh," *Political Science Quarterly*, LXXI (December, 1956), 539–52.

Code général des Impôts. Législation applicable au 15 août 1954. Paris, Imprimerie Nationale, 1954.

Colm, Gerhard, "The Basis of Federal Fiscal Policy," *Taxes—the Tax Magazine*, XVII (June, 1939), 338–40, 369 f.

—— "Conflicting Theories of Corporate Income Taxation," *Law and Contemporary Problems*, VII (Spring, 1940), 281–90.

—— Essays in Public Finance and Fiscal Policy. New York, Oxford, 1955. Chaps. 3 and 5.

—— "Methods of Financing Unemployment Compensation," *Social Research*, II (May, 1935), 148–67.

—— "Public Revenue and Public Expenditure in National Income," in Studies in Income and Wealth. Conference on Research in National Income and Wealth. New York, National Bureau of Economic Research. Vol. I (1937), pp. 175–227.

"Commentaire des dispositions législatives et règlementaires concernant la taxe sur la valeur ajoutée" (Preface by M. Lauré), *Recueil Sirey, 1954* (Paris, 1954), pp. 1–36.

"Les Contrôles fiscaux," *La revue fiduciaire*, No. 315 (November, 1954), pp. 1–104.

Copeland, M. A. "Concepts of National Income," in Studies in Income and Wealth. Conference on Research in National Income and Wealth. New York, National Bureau of Economic Research. Vol. I (1937), pp. 3–34.

Decrees No. 53-942 of September 30, 1953 and No. 53-1003 of October 7, 1953, according to the instructions of the General Administration of Indirect Taxes, No. 225, B 2/1, and No. 226, B 2/1, as reported in *La revue fiduciaire, monographies*, No. 48 (October 12, 1953), pp. 1–14.

Dellas, Jean. "Les taxes sur le chiffre d'affaires dans l'économie contemporaine," *Revue de science et de législation financières*, XL, No. 1 (1948), 66–100.

De Viti de Marco, Antonio. First Principles of Public Finance. Trans. from the Italian by Edith Pavlo Marget. New York, Harcourt, 1936.

Due, John F. The General Manufacturers Sales Tax in Canada. Toronto, Canadian Tax Foundation, 1951.

—— "A General Sales Tax and the Level of Employment: A Reconsideration," *National Tax Journal*, II (June, 1949), 122–30.

—— "Retail Sales Taxation in Theory and Practice," *ibid.*, III (December, 1950), 314–25.

—— Sales Taxation. Urbana, Ill., University of Illinois Press, 1957.

—— "Sales Taxation and the Consumer," *The American Economic Review*, LIII (December, 1963), 1078-84.

Due, John F. The Theory of Incidence of Sales Taxation. New York, King's Crown Press, 1942.

———"Toward a General Theory of Sales Tax Incidence," *Quarterly Journal of Economics*, LXVII (May, 1953), 253–66.

Earle, E. M., ed. Modern France. Princeton, N.J., Princeton University Press, 1951.

European Coal and Steel Community, High Authority. Report on the Problems Raised by the Different Turnover Tax Systems Applied within the Common Market. Report prepared by the Committee of Experts set up under Order No. 1-53 of the High Authority, dated March 5, 1953. Brussels, Publishing Services of the European Economic Community, 1953.

European Economic Community, Commission. Rapport du Comité Fiscal et Financier. Brussels, Publishing Services of the European Economic Community, 1962.

"Final Report of the Committee of the National Tax Association on Federal Taxation of Corporations," in Proceedings of the Thirty-Second Annual Conference on Taxation of the National Tax Association, 1939. Columbia, S.C., 1940, pp. 534–82.

Firmin, Peter A. The Michigan Business Receipts Tax. Michigan Business Report No. 24. Ann Arbor, Mich., Bureau of Business Research, School of Business Administration, University of Michigan, 1953.

Garrigou-Lagrange, André "Évolution du système fiscal français au vingtièmé siècle," *Revue de science et de législation financières*, LIII, No. 2 (1961), 198–210.

Giraudeau, Roger. "Considérations sur récentes fluctuations saisonnières du rendement des taxes sur le chiffre d'affaires," *Revue de science et de législation financières*, XLI, No. 4 (Paris, 1949), 458–82.

Goode, Richard. "Anti-Inflationary Implications of Alternative Forms of Taxation," *The American Economic Review*, XLII (May, 1952), 147–60.

——— The Corporate Income Tax. New York, Wiley, 1951.

——— "Taxation of Saving and Consumption in Underdeveloped Countries," *National Tax Journal*, XIV (December, 1961), 305–22.

Gornick, Allen L. Basic Discussion of the Michigan Business Receipts Tax— Its Bases and Economic Theory. Address delivered at the University of Michigan Law School Institute, July 30, 1953, pp. 1–25.

Grabower, Rolf. Die Gesichte der Umsatzsteuer und ihre gegenwärtige Gestaltung im Inland und im Ausland. Berlin, Carl Hemanns, 1925. Pp. 286–88.

Grossetête, J. "Chronique de législation fiscale," *Revue de science et de législation financières*, XLI, No. 2 (1949), 218–26.

Groves, Harold M. "Neutrality in Taxation," *National Tax Journal*, I (March, 1948), 18–24.

——— "Personal versus Corporate Income Taxes," *The American Economic Review*, XXXVI (May, 1946), 241–49.

—— Postwar Taxation and Economic Progress. 1st ed. New York and London, McGraw, 1946.

—— Trouble Spots in Taxation. Princeton, N.J., Princeton University Press, for the University of Cincinnati, 1948.

"Guide des taxes sur le chiffre d'affaires," *La revue fiduciaire*, I, No. 321 (June, 1955), 1–80; II, No. 324 (September, 1955), 1–79; III, No. 325 (October, 1955), 1–94; IV, No. 399 (October, 1961), 1–304.

Haberler, Gottfried. "National Income, Saving and Investment," in Studies in Income and Wealth. Conference on Research in National Income and Wealth. New York, National Bureau of Economic Research. Vol. II (1938), pp. 139–66.

—— and Everett H. Hagen. "Taxes, Government Expenditures, and National Income," in Studies in Income and Wealth. Conference on Research in National Income and Wealth. New York, National Bureau of Economic Research. Vol. VIII (1946), pp. 3–31.

Haig, Robert M. The Public Finances of Post-War France. New York, Columbia University Press, 1929.

Hansen, Alvin Harvey. Fiscal Policy and Business Cycles. New York, Norton, 1941. P. 436.

Heller, Jack, and Kenneth M. Kauffman. Tax Incentives for Industry in Less Developed Countries. Harvard Law School International Program in Taxation. Chicago, Commerce Clearing House, 1963.

Hollander, J. H., ed. Letters of David Ricardo to John Ramsey McCulloch, 1816–1863. Publications of the American Economic Association, Vol. X, Nos. 5 and 6. New York, American Economic Association, 1896. Especially p. 60.

Houghteling, James L., Jr. "The Income Tax in France," in Public Policy. Cambridge, Mass., Harvard Graduate School of Public Administration, Vol. V (1954), pp. 307–48.

"Interim Report of the Committee on Personal Property Taxation on Possible Substitutes for Ad Valorem Taxation of Tangible Personal Property Used in Business," in Proceedings of the Forty-Fifth Annual Conference on Taxation of the National Tax Association, 1952. Sacramento, Calif., 1953, pp. 76–106.

International Bureau of Fiscal Documentation. The EEC Reports on Tax Harmonization. Amsterdam, International Bureau of Fiscal Documentation, 1963.

Ito, Hanya. "Direct Taxes in Japan and the Shoup Report," *Public Finance,* VIII, No. 4 (1953), 382–83.

—— "Theorie und Technik der Nettoumsatzsteuer in Japan," *Finanzarchiv,* XV, No. 3 (1955), 447–78.

—— "The Value-Added Tax in Japan," *The Annals of the Hitotsubashi Academy,* No. 1 (October, 1950), pp. 43–59.

Jacoby, Neil Herman. Retail Sales Taxation. Chicago, Commerce Clearing House, 1938.

Jensen, Jens P. Government Finance. New York, Crowell, 1937.

Kaldor, Nicholas. An Expenditure Tax. London, Allen & Unwin, 1955.

Keynes, John Maynard. The General Theory of Employment, Interest, and Money. New York, Harcourt, 1936.

Kindleberger, Charles P. International Economics, 3d ed. Homewood, Ill., Richard D. Irwin, 1963.

Krier, H. "Le financement du réarmement dans une économie de reconstruction," Revue de science et de législation financières, XLIII, No. 1 (1951), 116–38.

Kuznets, Simon. "Discussion," in Studies in Income and Wealth. Conference on Research in National Income and Wealth. New York, National Bureau of Economic Research. Vol. I (1937), pp. 230–38.

―――― "National Income: a New Version," The Review of Economics and Statistics, XXX (August, 1948), 151–79.

―――― "On the Valuation of Social Income—Reflections on Professor Hicks' Article, Parts I and II," Economica, XV (February and May, 1948), 116–31.

Kuznets, Simon, assisted by Lillian Epstein and Elizabeth Jenks. National Income and Its Composition, 1919–38. New York, National Bureau of Economic Research, 1941. Vol. I.

Larguier, Émile. Traité des taxes à la production. Paris, Rousseau, 1939.

Laufenburger, Henry. "Chronique de législation fiscale," Revue de science et de législation financières, XLI, No. 4, (1949), 502–7.

―――― "Finances et fiscalité de guerre," ibid., XXXVIII, No. 2 (1940–46), 191–200.

―――― "La fiscalité française," ibid., XLII, No. 1 (1950), 106–17.

―――― "Technical and Political Aspects of Reform on Taxation in France," National Tax Journal, II (September, 1953), 273–85.

Lauré, Maurice. Au secours de la T.V.A. Paris, Presses Universitaires de France, 1957.

―――― "Impôts et productivité" (Conférence prononcée le mardi 9 décembre 1952 devant les membres de la Société industrielle de Mulhouse), extract from Bulletin No. 1, 1953 industrielle de Mulhouse, pp. 1–28.

―――― La taxe sur la valeur ajoutée. Paris, Recueil Sirey, 1952.

Levin, Jonathan V. The Export Economies: Their Pattern of Development in Historical Perspective. Harvard Law School International Program in Taxation. Cambridge, Mass., Harvard University Press, 1960.

Levy, Michael E. Income Tax Exemptions: Analysis of the Effects of Personal Exemptions on the Income Tax Structure. Amsterdam, North Holland Publishing Co., 1960.

Lindeman, John, "Income Measurement as Affected by Government Operations," in Studies in Income and Wealth. Conference on Research in National Income and Wealth. New York, National Bureau of Economic Research. Vol. VI (1943), pp. 2–22.

Local Autonomy Agency and Local Finance Commission. Local Tax Law. Tokyo, 1950. Pp. 12–49.

Lock, Clarence W. "Administrative History of Michigan's Business Activities Tax," in Proceedings of the Forty-Eighth Annual Conference on Taxation of the National Tax Association, 1955. Sacramento, Calif., 1956, pp. 20–25.

———, Donovan J. Rau, and Howard D. Hamilton. "The Michigan Value-Added Tax," *National Tax Journal,* VIII (December, 1955), 357–71.

Lutz, Harley L. Public Finance. New York and London, Appleton, 1929. *Passim.*

Macaulay, Hugh Holleman, Jr. Fringe Benefits and Their Federal Tax Treatment. New York, Columbia University Press, 1959.

McCracken, Paul W., ed. Taxes and Economic Growth in Michigan. Kalamazoo, W. E. Upjohn Institute for Employment Research, 1960.

McGrew, J. W. "Effect of a Food Exemption on the Incidence of a Retail Sales tax," *National Tax Journal,* II (December, 1949), 362–67.

Marshall, Alfred. Principles of Economics. 8th ed. London, Macmillan, 1938.

Martel, J. S. "What Should Be Done about the Personal Property Tax?" in Proceedings of the Forty-Third Annual Association Conference on Taxation of the National Tax Association, 1950. Sacramento, Calif., 1951, pp. 82–87.

Martin, James W. "Distribution of the Consumption Tax Load," *Law and Contemporary Problems,* VIII (Summer, 1941), 445–56.

Masoin, M. and E. Morselli. Impôts sur transactions, transmissions et chiffre d'affaires: problèmes du Marché Commun et de l'intégration internationale. Padua, Italy, Archives Internationales des Finances Publiques, 1959.

Meade, James E. Problems of Economic Union. Chicago, University of Chicago Press, 1952.

——— "Trade and Welfare," in Theory of International Economics. Vol. II. London, Oxford, 1955. *Passim.*

Means, G. C., Lauchlin Currie, and R. R. Nathan. "Problems in Estimating National Income Arising from Production by Government," in Studies in Income and Wealth. Conference on Research in National Income and Wealth. New York, National Bureau of Economic Research Vol. II (1938), pp. 267–91.

Mégret, Jean. Précis de droit fiscal. Paris Éditions du Prétoires, 1949.

Merrill, John F. "The Tax System of New York State as Viewed by the Administrator," Proceedings of the Twenty-Second Annual Conference on Taxation of the National Tax Association, 1929. Columbia, S.C., 1930, pp. 116–124.

Michigan Department of Revenue. Act. No. 150, Public Acts of 1953: An Act to Provide for the Raising of Additional Public Revenue by Prescribing Certain Specific Taxes on Income. State of Michigan, 1953.

Michigan Department of Revenue. Annual Reports. Thirteenth through Twenty-Second Reports. Lansing, Mich., 1954–63.

—— Michigan Business Activities Tax, Act No. 150, Public Acts of 1953, as Amended. State of Michigan, 1957.

—— Michigan Business Activities Tax, Act No. 150, Public Acts of 1953, as Amended: Rules and Regulations. State of Michigan, 1959.

Michigan State Tax Reporter. Vol. I. Chicago, Commerce Clearing House, 1964.

Michigan Tax Study Staff Papers. Lansing, Mich., 1958.

Mill, John Stuart. Principles of Political Economy. 5th ed. 2 vols. New York, Appleton, 1890. *Passim.*

Ministère des Finances. "Les impôts indirectes en 1961 et diverse renseigne-ments statistiques," *Statistiques et études financières, Supplément,* No. 165 (September, 1962).

—— *Statistiques et études financières.* Issues of January, 1955, through December, 1963.

Möller, Hans. Das Ursprungs- und Bestimmungslandprincips. Mimeographed study, University of Munich, 1961.

Morange, Georges. "La refonte des administrations fiscales," *Recueil Dalloz: Chronique, 1948* (Paris, 1948), pp. 125–28.

—— "La réforme du système fiscal français," *Revue de science et de législation financières,* XL, No. 1 (1948), 53–76.

Mount, Wadsworth W., with discussion by Franzy Eakin. "A Re-examination of Taxation Fundamentals," in American Management Series, No. 67. New York, American Management Association, 1941. Pp. 6–21.

Musgrave, R. A. "On Incidence," *The Journal of Political Economy,* LXI (August, 1953), 306–23.

—— The Theory of Public Finance. New York, McGraw, 1959.

National Industrial Conference Board. General Sales or Turnover Taxation. New York, National Industrial Conference Board, 1929. *Passim.*

Nelson, R. W., and Donald Jackson. "Allocation of Benefits from Govern-ment Expenditures," in Studies in Income and Wealth. Conference on Re-search in National Income and Wealth. New York, National Bureau of Economic Research. Vol. II (1938), pp. 317–31.

Nezis, M. A. "Rapport de M. A. Nezis, Directeur au Ministère grec des Finances," *Cahiers de droit fiscal international, rapports pour le septième Congrès international de Droit financier,* XXIV (Paris, 1953), 61–72.

"La notion de livraison à soi-même," *La revue fiduciaire,* No. 298 (June, 1953), pp. 41–51.

"Nouveau régime de la taxe à la production," *Bulletin fiduciaire,* No. 246 (January, 1949).

"Obligations des vendeurs, utilisations des bulletins de commande," *La revue fiduciaire, monographies,* No. 45 (June 2, 1953), pp. 1–12.

"Les options fiscales des industriels et commerçants," *La revue fiduciaire,* No. 315 (November, 1955), pp. 33–68.

"Ordonnance No. 58-1374 du 30 décembre 1958 (arts. 32–41), portant loi de finances pour 1959," *Journal officiel de la République française* (December 31, 1958), pp. 12075–76.

Organisation for European Economic Co-operation. Economic Conditions in France. Published annually. Paris, Organisation for European Economic Co-operation. Editions for 1953, 1958, 1960.

Organische Steuerreform. Bericht des Wissenschaftlichen Beirates beim Bundesministerium der Finanzen an der Herrn Bundesminister der Finanzen. Bonn, Bundesministerium der Finanzen, February 14, 1953. Pp. 59–62.

"Paiement volontaire de la taxe à la production," *La revue fiduciaire*, No. 270 (January, 1951), pp. 45–59.

Papke, James A. "Michigan's Value-Added Tax after Seven Years," *National Tax Journal*, XIII (December, 1960), 350–63.

Paton, W. A. "The Cost Approach to Inventories," *Journal of Accountancy*, LXII (October, 1941), 300–07.

Patouillet, J. "Aperçu sur les modifications apportées aux taxes sur le chiffre d'affaires," *Recueil Dalloz: Chronique, 1948* (Paris, 1948), pp. 109–11.

——— "La notion de producteur dans la taxe à la production," *Recueil Dalloz: Chronique, 1946* (Paris, 1946), pp. 69–72.

——— "La suppression du régime de la suspension de taxes en matière de taxe à la production," *Recueil Dalloz: Chronique, 1949* (Paris, 1949), pp. 9–16.

Petits Codes Dalloz: Code de Commerce. 58th ed. Paris, Jurisprudence Générale Dalloz, 1962.

Pigou, A. C. A Study in Public Finance. 3d ed. London, Macmillan, and New York, St. Martin's Press, 1956.

"Poujadists Leap from Street Brawls to Parliament," *Business Week*, No. 1376 (January 14, 1956), pp. 28–30.

"Preliminary Report of the Committee Appointed by the National Tax Association to Prepare a Plan of a Model System of State and Local Taxation," in Proceedings of the Twelfth Annual Conference on Taxation of the National Tax Association, 1919. New York, 1920, pp. 2126-69.

Prest, A. R. "A Value Added Tax Coupled with a Reduction in Taxes on Business Profits," *British Tax Review* (September–October, 1963), pp. 336–47.

Preston, H. M. "The Michigan Business Activities Tax as Viewed by Operators of Small Establishments," in Proceedings of the Forty-Eighth Annual Conference on Taxation of the National Tax Association, 1955. Sacramento, Calif., 1956, pp. 34, 35.

"Productivity—the Hot New Issue," *Business Week*, No. 1436 (March 9, 1957), pp. 25–26.

"Projet de loi portant réforme fiscale," *La revue fiduciaire, feuillets hebdomadaires d'information*, No. 321 (May 23, 1953), pp. 1–4.

Projet de loi portant réforme fiscale, No. 4579. Annexe au procès-verbal de la séance du 31 octobre 1952, deuxième législature, 1952. Paris, Imprimerie Nationale, 1952.

Rädler, Albert J. Die direkten Steuern der Kapitalgesellschaften und die Probleme der Steueranpassung in den sechs Staaten der Europäischen Wirtschaftsgemeinschaft. Amsterdam, Internationales Steuerdocumentationsbüro, 1960. Pt. III.

Recueil des arrêts du Conseil d'État, 1948–50. Paris, Recueil Sirey, 1948–50.

"La réforme de la fiscalité immobilière," Impôts et sociétés, Nos. 8–9, N.S. (August–September, 1963), pp. 1–170.

"La réforme des taxes sur le chiffre d'affaires," La revue fiduciaire, feuillets hebdomadaires d'information, No. 635 (June 3, 1960), pp. 1–8.

"Réforme des taxes sur le chiffre d'affaires, décrets et instructions d'application," Impôts et sociétés, Bulletin hebdomadaire, No. 5642 (July 6, 1955), pp. 255–90.

"La réforme du régime des taxes sur le chiffre d'affaires," La revue fiduciaire, No. 311-12 (July–August, 1954), pp. 1–64.

"Réforme fiscale," Journal officiel de la République française (May 3, 1955), pp. 4371–75.

"La règle du butoir et la T.V.A.," Impôts et sociétés, No. 131 (December, 1955), pp. 3469–74.

Report of the Citizens' Advisory Committee of the Michigan Tax Study, 1958, to the Special Legislative Committee on Taxation, House of Representatives. Lansing, Speaker-Hines and Thomas, 1959.

"Report of the Committee on Personal Property Taxation on Possible Substitutes for Ad Valorem Taxation of Tangible Personal Property Used in Business," in Proceedings of the Forty-Sixth Annual Conference on Taxation of the National Tax Association, 1953. Sacramento, Calif., 1954, pp. 365–407.

"Les restitutions de taxes acquitées sur affaires resiliées ou impayées," La revue fiduciaire, No. 294 (February, 1953), pp. 35–42.

"Revamping France's Taxes," Business Week, No. 1333 (March 19, 1955), pp. 152–54.

Ritschl, Hans. "Gutachten zur Grossen Steuerreform," Wirtschaftsdienst, XXXIII (October, 1953), 623–30.

Rolph, Earl R. "The Concept of Transfers in National Income Estimates," Quarterly Journal of Economics, LXII (May, 1948), 327–61.

——— "A Proposed Revision of Excise-Tax Theory," The Journal of Political Economy, LX (April, 1952), 102–17.

Ruggles, Richard. An Introduction to National Income and Income Analysis. 1st ed. New York, McGraw, 1949.

Say, Jean-Baptiste. A Treatise on Political Economy. Trans. from the 4th ed. in French by C. H. Prinsep. 3d American ed. Philadelphia, John Grigg, 1827. Passim, especially p. 246.

Schmölders, Günter. "À propos de la réforme fiscale en Allemagne, idées, et propositions," trans. from the German by Jacques Bertrand, *Revue de science et de législation financières*, XLV (Paris, 1953), 624–38.

———— Organische Steuerreform: Grundlagen, Vorarbeiten, Gesetzentwürfe. Berlin and Frankfurt, Franz Vahlen, 1953, Pp. 165–98.

———— "Die Veredelung der Umsatzsteuer," *Public Finance*, IX, No. 2 (1954), 107–22.

Schulte, Maria-Dolores. Der Einfluss Unterschiedlicher Steuersysteme auf den Wettbewerb innerhalb eines Gemeinsamen Marktes Dargestellt anhand der in Frankreich und in der Bundesrepublik Deutschland verwirklichten Besteuerungsformen. Ph.D. dissertation, University of Munich, Munich, 1961.

———— Die Wirtschaftspolitischen Grundlagen des Bestimmungsland- und des Ursprungslandprincips. Paper delivered before the Institut International de Finances Publiques, Luxembourg, 1963. (To be published in Travaux de l'Institut International de Finances Publiques.)

Seligman, Edwin R. A. Essays in Taxation, 8th ed. New York, Macmillan, 1919.

———— Progressive Taxation in Theory and Practice. Publications of the American Economic Association, Vol. IX, Nos. 1 and 2. Baltimore, American Economic Association, 1894.

Shoup, Carl S. "Business Taxes," in Encyclopaedia of the Social Sciences. Vol. III (New York, 1930), pp. 122–24.

———— "Discussion," *The American Economic Review,* XLII (May, 1952), 162–65.

———— "The Distinction between 'Net' and 'Gross' in Income Taxation," in Studies in Income and Wealth. Conference on Research in National Income and Wealth. New York, National Bureau of Economic Research. Vol. I (1937), pp. 251–81.

———— Federal Finances in the Coming Decade. New York, Columbia University Press, 1941.

———— "Incidence of the Corporation Income Tax: Capital Structure and Turnover Rates," *National Tax Journal,* I (March, 1948), 12–17.

———— Principles of National Income Analysis. Boston, Houghton, 1947.

———— "Ricardo on the Taxation of Profits," *Public Finance,* V, No. 2 (1950), 1–18.

———— The Sales Tax in France. New York, Columbia University Press, 1930.

———— The Sales Tax in the American States, A Study Made under the Direction of Robert Murray Haig. New York, Columbia University Press, 1934.

———— "Some Considerations on the Incidence of the Corporation Income Tax," *The Journal of Finance,* VI (June, 1951), 187–96.

———— "Taxation Aspects of International Economic Integration," in Travaux de l'Institut International de Finances Publiques, neuvième Session, Frankfurt, 1953. La Haye, W. P. Van Stockum et Fils, 1953. Pp. 89–118.

Shoup, Carl S. "Taxation in France," *National Tax Journal,* VIII (December, 1955), 325–44.

—— "Taxes Available to Avert Inflation," in Carl S. Shoup, Milton Friedman, and Ruth P. Mack, Taxing to Prevent Inflation. New York, Columbia University Press, 1943. Pt. II, pp. 76–110.

—— "Tax Reform in Japan," in Proceedings of the Forty-Second Annual Conference on Taxation of the National Tax Association, 1949. Sacramento, Calif., 1950, pp. 400–13.

—— "Theory and Background of the Value-Added Tax," in Proceedings of the Forty-Eighth Annual Conferences on Taxation of the National Tax Association, 1955. Sacramento, Calif., 1956, pp. 7–19.

—— The Theory of Harmonization of Fiscal Systems. Paper delivered before the Institut International de Finances Publiques, Luxembourg, 1963. (To be published in Travaux de l'Institut International de Finances Publiques.)

Shoup Mission. Report on Japanese Taxation. 4 vols. Tokyo, Supreme Commander for the Allied Powers, 1949. (Vol. II, pp. 197–204, discusses value-added tax.)

—— Second Report on Japanese Taxation. Toyko, Japan Tax Association, 1950. Pp. 17–19 and *passim*. . .

Shultz, William J., and C. Lowell Harriss. American Public Finance. 6th ed. New York, Prentice-Hall, 1954.

Simon, Herbert A., and Charles P. Bonini. "The Size Distribution of Business Firms," *The American Economic Review*, XLVIII (September, 1958), 608–17.

Simons, Henry C. Personal Income Taxation. Chicago, The University of Chicago Press, 1938.

Simpson, Herbert D. "The Changing Pattern of Property Taxation," *The American Economic Review*, XXIX (September, 1939), 454–67.

Smith, Adam. An Inquiry into the Nature and Causes of the Wealth of Nations. New York, The Modern Library, Random House, 1937. Pp. 271–2.

Smith, Dan Throop. Effects of Taxation: Corporate Financial Policy. Boston, Harvard University, Graduate School of Business Administration, Division of Research, 1952.

Sraffa, Piero, ed., with the collaboration of M. H. Dobb. The Works and Correspondence of David Ricardo. Cambridge, Eng., Royal Economic Society, 1951. 9 vols. Vol. I, especially pp. 388–89 and pp. 421 f., and Vol. IX, especially p. 173, n. 2.

Stapchinskas, J. P. "Taxation of Business in Michigan: Viewpoints of Businessmen," in Proceedings of the Forty-Eighth Annual Conference of the National Tax Association, 1955. Sacramento, Calif., 1956, pp. 25–28.

Stephenson, E. C. "The Michigan Business Activities Tax: A Retailer's Viewpoint," in Proceedings of the Forty-Eighth Annual Conference of the National Tax Association, 1955. Sacramento, Calif., 1956, pp. 29–33.

Stockfisch, J. A. "The Capitalization and Investment Aspects of Excise Taxes under Competition," *The American Economic Review*, XLIV (June, 1954), 287–300.

Stout, D. K. "Value Added Taxation, Exporting and Growth," *British Tax Review* (September–October, 1963), pp. 314–35.

Strayer, Paul I. "An Appraisal of Current Fiscal Theory," *The American Economic Review*, XLII (May, 1952), 138–46.

Studenski, Paul. "Characteristics, Developments and Present Status of Consumption Taxes," *Law and Contemporary Problems*, VIII (Summer, 1941), 417–29.

———— "Government as a Producer," *The Annals of the American Academy of Political and Social Science*, CCIX (November, 1939), 23–24.

———— "Modern Fiscal Systems, Their Characteristics and Trends of Development," *ibid.*, CLXXXIII (January, 1936), 27–38.

———— The Place of a "Value-Added" Tax in a War Time Fiscal Program. Preliminary Memorandum, mimeographed, New York University, April 6, 1942.

———— "Taxation and Business Enterprises," in Financial Management Series, No. 58. New York, American Management Association, 1939. Pp. 3–19.

———— Testimony, Hearings before the U.S. Congress, Ways and Means Committee, House of Representatives, Relative to the Social Security Act Amendments of 1939. 76th Congress, 1st Session. Washington, D.C., 1939. Vol. II, pp. 950–77.

———— "Toward a Theory of Business Taxation," *The Journal of Political Economy*, XLVII (October, 1940), 621–54.

Sullivan, Clara K. "Concepts of Sales Taxation," in Readings on Taxation in Developing Countries, ed. by Richard Bird and Oliver Oldman. Baltimore, The Johns Hopkins Press, 1964. Pp. 319–58.

———— The Search for Tax Principles in the European Economic Community. Harvard Law School International Program in Taxation. Chicago, Commerce Clearing House, 1963.

"Taxe à la production: déduction des investissements; régime des entrepreneurs de travaux immobiliers," *La revue fiduciaire, monographies*, No. 48 (October 12, 1953), pp. 1–14.

Terhalle, Fritz. Finanzwissenschaft. Jena, G. Fischer, 1930. Pp. 432–34.

Tobin, Charles J. "The New York State Tax Situation as Viewed by the Taxpayers," in Proceedings of the Twenty-Second Annual Conference on Taxation of the National Tax Association, 1929, Columbia, S.C., 1930, pp. 82–116.

Treaty Establishing the European Economic Community and Connected Documents. Brussels, Publishing Services of the European Communities, n.d.

United Nations, Economic Commission for Europe. "Current Economic Developments in Europe," *Economic Bulletin for Europe*, IX (August, 1957), 1–34; X (May, 1958), 1–40.

United Nations, Economic Commission for Europe. Economic Survey of Europe in 1957. Geneva, United Nations, 1958. Chaps. II and III.

United Nations Statistical Office. Monthly Bulletin of Statistics. January, 1955–December, 1963.

—— Statistics of National Income and Expenditure. Series H, No. 8. New York, September, 1955.

United States Bureau of the Census. 1949 Annual Survey of Manufactures. Series MAS-49-3. Preliminary Report. August 17, 1951.

United States Bureau of Foreign Commerce. "Establishing a Business in France," Economic Reports of World Trade Information Service, Pt. I, No. 58–59 (January, 1958), pp. 1–8.

United States Congress. Congressional Record. 67th Congress, 1st Session. Washington, D.C., 1921. Vol. LXI, Pt. 7 (October 21–November 9, 1921), pp. 6828–7298.

—— House Document 160. "Carrier Taxation." 79th Congress, 1st Session. Washington, D.C., 1944.

United States Department of Commerce, Office of Business Economics. National Income, 1954 Edition. Washington, D.C., Government Printing Office, 1954.

—— Statistical Abstract of the United States: 1963. 84th ed. Washington, D.C., Government Printing Office, 1963.

——U.S. Income and Ouput. Washington, D.C., Government Printing Office, 1958.

United States Treasury Department, Division of Tax Research. "Considerations Respecting a Federal Retail Sales Tax," Hearings before the U.S. Congress, Ways and Means Committee, House of Representatives, on Revenue Revision of 1943. 78th Congress, 1st Session. Washington, D.C., 1943. Pp. 1095–1272.

—— "Federal Manufacturers' Wholesale and Retail Sales Taxes," Memorandum Submitted by Randolph Paul. Hearings on Revenue Revision of 1942, Ways and Means Committee, House of Representatives. 77th Congress, 2d Session. Washington, D.C., 1942. Vol. I, pp. 345–55.

—— "Proposed Manufacturers' Excise Tax, Revenue Bill of 1932. Ways and Means Committee Report," Hearings before the U.S. Congress, Ways and Means Committee, House of Representatives, on Revenue Revision of 1942. 77th Congress, 2d Session. Washington, D.C., 1942. Vol. I, pp. 414–39.

Van den Berge, W. H. "La taxe sur le chiffre d'affaires aux Pays-Bas et sa répercussion sur l'économie," Public Finance, II (1947), 48–67.

Vedel, Georges. "Les aspects fiscaux du Marché Commun," Bulletin for International Fiscal Documentation, XII (1958), 321–39.

Vickrey, William. Agenda for Progressive Taxation. New York, Ronald Press, 1947.

Von Mering, O. The Shifting and Incidence of Taxation. Philadelphia, Blakiston, 1942.

"Vorläufiger Reichswirtschaftsrat," *Verhandlungen des Reichstags, Anlagen zu den Stenographischen Berichten,* No. 200 (1920/21).

Wald, Haskell P. "The Classical Indictment of Indirect Taxation," *Quarterly Journal of Economics,* LIX (August, 1945), 577–96.

Walker, David. "The Direct-Indirect Tax Problem: Fifteen Years of Controversy," *Public Finance,* X, No. 2 (1955), 153–76.

Warburton, Clark. "Accounting Methodology in the Measurement of National Income," in Studies in Income and Wealth. Conference on Research in National Income and Wealth. New York, National Bureau of Economic Research. Vol. I (1937), pp. 67–110.

—— "Discussion," in Studies in Income and Wealth. Conference on Research in National Income and Wealth. New York, National Bureau of Economic Research. Vol. VI (1943), pp. 23–37.

Wells, Paul. "General Equilibrium Analysis of Excise Taxes," *The American Economic Review,* XLV (June, 1955), 345–49.

Weston, J. Fred. "Incidence and Effects of the Corporate Income Tax," *National Tax Journal,* II (December, 1940), 300–45.

Wheatcroft, G. S. A. "Some Administrative Problems of an Added Value Tax," *British Tax Review* (September-October, 1963), pp. 348–49.

"Why Business is Finding More Uses for Foundations," *Business Week,* No. 1294 (June 19, 1954), pp. 166–78.

World Tax Series, Harvard Law School International Program in Taxation. Taxation in France, by Martin S. Norr. Chap. XIV. (To be published.)

—— Taxation in the Federal Republic of Germany, by Henry J. Gumpel. Chicago, Commerce Clearing House, 1963.

Zoller, J. F. "Discussion," in Proceedings of the Twenty-Second Annual Conference on Taxation of the National Tax Association, 1929. Columbia S.C., 1930, pp. 124–31.

Zurcher, Arnold J., Jr. History of Value-Added Taxation. Pamphlet, Harvard Law School, September, 1953.

Index

Ability to pay principle: personal taxation and, 4, 47; tax burden distribution, and, 20, 168; income principle and, 28; tax equity and, 152–53, 154, 173

Adams, Thomas S.: credit method suggested by, 17; on value-added taxation proposal, 41, 42; on tax simplicity, 151; on cost-of-service variant of benefit principle, 156, 157, 165; classification of government expenditures, 161; on distribution of tax burden, 168; on dual approach to general taxation, 175; on tax base, 181, 188–89, 228; on tax administration, 214; tax incidence question, 269–70; gross product type of value-added tax recommended by, 285

Addition procedure, 7–9, 286; in collection of consumption tax, 24–26; in implementation of income type of sales tax, 28; in proposed value-added tax in Japan, 137–39, 147; net income type tax base and, 199–203, 210

Administration of tax, 214–62; tax on value added as collection device, 6–10; evaluation of value-added and single-stage procedures, 15; in proposed value-added tax for Japan, 141; number of returns, 219–21; tax rate, 221–24; taxpayers' identification, 224–27; tax base determination, 227–61; exclusions and exemptions, 253–61

Aggregate tax base: controversies in definition of, 192–98; allocation of, among individual firms, 198–213; *see also* Tax base

Agriculture: tax legislation in France, 65, 67, 71, 77, 89–90; tax legislation in Japan, 143

Allocation of resources, anticipated effects of tax on, 271–80

Arant, Roscoe: recommendation on value-added tax, 45–46, 214, 270

Argentina, 13, 17, $30n$

Artisans, tax exemptions for, in France, 65, 107

Assujettis partiels, 99

Bad debts, 101, 239

Banks: under Japanese value-added tax, 136, 137; computation of tax base for commercial banks, 207–8; under Michigan Business Activities Tax, 302

Base of tax, *see* Tax base

Benefit principle of taxation, 3, 4, 37–38, 47, 49, 300, 310; income principle and, 28; in proposed value-added tax for Japan, 130, 138; in justification of various types of taxes, 155–156; cost-of-service variant of, 156–169; general-welfare theory, 169–76; tax as price of government services and, 173–74; consumption-type tax and, 177–79

British Purchase Tax, 231–32

Brokerage services, French legislation regarding, 68, 108

About the Author:

Clara K. Sullivan is Research Economist, International Program in Taxation, Law School, Harvard University, and Senior Economist, International Economic Integration Program, Columbia University.